D0810747

THE
FIVE OF
HEARTS

4=

THE
FIVE OF
HEARTS

AN INTIMATE
PORTRAIT OF HENRY ADAMS
AND HIS FRIENDS
1880-1918

PATRICIA O'TOOLE

CLARKSON POTTER /PUBLISHERS
NEW YORK

GRATEFUL ACKNOWLEDGMENT IS MADE TO THE HARVARD UNIVERSITY PRESS FOR PERMISSION TO REPRINT MATERIAL FROM THE SIX-VOLUME EDITION OF *THE LETTERS OF HENRY ADAMS,* EDITED BY J. C. LEVENSON, ERNEST SAMUELS, CHARLES VANDERSEE, AND VIOLA HOPKINS WINNER COPYRIGHT © 1982 AND 1988; AND FROM THE FOUR-VOLUME *LETTERS OF HENRY JAMES,* EDITED BY LEON EDEL COPYRIGHT © 1974, 1975, 1980, AND 1984. QUOTATIONS FROM THE ADAMS PAPERS ARE FROM THE MICROFILM EDITION, BY PERMISSION OF THE MASSACHUSETTS HISTORICAL SOCIETY.

COPYRIGHT © 1990 BY PATRICIA O'TOOLE

ALL RIGHTS RESERVED. NO PART OF THIS BOOK MAY BE REPRODUCED OR TRANSMITTED IN ANY FORM OR BY ANY MEANS, ELECTRONIC OR MECHANICAL, INCLUDING PHOTOCOPYING, RECORDING, OR BY ANY INFORMATION STORAGE AND RETRIEVAL SYSTEM, WITHOUT PERMISSION IN WRITING FROM THE PUBLISHER.

PUBLISHED BY CLARKSON N. POTTER, INC., DISTRIBUTED BY CROWN PUBLISHERS, INC., 201 EAST 50TH STREET, NEW YORK, NEW YORK 10022

CLARKSON N. POTTER, POTTER AND COLOPHON ARE TRADEMARKS OF CLARKSON N. POTTER, INC.

MANUFACTURED IN THE UNITED STATES OF AMERICA

LIBRARY OF CONGRESS CATALOGING-IN-PUBLICATION DATA

O'TOOLE, PATRICIA.
THE FIVE OF HEARTS: AN INTIMATE PORTRAIT OF HENRY ADAMS AND HIS FRIENDS, 1880–1918 / BY PATRICIA O'TOOLE.
P. CM.
1. ADAMS, HENRY. 1838–1918—FRIENDS AND ASSOCIATES. 2. ADAMS. HENRY, 1838–1918—FAMILY. 3. HAY, JOHN. 1838–1905—FAMILY. 4. HISTORIANS—UNITED STATES—BIOGRAPHY. 5. ADAMS FAMILY. 6. HAY FAMILY. I. TITLE.
E175.5.A2076 1990   89-16378
973'.07202—DC20   CIP

ISBN 0-517-56350-9

10 9 8 7 6 5 4 3 2 1

FIRST EDITION

To my friends

Contents

No man is an island.

JOHN DONNE

To be born is to be wrecked on an island.

J. M. BARRIE

Preface

The Five of Hearts entered my life in 1983, when I read *Descent from Glory: Four Generations of the John Adams Family* by Paul C. Nagel. In a few paragraphs, Nagel sketched a group of five men and women who came together in Washington, D.C., during the winter of 1880–81 and struck up a friendship that lasted for the rest of their lives. The most famous of them was Henry Adams, historian and man of letters, great-grandson of one president and grandson of another, a man who claimed to want nothing to do with politics yet chose to live in the shadow of the White House. Henry's wife, Marian Hooper Adams (known as "Clover"), presided over the capital's most exclusive salon, possessed a stinging wit, and was a gifted photographer. A victim of what modern medicine would probably diagnose as a manic-depressive mood disorder, Clover took her life at the age of forty-two. John Hay, charming, wry, enormously capable but unable to attach himself to a career, nevertheless managed to achieve distinction in two worlds, literature and diplomacy. He began as a secretary in the White House of Abraham Lincoln, wrote for and edited the New York *Tribune*, coauthored a ten-volume life of Lincoln, and ended his career as secretary of state to William McKinley and Theodore Roosevelt, overseeing the emergence of the United States as a world power. His wife, Clara Stone Hay, heiress to an

Ohio industrial fortune, was the soul of piety, deeply devoted to her family, and ill at ease in the society her husband craved. The fifth member of the quintet was Clarence King, a brilliant geologist. His survey of a large stretch of the route followed by the first transcontinental railroad was a landmark of nineteenth-century science and a key to the settlement of the American West. Superbly equipped to succeed as a mining entrepreneur, King died a pauper. He led another life as well—one that his close friends Hay and Adams knew nothing about until his death. In New York, where he kept an office on Wall Street and belonged to several of the city's most genteel men's clubs, King also had a black common-law wife who bore him five children.

Wanting to know more about the relationship of this striking assortment of personalities, I went to the library in search of a book about the Five of Hearts. No such thing existed. And when I turned to biographies of King and Hay and the Adamses, each new piece of information about the Five of Hearts seemed to widen the scope of their story. Like the Bloomsbury group in London and Gertrude Stein's circle in Paris, the Hearts had a genius for befriending everyone worth knowing. Over the course of their lives they knew Mark Twain and Walt Whitman, Henry James and Edith Wharton, Bret Harte and William Dean Howells, Horace Greeley, Robert Louis Stevenson, Rudyard Kipling, John Ruskin and Matthew Arnold, painters (John La Farge and John Singer Sargent), architects (Henry Hobson Richardson and Stanford White), the sculptor Augustus Saint-Gaudens, Bernard Berenson, the royal family of Tahiti, every president from Abraham Lincoln to Theodore Roosevelt, Andrew Carnegie, Carl Schurz, Henry Cabot Lodge, and scores of cabinet members and diplomats.

Though there was a paucity of published material about the Five of Hearts, I quickly discovered that they and their friends had left a trail of paper reaching from Massachusetts to California: thousands of letters, diary entries, memoirs, literary manuscripts, and documents as diverse as receipts, death certificates, menus, court testimony, and architectural drawings. The story that emerges from these sources (which are described more fully at the back of the book) is really two stories. The first is a group biography, a portrait of an elite who helped to define American culture and politics in the years between the Civil War and World War I. The second unfolds not in a particular time or place but along a purely human axis, with intimacy at one pole and isolation at the other. This latter tale is one of abounding love, the riches of friendship, tenderness, loyalties verging on passion, generosity, and, at the opposite pole, a story of secrets, loneliness, betrayal, madness, and suicide.

In the preface of his life of Samuel Johnson, W. Jackson Bate writes that biography allows the reader "to touch hands with others, to learn from each other's experience and to get whatever encouragement we can." A biography of a circle of friends is doubly rewarding in this respect since it allows us to touch their hands and to see how they held out their hands to each other.

In piecing together the relationships of the Five of Hearts, I discovered as much about my feelings as theirs. Deeply moved by Henry Adams's kindness toward Clarence King after King's nervous collapse, I glimpsed the magnitude of my own hope for the same tenderness in time of desperation. Biases—mine and theirs—lurked everywhere. The impulses of educated Americans in the late twentieth century are infinitely more egalitarian than the attitudes of their nineteenth-century counterparts, which presents special difficulties in dealing with the elitism of a circle like the Five of Hearts. In particular I recoiled from Adams's anti-Semitic outbursts, King's contempt for women, and John Hay's scorn for immigrants. But one can try to account for a prejudice without endorsing it, and however disagreeable, these attitudes deserve to be put in context. This I have endeavored to do.

When William Roscoe Thayer, the first biographer of John Hay, asked the elderly Henry Adams about the Five of Hearts, Adams was brusque and enigmatic. The only record he cared to leave, he said, was the Saint-Gaudens sculpture he had commissioned decades earlier for Clover's grave. "People who want to know us—we are not eager for notoriety at any time—can go there and we shall tell no lies." As far as I know, I have told no lies. And since the Five of Hearts left a record considerably more complete than the haunting bronze figure in Washington's Rock Creek Church Cemetery, I hope I have caught something of the truth.

Prologue: Farewells

For twenty hours it snowed. Then it rained, and by the time the sun rose on March 4, 1881, the streets of Washington had turned to rivers. It was a day to stay home by the fire, which is precisely what Mr. and Mrs. Henry Adams of Lafayette Square intended to do. A gunshot echoed through their neighborhood at ten thirty in the morning, and if the sound drew them to their windows, they saw, across the square in front of the White House, a crowd of thousands—men in black hats, women with dripping umbrellas, and soldiers on horseback, their dark capes pinned back to show a flash of red.

The gunshot signaled the start of the inaugural parade in honor of James Abram Garfield, Civil War hero, Ohio Republican, and twentieth president of the United States. Among the celebrants sloshing down Pennsylvania Avenue toward the Capitol, it would have been difficult to find a happier man than the nineteenth president, Rutherford B. Hayes. Having come into the White House under the cloud of an election variously described as "disputed" and "stolen," Hayes had passed his quadrennium without ever acquiring a taste for the presidency. As Garfield solemnly swore to uphold the Constitution, Hayes was heard mumbling cheerfully to himself, "Out of a scrape, out of a scrape."

Snug by their hearth on that sodden Friday, sunk into dark red leather armchairs cut low and small to match their diminutive figures, Henry and Clover Adams were only dimly aware of distant fifes and drums. By Clover's reckoning, the odds were ten to one that they would see nothing of their new neighbor in the White House or his administration. "In this ever-shifting panorama of course we shall find new combinations," she wrote to her father, "but we shall hardly have the intimate cosy set that we did."

So it seemed. After more than a year abroad, the Adamses had returned to the capital just in time to grow deeply attached to John Hay and Clarence King, who were leaving the government with the changing of the presidential guard. Hay and King had encountered the Adamses a few times in the past, but when Henry and Clover moved into a rented house at 1607 H Street in December 1880, the two men became constant callers. Hay, an assistant secretary of state, would leave his desk at four-thirty, walk north across Lafayette Park, and in five minutes pass between the fluted columns of the portico at 1607, a graceful mansion known to Washingtonians as "the little White House." By the time he arrived, Clover was usually deep in conversation with King, the director of the U.S. Geological Survey, or with Hay's wife, Clara, who made frequent visits from the Hays' home in Cleveland. At five o'clock, when Henry Adams emerged from his study, tea began. Tea often stretched into dinner, and dinner flowed into a party lasting till midnight. Delighted with their delight in each other, the friends sealed their bond with a name: "the Five of Hearts." Although the origin of the phrase went unrecorded, it almost certainly sprang from their familiarity with two other playing-card epithets. Henry Wadsworth Longfellow, a friend of Clover's father, had belonged to a circle known as "the Five of Clubs," and a bit of Wild West derring-do had won Clarence King the title of "the King of Diamonds."

An outsider would have been hard put to understand the intense affections of the Five of Hearts. Apart from their age (all were close to forty except Clara, who was thirty-one) and apart from the Boston Brahminism that linked Henry and Clover Adams, the quintet had little in common. As a Westerner, John Hay belonged to a species considered innately inferior by Henry Adams, son of Beacon Hill. Clarence King thought the silent and darkly handsome Mrs.

Henry and Clover Adams's rented house at 1607 H Street, on Washington's Lafayette Square, where the Five of Hearts became friends in the winter of 1880–81.
LIBRARY OF CONGRESS

Hay "calm and grand," but her ardent domesticity held no appeal for Clover Adams. While Clara filled her Washington days at ladies' luncheons, Clover stayed home and read. Clara seemed a strange companion for her loquacious husband and his witty friends, who talked unceasingly and punned without mercy. (When one of the Adamses' Skye terriers developed an eye problem, Hay pronounced it a case of "cataract." King leaned toward a diagnosis of "tom-cataract.") Clover, impatient with Hay's reverence for the novels of Henry James, declared that James's trouble was not that he bit off more than he could chaw but that "he chaws more than he bites off."

King, a blue-eyed bachelor who wore his blondish beard and thinning hair cropped close, was the very thing Hay and Adams were not: a man of action. While Hay and Adams were content to write history, King intended to make it. At twenty-five he had begun directing the largest scientific study the federal government had ever undertaken, a geological survey along the route of the first transcontinental railroad. Awed by King's drive and intelligence, Henry Adams and John Hay predicted that their friend would have whatever prize he chose.

King already knew what he wanted. As soon as he left the U.S. Geological Survey, he would head for Mexico in search of the fabled lost silver mines of the conquistadors. Sitting with the Hearts in Henry and Clover's comfortable drawing room, he spun dreams of the day when he would have a wife and children, like John Hay, and live like the Adamses in a mansion filled with choice English paintings and the finest rugs from Kashmir and Kurdistan. His fortune made, he would devote himself to scientific research.

Out of loyalties dating from his years as a junior secretary in the White House of Abraham Lincoln, Hay had come to Washington in 1879 to fill an unexpected vacancy in the State Department. Now he was going back to Cleveland by way of New York, where he would spend a few months standing in for the editor of the *Tribune,* who was going away for a honeymoon. Once home, Hay had no ambition except to pick up where he had left off: managing his father-in-law's millions and collaborating with an old colleague on a life of Lincoln.

Henry and Clover also meant to resume the life they had led before their long stay in Europe. They rode in the morning, breakfasted at noon; and at one o'clock Henry retreated to his study to write a history of the United States in the opening years of the nineteenth century. Such an existence was idyllic, he thought—"like a dream of the golden age." Henry fervently believed that the future of the world lay in the United States and that the future of the United States lay in Washington. He reveled in the expectation and fancied himself one of "the first rays of light" that would one day set fire to the world.

As winter turned to spring and President Garfield settled into the White House, the Five of Hearts said farewell. "Five o'clock tea is a bore," Clover pouted when they had gone. But there would be other endings, just as there had been other beginnings.

PART ONE

GRAVITATIONS

1

A Family Fugitive

*H*enry Brooks Adams began life with all the blessings and burdens of a famous family. John Adams and John Quincy Adams, his paternal great-grandfather and grandfather, had been presidents of the United States, and it appeared possible that his father, Charles Francis Adams, would be the same. There was money, too, for the Adamses had prospered during their two centuries in Massachusetts, and Henry's maternal grandfather, Peter Chardon Brooks, was said to be the richest man in Boston.

The fourth of seven children, Henry was born on February 16, 1838. Like generations of Adams males before him, he spent his late adolescence at Harvard College, receiving a degree in 1858. He went to Europe, traveled, and studied in Germany with thoughts of becoming a lawyer. In 1860, when he returned to the Adams keep in Quincy, he was filled with doubt on all but one point: the law was not for him.

The young man's strongest inclinations were literary, though he had no idea what to do about them. Pure literature seemed beyond the reach of a self-conscious beginner of twenty-two, and his father disapproved of journalism, contending that the ephemeral nature of newspapers and magazines deprived journalists of any chance for real influence. As an old man, Henry liked to say that he had had the good fortune to be born a fourth child, a status so trifling that he could fritter away his life and "never be missed." In truth, his first opportunity for choosing a career left him paralyzed, and he was relieved when his father chose for him. Charles Francis needed a secretary; Henry consented to serve.

In the autumn of 1860, Charles Francis was elected to a second term in Congress and took his family, secretary included, to Washington, where Henry quickly fell in with another young secretary uncertain of his destiny. Like Adams, John Milton Hay had been born in 1838 and felt drawn to things literary. He left Brown University in 1858 with a Phi Beta Kappa key and a deep yearning to fulfill the promise his fellow students had seen when they elected him class poet. Back home in the Mississippi River hamlet of Warsaw, Illinois, Hay sank into a deep depression. He had no employment prospects, and as he reflected on the "heartless materialism" around him, literary dreams seemed absurd. In a few years, he bitterly predicted, his poetic eye would not be "rolling in a fine frenzy, but steadily fixed on the pole-star of humanity, $!" Too unhappy to choose an occupation, he consigned his fate to his father and was soon apprenticed to an uncle who was a prominent attorney in Springfield, Illinois. Abraham Lincoln had been a partner in the firm, and when Lincoln ran for president in 1860, Hay poured his poetic idealism into the noble cause of ending slavery. After the election, Lincoln rewarded him with a post as assistant secretary in the White House.

Hay had confidence in Lincoln, but Adams watched anxiously as the new president fumbled with his white kid gloves at the inaugural ball. As far as Adams could see, Lincoln's "long, awkward figure" and his "plain, ploughed face" showed no sign of force. Six weeks later civil war erupted, and soon afterward Lincoln asked Charles Francis to serve as American minister to England. Henry's friendship with John Hay would have to wait.

Lincoln charged the new minister with a delicate mission. Britain proclaimed itself neutral in the American conflict, which meant that it recognized the Confederacy as well as the Union. Certain parties in England, reasoning that a divided America would enhance the power of Britain, were agitating for British aid to the Confederacy. It fell to Charles Francis to try to preserve England's neutrality.

As his father's personal secretary, Henry was not officially part of the staff of the American legation in London, but his duties gave him an insider's view of the diplomatic chess being played on the board of the American Civil War. Canny and tactful, Charles Francis would accomplish his mission in spite of schemers and intriguers on both sides of the Atlantic. Henry watched with admiration for his father and mounting disgust for the politicians who stood in his way. Power, Henry decided, was "a diseased appetite, like a passion for drink or perverted tastes." Its effect was "an aggravation of self, a sort of tumor that ends by killing the victim's sympathies." His antipathy would last a lifetime.

Away from the legation, Henry dined with Charles Dickens and Robert Browning, and he cultivated Sir Charles Lyell, a geologist devoted to amassing evidence for the shocking new evolutionary theory of Charles Darwin. He met John Stuart Mill, the philosopher whose political ideas squared perfectly with the deepest hopes and fears of the Adams family. Mill admired democracies because they allowed the brightest and best to gain more influence than they could in hereditary aristocracies. But he fretted that representative government naturally tended toward "collective mediocrity"—the dreaded tyranny of a majority who made ignorant, self-serving decisions.

Henry's greatest social pleasures in England were the breakfasts and house parties given by Monckton Milnes, member of Parliament and man of letters. Voracious reader, astute critic, lover of art and books, orchestrator of "collisions" of dissonant minds, Milnes was Henry's ideal as a host. Among the sparkling monologists in the Milnes salon, Henry was a welcome guest: "they needed a listener," he deduced. Silent and thrilled, he heard Algernon Swinburne recite whole plays—forward and backward. Memories of these entertainments were banked for the day when Henry could orchestrate collisions in his own drawing room.

The future did little to reveal itself to Henry Adams during his seven years in London. Working for his father and living at home left him uncomfortably suspended between adolescence and adulthood. In mild rebellion he grew a beard and kept it despite his mother's protests. He also launched a secret campaign of defiance against his father, writing unsigned articles on British politics for American newspapers. Morally, it was an ambiguous enterprise. As secretary he had access to privileged information, exposure of which might compromise fragile negotiations and embarrass Charles Francis. Henry, longing to experiment with journalism, persuaded himself that his articles would help by presenting forceful briefs for his father's views.

For eight months Henry spent Saturdays in his rooms on the top floor of the legation residence, where he composed accounts of the week's political events. His undoing was a newspaper editor unable to resist trumpeting the Adams name. But when British newspapers pounced upon the transgression, they scolded the lad less for his politics than his manners, taking deepest offense at his complaint about the "thimblefuls of ice cream and hard seed cakes" served in English ballrooms. Afraid of being caught in a more damaging act, Henry put down his pen.

Though the minister bore the episode "very good-naturedly," Henry knew that another episode would be his ruin "for a long time." When Henry tried to explain his acute sense of failure to his older brother, Charles, Jr., Charles told him to stop whining. But Henry could not shake the feeling that he was "a humbug."

Humiliation notwithstanding, Henry's clandestine writing taught him that he enjoyed journalism no matter how little his father thought of it, and anonymity had offered a way to practice his new craft without fear of ridicule. To a perfectionist who had dismissed several earlier literary efforts as sadly wanting—unworthy of the House of Adams—a secret apprenticeship had incalculable worth.

Thin, thirty, and, by his own description, "very—very bald," Henry went back to the United States with his family in the summer of 1868, when his father decided to return to private life. Determined to break away from Boston and the Adams orbit, he settled on a career in journalism, wryly admitting that it was "the last resource of the educated poor who could not be artists and would not be tutors." New York, with its abundance of newspapers and magazines, was his ultimate destination, but he decided to go first to Washington, perhaps because he knew politics best. His father acquiesced, though he let it be known that he expected his son to grapple with "questions of public importance" and to do so "in a manner useful to the country." Charles Francis also warned him against Washington's "silly young women" and the time-thieving fripperies of capital society.

On his own at last, Henry bloomed. Cabinet members took him under their wing. Congressmen granted long interviews and, when it suited their purposes, assisted his investigations. In an analysis of the 1869–70 session of Congress, which appeared in the *North American Review,* he delivered blistering judgments with a self-assurance that would have been unthinkable a year or two before.

To the fledgling correspondent, it seemed that the government was out of control and no one would be held accountable. The president said he could not act because Congress would not pass laws, and Congress begged absolution because nothing could get past its fractious committees. The government was drifting, without "a course to steer, a port to seek," and the villain was President Ulysses S. Grant. Henry derided the lumpishness of Grant's mind and his refusal to see himself as anything more than a caretaker. Grant, Henry supposed, came as a rude shock to citizens who had expected the bold hero of Vicksburg to be a bold chief executive.

The incumbents were furious with the upstart's assessment, and the upstart basked in their fury. "I have smashed things generally and really exercised a distinct influence on public opinion," he boasted. When a senator lashed back in print, Henry's joy was complete: "To be abused by a Senator is my highest ambition."

The capital itself he considered "the drollest place in Christian lands." After seven years of London formality, unformed Washington offered "an easy and delightful repose." Cannons rolling through the streets for the four years of the Civil War had ground the pavement of the main thoroughfares to dust, rendering them even more impassable than the muddy side streets. Then, as later, society huddled around Lafayette Square, and beyond the square, "the country began." The country Henry saw as "a long, straggling caravan, stretching loosely toward the prairies, its few score of leaders far in advance and its millions of immigrants, negroes, and Indians far in the rear, somewhere in archaic time." Unlike New York and Boston, Washington had little wealth, which meant that men of modest means could live well and find ready acceptance by society. As for the "silly young women" disdained by his father, Henry charmed them sufficiently to win a reputation as one of the three best dancers in the capital. Journalism might be ephemeral, the nation might be dangerously adrift, but Henry Adams, for the first time in his life, enjoyed being Henry Adams.

The only one who asked more was his father. "You shoot over the heads of most people," Charles Francis complained. He also found Henry's style "savoring of conceit." Guessing that shyness compelled Henry to assume the pose of arrogance, Charles Francis warned that if he expected to influence men in public life, he would have to "remove this obstacle."

A younger Henry Adams would have been crushed. But with the buffer of five hundred miles between Washington and Quincy, and with abundant praise from editors and friends, Henry felt no need to alter his tone. And in spite of a growing disdain for the "dirty whirlpool" of politics, he had no desire to abandon Washington or journalism. In the summer of 1870, when the president of Harvard invited him to take a post as assistant professor of history, he promptly declined. He was flattered, he said, "but, having now chosen a career, I am determined to go on in it as far as it will lead me."

Two months later Harvard tried again. Henry's brothers thought he should take the job, as did his father, who had come to regard universities as "the field of widest influence in America." Under ordinary circumstances, the newly contented Henry Adams would have stayed in Washington, but that summer he had witnessed the unexpected death of his older sister, Louisa, who had contracted tetanus after being thrown from a carriage. Harvard was only a few miles from Quincy; perhaps his presence would soften his family's grief. The ferocious Washington correspondent, the man who loved smashing things, came tenderly home.

Telling an English friend of his appointment to teach medieval history, Henry confessed, "I am utterly and grossly ignorant . . . I gave the college fair warning of my ignorance, and the answer was that I knew just as much as anyone else in America knew on the subject." With his ready laugh, an endearingly poor memory for dates, and his refusal to require students to memorize page after page of text for recitation, Professor Adams was an immediate favorite. He was fearless in showing his ignorance. When a student asked for a definition of "transubstantiation," he shot back, "Good Heavens! How should I know! Look it up." His idea of a good examination question was one he could not answer. "It astounds me to see how some of my students answer questions which would play the deuce with me," he remarked to a friend. "You would be proud to know as much as they do."

With his teaching duties came the job of editing the *North American Review,* which had published several of his Washington essays. Perversely proud of its tiny circulation—four hundred at best—the magazine assumed that its subscribers included everyone who mattered. While Henry lamented that an editor was "a helpless drudge, whose successes, if he made any, belonged to his writers" and whose failure could mean bankruptcy, he quickly turned the *Review* into a pulpit for the reformist politics of the Adams family. He lashed out at monopolists and stock market manipulators, continued his assault on Ulysses S. Grant, and told his readers what to think of new books and scientific discoveries.

Beyond the iron railings of Harvard Yard, he made friends he would keep for life. He saw the sensitive Jameses, William and Henry, who were beginning their careers in philosophy and literature, and dined with William Dean Howells, whose novels he praised in the *Review*. He also befriended the tall, austere John La Farge, an artist struggling to perfect the manufacturing technique that would start a renaissance in stained glass.

In the spring of 1871, one of Henry's boyhood friends, Samuel Franklin Emmons, invited him to spend the summer out west with a party conducting a geological survey for the federal government. Eager to explore a new world and to rekindle the interest in geology that had begun with Sir Charles Lyell in England, Adams headed for Wyoming in July.

The West enthralled him. In the past he had poked fun at American crudities, but now he bragged to English friends about "country wilder than anything in Siberia." Even the climate was enchantingly hostile, with temperatures of a hundred degrees at noon and nights cold enough to leave crusts of ice in the water pails. He wore moccasins ("though they spoil the shape of the feet") and calmly wrote letters under the gaze of Indians on horseback.

The most exotic human being Adams encountered in his travels

Professor Henry Brooks Adams of Harvard in about 1875, when he was in his late thirties.
MASSACHUSETTS HISTORICAL SOCIETY

was Clarence King, director of the survey. At twenty-nine, King seemed to have everything, including the influence so prized by Charles Francis Adams. His Fortieth Parallel survey, underwritten by the government, was making the first accurate maps of a large part of the West and sizing up the region's mineral wealth, water resources, and agricultural prospects. A muscular five-foot-six, King had boundless energy and no discernible fears. He had once trapped a bear in a cave, climbed in after it, and, after coolly waiting for his eyes to adjust to the darkness, dispatched it with a single shot.

An aesthete with a particular fondness for painting, King saw to it that photographers and landscape painters accompanied the survey, and he strove to give his camps an air of refinement. In the evening, after a long, gritty day in the field, he donned silk hose, gleaming shoes, and a suit freshly pressed by his valet. Materializing at the campfire, he looked to an astonished Henry Adams like "a bird of paradise rising in the sage-brush." When a visitor teased the geologist about his fancy duds and the overweening ambition of his chuckwagon, King treated him to a haughty lecture: "It is all very well for you, who lead a civilized life nine or ten months in the year, and only get into the field for a few weeks at a time, to let yourself down to the pioneer level . . . But I, who have been for years constantly in the field, would have lost my good habits altogether if I had not taken every possible opportunity to practice them."

On meeting Clarence King, Adams felt the same instant connection he had experienced when he shook hands with John Hay. Friendship with King "was never a matter of growth or doubt," Adams said. It was whole from the start.

Back in Cambridge for his second year of teaching, Henry resumed a budding relationship with the Hoopers, a family whose Bay Colony roots went as deep as his own. Though he had known them for years, he owed the new closeness to Ephraim Whitman Gurney, dean of the Harvard faculty and husband of Ellen Hooper. Through the Gurneys Henry came to know Ellen's brother Edward (Ned) and sister Marian, called Clover by family and friends. Born September 13, 1843, Clover was the youngest of the Hoopers. At five-feet-two, she stood two inches shorter than Henry. With her large nose, full cheeks, and prominent chin, she was not pretty, but she possessed

Marian ("Clover") Hooper at Beverly Farms in 1869. She was twenty-seven.
MASSACHUSETTS HISTORICAL SOCIETY

highly developed artistic tastes and a wit so adroit that Henry Adams dove into love. As he told one of his brothers, "On coming to know Clover Hooper, I found her so far away superior to any woman I had ever met, that I did not think it worthwhile to resist . . . the devil and all his imps couldn't resist the fascination of a clever woman who chooses to be loved." On February 27, 1872, while his parents were far away in Europe, Henry asked Clover to marry him.

2

A Charming Blue

On Thursday, June 27, 1872, a party of thirteen gathered at the summer home of Dr. Robert Hooper in Beverly Farms, Massachusetts, for the wedding of his daughter Marian to Henry Brooks Adams. "The ceremony lasted in the neighborhood of two minutes," the groom's brother Charles grumbled in a letter to their father. The luncheon that followed lacked a seating plan, the champagne was insufficiently chilled and meagerly dispensed, the main dish mere roast chicken—served cold and carved by the bride. In all, Charles sniffed, "the aspect of affairs tended toward the commonplace."

To the bride and groom, it had been a splendid day. The thermometers on Boston's North Shore registered a comfortable sixty-five degrees, a gentle wind ruffled the sea, gray skies deepened the soft blues of the Morris wallpaper in the parlor. From the abbreviated exchange of vows to the informality of the meal, everything had gone in accordance with the couple's wishes. Thanking her father in a note written the next day, Clover said she and Henry thought the occasion "went off charmingly." The new husband pronounced the event "very jolly" and fancied that he and his wife had "established a precedent for quiet weddings."

The mean-spirited review filed by Charles Adams had less to do with the absence of the Hooper family's social finesse than with Clover's presence in Henry's life. Before Henry fell in love, he and Charles had been fellow knights in a glorious crusade. With the *North American Review* as their lance they had attacked the chicanery of railroad magnates and Wall Street manipulators, and they had worked zealously to make their father a candidate for the Democratic presidential nomination in 1872. By denying Ulysses S. Grant a second term, they dreamed not only of adding a third president to the Adams dynasty but of ridding the country of political and financial corruption. In choosing the summer of 1872 as the moment to begin a honeymoon year abroad, Henry dramatically abandoned his brother on the family battleground.

Charles had a further reason to be upset. On hearing of Henry's engagement to Clover, he had burst out, "Heavens!—no—they're all crazy as coots. She'll kill herself, just like her aunt!" The aunt, Susan Sturgis Bigelow, had taken arsenic at twenty-eight, ending her own life and that of an unborn child. Another aunt, Carrie Sturgis Tappan, was considered highly eccentric if not unstable, and Clover's mother, the fragile Ellen Sturgis Hooper, had died of tuberculosis in her mid-thirties.

The family's tragic history had not been concealed from Henry. "I know better than anyone the risks I run," he told his younger brother Brooks. "But I have weighed them carefully and accept them." He claimed not to care what the world thought of the marriage as long as people left him alone. But the truth was that he worried deeply about the reactions of family and friends. Fearing that Clover would fall victim to the savage candor that passed for conversation in the Adams household, he put Brooks on notice: "I shall expect you to be very kind to Clover, and not rough, for that is not her style." Describing his fiancée to an English friend, he seemed bent on exposing every flaw, as if to disarm all possible opposition in advance.

> She is certainly not handsome; nor would she be called quite plain, I think. She is 28 years old. She knows her own mind uncommon well. She does not talk *very* American. Her manners are quiet. She reads German—also Latin—also, I fear, a little Greek, but very little. She talks garrulously, but on the whole pretty sensibly. She is very open to instruction. *We* shall improve her. She dresses badly. She decidedly has humor and will appreciate *our* wit. She has enough money to be quite

independent. She rules me as only American women rule men, and I cower before her. Lord! how she would lash me if she read the above.

Though Clover's intellect was "quick and active," Henry had observed that she lacked thorough knowledge of any subject. Her mind, like the minds of other women he had known, struck him as "a queer mixture of odds and ends, poorly mastered and utterly unconnected." (Henry James, who shared Adams's reservations, had once declared Clover that rarest of creatures, a woman with "intellectual grace.")

Like virtually all of her female contemporaries on Beacon Hill, Clover had not gone to college, which was held to be injurious to girls by subjecting them to pressure and anxiety at the moment Nature had reserved for perfecting their reproductive systems. In 1872, Edward H. Clarke, a prominent Boston physician, warned the New-England Women's Club that invalidism and early menopause occurred more frequently among female college graduates than other women, and he painted a hellish prospect for those who stopped menstruating before Nature intended. Skin toughened, the body hardened, maternal instincts dwindled, and one acquired an "Amazonian coarseness and force." Altogether, said Dr. Clarke, such females were "analogous to the sexless class of termites."

Boston feminists, Julia Ward Howe among them, were quick to react. Mrs. Howe, who had turned her reforming energies from abolitionism to women's suffrage, urged that men and women be educated together in order to enjoy each other to the fullest in marriage. Elizabeth Stuart Phelps, a novelist, argued that women were less likely to be harmed by education than by "the change from intellectual activity to intellectual inanition. . . . The sense of perplexed disappointment, of baffled intelligence, of unoccupied powers, of blunted aspirations . . . is enough to create any illness which nervous wear and misery can create."

Clover's aunt Carrie Tappan counted herself one of the baffled and blunted. After a childhood of rowing and riding with boys, she felt betrayed when they went off to Harvard without her. Barred from academic pursuits, she wrote melancholy poetry and turned her inquisitiveness to the shadowy, faintly disreputable world of psychic phenomena.

Clover's school days were passed very happily at a progressive Cambridge establishment run by the wife of Louis Agassiz, a distinguished Harvard naturalist who had taught paleontology to Henry Adams. Like her sister Ellen and the daughters of many Boston notables, Clover studied the classics, learned French and German, and was introduced to the sciences by Professor Agassiz himself.

If Clover yearned for more education when she met Henry, she did not say so, and once he proposed, she yearned only to share her joy. "I love you more because I love Henry Adams very much," she sang to a friend. In a letter to her sister, she recounted a dream in which the two of them sat side by side, separated by a high wall of ice. Ellen's ice melted with her marriage to Whitman Gurney, but Clover's ice was in the shade and could not thaw. Then a blinding sunset forced her to cover her eyes. When she took her hands from her face, "there sat Henry Adams holding them and the ice has all melted away and I am going to sit in the Sun as long as it shines thro'."

As a marriage prospect, Clover's greatest attraction was money, which Henry, with a comfortable income of his own, did not need. For Clover, the heady truth was that Henry Adams loved her for herself. A "charming blue," one of his friends had dubbed her, and in fact he was captivated by her bluestocking qualities—her wide curiosity and a healthy scorn of convention.

Clover's gift to Henry was a new and enfolding sense of well-being. The Hoopers accepted him as he was—undoubtedly a delectable shock to one accustomed to the rigors of a family in which self-improvement was a relentless imperative. The Hoopers, believing that the fortune accumulated by their seafaring ancestors was meant to be enjoyed, cared more for pleasure than influence and freely indulged their passion for art. Ned was a founding trustee of Boston's Museum of Fine Arts, an early enthusiast of Winslow Homer, and one of the first Americans to appreciate the eerie engravings of William Blake. Fascinated by their taste, grateful for their affection, Henry gave the Hoopers an unabashed adoration that Charles Adams would never forgive.

For ten days the newlyweds stayed at Cotuit Point on Cape Cod, walking in the woods, calling on friends, and lolling on a large yacht left at their disposal by Clover's uncle. They kept their sexual dis-

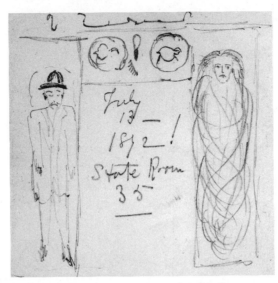

Henry and Clover Adams crossing the Atlantic on their honeymoon, as sketched in pencil by Clover. MASSACHUSETTS HISTORICAL SOCIETY

coveries to themselves, but for Henry at least, the experience came as a relief. Just before asking Clover to marry him, he had wondered anxiously how men and women reconciled themselves to sexual intimacy, which he referred to as "the brutalities of marriage." The reassuring surprise of life with Clover was that she seemed as familiar as his oldest furniture. "It is rather a sell to find that marriage is a very quiet institution," he wrote a friend a few weeks after the wedding.

Clover was less serene. She wrote chipper notes home, but she deeply missed her father and worried because she knew he missed her. Widowed for nearly twenty-five years, Dr. Hooper was more attached to Clover than to his other children. Clover was five when her mother died—four years younger than Ned, five years younger than Ellen—and she had always lived at home. Her father's closest companion, Clover rode with him, managed his household, and served as hostess when his friends Ralph Waldo Emerson and Henry Wadsworth Longfellow came for dinner. At sixty-two he was unlikely to return to medicine, the career for which he had trained but never practiced except as a volunteer.

While there was little Henry could do to ease the pain of separation, he showed a tender understanding of the tie between father and daughter. "I wish it were in my power to make the loss of Clover less trying to you," he wrote Dr. Hooper the day after the wedding, "but I know no other way of doing it than by making her as happy as I can."

The first sign of Clover's unhappiness spilled out inadvertently during the ocean voyage that followed their Cape Cod idyll. In a cartoon depicting the miseries of seasickness, Clover sketched two figures lying stiffly in coffinlike berths on opposite sides of the stateroom. With his eyes closed and hat on, Henry wears a distinctly comic expression, but Clover, hair disheveled and body tightly bound by blankets, stares wide-eyed into infinity. Intending the drawing for her father's amusement, Clover seemed to have no sense of the panic and isolation it revealed.

Still, homesickness did not entirely rule out happiness, and Clover's letters often contained evidence of both. From Lake Como she reported that Henry rowed her "for hours in and out of strange places, picturesque villas with stone saints and popes guarding the entrance, here a cove, there a waterfall. When we are hungry, we land and ransack a town for figs, and so the day slips by." Yet she was glad to learn that her father missed her, she said, "because I long to see you, and it wouldn't be nice to have it all on my side."

In Geneva, where Charles Francis Adams, Sr., was representing the United States at the arbitration of a dispute with England, Clover had her first encounter with Henry's parents. It did not go well. Afraid that the dresses in her trunks were too plain for the ballrooms frequented by the diplomatic corps, Clover begged to be excused from these formal occasions. She had her way, but the elder Adamses did not hide their displeasure. Henry's mother, Clover noted, was "quite disgusted."

By early December, Henry and Clover were ready for the most adventurous stretch of their honeymoon, a three-month cruise on the Nile. Henry had learned the rudiments of photography especially for the excursion, and Clover planned to sketch and keep a journal. But from their first day in Cairo's dusty streets, which teemed with bad-tempered camels, veiled women, swarthy complexions, and a babble of alien tongues, Clover felt menaced. A visit to a mosque took on the character of a nightmare. Dervishes in long gowns and

high white hats "spun round and round" while other "wild creatures" snorted like beasts and swung themselves "backward and
forward, almost touching the ground with their heads." For more
than half an hour they whirled faster and faster until she felt "surrounded by maniacs." Apologizing to her father for a lapse in correspondence, she explained, "I have found it impossible to get my
ideas straightened out at all." As she contemplated the long voyage
that lay ahead, she was filled with anxiety. "I can't imagine how
anybody can write letters from the Nile, as everyone knows about
the Pyramids and Sphinxes and ruins, and it is so useless to try and
say anything new about them."

On December 10, the Adamses set out on their chartered boat, the
Isis, a modern version of an ancient shallow-water craft known as a
dahabeah. Flat-bottomed and fitted with two masts, *dahabeahs* could
be sailed, rowed, poled, or towed. With a crew of at least twelve, the
Isis afforded numerous pleasures, and on many days Clover surrendered to them. The food she found "worthy of Paris," the climate
sunny and soft. In the long stretches of river between ruins, she and
Henry read on deck, and as Christmas drew near, the crew festooned
their cabin with palm fronds. When the *Isis* tied up along the banks,
the Adamses frequently dined with other Americans. On many days
they hiked and picnicked with Mr. and Mrs. Samuel Ward of New
York, and from time to time they met up with the family of an
energetic, bespectacled fourteen-year-old, also from New York:
armed with a rifle he had received for Christmas, young Theodore
Roosevelt shot his first bird and declared himself "proportionately
delighted." Henry might have joined the lad with the rosy cheeks
and large, brilliant teeth, but his own shooting gear, ordered months
before in London, had failed to turn up.

The Adamses did not see him, but Ralph Waldo Emerson was also
on the Nile, traveling with his daughter and cursing Egypt as an
affront to his New England soul. He loathed the tawny landscape,
the cloudless sky, the absence of trees. The trip was "a perpetual
humiliation, satirizing and whipping our ignorance," he scratched in
his journal. "The people despise us because we are helpless babies
who cannot speak or understand a word they say; the Sphinxes scorn
dunces; the obelisks, the temple-walls defy us with their histories
which we cannot spell."

When other travelers told the Adamses of the old philosopher's testiness, Clover was shocked. "I confess that temples do begin to pall—but that is an aside—so much the worse for me!" she told her father. "How true it is that the mind sees what it has means of seeing. I get so little, while others about me are so intelligent and cultivated that everything appeals to them." Where Emerson at seventy could admit that he disliked Egypt precisely because it humiliated him, Clover felt the same humiliation and blamed herself.

She begged her father not to show her "silly and homesick" letters to anyone and worried that Henry's family would be offended by her silence. But, she told Dr. Hooper, "I cannot write except to you who are used to my stupidity and shortcomings." By this time, she was agonizing over more than epistolary failures. "I must confess I hate the process of seeing things which I am hopelessly ignorant of, and am disgusted by my want of curiosity. I like to watch pyramids, etc., from the boat, but excursions for hours in dust and heat have drawbacks to people so painfully wanting in enthusiasm as I am." Unable to compose a proper account of her visit to Luxor, she lamented, "I never seem to get impressions that are worth anything, and feel as if I were blind and deaf and dumb too." No journal would be kept, no sketches made.

Several biographers have intimated that Clover suffered a nervous collapse on the Nile. Clearly the experience was an ordeal. But the only evidence of a breakdown is slight and oblique. For several weeks it appears that Clover wrote no letters; at least none have survived. Henry's correspondence also dropped off. In a note to a friend he mentioned that he had thought of writing an essay on Egyptian law but had given it up. "I have too much on my hands," he said, declining to elaborate.

Whatever the nature and the depth of Clover's despair, her spirits lifted on the Nile island of Philae, with its enormous sandstone boulders and colorful temples. For more than a week, she and Henry strolled among Philae's painted columns and Coptic shrines and basked in the sunshine of roofless temples. They rowed a bit and dined often with several American families, including the Wards and Roosevelts. Clover found the climate perfect and the ruins, set against deep-blue mountains, superb. South of Philae the Nile had been closed to tourists because of cholera, but when the quarantine was lifted and the Adamses extended their stay, Clover expressed no dismay.

By mid-March, when they boarded a steamer for Naples, Clover regretted "leaving palms and camels and turbans forever." Egypt was "a great success," she concluded. "We feel as if we had had a great bath of sunshine and warmth and rest, and are quite made over new." She even declared herself finished with homesickness. Henry, rarely mentioned in her bleakest letters, reappeared as her tender and devoted companion, buying her a Bedouin necklace and engaging himself with the question of where they would live when they returned to Boston.

Working their way north, they stopped in Rome, where they encountered their peripatetic friend Henry James, who had recently forsaken America for Europe. Homesick and aching with uncertainty over the "desolate exile" he had chosen for himself, James could not decide how he felt about the Adamses. He told one correspondent that "Henry A. can never be in the nature of things a very spacious or sympathetic companion and Mrs. A. strikes me as toned down and bedimmed from her ancient brilliancy." To his brother William, however, he said he found Professor Adams "improved," and he intuited that Clover, though her wit had been "clipped a little," had been "expanded in the 'affections'" by marriage.

Like other Americans, the Adamses made their way to the Roman studio of William Wetmore Story, an expatriate sculptor. "Oh! how he does spoil nice blocks of white marble," Clover moaned. Nor did she approve of the paintings of Elihu Vedder, another American settled in Rome. No longer signs of discontent, these dislikes were the confident judgments of a practiced connoisseur. From the moment the Adamses landed in Italy until they sailed home from England, Clover's letters brimmed with happy accounts of her purchases of ancient Italian terra-cotta figures, watercolors, Oriental rugs, and Japanese bronzes. Twenty-five crates of treasure would follow them home.

In Paris they settled into a sunny hotel on the Rue de Rivoli long enough to install plants on the balcony and hang their new watercolors. Their only unpleasantness arrived in the form of Henry's brother Charles. More than a year had passed since the wedding at Beverly Farms, but Charles had not lost his sneer. After surprising them early one morning, Charles told his wife he had torn Henry "out of the arms of his Clover, for he's always in clover now (Joke! ha! ha!)!" Marriage had turned Henry into "a damned solemn, pompous little ass," he fumed. Clover, who clung to Henry's hand and chattered more than Charles thought fitting, was "an infernal bore."

Arriving in Massachusetts in August 1873, Henry and Clover went straight to Dr. Hooper at Beverly Farms. A few days later, Henry journeyed to Quincy alone to see his parents. He expected that he and Clover would soon pay a visit together, but for the moment they were absorbed in life at Beverly and the logistics of setting up a household in Boston. Their new quarters at 91 Marlborough Street were not far from 114 Beacon Street, the home of Clover's father.

3

The King of Diamonds

No one was better equipped than Clarence King to understand the closeness between Clover Adams and her father. Born January 6, 1842, in Newport, Rhode Island, Clarence King was the son of James Rivers King, a China trader, and Florence Little King, a deeply religious woman with a taste for Romantic poetry. In 1848, James was lost at sea, together with his ship and a large share of the family's money. When the boy's infant sister died soon afterward, the grieving Florence resolved to devote her life to her son. It was a vow she kept, and it forged a bond her son never managed to break.

Determined to give the boy a superior education in spite of her limited means, Florence moved from one Connecticut town to another in search of fine public schools. Away from the classroom, Clarence spent hours roving through woods and fields, coming home with detailed descriptions of nature and dozens of questions. Florence encouraged these explorations, found science books for him, and read him poems about God and the majesty of Nature.

In the spring of 1859, on the eve of his graduation from Hartford High School, Clarence withdrew because of "illness." Quite unexpectedly he decided against going to college, moved to Brooklyn, and went to work for a flour broker in Manhattan. Though he found business "distasteful," he was determined to make his own way, he wrote to his closest school friend, James Gardiner. "I feel that I am my own man dependent on no one, and if I fail no one but myself is to blame. Then again if I succeed it is owing entirely to myself for not a soul has aided me."

The cause of this sudden display of independence was a man named George Howland. A moderately prosperous New York business-man, a widower with one son, Howland wanted to marry Florence King, who saw no reason to discourage the arrangement. Loathing the prospect of sharing his mother with a stepfather and a step-brother, seventeen-year-old Clarence intended to break away. To underscore the separation, he announced that he had chosen a new name for himself: henceforth he wanted to be known as "Clare," not "Clarence."

To the complicated hurts of his altered relationship with his mother were added the torments of sexual longing. The ideals of purity that he and Gardiner had piously set forth for themselves in Hartford seemed hopelessly unattainable in New York, where there was "more than one seductive, wicked, beautiful, fascinating, jolly, voluptuous, apparently modest artful woman to one poor chicken here; they show you their necks and bosoms without intending to and all sorts of abominable wiles they practice on a fellow that are mighty inflaming."

Disturbed by these inflammations and depressed by the invasion of George Howland, young Clare tried unsuccessfully to control his feelings. Self-government and self-discipline were not enough, he explained to Gardiner. They had placed his will "on a kind of throne," and pride in his will ground him down "into a low slav-ery." Only by wearing God's yoke did he expect to find real free-dom. He longed for another life, one in which all his yearnings would be satisfied by Christ's acceptance of his adoration.

Perhaps sensing that he would feel less turbulence if he left New York, Clare agreed to let Howland underwrite a two-year course of study at the Sheffield Scientific School of Yale College. He entered in the autumn of 1859 and left in the spring of 1861 with a degree, cum laude, in applied chemistry. No surer of his future than John Hay and Henry Adams had been of theirs, he knew only that he did not want to fight in the Civil War. Abolitionist convictions ran strong in his family, and he boasted that his grandmother had long boycotted

Southern oranges because of her belief that they contained "the blood of slaves," but he could not bear the thought of killing another human being. "God knows that for my country I *would* 'push a bayonet' and that I would not quail before death for my land, but the act would crucify in me many of my noblest impulses," he told Gardiner. Gardiner's suspicions to the contrary, it was not a matter of cowardice. "Constantly you force it on me that I don't want to lead men, that mine is not that kind of nature," he said. Insisting that leadership would be his "life's object," he begged Gardiner not to misjudge him: "Don't think that because I show you my tender side, my weak one if you will, that I have no fire, no firmness, no mental power."

In the spring of 1863, after two years of studying geology on his own, King was persuaded that he had found a profession with a shining future. As Henry Adams noted, the geologist's hammer was the key to El Dorado in nineteenth-century America—the only scientific means of unlocking the earth's treasure chests of gold, silver, copper, iron, and coal. At Yale, King had been enthralled by discussions of a pioneering geological survey in California, and he convinced Jim Gardiner that they should be a part of it. In April they boarded a train for Missouri, where they joined a wagon train to Virginia City, Nevada. By September, after trekking westward on foot through the Sierra Nevada range, they reached Sacramento and boarded a riverboat for San Francisco. When they discovered that one of their fellow passengers was a member of the California survey, the young men presented their letters of recommendation and asked for work.

None was available. Chronically short of funds, wholly dependent on the largess of the legislature, the California State Geological Survey proceeded by fits and starts. Gardiner decided to look for paid employment in San Francisco. With no hesitation, King put himself forward as a survey volunteer, an offer that was immediately accepted.

For the next three years King scrambled the Sierra Nevada in perfect happiness, his spirit enlarged by the "vastness of prospect" atop the mountain peaks and experiencing "a strange renewal of life" as he made each descent. These returns were "points of departure more marked and powerful than I can account for upon any reason-

Clarence King in his early twenties, fresh from the Sheffield Scientific School at Yale.
HUNTINGTON LIBRARY, SAN MARINO, CALIFORNIA

able ground," he wrote. "In spite of any scientific labor or presence of fatigue, the lifeless region, with its savage elements of sky, ice and rock, grasps one's nature, and, whether he will or no, compels it into a stern, strong accord. Then, as you come again into softer air, and enter the comforting presence of trees, and feel the grass under your feet, one fetter after another seems to unbind from your soul, leaving it free, joyous, grateful!"

In his knapsack he carried a Bible and a book of sermons, and the grandeur of the Sierra strengthened his reverence for the works of God. He viewed Nature as "the key to Art and Science, God the key to Nature." The beauties and mysteries of Nature were "a veil which He has drawn before us," to be looked at "with gentleness and humble admiration." Reluctant to share this fervor with his rough-and-ready companions, King hid it in a small volume that he titled *Notes on Yosemite* on the cover and *Notes on the life of Our Savior* on the flyleaf. In these private pages he summarized his Bible readings, meditated on the relation of God and Nature, and said nothing of Yosemite.

Still troubled by his sexual urges, King also concealed his attraction to the Indian women of the California mountains. It would be years before he could voice his sensuous memories of seeing a native woman "of splendid mould, soundly sleeping upon her back, a blanket covering her from the waist down, her bare body and large full breasts kindled into bronze under streaming light." Whenever he saw an Indian woman in her tent, he felt an overpowering desire to join her and talk about "Creation." Hearing of these impulses decades later, King's California colleagues finally understood his occasional disappearances from camp.

The Sierra idyll ended abruptly in the spring of 1866. George Howland died, and King hastened to his mother in New York. Howland's businesses had fallen into disarray, leaving King at the age of twenty-four with eleven dependents: his mother, a stepbrother, an infant half-sister, his maternal grandmother, assorted impecunious female relatives, and several servants. As soon as King grasped the hopelessness of Howland's affairs, he thought he should head for Colorado and a mining career. But his heart pulled him in another direction. Josiah Dwight Whitney, leader of the California survey, had suggested that the United States government would profit handsomely from a geological survey along the route of the transcontinental railroad. Once completed, the railroad would open vast Western territories for settlement, but no one knew what these lands contained. Compelled by the idea of finding out, King discussed the project with his old professors at Yale and, in January 1867, shortly after his twenty-fifth birthday, went to Washington to propose the survey to the secretary of war.

King was more qualified for this great task than his youth suggested. As a geologist, he had determined the age of California's gold-bearing deposits, a major advance for the mining industry. As an explorer and mountain climber, he held the record for the number of first ascents of Sierra Nevada peaks. And he had mastered an essential lesson of leadership. The state of California funded Whitney's work in hopes of gaining information that could be turned to practical use in mining and agriculture, but Whitney, more interested in pure science, had concentrated his first efforts on a study of fossils. When the initial appropriation ran out, Whitney had few admirers in the statehouse at Sacramento. Determined not to repeat Whitney's mistakes, King stressed the economic value of his survey. He and his party would pave the way for settlement by discovering where water could be had for irrigation, where cattle would thrive, and what the earth promised in the way of coal, metals, and other resources. Their focus would be the Fortieth Parallel, and they would survey a hundred-mile-wide swath stretching from the western slope of the Rockies to the eastern slope of the Sierra.

Impressed, Secretary of War Edwin M. Stanton persuaded a senator to add the survey to a pending appropriations bill, and in March 1867 Congress authorized the expenditure of $100,000 for the survey's first year. Handing King the letter that named him U.S. Geologist in charge of the Geological Exploration of the Fortieth Parallel, Stanton offered a word of advice: "the sooner you get out of town, the better—you are too young a man to be seen about Washington with this appointment in your pocket—there are four major-generals who want your place."

King dashed off a letter inviting his friend Jim Gardiner to join the survey and sped to Newport to share his elation with his mother. Their financial worries were over. As U.S. Geologist, King would draw a monthly salary of $250 and a per diem allowance in the field; he could get by on the allowance, and his salary would suffice for Florence Howland's ménage.

Beginning on the eastern slope of the Sierra Nevada and moving east along the Fortieth Parallel, the survey marched to the cadence of the calendar—fieldwork in the warm months, paperwork in the winter. King elected to spend the first winter in Virginia City, Nevada, where he wanted to study the played-out Comstock silver mine as well as help with the writing of the survey's first reports. With its plenitude of gaming tables, saloons, and bawdy houses, Virginia City did not measure up to its chaste name, but most men who had been long in the mountains were disinclined to hold the town to higher standards. Nonetheless, King and Gardiner passed up the fleshpots in favor of ice-cream sociables, prayer meetings, skating parties, and quiet gatherings in the parlor of a local judge. By winter's end, both young men had fallen in love with schoolteachers— King with a Miss Dean and Gardiner with a Miss Rogers.

In one of his private notebooks, King pondered the love between man and woman and decided that a satisfying marriage was built upon "physical mergence." Besides being a biological imperative and a divine good, physical union was the wellspring of intellectual companionship and an equality that allowed both parties to express their softer feelings. On Easter Sunday of 1868, just before leaving for the Fortieth Parallel, King presented a diamond ring to Miss Dean.

Deeply in love, King overflowed with tenderness when he learned that one of his old colleagues would soon marry: "My pleasure in thinking of you as loved and cherished by a good woman amounts to solid comfort. God grant that your new life may be hallowed and blessed by all the wealth of love and all the sweet comfort of domestic tranquility. I can bid you God speed in this move with more earnest thankfulness and more hearty good will than I once could for one of the best of God's own girls has promised bye and bye to crown my life with the same blessing."

In the autumn of 1868, King took Miss Dean to Newport to meet his mother. For reasons that one can only guess—jealousy, snobbery, financial fears—Florence Howland vehemently disapproved,

Clarence King mountaineering in the Sierra Nevada in 1870, when he was twenty-eight.
NEW YORK PUBLIC LIBRARY, RARE BOOKS AND MANUSCRIPTS DIVISION,
ASTOR, LENOX AND TILDEN FOUNDATIONS

and Miss Dean disappeared from King's life. The wound hurt for years. In an 1880 letter about the engagement of a friend, King bitterly remarked that he had lost the only woman he had ever wanted to marry through "too much attention to duty. Duty has stood between me and almost every good thing."

By 1872, the thirty-five men of the Fortieth Parallel survey had made the first accurate maps of thousands of square miles of Western terrain, catalogued hundreds of plant and animal specimens, discovered a glacier, and charted the region's mineral resources. Studying the supposedly exhausted Comstock lode, King concluded that its day had not yet passed. In a few years the Big Bonanza would prove him right. The party's official photographer and a succession of guest artists, including landscape painter Albert Bierstadt, added pictures to the record.

As director of the Fortieth Parallel survey, Clarence King, at left, believed in dressing for dinner. Adams, who spent a summer with the survey, saw him as "a bird of paradise rising in the sage-brush." NEW YORK PUBLIC LIBRARY, RARE BOOKS AND MANUSCRIPTS DIVISION, ASTOR, LENOX AND TILDEN FOUNDATIONS

Gardiner, who worked for the survey from the beginning, had ample opportunity to revise his opinion of his friend's cowardice. He saw King scorched by lightning, and he had waited in suspense while King hunted down a deserter from the survey's cavalry escort. The soldier, who had stolen away in the night, was miles ahead of him, but since the survey party was about to enter territory ruled by hostile Indians, King felt obliged to teach a lesson that would stave off further defections. With the sergeant in charge of the escort, King set off at a gallop. Near sundown, at the end of a hard ride through a hundred miles of desert and mountains, King spotted a trail leading to a mountain pass. Reasoning that the runaway would choose that route, King and his sergeant spent the night in the saddle, riding over the mountain to the far end of the pass. They reached their destination at sunrise and saw the fugitive calmly cooking breakfast near a spring in a willow grove. King left his horse in care of the sergeant, drew his revolver, and crept forward. The deserter saw him and fired. King charged and captured his quarry in a hand-to-hand struggle. Depositing the renegade in the nearest jail, King returned to camp with his point persuasively made.

From time to time, King wrote about his adventures for William Dean Howells of the *Atlantic,* giving many Easterners their first glimpse of the Far West. Through Clarence King they came to know glaciers, waterfalls, the furies of a mountain storm, Indian funeral customs, hard-bitten pioneers, and the deficiencies of frontier justice. In a tale of a barroom trial of an accused horse thief, King described the jury's deliberations and their verdict of innocent. "You'll have to do better than that!" they were told. Half an hour later, they supplied a verdict of guilty. "Correct!" said the court official. "You can come out. We hung him an hour ago." Before the day ended, the barkeep found the allegedly stolen animals behind the saloon, placidly chewing up decks of playing cards.

In 1872, when a collection of King's sketches appeared under the title *Mountaineering in the Sierra Nevada,* one of the few critics immune to the charms of the book was the author's new friend, Henry Adams. After a few brushes with rattlesnakes and hostile Indians, Adams complained in the *North American Review,* the reader grew "distinctly sleepy." Assuring his subscribers that King had more substance than his "trifle" suggested, Adams urged them to read the scientific tomes of the Fortieth Parallel survey. It was a dreary antidote, however kindly intended. Adams sounded more like his father than himself when he worried that King's literary dabbling would cost him influence with the congressmen who held the purse strings of the survey.

In the fall of 1872, King and his crew wrapped up the year's fieldwork and settled down for their customary winter of writing reports and preparing the survey's next volumes for publication. Sometimes they came East, but this year they were putting up in San Francisco, and when they arrived in October, they found the town buzzing with rumors of a fabulous diamond mine. From Rothschilds to Tiffanys, the mine was backed by all the right people. It had also passed the scrutiny of Henry Janin, a mining engineer well known for his professional skepticism. Though King knew of no spot in the West capable of yielding such riches, he joined the crowds gawking at a jewelry-store window aglow with diamonds, sapphires, and rubies said to have come from the mine.

As a frequent guest at the Union Club, gathering place of San Francisco's bankers and entrepreneurs, King heard every bonanza rumor wafting through the West, and he considered himself a shrewd judge of the men who peddled them. (No admirer of George Hearst, the mining baron, King remarked that when Hearst was stung in the privates by a scorpion, it was the scorpion that died.)

Neither King nor Gardiner believed the glittering evidence in the jeweler's showcase, but they could not guess how the swindlers, whoever they were, had managed to gull Janin, a diamond merchant of Charles Tiffany's renown, and a corps of sharp-witted financiers. The question nagged more than it might have since the geologists were about to write a report ruling out the possibility of precious gems along the Fortieth Parallel. Years before, after Josiah Whitney had flatly declared that petroleum would never be found in a certain part of California, a major oil discovery had cast doubt on all of his other "scientific" findings. King did not want to leave his work open to the same sort of attack.

King knew Henry Janin, and the next time they met, he casually asked where Janin liked to dine. King and Gardiner began posting themselves there in the evenings. A few nights later, when Janin turned up, King persuaded him to join their table. The surveyors had worried about how to bring up the diamond mine without arousing Janin's suspicions, but the engineer was bursting to tell them all he knew. He bragged that his thousand shares in the San Francisco and New York Mining and Commercial Company had quadrupled in value. Predicting that the mine would yield a million dollars' worth of gems a day, he urged King and Gardiner to invest before production began.

King coolly launched his interrogation. "Of course, you now know exactly where the place is?"

Janin did not. He had made the journey blindfolded, reaching the diamond mine only after a thirty-six-hour train trip and two days on horseback. The site was "a curious place," he said—"a level desert with a conical but flat-topped mountain rising right out of it, and on the mountain you find everything from garnets to diamonds!" He had turned up gem after gem merely by poking the surface with a pocket knife.

In his most offhanded manner, King remarked that it was a shame Janin had had such bad weather for the trip.

When Janin replied that the weather had been "splendid," King and Gardiner had the clue they needed. During the time of Janin's trip, the only dry mountainous area in the West was a patch near the convergence of the borders of Wyoming, Utah, and Colorado—approximately thirty-six hours by train from San Francisco. Back in their rooms, the two geologists pulled out topographical maps made by the Fortieth Parallel survey and quickly located a mesa fitting Janin's description in northwestern Colorado.

The next morning King, Gardiner, and two other trusted survey members crossed San Francisco Bay on a ferry and boarded the Central Pacific at Oakland. Taking care not to tip their hand to fellow passengers, they referred to the diamonds as "carboniferous fossils." Thirty-six hours later, in subzero temperatures, they disembarked at Green River, Wyoming. The blindfolded Janin had been led in circles for two days after his train ride, but King and his team headed straight for the sawed-off cone. Each time they forded a stream, the water dripping down the legs of their mules hardened into balls of ice that clacked like castanets in the bitter wind. They reached the mesa in the afternoon and by nightfall gathered a hundred rubies and four small diamonds. They also made a curious discovery: the gems were found in crevices and anthills marred by small scratches, suggesting that some sort of tool had been used to shove the stones into place. For three bone-chilling days they poked and probed until King was satisfied that the fraud was beyond question.

In the middle of their investigations they were visited by a stranger, a corpulent man in city dress. He had been watching them through a spyglass. An associate of George Hearst, the man had been trying for months to locate the secret diamond mine, and after observing King and his colleagues at work for hour after hour on the windswept mesa, he concluded that he had come to the right place. Without thinking, the geologists told him he was mistaken. The Golconda was a hoax. The stranger thought for a moment then remarked that the situation presented a superb opportunity to short the stock of the San Francisco and New York Mining and Commercial Company.

When the man left, King decided to go straight to San Francisco to stop further stock transactions. By riding all night, he and his party reached Green River just in time to board the dawn train for Oakland. They arrived in San Francisco late on November 10, roused Janin, and spent most of the night explaining their findings. In the morning, King informed the directors of the mining company that they were "victims of an unparalleled fraud." As evidence he offered a diamond partly burnished by a lapidary tool. Equally suspect was the wide array of minerals found in the same field. The prospectors had turned up four types of diamonds, plus rubies, garnets, spinels, sapphires, emeralds, and amethysts, which in King's professional opinion was an "impossible occurrence in nature." In short, someone had salted the field—one of the oldest tricks in the mining business.

Stunned, the directors insisted on a return to Colorado to confirm the findings. King agreed but warned that if they did not make a public announcement of the fraud as soon as they returned to California, he would. He had no intention of allowing them to dump their stock on the innocent.

When the announcement came, King softened Janin's humiliation by pointing out that the fraud was "the work of no common swindler, but of one who has known enough to select a spot where detection must be slow, and where every geological parallelism added a fresh probability of honesty." Furthermore, Janin had been given only an hour for prospecting.

Abashed, Janin explained his mistake by noting that two experts before him had inspected the diamond fields and attested to their worth. He had gone to the mine a believer, thinking his job was simply to estimate the yield. He had also trusted in the opinion of Charles Tiffany, who confessed with considerable embarrassment that his jewelers had overvalued the gems because of their unfamiliarity with raw diamonds. They had always worked with polished stones, imported from Amsterdam.

A grand jury was appointed to investigate the hoax. The perpetrators, a sly pair who had passed themselves off as grizzled prospectors of marginal intelligence, vanished before the grand jury returned its indictments.

For days after the announcement, the exploits of Clarence King competed for headlines with the death of the country's most famous newspaper editor, Horace Greeley of the New York *Tribune*. King's superiors in Washington were annoyed to learn of the hoax from the newspapers rather than from their geologist, but their vexation was swept away by a wave of public adulation. King's exposure of the hoax proved the value of the Fortieth Parallel survey, the *Nation* wrote. "This single exposure, the work of a few days in appearance, the result of several years in reality, has more than paid for the cost of the survey." Overnight, Clarence King was famous.

4

Death of a Hero

"My diamond shares of course turn out worthless, but I lose nothing," a relieved John Hay wrote home to Warsaw, Illinois, at the end of 1872. Together with almost everyone else who invested in the shimmering bubble popped by Clarence King, Hay was to be reimbursed. His other affairs, he added, "look a little better than they did, though I do not quite yet see daylight through them. I am about embarking, with powerful friends, in another enterprise, where the loss, if any, will be small, and the profit, if it comes, will be large."

At thirty-four, Hay still felt obliged to explain his finances to his father, as if to assure both of them that he would in fact succeed. As an editor and writer at the New York *Tribune,* he was well paid and deemed sufficiently respectable for membership in such clubs as the Century and the Knickerbocker—the bastions of his "powerful friends"—but the sting of early failure had not subsided.

In the first decade of his career, Hay had known both the pinnacle and the abyss. At twenty-two, the ink still fresh on his certificate of admission to the Illinois bar, Hay had gone to Washington to work as assistant to John George Nicolay, Abraham Lincoln's secretary.*

---

* Hay functioned as assistant secretary though he never held the title. By law, the president was entitled to only one secretary. Nicolay arranged for Hay to be appointed to a clerkship in the Department of the Interior and assigned to the White House. In 1864, the War Department

After Lincoln's inauguration on March 4, 1861, Hay and Nicolay became members of the household at 1600 Pennsylvania Avenue, and their admiration for the president grew with their intimacy. Hay, possessor of a Phi Beta Kappa key and a diploma from a fine Eastern university, could not restrain his laughter as he listened to the unworldly Lincoln attempt to converse with a delegation of Potawatomis by asking, "Where live now?" and "When go back Iowa?" But the Rail Splitter's power to cut to the core of any issue, however complicated, left the young secretary in permanent awe. Hay caught his first glimpse of Lincoln's wisdom in the early weeks of the Civil War, when the president explained to him that the debate over slavery was peripheral. The great question to be settled was "whether, in a free government, the minority have the right to break up the government whenever they choose." By preserving the Union, Lincoln intended to prove that popular government was not "an absurdity."

Haunted by the war, President Lincoln slept badly and often padded down the drafty second-floor corridor, clad only in nightshirt and slippers, to his secretaries' rooms at the east end of the White House. After a midnight visit in April 1864, Hay reported in his diary that Lincoln had come in laughing, "seemingly utterly unconscious that he, with his short shirt hanging about his long legs, and setting out behind like the tail feathers of an enormous ostrich, was infinitely funnier than anything in the book he was laughing at. What a man it is! Occupied all day with matters of vast moment, deeply anxious about the fate of the greatest army of the world, with his own fame and future hanging on the events of the passing hour, he yet has such a wealth of simple *bonhommie* and goodfellowship, that he gets out of bed and perambulates the house in his shirt to find us that we may share with him the fun."

In March 1865, at the beginning of Lincoln's second term, Secretary of State William Seward invited Hay to take a post as secretary of the American legation in Paris. Eager for relief from the demands imposed by the war, Hay accepted, but at Lincoln's request he delayed his departure in order to assist with the transition to the new

---

commissioned Hay as a major, giving him the title of assistant adjutant general of volunteers, detailed to the Executive Mansion. In 1865 he was promoted to lieutenant colonel, then colonel.

President Abraham Lincoln flanked by his chief assistants, John George Nicolay, left, and John Hay. Hay was twenty-two when he went to work in Lincoln's White House.
JOHN HAY COLLECTION, JOHN HAY LIBRARY, BROWN UNIVERSITY LIBRARY

administration. A few weeks later, on the night of April 14, while Hay and the president's son Robert sat talking in the White House, shouting crowds burst through the doors with the news that the president had been shot. The two young men dashed downstairs, commandeered a carriage, and drove to the house on Tenth Street where Lincoln lay dying. Hay stood by the bed until twenty-two minutes past seven in the morning, when Lincoln stopped breathing. Pitched into despair by Lincoln's death, Hay could not express his feelings even in the privacy of his diary. He fled Washington at the first opportunity.

Arriving in Paris at the end of July, the grieving Hay found fault with everything, from the sterility of the broad new boulevards to the stench of the older arrondissements. Emperor Napoleon III, with his lifeless eyes and "rotten threadbare uniform," struck him as grotesque. When an American traveler asked the legation to intercede in her dispute with a hotelkeeper, Hay advised her to drop the matter. The French, he explained with a signal want of diplomacy, "make their living by plundering foreigners."

Hay was no happier with himself than with the French. He felt less than honorable in the service of Lincoln's successor, Andrew Johnson, who seemed to be "doing his best to discredit his high office," Hay thought. It was Johnson's misfortune to preside over the bitter beginnings of Reconstruction, touching off clashes with Congress that nearly cost him the presidency. Apart from his low regard for Johnson, Hay felt underpaid for the style he was expected to maintain as a member of the diplomatic corps, and he recoiled from the picture of himself as a "whiteheaded old shyster of sixty loafing about the Capitol boring my Senator to get me an office to keep me from starving."

In confident moments, he dreamed of writing a novel and collaborating on a life of Lincoln with John George Nicolay, but an inability to act on his dreams kept him in constant anxiety. "I am confronted continually by the suggestion of middle age coming on me and finding me with no money, no home, no trade, nothing but the habits of the loafer," he fretted to his brother. "Up to a certain point it is a good and a pleasant thing to knock around the world, but one must know when to hang up the fiddle and the bow and take up the serious shovel and the lucrative hoe." The matter was particularly pressing in view of his previous disasters with shovels and hoes. A foray into the turpentine business had wiped out his savings— more than $4,000—and a small vineyard in Illinois, supervised by his father, had yet to turn a profit.

Determined to acquit himself in the world of business, Hay resigned in July 1866, barely a year after his arrival in Paris. With no employment prospects, he wrote to his Uncle Milton in Springfield, Illinois, asking to rejoin the law firm where his career had begun: "I have forgotten most of the law I read with you and would have to learn it all over again. I am not even a good clerk as I know very little about money or business. It is nearly an even chance whether I would ever get to be worth my salt at the bar." All he could offer was a willingness to try.

Milton Hay had no room for his nephew, publishers had no room for another book on Lincoln, employment failed to materialize, and after a few dispiriting months at home, John Hay was grateful to be asked to take another diplomatic assignment, in Vienna. His official title would be secretary of legation, the same as in Paris, but as acting chargé d'affaires he would earn $6,000 a year—more than double his pay in France. He sailed from New York on June 29, 1867.

Vienna pleased Hay no more than Paris. The emperor was "a stupidish fellow," the Austrians hopelessly smug in their "satisfaction with a very bad present." In 1869, moving on to the legation in Madrid, he quickly transferred his abuse to the Spanish. Lazy and devoid of "moral principle," they were led by politicians to whom decency meant nothing and an empress who succeeded with American envoys by keeping them "in a chronic priapism." Equally disgusted with the United States, Hay charged that President Ulysses S. Grant, who succeeded Johnson in 1869, was filling the diplomatic corps with "swine" and "nonentities." It was, he confided in a letter intended for his correspondent's fire, "very dreary to be an American and hate your home."

Treated to this barrage of bitterness, friends and family must have mourned the loss of their sweet Johnny Hay, the warm, sensitive youth who had sailed through innumerable tempests on his impeccable manners and his droll sense of humor. Surely the "idiots" he complained of in Europe did not put his grace to more strenuous tests than he had met at the hands of greedy office-seekers and the mercurial Mary Todd Lincoln. In the White House he had been more inclined to laugh than censure when megalomaniacs recommended themselves as major generals or when Mrs. Lincoln, in a show of temper, scratched his name from a list of dinner guests. Hay's angry outbursts from Europe were expressions of grief and rage, walls thrown up around a broken heart. Lincoln had saved the Union, but he had abandoned John Hay and bequeathed the nation to incompetents.

Hay did not recover until the spring of 1870, five years after the assassination. Finally able to look at his future with more optimism than fear, he resigned his post in Madrid and told his parents he was coming home to "do a little writing."

★   ★   ★

The "little writing" soon followed, though not in Warsaw, Illinois. Passing through New York in September, Hay dined with Whitelaw Reid, Horace Greeley's first lieutenant at the *Tribune*. Known, only half jokingly, as the Great Moral Organ, the *Tribune* still hewed to the high principles Greeley had set forth in 1841, when he founded the paper with a pledge to "advance the interests of the People, and to promote their Moral, Social and Political well-being." By eschewing lurid scandals and unsavory advertising, the *Tribune* meant to win "the hearty approval of the virtuous and refined." A vegetarian with a weedy-looking fringe of white whiskers along his jawline, Horace Greeley was easy to lampoon but impossible to ignore: the *Tribune* was read from coast to coast. As Ralph Waldo Emerson explained to Thomas Carlyle, "Greeley does the thinking for the whole West at $2 per year for his paper."

Whitelaw Reid, impressed by Hay's command of foreign affairs, offered him a job, and after a few weeks of mulling it over, Hay accepted. He had come home superbly accoutred for a newspaper career. Diplomacy had given him an understanding of the subtleties of ministerial pronouncements, and the hours he had spent writing letters and essays had polished his literary style and honed his powers of observation. In December, only a few weeks after Hay's arrival, Reid raised his pay from fifty to sixty-five dollars a week and sent him a note of praise: "I have seen now enough of your capacity in sudden emergencies and in a wide scope to be ready to repeat the assurance which I gave you at the beginning, that journalism is sure to prove your true field."

Since the *Tribune* seldom credited its writers, Hay's contributions are hard to trace, but one episode, his coverage of the great Chicago fire, suffices to confirm Reid's high opinion. The blaze began on Hay's thirty-third birthday, October 8, 1871. Reaching Chicago after a grueling thirty-eight-hour train trip from New York, Hay made the dismaying discovery that the fire had crippled most of the city's telegraph lines. The keepers of the lines, plowing their way through sheaves of unsent messages, refused to give one newspaper preference over another. Hay managed to persuade them to send one of his dispatches to the Associated Press, arguing that it would then be available to scores of newspapers. It was not the exclusive coverage the *Tribune* wanted, but it was more than most of his rivals achieved. Though he saw little chance for further transmissions, he worked sixteen hours a day, freshening his stories with new developments in anticipation of the moment when the wires were restored.

On October 15, one week after the fire began, Hay wrote his last dispatch. "I have here before me six miles, more or less, of the finest conflagration ever seen," he told *Tribune* readers. "I have smoking ruins . . . mountains of brick and mortar and forests of springing chimneys; but I turned from them all this morning to hunt for the spot where the fire started." Finding his way to Mrs. O'Leary's "mean little street," he observed that on one side, not a single house had burned, while on the other only one "squalid little hovel" remained: a "warped and weather-beaten shanty . . . made sacred by the curse that rested on it. . . . For out of that house, last Saturday night, came a woman with a lamp to the barn behind the house, to milk the cow with the crumpled temper, that kicked the lamp, that spilled the kerosene, that fired the straw that burned Chicago." Behind the house, Hay found Mr. O'Leary with two of his friends.

> His wife, Our Lady of the Lamp—freighted with heavier disaster than that which Psyche carried to the bedside of Eros—sat at the window, knitting. I approached the Man of the House and gave him good-day. He glanced up with sleepy, furtive eyes. I asked him what he knew about the origin of the fire. He glanced at his friends and said, civilly, he knew very little; he was waked up about 9 o'clock by the alarm, and fought from that time to save his house; at every sentence he turned to his friends and said, "I can prove it by them," to which his friends nodded assent. He seemed fearful that all Chicago was coming down upon him for prompt and integral payment of that $200,000,000 his cow had kicked over.

But it was poetry, not prose, that brought John Hay his first fame. At about the same time he joined the *Tribune,* Bret Harte wrote a comic ballad about two Western cardsharps outsmarted by an Oriental named Ah Sin. Called "Plain Language from Truthful James" but quickly retitled "The Heathen Chinee," the poem was printed by hundreds of newspapers across the country. Vendors hawked pamphlet versions on streetcorners, and scores of imitators took to their foolscap. Hay, drawing on his dormant poetic talents and the Pike County dialect he knew from his childhood on the Mississippi, dashed off a few ditties of his own. In "Jim Bludso of the Prairie Belle," the hero is a riverboat engineer "who weren't no saint," having "one wife in Natchez-under-the-Hill / And another one here, in Pike." But when the *Prairie Belle* caught fire, Jim steered for the riverbank and vowed to hold the wheel "Till the last galoot's ashore."

> *And, sure's you're born, they all got off*
> *Afore the smokestacks fell,—*
> *And Bludso's ghost went up alone*
> *In the smoke of the Prairie Belle.*

> *He seen his duty, a dead-sure thing,—*
> *And went for it thar and then;*
> *And Christ ain't a-going to be too hard*
> *On a man that died for men.*

"Little Breeches" was the sentimental saga of little Gabe, a four-year-old whose father had "larnt him to chaw terbacker / Jest to keep his milk-teeth white." Carried off into a stormy winter night by a team of startled horses, little Gabe was given up for lost when his desperate father flung himself "Crotch-deep in the snow, and prayed." Inspired to look in a nearby sheepfold, he found his boy, unharmed among the sleeping lambs. The child had only one complaint: "I want a chaw of terbacker / And that's what's the matter of me."

The *Tribune* printed Hay's verses, signing them J.H., and in a few weeks they were as famous as "The Heathen Chinee." Even Professor Henry Adams of Harvard was charmed; Hay's poems were "better than anything Bret Harte ever wrote," he told a friend. In the saloons of Newton, Kansas, where cowpokes recited the ballads and showed off their chaws of terbacker, an enterprising *fille de joie* began claiming the bard as her brother.

"That ridiculous rhyme of mine has had a ridiculous run," the

bard noted with amazement after "Little Breeches" appeared. "As
my initials are not known, and they generally get worn off on the
second reprint, I have not been disgraced by it." In a note to W. D.
Howells, who had published several of Hay's essays in the *Atlantic,*
Hay wondered whether Howells knew of "Little Breeches" and its
"appalling run. It is published every day in hundreds of newspapers.
Two political papers in the west have issued illustrated editions of it.
I mention this to show what a ravenous market there is for anything
of the sort."

Howells not only understood the market, he had done more than
any other Eastern editor to create it. A native of Ohio, he loved the
twangs and drawls of the West. In Mark Twain and Bret Harte and
the Sierra tales of Clarence King, he heard voices that were distinctly
American, voices owing as little as possible to the literary traditions
of England.

Howells wanted more rhymes, but Hay could not oblige. Perhaps
his Pike County vein had simply run out, or perhaps he was thrown
by the accusation, baseless though it was, that he had plagiarized
Bret Harte. A few days after Christmas 1870, he announced to Howells that he was out of the ballad business: "I wrote another one, and
Reid says it is very bad—in which I agree—so it is not to be published, and I will do no more songs."

It was Hay's early poetic idol, Walt Whitman, who had heard America singing and had encouraged her to celebrate herself. Whitman
was still listening in the lighthearted season of "Jim Bludso" and
"The Heathen Chinee," but the music he heard was decidedly more
somber. America echoed with "hollowness," he wrote in *Democratic
Vistas,* his 1871 meditation on the soul of the nation. "Genuine belief" had disappeared, hypocrisy was everywhere. The "depravity of
the business classes" was "infinitely greater" than Americans supposed, government agencies were "saturated in corruption, bribery,
falsehood, mal-administration. . . . The best class we show is but a
mob of fashionably dress'd speculators and vulgarians." While the
nation's prosperity had lifted the masses from their sloughs, Whitman thought America had failed "in its social aspects, and in really
grand religious, moral, literary, and esthetic results." The great west-

ward march, source of so much patriotic pride, seemed to him a pointless extravagance. "It is as if we were somehow being endow'd with a vast and more and more thoroughly-appointed body, and then left with little or no soul." The cure, he thought, lay in scientific breeding. Women must be freed from the "incredible holds and webs of silliness, millinery, and every kind of dyspeptic depletion" in order to fulfill the destiny of their sex. With a "strong and sweet Female Race, a race of perfect Mothers," the states could be kept supplied with "a copious race of superb American men and women, cheerful, religious, ahead of any yet known."

If Whitman's prescription was easy to ridicule, his diagnosis was not. Ahead of most of his countrymen, he saw that corruption—political, financial, social—was threatening to derail the great loco-motive of democracy. In Washington, bribes were no longer simply accepted, they were organized into auctions, with appointments, charters, rights-of-way, and other government favors going to the highest bidder. Those who demanded reform were regarded as fleas on the body politic. The reformers were "noisy but not numerous," one ravening senator noted; they could be "easily dealt with." To the airless mind of President Grant, the issue was not corruption versus reform but whether anyone really wanted reform. If Congress de-clined to pass laws putting civil-service positions beyond the reach of party patronage, he declared, he intended to drop the subject.

As Republicans and Democrats squared off for the presidential contest of 1872, a small band of idealists wished a plague upon both their houses. Parties bred machines, they reasoned, and the money and offices controlled by machines led inexorably to corruption. They aspired to smash the machines, clearing the way for a return to the pristine days of the Founding Fathers, when government reposed in the hands of the best people. The Republican party, heedless of the corruption swirling around Grant, whose associates were skimming profits from the Union Pacific Railroad and taking bribes in ex-change for concessions to operate army trading posts, nominated him to run for a second term. The Democrats, joined by a faction of liberal Republicans, invested their hopes in John Hay's employer, Horace Greeley.

As an editor of the *Tribune,* Hay was expected to manufacture enthusiasm for Greeley's candidacy, but he could not bring himself to feel it. For John Hay, Democrats were inextricably bound up with the ghastly night in April 1865 when John Wilkes Booth, a Democrat, assassinated Abraham Lincoln. On election day, Hay went as far as he could for Greeley. Unable to cast a ballot for him, he stayed away from the polls.

5

A Daughter of the Middle West

*U*lysses S. Grant swept twenty-nine of thirty-five states. Horace
Greeley, whose wife died a few weeks before election day, lost his
mind and was taken to an asylum in the country. "He acquiesced in
it himself and indeed told me that he supposed he must be mad,"
Whitelaw Reid wrote to John Hay. "It troubled him that he could
not convince me . . . the whole world was ruined, and he had caused
it, and that if it was not so, as I insisted, he must be mad." By
December Greeley was dead.

And by December John Hay was deeply in love. Through a New
York socialite who considered bachelorhood too cruel a fate for the
author of the tender "Little Breeches," Hay had been introduced to
Clara Louise Stone, a reserved and pious young woman whose robust figure, dark complexion, deep-brown eyes, and abundant dark
hair gave her the air of a Roman empress.

In the spring of 1873, when Clara's parents consented to her marriage, Hay vowed to "consecrate" his life to her. "My mind and
spirit are yours as well as my heart and life," he pledged. "I love you,
your soul and body, your goodness and your beauty. You *are* my
inspiration and reward. I worship you." Sometimes, he confessed,
he gazed at her until her eyes and mouth seemed "radiant and glo-
rified with some divine beauty and promise—until it seemed to me

49

that I could not live without falling at your feet and pouring out my full heart in worship." But honor compelled him to warn her: "You are crazy to give yourself to me—everything for nothing. You are wastefully generous. Ah, think what you give. Beauty and goodness and youth, a rich and noble nature, candor and honor and affection, and in return you get only the worship of a soul which has no existence but in you." The most he could offer was assurance that his love flowed from an honorable source—respect for her "firm and inflexible Christian character" and her purity. "If, like me, you had passed many years in the troubled current of the world, and met everywhere deceit and folly and sin, treachery and malice, then you would know how infinitely comforting it would be to meet one heart which is true and noble and kind, one which you could trust for time and for eternity."

The woman who inspired this passion was born December 29, 1849, eleven years after John Hay. Like him, she was a product of the strapping, energetic Middle West. As a young man, Clara's father, Amasa Stone, Jr., had moved from Massachusetts to Ohio in order to build railroad bridges. Cleveland was a boom town, inventive and industrious, and Stone's business prospered. He compounded his fortune by investing his profits in such promising new enterprises as Western Union and Standard Oil. A generous philanthropist, Stone underwrote a home for elderly women and an industrial school. After his only son, Adelbert, drowned at Yale, Stone gave $600,000 for the founding of Adelbert College, which evolved into Case-Western Reserve University.

Affluence enabled Amasa Stone and his wife, Julia, to put up a gingerbread palace on Euclid Avenue, the broad, leafy street where Cleveland's finest installed themselves in American translations of Italian villas, Loire Valley châteaux, and Elizabethan manor houses. They sent their sons to Harvard and Yale and finished their daughters at Cleveland Academy.

Growing up in this privileged enclave, a daughter was expected to acquire an appreciation of the arts, a sense of duty, and a cheerful acceptance of reality, however it presented itself. Clara Stone's school compositions show that she learned these lessons well. In "What the Cold Does," she noted that although it killed plants and people, one "ought not to complain" for without the cold there would be no ice

*The wealthy and pious Clara Louise Stone, twenty-four, on the eve of her wedding in
1874. John Hay boasted that she was "large, handsome and good."*
JOHN HAY COLLECTION, JOHN HAY LIBRARY, BROWN UNIVERSITY LIBRARY

skating. An imaginary conversation between needle and thread begins as a boasting contest and ends with a conciliatory proposition by the needle: "I think now that you are about as useful as I am and if anything more, so let us shake hands and be friends and never quarrel again about such a little thing." Clara's dreams of adventure flickered to life in an essay on traveling the world, but given a chance to describe a well-spent day, her thoughts ran to duty rather than excitement. She envisioned a girl who went to school early, recited perfectly, practiced the piano for two hours after school, and then helped her mother sew until dark. After supper the girl did her homework, checked it, and went to bed.

Clara worked as diligently as this paragon, though she remained a rather baffled grammarian. "You must leave off now and again, Clara, and start a new sentence," one of her teachers implored. Still, Clara loved books, and in June 1868, on the eve of her graduation from Cleveland Academy, she challenged one bit of conventional wisdom in "Literature versus Housekeeping."

> It is a very old idea that literary women cannot make good housekeepers. It seems natural to believe that a woman cannot attend to belles lettres and write poetry (for proficiency in these takes a great deal of time) and also find opportunity for her household duties. How absurd (it has been often said) for a woman to be taking care of crying children or getting a dinner and at the same time trying to write a book yet it can be done. Men have done it. Look at Oliver Goldsmith who while in the heighth [sic] of his literary glory was keeping house in lodgings and getting his own dinners. Housekeeping appears to be the particular end of woman and anything which interferes with that end should be set aside.
>
> In accomplishing this "particular end" one must needs have their wits about them as it is something which cannot well be shirked especially management of servants who as all know soon become quite as knowing as the mistress if she has not learned the art of controlling them. But is there any real reason to think that a woman with a well balanced mind and ideas concerning the economy of her hours may not find time for other affairs beside those of housekeeping.
>
> Literary women have always been and always will be the subject of ridicule. They are generally called blue-stockings, are described as slatternly in their dress and always as having their fingertips dabbled with ink. But ridicule is not argument. There is certainly no need of all this for a woman can keep herself dressed up neatly if she is an authoress as if she had nothing to do with ink.

Clara added that she would have enjoyed being part of the Blue Stocking Circle, an eighteenth-century group of London women who organized evenings for the sole purpose of intelligent conversation. How refreshing it would be, she thought, to discuss Plato instead of "trials with servants and the annoyances of providing family groceries." While agreeing that modern women should learn chemistry to understand cooking, arithmetic for keeping family accounts, and Greek and Latin to discipline the mind, Clara believed that none of these mattered as much as the world of letters. "A love of literature is a constant source of pleasure, for a favorite poet or historian often brings refreshment and relief in the midst of the trials and fatigues of household duties," she declared. On an even loftier plane, literature enlarged a woman's understanding of "the relation she bears to her fellow beings."

The relation of Clara Stone and John Hay incorporated this love of literature. As a long-distance suitor, writing to Euclid Avenue from his office at the *Tribune,* Hay delighted in passing along books he thought she would enjoy. The couple shared an unqualified admiration for the works of William Dean Howells and Henry James, and when Clara planned a trip out West, Hay forwarded his friend Clarence King's book, *Mountaineering in the Sierra Nevada.*

In the summer of 1873, the relationship was put to its first test. Clara had postponed their wedding, perhaps more than once, and Hay was growing impatient. As he explained to his friend George Nicolay, "There will be an internecine war before Mrs. Stone consents to give up her daughter—wherein I sympathize with her." Julia Stone approved of Hay but dreaded the prospect of Clara's move to New York. In spite of Mrs. Stone's opposition, Hay jauntily predicted victory "before many centuries" and praised his fiancee as "a very estimable young person—large, handsome and good."*

Writing to Clara during that troubled summer, Hay could not resist a bit of sarcasm. If she persisted in procrastinating, he said,

* Various authors have interpreted that description as a sign that Hay was less attracted to Clara than to Amasa Stone's millions. But Hay's correspondence contains other complimentary references to amply proportioned women, and when he wrote to a friend after the wedding—describing Clara as "large, handsome and very comfortable"—he enclosed her photograph, a step he would hardly have taken had he been embarrassed by her stoutness. (John Hay to Alvey A. Adee, November 28, 1874.)

"We must love each other less, write more seldom, think of each other much less frequently. How do you like this proposition?" He also pointed out that the happiest relationships he knew were those in which "the husband is all selfishness and the wife all devotion. Shall we try to cultivate these talents, you and I? My own precious love, I cannot be made over again, and so you must take me as I am. If there is any selfishness in your nature it will be aggravated by living with me."

The difficulties passed, and on Wednesday evening, February 4, 1874, in her parents' parlor, Clara Stone became Mrs. John Hay. The newspapers, which noted only that the occasion was elegant and decorous, were most impressed by Colonel Hay's New York guests, who noticed the excellence of the French on local restaurant menus.

One week after the wedding the Hays arrived at their first home, a sunny spacious apartment at 111 East 25th Street in Manhattan. "Lady Clara was in fine spirits and was struck so favorably that I hope the impression may last for some time," Hay wrote to her sister, Flora. "She spent the afternoon in delightful pottering and has not yet got all the sunshine out of her temper." There were invitations, including one to dine at the Clarendon Hotel with Mr. and Mrs. Henry Adams of Boston, but Hay was glad that they had married just before Lent, when the social season would come to a halt. Then they would have no obligation to spend their evenings anywhere but at home.

As feared, Mrs. Stone was distraught, assailed by headaches and unable to sleep, but Clara's sister suggested that Mrs. Stone's feelings were not the only ones to be considered. Taking Hay into her confidence, Flora explained that when Clara was a child, she was "shy and diffident, never thought *she* could be or do anything, and the general public, not having as much faith as we, did not encourage her much. Now, however, I can fairly see her blossom out in the sunshine of her happy life."

The sunshine bathed John as well as Clara. Amasa Stone expressed his affection for his son-in-law with a gift of $10,000 in railroad bonds, the *Tribune* rewarded him with regular pay increases, and he enjoyed wide literary acclaim for his Pike County ballads as well as his book, *Castilian Days,* a collection of essays written during his days in Madrid. Mark Twain, Bret Harte, and W. D. Howells—the

By the time he married, at thirty-five, John Hay had served in the White House, held diplomatic posts in three countries, and won fame as a poet and journalist.

JOHN HAY COLLECTION, JOHN HAY LIBRARY, BROWN UNIVERSITY LIBRARY

most celebrated *litterateurs* of the day—admired John Hay. Twain's admiration verged on idolatry. Hay not only possessed a "winning naturalness" and "a charm of manner," Twain thought, he was "a picture to look at, for beauty of feature, perfection of form, and grace of carriage and movement."

(Clara Hay, however, gave Twain a permanent fright. Late in life, writing his autobiography, he recalled a Sunday morning decades earlier when "Mrs. Hay, gravely clad, gloved, bonneted, and just from church, and fragrant with the odors of Presbyterian sanctity," happened onto her husband and Mark Twain as they were "chatting, laughing and carrying on." The two men sprang to their feet, ready "to say the pretty and polite thing and offer the homage due," but "the comely young matron forestalled us. She came forward, smileless, with disapproval written all over her face, said most coldly, 'Good morning, Mr. Clemens,' and passed on out." Overcome by sheepishness—one wonders about the nature of the conversation interrupted by Mrs. Hay—Twain could think of nothing to say. Hay, torn between loyalty to his wife and a hostly impulse to ease his guest's discomfort, explained that Clara was "very strict about Sunday.")

The Hays finished their first year of marriage with the happy suspicion, soon confirmed, that they were to become parents. The only cloud in their benignant sky was notable mostly for its silver lining: Amasa Stone wanted Hay to move to Cleveland and join his business, in exchange for which Hay was promised "immediate wealth." While Hay felt no deep attachment to the *Tribune* or to journalism, he did not rush to accept Stone's offer. Perhaps he was reluctant to trade his independence for life in the shadow of his powerful father-in-law. Or perhaps he feared that a quick acceptance would lend credence to the rumor that he had married for money—a million dollars, the gossips said. Whatever Hay's hesitations, he set them aside in the spring of 1875, when Stone's deteriorating health made it difficult to refuse his importunings.

In the beginning, Hay delighted in his Cleveland life. He adored his first child, Helen, who had arrived in March, and he and Clara and the baby were elegantly ensconced in a house on Euclid Avenue, courtesy of Amasa Stone. The work Stone assigned to his son-in-law was trifling—"merely the care of investments which are so safe that they require no care," he told a friend. After years of showing no interest, publishers had begun pressing Hay and Nicolay for a biography of Lincoln, and at last there would be time to write it. As Christmas drew near, Hay totted up his blessings and pronounced himself "hedged about with good things."

But sometime during the spring of 1876, Hay began to suffer from a constellation of ailments suggesting that he was not entirely at ease in his luxurious new life. Headaches, exhaustion, insomnia, and depression came and went for no apparent reason. Disgusted with himself after six trying months, Hay stopped talking about the symptoms, even to Clara.

Toward the end of the year, two events forced Hay's attentions in other directions. On November 1, Clara gave birth to their first son, Adelbert, a "fine little man-child, ugly and strong, lean and big-boned," and sufficiently fierce of mien to be "a railroad maker and statesman," Hay wrote to Whitelaw Reid. The mother was in splendid form: "The babies take none of her health or good looks away from her," Hay noted with gratitude. On December 29, Clara turned twenty-seven. It was a day of heavy snow and ripping winds. At seven thirty that evening, in northeastern Ohio, a Lake Shore and Michigan Southern Railroad locomotive crept through a large snowdrift and onto a long bridge spanning the Ashtabula River gorge. The engineer heard a crack and felt the bridge give way. By slamming the throttle wide open, he made it past the break, then watched in horror as the rest of the train plunged into the river seventy feet below. Heating stoves exploded. Fire raced through the cars. Before the night ended, some eighty persons were dead, another sixty injured. It was the worst railroad accident on record, and Amasa Stone had built the bridge.

For several years, Stone had also been president of the Lake Shore and Michigan Southern. When investigators of the Ashtabula accident discovered that the railroad had not regularly inspected the bridge, they naturally concluded that inspections might have prevented the disaster. Worse, the chief engineer on the bridge-building project testified that Stone had refused to listen to concerns about using iron rather than wood to fabricate a span of such great length. Nor had Stone wanted to hear about problems with bridge beams purchased from a firm partly owned by his brother.

Stone denied knowledge of the defective beams and pointed out that he himself owned no part of the ironworks in question. He also speculated that the bridge collapse had not been caused by structural flaws. There had been a second locomotive behind the tender of the first locomotive, and Stone argued that it had derailed, subjecting the bridge to extraordinary stress. But an engineer who survived the wreck testified that the second locomotive held the rails until it slid into the chasm. The court ordered the railroad to pay damages of $600,000.

Stone fled to Europe, sparing himself a fusillade of criticism by newspapers and magazines. Henry Adams's brother Charles, an authority on railroads, accused Stone of dishonesty and criminal neglect. W. D. Howells, who had moved from the *Atlantic* to *Harper's,* used his editor's column to blame the tragedy on naked greed, and he praised the court for hitting railroad titans in the one place it was sure to hurt, the pocketbook.

After hearing from an angry John Hay, Howells recanted. A "friend" who was "thoroughly informed of all the facts" had set him straight, he explained in the July 1877 issue of *Harper's*. The friend had made him aware that the railroad began compensating victims and their families the day after the catastrophe—well before the court levied its penalties. In addition, the court's verdict rested largely on the testimony of disgruntled former employees of Amasa Stone. After presenting Hay's brief, Howells expressed his pleasure at learning of the "really careful management" of the railroad and the "high character" of its officials.

Restored to favor, Howells soon found himself invited to Cleveland for the premier of his play, *Counterfeit Presentment*. "My wife never lets me read anything of yours to myself," Hay said in his invitation. "It is her proud prerogative to read aloud to me every word you write."

The rest of Ohio shared Clara Hay's enthusiasm for this native son. Howells had conquered the summit of cultural summits, literary Boston, and Ohioans chose to read his triumph as a sign that they too had arrived. Because of Howells, Midwesterners were no longer obliged to squirm in silence when an Eastern visitor professed surprise, as Howells's bride-to-be once had, at seeing a copy of *Harper's* or the *Atlantic* west of the Alleghenies. They could drop the name of the lad from Columbus, who had edited both.

In November 1877, soon after Howells and his wife stayed with the Hays, John and Clara journeyed to Cambridge to return the visit. Clara arrived with a new autograph book, for which Howells obligingly composed a short poem. Hay came, he told Howells, in the hope of learning "how the deuce you write such delicious things." Once he knew the secret, he added, "I will come home happy and write some myself."

But for most of the next two years, happiness eluded John Hay. Though he turned out more than fifty thousand words of the Lincoln biography, he was plagued by nervous symptoms and bouts of gloom. He traveled to Philadelphia to consult S. Weir Mitchell, an eminent specialist in maladies of the nerves, who found nothing wrong but suggested that Hay spend the summer of 1878 away from his work. Leaving Clara at home with the babies, Hay and his brother Leonard stayed in England for a month, explored Holland and Belgium, took a month-long rest cure at Schlangenbad in Germany, and toured Italy, Switzerland, and Scotland.

"After I got back I imagined I felt better for a month or so," Hay reported to Nicolay early in 1879, "but the other day I had the most ridiculous attack I have ever had—thought I was dead for half an hour. The Doctor said it was nothing at all serious—simply the effect of the cold. But I feel rickety yet. I have been trying my best to get to work again with very indifferent success." His symptoms were undoubtedly aggravated by his relations with Amasa Stone. Long uncertain, Stone's health worsened after the Ashtabula disaster, which forced him to rely more heavily on his son-in-law. But Stone would not bow out entirely, which left Hay with insufficient authority to carry out his expanding responsibilities. As a prime beneficiary of Stone's largess, Hay was not in a strong position to complain.

Hay himself saw no link between his delicate nerves and the tensions of life on Euclid Avenue. In October 1879, when Secretary of State William Evarts asked him to fill in for eighteen months as assistant secretary, Hay declined on grounds of sheer happiness with his family and Cleveland. His only regret centered on the loyalty he felt to the Republican Party and the memory of Lincoln. The vacancy had arisen with the departure of Frederick Seward, who was Hay's friend as well as the son of Lincoln's secretary of state, to whom Hay owed his early diplomatic career. Describing the situation to Howells, Hay fretted that his refusal would be considered "frivolous and vain. In that case I shall have to accept—and I stand like a hydrophobical on the edge of a bathtub. It is enough to make a man perish with self contempt, to see such vacillation and lack of self-knowledge."

In November, when Secretary Evarts repeated his request, Hay packed his bags for Washington.

6

Infinite Mirth

*H*ay settled into a suite at Wormley's, a cozy hotel at Fifteenth and H streets, just east of Lafayette Square. Owned by a family of mulattoes, Wormley's was renowned for its table, its encyclopedic wine cellar, and impeccable service. A State Department official had promised that for eight dollars a day, Hay would have every amenity save one: Wormley's suffered from a shortage of the "high-toned Southern Congressmen" whose nocturnal poker games enlivened the air of most Washington hostelries.

The capital had scarcely changed since Hay first saw it on the eve of Lincoln's inauguration in 1861. The population had tripled, to 177,000, and asphalt had at last begun to overtake the mud of the streets, but the city still exuded an air of impermanence. Pondering the contrast between the grandeur of the Capitol and the scruffy rooming houses lining the streets, more than one visitor shared an English tourist's suspicion that Washington was a Potemkin village, "run up in the night," dismantled when Congress adjourned, then "packed up till wanted again."

Insofar as this encampment had a permanent core, it was Lafayette Square, which John Hay crossed every morning on his way to the State Department. Anchored by the White House and Pennsylvania Avenue on the south, the square was a handsome composition of

Federal-style houses, mostly brick, which had sheltered public figures as diverse as Daniel Webster, Henry Clay, John C. Calhoun, and Dolley Madison. On the night of Lincoln's assassination, a conspirator of John Wilkes Booth had also tried to murder Secretary of State William Seward in his house on Madison Place, the eastern edge of the square. His neck encased in a brace as the result of a carriage accident, Seward was slashed in the face and head but survived. On the opposite side of the square, along Jackson Place, James Blair had organized one of the first scientific expeditions to the southern reaches of South America and the coast of Antarctica, setting out in 1838, the year John Hay and Henry Adams were born. To the north lay H Street and the gold-capped steeple of St. John's Church, the unofficial house of worship for presidents and their families.

Hay's office, near the southwestern corner of Lafayette Square, was deep in the colossal new gingerbread fantasia known as the State, War and Navy Building.* Pillared, porticoed, corniced, and capitaled to a fare-thee-well, the edifice looked less like a bastion of state than a playhouse—the sequel, perhaps, to mad King Ludwig's fairy-tale castle in Bavaria. What Hay made of this ne plus ultra of Second Empire architecture he did not say, but after only two weeks at his desk he was ready to return to Cleveland. The satisfactions of public service did not begin to fill the holes left by his absent family, he told Clara's father. "I shall be very glad when I can decently give up this place and go home." Apart from missing Clara and the babies, he dreaded the daily onslaught of callers who begged favors he could not grant—women, "gentle and ladylike and poor," who came in search of clerical work, and a parade of would-be consuls and legation secretaries. "Oh dear! if you could sit by my desk one single day and see the clamorous greedy host that comes continually for offices that are not worth having, you would know how sick and disgusted with human nature I feel when evening comes," he told Clara.

Among the clamorous was his old friend and fellow balladeer, Bret Harte. After the sensation of "The Heathen Chinee," the *Atlantic* had signed Harte for the stratospheric sum of $10,000 a year,

---

* Completed in 1888, the structure was later named the Executive Office Building and still later became known as the Old Executive Office Building.

but success exacerbated his taste for drink, and by the mid-1870s, the debts of Bret Harte were as famous as his yarns of the Wild West. Mark Twain, one of his angriest creditors, began calling him "the Immortal Bilk." When Harte promised to sober up, W. D. Howells, Clarence King, and other friends recommended him for a minor diplomatic post in hopes that the combination of a salary and minimal responsibilities would enable him to resume his writing. In 1878 Harte went to Germany as American consul at Crefeld, near Dusseldorf. The locals showed no deference to the author of "The Outcasts of Poker Flat," the damp air of the Rhine bothered his neuralgia, and Harte was soon plumping for a new post. Hay, after weeks of pulling strings to arrange a transfer, complained that he had received a letter from Harte "showing that his ideas were so lofty that nothing I could do would suit him." Like the greediest of the greedy who badgered the assistant secretary of state, Harte had his eye on the balmy climes of Spain and southern France. The best Hay could offer was Glasgow. To his surprise, Harte quietly accepted.

Before going to Washington, Hay had considered running for Congress, a notion heartily endorsed by Mark Twain, who told their mutual friend W. D. Howells that the "presence of such a man in politics is like a vase of attar of roses in a glue-factory—it can't extinguish the stink, but it modifies it." But as 1879 came to a close, Hay decided that he wanted no part in the glue factory. The more he saw of congressmen, the more "distasteful" he found them, he told Clara. "I do not want or need any office in the world." When Clara worried that Ohio Republicans would draft him unless he declared his intention not to run, Hay assured her otherwise: "If I do not work for it, I will not get it."

Away from the State Department, Hay spent most of his time in the company of Clarence King, who was also staying at Wormley's. They had known each other in New York, during Hay's *Tribune* days, when they passed many evenings together at the Century Club and won a mild notoriety for a midnight game of leapfrog over the ashcans outside another gentlemen's club. In 1878, after completing the Fortieth Parallel survey, King had come to the capital to campaign for the creation of the U.S. Geological Survey, which would coordinate the growing number of geological expeditions conducted by the government. He had intended to leave Washington as soon as the agency won congressional approval, but when an incompetent scientist appeared to have mustered enough political support to win the directorship of the new bureau, King had seen no way to block the appointment short of putting himself forward as a candidate. He prevailed and postponed his business plans. Reunited in Washington, King and Hay quickly became inseparable. They breakfasted, walked, ate dinner, and paid social calls together, and with another friend of King's, they soon rented a house at 1400 Massachusetts Avenue. Life in their new "bachelor castle" proceeded "in a scrambling sort of way," Hay warned Mr. and Mrs. W. D. Howells in an invitation to dinner, but he promised that an evening with the genial King would be worth their while even if "the feast consisted of a cold potato."

While Hay had drifted from diplomacy to journalism to his sinecure in Cleveland, King had leaped from one pinnacle to another, and Hay overflowed with admiration. The Fortieth Parallel survey was not only exemplary science, it had sealed the bond between East and West—a critical achievement in the eyes of political leaders whose memories of the Civil War stirred fears of Western secession. At ease in the literary realm of Howells, able to discuss the most arcane details of Oriental art, a superb outdoorsman, King seemed to have left no territory unconquered. In spite of his desire to leave government, he embraced his administrative duties at the U.S. Geological Survey with as much ardor as if he planned to stay forever. He devised uniform standards for fieldwork, eliminated duplications among surveys in progress, and undertook an ambitious study of the nation's mineral wealth for the 1880 census.

As a scientist, King was one of a handful who challenged the assumption of gradual change that underlay Darwin's theory of evolution. After examining volcanoes, mountains, and other terrestrial upheavals, King concluded that cataclysmic events such as earthquakes had also left their mark on the evolution of plants and animals. Outlining his ideas at the 1877 commencement exercises of his alma mater, the Sheffield Scientific School at Yale, King sounded a theme that would preoccupy social thinkers for the rest of the century: "When catastrophic change burst in upon the ages of uniformity and sounded in the ear of every living thing the words 'Change or die,' plasticity became the sole principle of salvation." To John Hay, no one seemed more adaptable, more versatile, more splendidly equipped for change than Clarence King.

King returned the admiration. For all his discontent and indecision, Hay represented precisely what King wanted for the next stage of his life: stability. Since breaking off his engagement to Miss Dean of Virginia City, King had struggled to resign himself to life without marriage, but he still longed for a wife like the "calm and grand" Clara Hay, who struck him as a rare combination of head and heart and the embodiment of "the best of the 19th century."

Full of plans for cattle ranches and mining ventures, sure that his knowledge of the West would enable him to make fortunes of his own, King felt little envy of the wealth Hay had acquired by marriage. King was less compelled by the fact of Hay's money than by the uses to which he put it. Unharried by any desire to build an empire of his own, Hay contented himself with incremental gains on his father-in-law's millions and directed his energies to other pursuits, such as the Lincoln biography he was writing with Nicolay. King meant to pursue a similar course. Once rich, he would collect art and subsidize serious scientific work—theoretical research of the sort abjured by practical-minded legislators.

King and Hay were also united in their antipathy to Washington society. As the capital of a democracy, Washington prided itself on keeping its doors wide open and liked to boast that this accessibility made for the most captivating society in the nation. Those who held such a view were "very much mistaken," said a *New York Times* correspondent. "The truth is that more uneducated, rude, and vulgar men and women find their way into the social gatherings of the capital than to those of any other city in the Union." A Washington party was bound to be a crush of "over-dressed, loud-mouthed, vulgar people"—adventurers, swindlers, and the elderly debauchés who made up the diplomatic corps. Hay tried to like the spectacle of it, if only because he thought Clara would, and his letters to Euclid Avenue brimmed with descriptions of blazing jewels, ambitious ball-gowns, and diplomats in brilliant regalia. Bored and annoyed by the social demands of his office, Hay sometimes forgot engagements, and he made a game of inventing devious methods of skipping dinner courses without attracting the notice of his hostess. King was not

nearly so restrained, and the primmer the crowd, the greater his urge
to test the limits of propriety. He loved to tell crude tales of the West,
especially one about a campfire repast consisting entirely of baked
beans. "Pitch in, my boy, pitch in!" he had urged a forlorn-looking
diner. "Sow the wind! Reap the whirlwind!" Boasting of his marks-
manship, he had brought a hush to a fashionable drawing room by
raising a rifle and taking aim at a chandelier. When an anxious guest
asked if the gun were loaded, King withered her with a smile and an
offer to load it if she wished.

Hay did not comment on these performances, but he was aware of
the friction between women and Clarence King. Clara's mother and
sister were afraid of him, and King appeared to have a few trepida-
tions of his own. Hearing a rumor that one of Lafayette Square's
most delightful young women, Emily Beale, was in love with King,
Hay asked him what he thought of her. "To see her walk across a
room, you would think someone had tilted up a coffin on end and
propelled the corpse spasmodically forward," King replied, effec-
tively closing the subject of Miss Beale. A few weeks later, when she
declared herself to King, he vowed to Hay that he would never again
call at her family's house.

In the autumn of 1880 Henry and Clover Adams returned to Washington after spending more than a year in Europe, where Henry had
scoured diplomatic archives for a history of the United States during
the presidencies of Jefferson and Madison. The Adamses rented a
house on the northern border of Lafayette Square, at 1607 H Street,
with only Lafayette Park between them and the White House. It was
"a solid old pile," Clover told her father, built around stout chimneys and sheathed in walls fourteen inches thick. The house had six
bedrooms, rear porches on all three stories, and, in the words of their
delighted new cook, a "powerful large" kitchen.

Henry and Clover stayed at Wormley's while painters, plasterers,
and carpenters renovated their new quarters. By December the Adamses and their four servants were ready to receive the fifteen wag-
onloads of furnishings they had left in storage. Oriental and Middle
Eastern carpets—Bokharas and Baluchistans, Kashmirs and
Kurdistans—were unrolled on the floors, and around the drawing
room they stationed their dark red, low-slung leather armchairs. Art

was everywhere: Japanese vases, Oriental bronzes, porcelain, drawings by Rembrandt and Michelangelo, oils by Turner and Constable. More than forty watercolors hung on the thirteen-foot-high walls of the library, and nearly three dozen prints lined Henry's study. The indoor flora and fauna consisted of potted palms and a pair of Skye terriers named Boojum and Pollywog.

The Adamses had first come to live in the capital in 1877, after Henry gave up the editorship of the *North American Review* and his teaching position at Harvard in order to edit the papers of Albert Gallatin, Jefferson's secretary of the treasury. For Clover, leaving Boston meant separation from her adored father, Dr. Robert Hooper, but Henry descended from Beacon Hill with no regrets. "I gravitate to a capital by a primary law of nature," he told one of his English friends. "This is the only place in America where society amuses me, or where life offers variety."

On the surface, variety seemed a peculiar claim to make for a town that trafficked only in politics. Art, intellect, and commerce, which rounded out the lives of older capitals such as London and Paris, had almost no practitioners in the District of Columbia. Libraries were scarce and small, a proper concert hall had yet to be built, and with the exception of the Corcoran Gallery, museums of art did not exist. But if Washington lacked finesse, it compensated with an unending procession of new faces. Congressmen came and went. So did senators, cabinet secretaries, and diplomats. Henry and Clover Adams could sit on the banks of this stream of humanity and dip their nets whenever they were, to use one of their favorite words, "amused."

In leaving the *North American Review,* Henry said farewell to politics, and years later, when he wrote of his reformist crusades in *The Education of Henry Adams,* he would dismiss his political journalism as one more failed experiment. But in truth his departure from politics was less a defeat than a liberation. Once he stopped seeing his pen as an instrument of reform, he felt free to wander all the corridors of literary expression. As soon as he divorced himself from politics, he started working on the Gallatin papers and a companion biography, and he laid plans for his epic history of the United States in the opening years of the nineteenth century.

Like John Hay, Henry Adams viewed his career as a series of accidents. In his youth he had dreamed that he and his brothers and their friends would form the nucleus of "a national set of young men, like ourselves or better, to start new influences not only in politics, but in literature, in law, in society, and throughout the whole social organism of the country. A national school of our own generation." When the nation failed to take note, Adams settled for the work that came his way, serving as his father's secretary, a Washington correspondent, a magazine editor, and a professor of history. Not until his thirty-ninth year did he hit upon the plan of going to Washington and immersing himself in a labor that would take a decade to complete.

By all measures, the Adamses' move to Washington was a splendid success. They started their days on horseback, exploring the wilds of Rock Creek Park or, with the aid of maps supplied by a general of their acquaintance, riding trails cut by the Union army during the Civil War. After a noon breakfast frequently shared with guests, Henry went off to the State Department archives to work on his history. At five o'clock he returned for tea and more guests, and in the evening they either dined out or entertained. In the summer, when Washingtonians fled the heat, the Adamses decamped to their cottage at Beverly Farms on Boston's North Shore, near Clover's father and her sister and brother.

Now that they were home, Henry and Clover were eager to pick up where they had left off. They had finished with Europe forever, Clover told her father. "The more we travel, the more profoundly impressed we are with the surpassing-solid comfort of the average American household and its freedom from sham. They beat us on churches and pictures in the Old World, but in food, clothing, furniture, manners and morals, it seems to us we have the 'inside track.'" Washington promised more of these comforts than Boston or New York. With an annual income of $25,000—five times a senator's pay—the Adamses could, said Clover, "strut around as if we were millionaires."

As soon as the Adamses were settled on H Street, Clarence King and John Hay came to tea almost every day. More often than not, they were joined by Clara Hay, who spent much of the winter of 1880–81 in Washington. Apart from a few stray remarks in Clover's letters to her father, the quintet who came to call themselves the Five of Hearts

Pieces from the Five of Hearts' tea service, which Clarence King gave the Adamses in 1885. © 1988 STUART SYMINGTON, JR. ALL RIGHTS RESERVED.

left no records of their gatherings, but by spring, when Hay and King left office, they had begun a lifelong friendship. Like most groups of friends, particularly collections of strong-minded individuals, the Five of Hearts owned a few common traits and an abundance of differences. Their strongest shared resemblance was physical: all of them were short. Henry Adams stood five-feet-four, Clover five-feet-two. Hay was Clover's height, and a bit shorter than his wife. King, five-six and well muscled, was the burliest of the lot but still small enough to sit comfortably in the Adamses' little red armchairs. In age they ranged from forty-two (Hay and Adams) to thirty-one (Clara). King was thirty-eight, a year older than Clover.

They were sensitive, intelligent, charming, and, with the exception of Clara Hay, articulate and highly amusing. (Mrs. Hay had her uses in such company. As Henry Adams knew from his own silent forays into the London drawing room of Monckton Milnes, a dazzling talker was nothing without an audience. Clover, noting that Mrs. Hay "never speaks," speculated that it was just as well since Mr. Hay "chats for two.")

Each of the men had attained a degree of literary eminence, Adams at the *North American Review*, King with *Mountaineering in the Sierra*

Nevada, and Hay with his comic ballads and *Castilian Days,* the volume of essays written during his stay in Madrid.

All five were enthusiastically American, albeit with an elitist point of view. "I wish," said Clarence King, "that it could be engraved upon my tombstone that I am to the last fibre aristocratic in my belief, that I think the only fine thing to do with the masses is to govern and educate them into some semblance of their social superiors." To Henry Adams, whose sympathies lay with the Democratic Party, it seemed that the noble experiment of the Founding Fathers was being perverted by the growing political power of the rich, particularly financiers, and most particularly Jewish financiers. Adams would outlive this prejudice, but for much of his life, Jews were a lightning rod for his feelings about the demise of the democratic ideal. John Hay, unswervingly Republican, worried less about the rich than about the trade unionists, anarchists, and other castoffs borne on the immigrant tide. Immigrants, ran the conservative Republican argument, lacked the experience for the successful practice of democracy. Behind such claims it was easy to see the fear that the sheer number of immigrants spelled the end of a political system long dictated by an elite. As one visiting Englishman noted, clouds of melancholy and petulance hung over the American upper classes in the 1880s as they began to understand that their ballots carried no more political weight than those of any other voters.

As a son of Beacon Hill and Harvard, Henry Adams would never understand, much less endorse, the Western political ascendancy of which John Hay was a part. To someone who had polished his manners in the best London houses, men such as Ulysses S. Grant, Rutherford B. Hayes, and the other Ohioans who came to the White House after the Civil War seemed hopeless primitives, and Henry agreed with his brother Charles's characterization of Western politicians as men of "mixed ability, cant, vulgarity and shrewdness." Describing the "amiable and clever" John Hay of Cleveland to an English friend, Adams said that his only fault was political: "he has always managed to keep in what I think precious bad company. I never could understand why, except that I never knew more than two or three men born west of the Alleghenies who knew the difference between a gentleman and a swindler. This curious obliquity makes him a particularly charming companion to me, as he knows intimately scores of men whom I would not touch with a pole, but who are more amusing than my crowd."

Clara Hay and Clover Adams had no politics apart from the politics of their husbands. Nor did they have the right to vote. But except for their disenfranchisement, the two women had little in common. Contented with a world centered on family, home, and church, Clara was the very model of the woman celebrated in the popular Victorian poem "The Angel in the House." Clover, with no children, no religious faith, and no outlet for her abundant intellectual energy, knew depths of restlessness and resentment unfathomed by the placid Mrs. Hay. Clover detested the luncheons and musicales that delighted Clara, though she graciously put aside her feelings and consented to pour when the visitor from Cleveland hosted a reception.

Clover also introduced Clara to the creations of Charles Worth, the Parisian couturier favored by wealthy Americans. Worth had won her eternal loyalty on a day when he had focused his attentions entirely on her, oblivious of the Mrs. Astor and the Mrs. Vanderbilt in his waiting room. A blue-and-green Worth gown acquired on her last stay in France not only filled her soul but "seals it hermetically," she claimed. As she could demonstrate to Mrs. Hay, and to Clarence King, who shared Clover's sartorial passion, the inside had been finished as meticulously as the outside. When the dress began to fray and fade, she said, she would wear it wrong side out.

King boasted of once owning a coat so fine that a dying Paiute Indian chief had asked to be buried in it. King obliged and a few days after the funeral noticed it on the back of another member of the tribe. The brave had so admired King's coat that he robbed the grave.

It was hard to tell when King's narrative instincts caused him to stretch the truth, but neither the Adamses nor the Hays were inclined to subject their favorite Heart to rigorous scrutiny. With his unbroken chain of successes, King was an object of veneration to Hay and Adams. "When the Lord *might* have made other men like him," Henry wondered, "why the D. didn't he?" Clover, listening to the hero worship, mockingly declared that she "never knew such fanatic adoration could exist in this practical age." Henry noted that women "were jealous of the power [King] had over men; but women were many and Kings were one. The men worshipped not so much their friend, as the ideal American they all wanted to be."

Above all, Hay and Adams admired King because his life showed no gap between idea and act: he thought, then he did. In politics, the only sphere in which Adams had tried to exert influence, his thoughts invariably led to the conclusion that action was futile. Hay was less despairing but found it easier to carry out the wishes of others than to steer his own course, which made him as Hamlet-like as Henry Adams. In the realm of public service, which all three men considered an obligation of their class, only King had discharged his duties with a sense of satisfaction. Adams still waited for someone in government to ask his help, and Hay could not wait to leave Washington. In December 1880, when President-elect James Garfield asked Hay to move from the State Department to the White House to fill the post of secretary, Hay had turned him down with bitterness and no trace of regret. "The constant contact with envy, meanness, ignorance, and the swinish selfishness which ignorance breeds, needs a stronger heart and a more obedient nervous system than I can boast," he told Garfield. Hay did not intend to hold public office again. In the future he would give as much time and money to politics as his circumstances allowed, and that, he insisted, "is all anybody can ask of me." It was an honorable plan but far from the triumphs of Clarence King, surveyor of the Fortieth Parallel and father of the U.S. Geological Survey.

If King's gift to the Five of Hearts was, as Adams put it, a "bubbling energy which swept everyone into the current of his interest," their gift to him was escape from the dinners and parties that posed such vexing challenges to his bachelorhood. The hospitality of the Adamses' hearth was legendary in Washington, and no one contributed more to the legend than the multitudes excluded from Clover's guest lists. To the Adamses' friend Henry James, who transformed Clover into Mrs. Bonnycastle in a short story called "Pandora," she was "the lady of infinite mirth." As James discerned, her salon "left out, on the whole, more than it took in," and the rare senator allowed entrance was scrutinized with "a mixture of alarm and indulgence." Mr. Bonnycastle also surveyed Washington from lordly heights, but with singular broad-mindedness: "Hang it," he told his spouse, "let us be vulgar and have some fun—let us invite the President."

Asking the Adamses to dinner by no means guaranteed a return invitation, and Clover had little regard for the social convention that permitted strangers to leave their cards in the hope of winning a summons from the hostess. The exclusionary impulse noted by Henry James was genuine, but it was not, as many assumed, a simple matter of snobbery. Lacking the snob's preoccupation with wealth and power, the Adamses screened guests by a single criterion: did they amuse? In life as in letters, Henry Adams was a devotee of form. Life could have interest and meaning only when it had shape, and finding the right shape meant choosing what—or whom—to exclude. A bore, like an ill-chosen word, was an error of aesthetics.

There is nothing like a secret for reinforcing a sense of exclusivity, and in the winter of 1880–81, Clarence King and the Hays, as the *crème de la crème* of the drawing room at 1607 H Street, were made privy to a confidence shared only by Henry and Clover Adams and two or three others. In 1880, while the Adamses were safely out of the country, a New York publisher named Henry Holt had brought out an anonymously written political satire called *Democracy*. An instant bestseller, the novel also turned into a national guessing game as newspapers and magazines speculated on the author's identity. John Hay and Clarence King, well known for their objections to Washington society, found themselves on the list of suspects, as did the sharp-tongued Clover Adams. No one in the country guessed that the culprit was Henry Adams.

The protagonist of *Democracy* was Mrs. Lightfoot Lee, an attractive young widow with Henry's unblinking intelligence and Clover's sensitive nerves. Bored with Europe, convinced she was "American to the tips of her fingers," Madeleine Lee decided to move from New York to Washington. Like a passenger on an ocean liner, she was unable to rest until she had visited the engine room and talked with the engineer: "She wanted to see with her own eyes the action of the primary forces; to touch with her own hand the massive machinery of society. . . . She was bent upon getting to the heart of the great mystery of democracy and government. She cared little where her pursuit might lead her."

Madeleine rented a home on Lafayette Square and quickly met her principal object of study, Senator Silas P. Ratcliffe of Peoria, Illinois. (Names do not sit lightly on the characters of *Democracy*; the "Rat" and the "Peon" signified, and Adams expressed his resentment of the rising financial power of American and European Jews by naming a Jewish character Schneidekoupon—literally, "coupon clipper," a derisive term for one who lives on investments.) A man of silver hair and vast experience, Ratcliffe fascinated Madeleine Lee. She was eager to learn, the senator an obliging teacher. Patiently he explained that "no representative government can long be much better or much worse than the society it represents. Purify society and you purify the government. But try to purify the government artificially and you only aggravate failure." In another lesson Ratcliffe admitted his part in an election fraud during the Civil War, justifying his wrongdoing on the ground that it guaranteed a higher good—the preservation of the Union. A shaken Mrs. Lee was left to wonder where her political ideals fit in "this wilderness of stunted natures where no straight road was to be found, but only the tortuous and aimless tracks of beasts and things that crawl."

In spite of the moral perversities of government in action, Mrs. Lee clung to her faith in democracy, sure that underneath "the scum floating on the surface . . . there was a sort of healthy ocean current of honest purpose which swept the scum before it and kept the mass pure." Longing to have this faith affirmed by a member of the Washington priesthood, she cornered one of Ratcliffe's Senate colleagues, a sage New Englander, and posed her deepest question: Is America right or wrong?

"I grant it is an experiment," he told her, "but it is the only direction society can take that is worth its taking; the only conception of its duty large enough to satisfy its instincts. . . . Every other possible step is backward, and I do not care to repeat the past."

The question and the answer were pure Henry Adams. He had failed as a reformer and declared himself shut of politics, but as a historian he hoped to influence the future of his country by showing where it had gone wrong in the past. Though Adams would never find a way to practice his political faith outside his writing, Madeleine

Lee thought that she knew the solution to the problem presented by Senator Ratcliffe. By becoming his wife, she could reform him, after which he would reform democracy. Friends who recognized the perils of her delusion intervened, showing her a letter detailing the senator's acceptance of a $100,000 bribe in exchange for a favorable vote. At last the student of democracy grasped that neither Silas Ratcliffe nor the system he represented could be remodeled to her pristine tastes. She called off the marriage and announced her wish to flee to Egypt: "democracy has shaken my nerves to pieces. Oh, what rest it would be to live in the Great Pyramid and look out for ever at the polar star!"

Separated from Washington by thousands of miles and thousands of years, ancient Egypt furnished the novelist with a neat antithesis to modernity and change. Egypt and the Pyramids also set off deeper vibrations in the author, though the Hays and Clarence King probably did not understand them at the time. Like the author, Madeleine Lee was a fearless seeker of truth. In pursuing it, however, and in not caring where the chase might lead, she sometimes verged on the desperation that had burst out of Clover Adams on the Nile. Presented with proof that Ratcliffe had taken a bribe, Mrs. Lee had cried out, "Oh, how I wish I were dead! how I wish the universe were annihilated." Egypt was the site of the deepest unhappiness Clover experienced on her honeymoon, the Great Pyramid a tomb. Behind Madeleine Lee's longing for these places it is possible to see an anxious husband's desire to bury the unmanageable feelings of his wife in the place where he first encountered them.

But in the jolly winter of 1880–81, *Democracy* was a wonderful lark. To Henry's delight, the first edition had gone through nine printings, and pirated versions had begun to turn up on newsstands. In private the Five of Hearts could amuse themselves by trading stories of offended Washington matrons who believed that *Democracy* was the work of an unscrupulous newspaperman, and together they could laugh at the Boston *Transcript,* which sniffed that the author had obviously not mingled in "the best society of the Capital."

By the end of April, the uproarious fun of the Five of Hearts had come to an end. King "beams with joy at being out of office,"

*John Hay holding a copy of the French edition of Henry Adams's anonymous best-seller,
Democracy. This portrait, taken by Clover Adams, was one of many Five of Hearts
jokes about the authorship of the novel, which various accusers attributed to Hay, King,
and both Adamses.* MASSACHUSETTS HISTORICAL SOCIETY

Clover reported to her father. "He and Mr. Hay were as eager to get
out as most fools to get in." Clara Hay returned to Cleveland, and
her husband, almost fatally incapable of refusing a friend, allowed
himself to be talked into editing the New York *Tribune* for six
months while Whitelaw Reid honeymooned in Europe. King was
also in New York, preparing the U.S. Census report on precious
metals, combing art galleries in search of bric-a-brac, and carrying
out what he called a "scientific experiment in Wall Street." Acting on
a tip from a friend, he had invested $10,000 and lost it in twenty-four
hours. "Would you refrain from bric-a-brac till you had recouped,
or would you . . . put your little remnant into a yellow pot with
relief dragons?" he asked Hay. His good cheer was rooted in his
optimism. While he finished up the report for the census, he was also
planning a grand enterprise in Mexico, where he would rework the
fabulous silver mines abandoned centuries before by the conquistadors. What was $10,000 when millions lay waiting in the mountains
of Mexico?

In Washington Henry toiled at his history, and Clover, bored without King and the Hays, passed up tea in favor of long afternoon rides, often staying out until sunset. Years after the winter when the Five of Hearts invented itself in Lafayette Square, Henry remarked that friendship requires "a certain parallelism of life, a community of thought." The community of thought—a web of patrician convictions and a love of what Adams called "taste and dexterity"—endured. But the lives would veer sharply from parallel.

PART TWO

DISTANCES

7

Arrivals and Departures

The first chilly mists of autumn were rolling through the marshes when Clarence King appeared on the Beverly Farms porch of Henry and Clover Adams in September 1881. King, exhausted, had to be put to bed and nursed. For months the geologist had crisscrossed the West, braving malaria, dysentery, floods, and recalcitrant mules in his quest for fortune. Backed by two Boston financiers, King owned interests in a half dozen gold and silver mines stretching from northern California to central Mexico.

The mines were as remote from civilization as from each other, and conditions at the sites ran a short gamut from difficult to hostile. King's silver mine in the western Mexican province of Sinaloa lay at the end of a long trail that could be traveled only on foot or by mule. Spanish explorers had christened the place Yedras—poison ivy—a name that was still uncomfortably apt. The mine itself had flooded long ago, when another band of treasure hunters accidentally bored into an underground stream. Before production could resume, the makings of giant pumps and a sawmill had to be carried in, one mule-load at a time. Three hundred miles to the southeast, at Sombrerete in Zacatecas, it took four thousand mule trips to transport the gear needed to reopen the mine.

While Clover worried that King's entrepreneurial ambitions were making him "reckless of life and strength," Henry and John Hay were more thrilled than alarmed. Each time King triumphed over an obstacle that neither of them could have conquered, their lofty opinion of him won ringing confirmation. The search for mining properties had proved no challenge at all. King simply contacted an old friend who specialized in evaluating the potential of abandoned mines. Raising capital had been equally uncomplicated; riding on his success with the U.S. Geological Survey, King had only to outline his plans and financiers put up millions. Even language barriers melted before Clarence King. Knowing he would have to supervise native laborers, King spent a stagecoach ride from Tucson to Mexico memorizing words from a Spanish dictionary. Of grammar he knew nothing, but he invented what Hay called "a highly effective and picturesque jargon which delighted the Mexicans and carried him triumphantly to the mines."

Hay could not resist investing in one of King's Mexican ventures, and Adams bought into another. In the summer of 1881, when Adams received his first profits, he declared himself as excited as a child on seeing a rabbit pulled from a hat. In the past, he said, he had viewed mining investments "in much the same light as I do a lent umbrella." But the arrival of a $1,333 check from the Minas Prietas Mining Company made him think he would enjoy having "more money grow mouldy in the same way."

Henry's enthusiasm was the tonic King needed when the Adamses tucked him into bed at Beverly Farms. While he still believed he would profit from all his ventures, early results suggested that he would not realize his dream of reaping untold wealth from lost treasures. But a few days of Henry and Clover's tenderness left him feeling restored. "It is awfully comfortable and regulating to the mind to stay with you," he wrote Henry after returning to his business office in New York. "I feel calmer and more like marrying for a week afterward."

King's visit marked a turning point for the Adamses, too. After King and the Hays had left Lafayette Square in the spring, Henry had immersed himself in his history, daring to hope that his epic would rival Edward Gibbon's classic account of the fall of Rome. Clover decided to read Gibbon—"a bone which will take months to gnaw,"

Pitch Pine Hill, the Adamses' summerhouse at Beverly Farms, by Clover.
MASSACHUSETTS HISTORICAL SOCIETY

she told her father—but books seemed a poor substitute for the companionship of the Five of Hearts. In an outburst reminiscent of her unhappiest days on the Nile, Clover complained that her life was nothing but "read, read, read, till I loathe the very sight of a book."

In the summer, when the Adamses transplanted themselves to Beverly Farms, Henry passed his days amid the musty, yellowed pages of early-nineteenth-century newspapers while Clover cared for two of her brother Ned's five daughters. It was an unsettling task. They were two and four, and their mother had died a few months before. Clover had shielded herself from that event, leaving Ned to sorrow alone in Cambridge despite her devotion to him. To her father, Clover explained that she was staying in Washington because Henry refused to let her travel alone and she was "not willing to pull him up from his work." If the death of Ned's wife stirred painful childhood memories of her own mother's death, the act of facing little girls crushed by the same blow may have been more than she could bear.

A summer spent caring for children raised other anxieties. Nearing thirty-eight, Clover had moved into uncomfortably ambiguous terrain—past the typical age of childbearing but not yet into the realm of biological impossibility. Her attitudes toward motherhood swung from one extreme to the other. At one moment she disowned all interest in news of births, at another she cried out, "If any woman ever says to you that she doesn't want children, it isn't true. *All* women want children!" The contradictions paled beside the intensity of her feelings.

Henry shared Clover's conflict. He had married in 1872 with the hope of having children but by 1876 had realized that his desires might go unfulfilled. In answer to news of a birth and a death, his normally fluid pen developed a stammer: "I wish—wish—wish— well, I wish various things, but among others that the mystery of Birth and the Grave were either less important to us, or more en- couraging." Tiring of questions about his reproductive intentions, he sought to head off inquisitive friends by making pointed decla- rations of his happiness. He told one acquaintance that he had "never cared enough about children to be unhappy either at having or not having them, and if it were not that half the world will never leave the other half at peace, I should never think about the subject." On another occasion he announced that he and Clover were "quite well, very busy, and very happy. One consequence of having no children is that husband and wife become very dependent on each other and live very much together."

The reasons for Henry and Clover's childlessness remain un- known. Gossips suggested that Henry was impotent; if so, it seems unlikely that he would have felt so comfortable in his first days of marriage. A gynecological treatise found in Henry's library has led to speculation that the difficulty was Clover's, though the book offered no clue to a specific problem.

Whatever the state of their feelings about parenthood in the sum- mer of 1881, the Adamses said remarkably little about their young charges. Henry mentioned them only once in his correspondence, explaining to a friend that he hesitated to extend an invitation be- cause of their presence. With the entire Hooper clan summering nearby, Clover wrote few letters, but when she resumed writing to her father in the fall, she said nothing of the experience with her nieces.

John Hay had intended to laze away the spring and summer of 1881 as editor of the New York *Tribune*. Standing in for Whitelaw Reid,

Hay had not expected to work full time or even stay in New York. Reid had asked him "merely to give direction" to policy and promised that "an hour a day would cover all the serious work." Hay took him at his word, spending most of his time in Cleveland, where he worked on the Lincoln biography. But on July 2, in what Henry Adams called "one of the disregarded chances of life," a malcontent named Charles Guiteau fired two bullets into President Garfield. Hay raced to New York to supervise the *Tribune*'s coverage of the event.

Bulletins on the president's condition were posted outside the *Tribune*'s offices on Park Row. A few blocks away, on Wall Street, stock prices plunged 5 percent, scaring nearly everyone but Hay's father-in-law, Amasa Stone. When Hay asked him how the assassination attempt would affect a recent investment, Stone offered chilling reassurance: "I think you are all right . . . although you might have bought lower at a later date, and still lower should Prest. Garfield die."

Garfield died on September 19. The stock market, which had anticipated his demise for some time, showed almost no change and closed early.

Contemplating the new president, Chester Alan Arthur, Clarence King decided the nation was in good hands. Calling himself "a sort of Saul of Tarsus," King told Adams he was finally ready to embrace the cause of political reform. "Why? because reform is getting within the possibilities. So long as it was a thin gray streak of dawn in the East, a chilly three o'clock in the morning thing, I felt it to be futile to get up and spoil people's sleep by crying out 'awake! arise! behold there will be breakfast.' Now that one can see to read and the regular rank and file are up and dressing and the machine men are seeing which way the wind blows there will be reform and I . . . will help to do the thing."

King did not know his man. A dandy who owned a hundred pairs of trousers, Arthur had risen through Republican Party ranks during his tenure as customs inspector for the Port of New York. All who were caught importing goods without paying duty were invited to escape large fines by making contributions to the Republican Party and the pockets of the many-trousered Chester Arthur. Henry Adams, noting that reformers "vanished like smoke" when Arthur took

office, joked that he too would throw in his lot with the new president, "whose social charms we now understand to be most extraordinary, although only last spring we were assured by the same people
that he was a vulgar and a dull animal."

From Europe, Whitelaw Reid signaled his satisfaction with Hay's
management of the assassination coverage and most other editorial
matters, but the two men found themselves at odds over a book
review. Mark Twain, almost finished with *The Prince and the Pauper,*
asked his friend W. D. Howells to review it for the *Tribune.* Howells
put the proposition to Hay, saying that he would use the occasion to
write about the "unappreciated serious side" of Twain's "curious
genius." From his own dealings with Howells after the Ashtabula
train disaster, Hay knew that Howells was incapable of dispassion
where friends were concerned, but he was inclined to accommodate
the request. As he explained to Reid, "I took into account your
disapproval of Mark in general and your friendship for Howells—
and decided for the benefit of the *Tribune.*" If Reid disapproved, Hay
suggested he balance the scales by assigning Twain's archenemy,
Bret Harte, to review Twain's next opus. Reid protested. "[I]t isn't
good journalism to let a warm personal friend, and in some matters
literary partner, write a critical review of him in a paper wh. has
good reason to think little of his delicacy and highly of his greed. So,
if you haven't printed it yet, I wld. think of this point before doing
so." Hay stood by his decision, and on October 25 the *Tribune*
allotted more than three columns to Howells's unsigned hymn to
Twain.

When the review appeared, the Five of Hearts were enjoying a
reunion in New York. Henry and Clover had stopped off en route
from Beverly Farms to Washington, Clara Hay was visiting from
Cleveland, and King was in Wall Street tending the financial side of
his mining affairs. On Broadway they saw *Patience,* Gilbert and Sullivan's new satire of the foppery of Oscar Wilde. In Tiffany's, Clover
gaped at leg garters decked with diamonds. Dining twice at Delmonico's, they sampled duck with fried hominy and turkey stuffed
with chestnuts.

They talked about Henry James, now a confirmed Londoner, who
was about to make his first visit to the United States in six years.
One of Clover's New York friends, who had disapproved of the

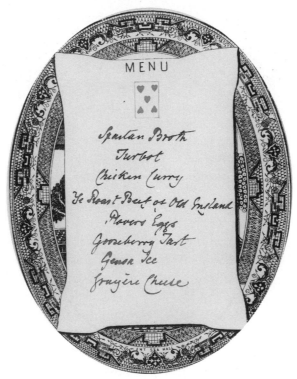

MENU

Spartan Broth
Turbot
Chicken Curry
Ye Roast Beef of Old England
Plovers Eggs
Gooseberry Tart
Genoa Ice
Gruyère Cheese

Menu card from a Five of Hearts dinner party. The Hays preserved the card, but nothing is known of the occasion. JOHN HAY COLLECTION, JOHN HAY LIBRARY, BROWN UNIVERSITY LIBRARY

forward heroine of *Daisy Miller,* pointedly asked if the novelist were coming home in search of "*raw* material." James's latest novel, *The Portrait of a Lady,* would soon be the object of an enthusiastic *Tribune* review (also unsigned) by his friend John Hay. In Hay's view, the novel would "remain one of the notable books of the time" and as such deserved comparison with "the gravest and most serious works of imagination which have been devoted to the study of the social conditions of the age and the moral aspects of our civilization." Clover strenuously disagreed. Where Hay saw nuance and subtlety, she saw a thin plot and overstuffed prose. James's *Portrait* was "nice" and "charming," she conceded, "but I'm ageing fast and prefer what Sir Walter called the 'big bow-wow style.'" Henry had not enjoyed the novel either but decided to give it the benefit of the doubt since friends whose judgment he respected found reason to "admire it warmly, and find it deeply interesting."

Knowing nothing of the Adamses' reservations, James wrote Clover—his "Voltaire in petticoats"—that he was exhilarated by the prospect of seeing her and Henry "in the Washington to which you so fondly cling." Though he did not plan to come until after Christmas, he added, "I cannot longer delay to let you know of my arrival—conscious as I am that it is fraught with happy consequences for you."

Back on Lafayette Square, Adams learned that his friend and former student, Henry Cabot Lodge, had just lost a close race for a seat in the Massachusetts senate. Sending his consolations, Adams said he had "never known a young man go into politics who was not the worse for it. They all try to be honest, and then are tripped up by the dishonest; or they try to be dishonest (i.e. practical politicians) and degrade their own natures." The Adams family's political experiences and his own years in Washington had convinced him that "no man should be in politics unless he would honestly rather not be there. Public service should be a *corvée*; a disagreeable necessity. The satisfaction should consist in getting out of it." It was an interesting letter in view of Henry's summer at Beverly Farms. The distance Henry claimed between himself and politics strongly resembled the distance he tried to achieve from fatherhood: what he privately concluded he could not have, he publicly announced he did not want.

Disagreeable or not, politics enthralled the Adamses in the waning months of 1881. Beyond the blazing red and yellow maples of Lafayette Park, they could see the White House, where garlands of black crepe decked every window, column, and cornice. When the trial of President Garfield's assassin began on November 14, Henry and Clover were as eager to attend as the rest of Washington.

Charles Julius Guiteau was a sad case—forty years old, a failure at journalism, law, and public speaking. His discontent with Garfield had begun when James G. Blaine, the secretary of state, refused to consider Guiteau for the job of American consul in Paris, a post for which he possessed not a single qualification. Guiteau protested in a letter to Garfield, who did not respond. Brooding on a bench in Lafayette Park, Guiteau concluded that the president must be murdered and that God had chosen him for the task. The trial would center on the question of Guiteau's sanity. If found insane, as his attorneys hoped, he would be locked away in an asylum. If the prosecution proved that Guiteau was sane, he would be held accountable and go to the gallows.

At the courthouse the assassin signed autographs, cursed, and lost his temper so often that the judge threatened to have him gagged. Four days into the proceedings, while traveling between the courthouse and the jail, Guiteau was slightly wounded in an attempt on his life. Clover, worried about the "sporadic gunpowder lying around," said she and Henry had given up their thoughts of attending the trial. But when they received an invitation from Dr. Charles Folsom, a physician of their acquaintance who served on the National Board of Health, they could not resist.

On December 7 a marshal ushered Clover to a seat near an open window, and Henry sat among the expert witnesses. "It was intensely interesting," Clover reported to her father. "The assassin was in front of me, so I could only get his profile—a large strong nose, a high straight forehead, and a good height from top of ear to top of head. He bullied and badgered everyone; banged his fist on the table; broke off in reading a paper, saying, 'Arthur's message has the true ring. I think he'll give us the best administration we ever had.'" Several "nice, intelligent men" from Guiteau's home state of Illinois testified that "no suspicion of insanity had heretofore rested on the family," which in Clover's view smashed the defense argument of hereditary insanity.

When the court was adjourned for the day, the Adamses watched as guards led Guiteau past the jeering crowds on the sidewalk to the van that would return him to jail. Dr. Folsom, on his way to the jail to examine Guiteau, invited the Adamses to accompany him. Henry immediately agreed. After some hesitation, Clover decided to join them. "As we entered the jail, we came into a large hall," she told her father. "In one corner I noticed a group of four or five men, one sitting in a rocking chair, whose face seemed to me of the Guiteau type, though I had not got a front view in Court. As we entered he got up and came forward very courteously, saying, 'How do you do, Doctor?' and shook his hand. Dr. Folsom introduced Henry and me, and supposing it must be the jailer I met his offered hand. I felt rather overwhelmed as it broke upon me who the man was."

Clearly upset, Clover called Guiteau a "beast" three times in her

The Adamses' view of the White House in 1881, after the assassination of President Garfield. R. B. HAYES PRESIDENTIAL CENTER

letter and repeated that her mistake had resulted from not seeing Guiteau clearly in court. She implored Dr. Hooper to tell the story carefully: "I don't wish to have it repeated that I shook hands with the accursed beast, without the context being given. Someone would write on that they 'were sorry to hear that I had asked Guiteau to tea.' "

Like most Americans, Clover wanted Guiteau pronounced sane so that he would be punished for his crime (which happened, despite his bizarre behavior during the trial). But she also may have resisted the idea of hereditary insanity for deeper reasons since it posed disturbing questions about her family history of suicide and melancholy.

The autumn of 1881 also marked the beginning of Henry and Clover's friendship with Elizabeth Sherman Cameron. Tall, beautiful, and barely twenty-four, Lizzie was unhappily married to Senator J. Donald Cameron of Pennsylvania, a machine politician of the stripe Adams had in mind when he advised Lodge to swear off politics. Don's father, Simon Cameron, had been removed from his post as President Lincoln's secretary of war for corruption in awarding military contracts. Simon later won election to the U.S. Senate and in 1876 persuaded his friend President Grant to appoint Don as secretary of war to fill an unexpected vacancy. That fall, during the heated dispute over the results of the Hayes–Tilden election, Don put federal troops at the disposal of Republican Party functionaries in two of the four states where electoral votes were being challenged. When the victorious Hayes declined to reward Don's initiative with a cabinet appointment, Simon Cameron came up with a consolation prize— his own Senate seat. Simon resigned, the Pennsylvania legislature elected Don to serve out his term, and Don took his father's place in the Senate amid sneers about the power of "the Cameron Transfer Company."

"Beauty and the Beast," a gossip columnist called Lizzie and Don. She was five-feet-eight, a slim brunette with compelling gray eyes. He stood six-two, had sandy-red hair, and under his large Roman nose wore a drooping mustache that made him look permanently out of sorts. She was twenty when they married in 1878. He was forty-four, a widower with five children, one of whom was a contemporary of Lizzie's.

A member of the formidable Sherman clan of Ohio, Lizzie was the niece of General William Tecumseh Sherman and his brother John, who served in both houses of Congress and two Cabinet posts. Lizzie had wanted to marry another man, but the Shermans, suspecting him of a fondness for alcohol, ended the relationship. Bowing to the pressure of family members eager for a match with a powerful senator, she finally agreed to marry Don Cameron. On her wedding day she begged that the ceremony be called off, but the Shermans held firm: Lizzie had given her word. Lizzie and Don passed their wedding night aboard a luxury railroad car; years later she confided to a friend that his clumsy insistence had left her feeling like the victim of a rape. A second cruel surprise soon made itself felt: the senator downed a fifth of bourbon a day.

It would have been unthinkable for Lizzie to confide her unhappiness to her new friends on Lafayette Square, but the Adamses could not have failed to notice her eagerness for their companionship. An intelligent listener, full of questions and appreciative laughter, she quickly won their affection. In the earliest weeks of their friendship, Senator Cameron was away, politicking in Pennsylvania, but as soon as he returned the Adamses asked him to tea. Apart from the senator's enthusiasm for one of their terriers, Clover saw "noth-

ing to please one" and feared that Lizzie had "drawn a blank in Don
. . . for all his money and fine house." Henry felt likewise but decided to tolerate the senator for Lizzie's sake. "I adore her and respect
the way she has kept out of scandal and mud, and done her duty by
the lump of clay she promised to love and respect," he told Hay.

Waiting out the fall of 1881 much as they had waited out the spring,
Hay and King were now as eager to leave New York as they had
been to exit Washington. Garfield's assassination had forced Hay to
spend weeks away from the quiet pleasures of Euclid Avenue, and
his departure had been further delayed by news from Whitelaw Reid.
Mrs. Reid, newly pregnant, had been advised to postpone her voyage home from Europe.

King, still fatigued by his Western travels and discouraged by
mining setbacks, sometimes talked vaguely of marriage and sometimes dreamed of an escape to Europe. Approaching forty, he was
still a favorite at the Century Club, but an evening there inevitably
wound to a lonely end. When his contemporaries went home to their
wives, King skulked downtown alone to his hotel room at the
Brevoort House.

Believing that the time had come for King to marry, Hay took
him for tea with a cousin who lived in New York. King's behavior
was "angelic," and the cousin "had long loved him in secret," Hay
reported to Clover. When nothing came of the meeting, Hay supposed that the problem was distraction; King always seemed to have
more to do than "a juggler with four knives in the air."

King seemed to want a wife like Clara Hay, whose "rooted repose" and "tranquility" made even Nirvana "seem fidgety," he said.
"Only once in a million times does Providence pour out the *full cup*
for man to drink," he told Hay. "For you it has."

Worried about King's loneliness and eager to preserve the alliance
of the Five of Hearts, Hay went to a New York printer and ordered
stationery embossed with a small red replica of the five of hearts
found in a deck of playing cards. "I had a few sheets of paper made
for the official correspondence of the Club and send a sample by mail
to you today for your approval," he wrote to Clover in November
1881. About to meet King for lunch, Hay promised that the New
York and Cleveland branches of the Five of Hearts would "remem-

ber the Residency-Branch with affection tempered with due respect."
King looked at the stationery and predicted that when the Adamses'
"sedate servant-man" saw the envelope, he would suspect that
Henry's great literary labor was a book on poker.

A few weeks later, in a howling snowstorm, Hay boarded the
train for Ohio. A bad cold had forced King to cancel their farewell
lunch at the Union League Club, but Hay had gone to see him at the
Brevoort. "I stayed till the last minute," he told Clover, "and then
drove away with a heavy heart."

8

"My Facts Are Facts, Too"

For the Adamses, 1882 opened with a visit from Henry James. He had come home mainly to see his parents in Massachusetts, but he also meant to explore New York City, where he had been born, and Washington, which he had never seen. The Adamses booked him a sunny suite of rooms near Lafayette Square, and he was soon a fixture of the "very pretty little life" he found at 1607 H Street. He marveled at Clover's "perennial afternoon tea" and observed that in their native air, the Adamses "bloom, expand, emit a genial fragrance." During their last trip abroad, they had tired him with their long list of grievances against the Old World, but James needed only a few days in Washington to understand why they preferred it to London. As he put it to Sir John Clark, a Scottish friend of the Adamses, "they are, vulgarly speaking 'someone' here, and . . . are nothing in your complicated Kingdom."

At first James found Washington a refreshing change from New York, where life moved at a frenetic pace and money was the measure of everyone and everything. "I believe that Washington is the place in the world where money—or the absence of it, matters least," he told Sir John. Essentially "social and conversational," the capital was "the only place in America where there is no business, where an air of leisure hangs over the enormous streets." Before long, however, James felt "woefully and wickedly *bored*" and "horribly home-sick for the ancient world." The layout of Washington was "bristling and geometrical," the Capitol "rather wanting in tone." In the "hideous" interior of Congress, he winced at paintings and sculptures of statesmen that created an effect "too serious for a joke and too comic for a Valhalla."

"That young emigrant has much to learn here," Clover fumed. "He may in time get into the 'swim' here, but I doubt it." She guessed that the novelist preferred "a quiet corner with a pen where he can create men and women who say neat things and have refined tastes" to the "real, live, vulgar" America.

The truth was that James showed a larger appetite for "real, live, vulgar" Americans than the Adamses did. They groaned when he accepted invitations from people they shunned, though he noticed that they pumped him dry when he returned. After one dinner, he said, "they mobbed me for revelations; and after I had dined with Blaine, to meet the president, they fairly hung on my lips." Unhappily for Henry and Clover, the bland Chester Arthur failed to excite the novelist's descriptive powers. In his "well-made coat and well-cut whiskers," he merely struck James as an agreeable man with a "desire to please."

James also called on Oscar Wilde, who was touring America and doing his best to live up to Gilbert and Sullivan's parody of his outlandishness. When James mentioned his homesickness for London, Wilde replied, "Really? You care for *places?* The *world* is my home." James reported to the Adamses that Wilde was a "fatuous fool" and a "tenth-rate cad," judgments Clover repeated with glee. Clover had resolved not to entertain Wilde during his Washington sojourn, insisting that she "must keep out thieves and noodles," but she managed to catch a titillating glimpse of him one day on Pennsylvania Avenue. She was out walking, she told her father, and there was Wilde, tall and slender, "*cafe au lait* in the face, long hair, dressed in stockings and tights, a brown plush tunic, a big yellow sunflower pinned above his heart, a queer cap on his head: turning to look after him,—as you taught me was very vulgar,—I saw a large blue card on his back, 'Oscar on a wild toot.'"

In the spring, when James boarded a liner for England, his parting thoughts were of Clover. He had chosen her to receive his last American letter, he explained, because he considered her the incarnation of her native land. In view of his love for England, Clover considered the gesture "a most equivocal compliment" and was left to wonder, "Am I then vulgar, dreary, and impossible to live with?"

And that, in the mind of Clover Adams, was the end of Henry James. When the death of his father in December 1882 brought him back to the United States, he revisited Washington and once more made his way up H Street to the Adamses' little round dinner table. But Clover no longer cared to repeat his gossip or even to disapprove of his disapproval of America.

The loss was Clover's. In her impatience with James's Continental tastes and ruminative style, she deprived herself of his vast sympathy for natures much like her own. The heroines of his novels are intelligent, spirited women striving for self-expression, yearning for some acknowledgment of their value as individuals.

As for what the self was, and what expressed it, James was undecided. In *The Portrait of a Lady,* the worldly Madame Merle maintained that the self had no discernible boundaries. "It overflows into everything that belongs to us—and then it flows back again," she explained to young Isabel Archer, a visitor from America. "I know that a large part of myself is in the dresses I choose to wear. I've a great respect for *things!* One's self—for other people—is one's expression of one's self; and one's house, one's clothes, the book one reads, the company one keeps—these things are all expressive."

Miss Archer was appalled. "Nothing that belongs to me is any measure of me; on the contrary, it's a limit, a barrier, and a perfectly arbitrary one," she insisted. "Certainly, the clothes which, as you say, I choose to wear, don't express me; and heaven forbid they should!"

James's failure to resolve the debate between Madame Merle and Isabel Archer mattered less than his identification of self-expression as a fundamental human impulse, one that compelled women as much as men. He would have been most touched by Clover's instruction to her father in a letter written at the end of 1881. "Save this," she said, achingly aware that her accounts of politics and society were superior to the versions that appeared in the newspapers. "My facts are facts, too, which all the special correspondents' are not."

Barred from the world of work, Clover, like most of her female contemporaries, sought self-expression in private realms. She wrote letters, served as gatekeeper of an exclusive drawing room, and collected art with a gusto not apparent in any other part of her life. In 1882, when an English friend presented the Adamses with a small painting by Richard Bonington, Clover was ecstatic. "That makes our fourth, and in Europe Bonington is 'heads even' with Turner in reputation," she boasted. "We shall at this rate leave fine pickings for our heirs." She could not resist adding that a neighbor had paid her taste the ultimate compliment: "My dear, I dislike auctions very much, but I mean to go to yours after you die."

Her prize acquisition, made a few weeks after the Bonington was shipped from England, began with a mysterious unsigned note directing her to a house where she would find an armoire, a secretary, and two portraits by Sir Joshua Reynolds for sale at "reasonable" prices. Curious but wary, Clover asked Henry and a friend to go with her. When they reached the house, a dilapidated stucco affair on F Street, the servants showed the merchandise but proved unable to answer questions about it. Mystified and slightly irritated, Clover decided to leave. But while she had been interrogating the help, Henry had turned up a clue: a book inscribed with the signature of Theodore Dwight, librarian of the State Department. Henry had met Dwight in the course of researching his history.

Dwight was summoned to tea. As far as he knew, the portraits were genuine Reynoldses, and the armoire and the secretary were Flemish antiques. The seller, a friend of his, was an elderly woman in straitened circumstances.

Clover hurried back to the house and bought everything, paying for her purchases with money Dr. Hooper had sent her for Christmas. The portraits, priced at $150 apiece, were dirty and cracked, and Clover wondered whether they could be restored. As for their provenance, she had learned only that the subjects were the seller's ancestors, named something like Grover or Grove or Groves. "Do you think I've wasted your cheque?" she asked her father.

Two weeks later, Clover was flushed with triumph. "Eureka! Eureka!" she wrote to Dr. Hooper. Dwight had unearthed a biography of Sir Joshua which revealed that a Mr. and Mrs. Groves sat for the painter in August 1755. It was also clear that the paintings had been in the family ever since. "I am their first purchaser!" Clover exulted.

Once the restorers wiped away a century of grime, even Henry, who disliked portraits, conceded that the pictures of Mr. and Mrs. Groves were "charmingly modelled and very dignified." Clover hung them side by side between the windows of the library. "Henry," she teased, "can look the other way."

H. H. Richardson, a celebrated architect who had known Henry Adams since their days at Harvard, was building a house in Washington for another college friend, and he gave Clover the double-edged thrill of praising her eye while damning his client, who had been offered the paintings a few months earlier. Though Clover basked in Richardson's blessing, she hardly needed it to bolster the confidence she felt in her artistic judgment. A true connoisseur, she recognized genius with or without the stamp of fame. She had met John Singer Sargent when he was twenty-three and immediately understood his promise. Also capable of appreciating the merits of art she disliked, she once urged her father to alert the Museum of Fine Arts in Boston to the availability of a macabre Audubon oil painting of "dead birds, some in an overturned basket, some on the ground, a spray of purple convulvulus on the left background." Even as she jested that neither she nor Henry cared for "still life," she could admire the painting's delicacy of execution.

The rest of the Five of Hearts shared Clover's love of art, but only Clarence King fancied himself her equal as a connoisseur. He wrote her about his purchases of paintings and bric-a-brac, discussed art-works for sale, and occasionally engaged her in his fantasies of feminine adornment. He had a special fondness for peignoirs, which, he told Clover, he had learned to love "on a female in the overland Pullman: she was the wife of a French banker in San Francisco. She had parted from her lover (as she informed me) but three weeks before and was consoling herself mornings by the most becoming imaginable peignoirs. Since then I have always striven to introduce them into my family. Lately my Mother has had three separate dress makers cut them but all were failures. The back seam, which must be straight from one end to the other and float off in a captivating curve, flops hither and yon . . . and spoils the effect." He hoped that his Mexican wanderings would turn up a sufficiently "loose jointed" fabric for a more successful attempt, and when he found the right material, he would give some to Clover.

Though King said he associated peignoirs with the "gilded vice" of French short stories, his lack of self-consciousness in discussing them with Clover suggests that he meant to speak to her as one aesthete to another. Clover took a deep pleasure in the artistry of her gowns from the Parisian house of Worth, and she grew lyrical over a large turquoise that reminded her of a summer sky. In a single breath she could speak of reading the *Iliad* in Greek and trimming her new spring bonnet, conveying the impression that she valued both as aesthetic experiences.

Clover also responded intensely to the beauty of flowers. During her first spring at 1607 H Street, she designed a garden with advice from historian George Bancroft, an avid amateur horticulturalist who had developed the American Beauty rose in his backyard near Lafayette Square. By planting lilies of the valley and daffodils for early spring, chrysanthemums for fall, and roses that bloomed until Christmas, Clover had flowers for most of the months she and Henry spent in Washington. Each spring she eagerly waited for the capital's magnolias to flower and combed the wilds of Rock Creek Park in search of the first dogwood petals.

But the more Clover indulged her aesthetic side, the less she cared for the social life she had cherished when the Five of Hearts assembled at her hearth. "Life is like a prolonged circus here now," she told Dr. Hooper early in 1882. "[P]lease copy at once the following on a post-card and mail to me: 'My dear child: Let me beg of you not to make calls and as few new acquaintances as possible. I know better than you the delicacy of your constitution. Ride on horseback daily but avoid visiting and evening parties. Medicus.'" A few months later, amid birdsong and wildflowers, she wished that "the sap which makes the trees and bushes so lively in the springtime ran as gaily in human legs and arms." She and Henry seldom dined alone at home, but Clover ventured out less and less. Picnics were deemed too strenuous, musical parties seemed pointless since no one listened to the music, and she complained that ladies' luncheons were "a style of killing time which I detest."

Even politics ceased to amuse. "Congress bumbles on," she sourly observed. "Everyone laughs at its assumed spasms of virtue, no one is deceived by any reform pretenses." Portly President Arthur, a coxcomb from his impeccable cravat to the tips of his gleaming shoes, was an object of particular derision. "There goes our chuckle-headed sovereign on his way from church!" Clover scoffed one Sunday morning as the parishioners of St. John's streamed into Lafayette Square. "He doesn't look as if he fed only on spiritual food."

Chester Arthur appointed the Adamses' friend Frederick T. Frelinghuysen as secretary of state, and in the spring of 1882, Frelinghuysen offered Henry the post of minister to Costa Rica, which included responsibility for most of Central America. Clover wistfully said she wished they wanted it—"it would be so new and fresh." But they did not want it. Henry was engrossed in what he called his "little historical mud-pie," doing his best to give it "shape and cohesion." A happy prisoner of routine, he rode for two hours a day, wrote for five, and then allowed himself to "chatter all I can with all who care to waste their eternal souls in that frivolity," he told a friend. "Nothing surprises me more, as time goes on, than to find how little the world seems to object to me, or indeed to interfere in any way with my concerns."

Clover's happiness proved more elusive. Society could still furnish unexpected delights, such as the dinner party at which General Sherman recreated his march to the sea on the host's tablecloth. Pushing battalions of silverware this way and that, the fiery general sent the rebel army clattering to the floor with the sweep of a pudding knife. But the prospect of more of these charming moments meant little to Clover as she pondered invitations during the winter of 1882–83, and her peevishness grew with her boredom. After meeting most of the diplomatic corps at a British Legation dinner, she declared that centuries of aristocratic breeding had left the "little secretaries" with brains "attenuated to a startling degree." When her sister Ellen asked if Washingtonians would contribute money for a women's annex to Harvard, Clover said it was useless "to expect anything from 'Washington nabobs'. . . . No one here cares for higher education—for women or men either; they'd laugh in one's face. I wouldn't even hint at it." Sending Henry alone to a large party, Clover justified her absence by noting that "hot rooms and crowds always take so much more from one than they give." A chronic ear infection furnished a perennial excuse for avoiding other social occasions though it did not seem to rule out her daily rides.

In that trying winter, Clover found her greatest pleasures in the autobiography of George Sand. She raced through all twenty volumes, in French, in the space of a few weeks, intrigued by the exploits of Madame Sand, who donned men's clothes and boldly explored Paris. Clover particularly enjoyed the thought that Dr. Hooper and George Sand might have crossed paths during his days as a medical student in the Latin Quarter. "She must have jostled you daily," Clover told him. She quizzed her guests about Sand and passed along all tidbits to her father, who had begun reading the work at Clover's suggestion. "Madame Sand looked like a sheep," she reported after meeting someone who had known her; she "had no conversation, scarcely talked at all, but watched others."

Striding through the *allées* of Paris in a man's suit and the most comfortable boots she ever owned, Sand had not wished to be a man but to observe without being observed, an impulse Clover shared. Writing to her father, Clover kept a voyeur's distance from her window: close enough to see who passed by on H Street but far enough back to avoid being seen. "I'm sitting by an open window behind a screen of roses and heliotrope," she confided one Sunday morning, "partly writing to you and keeping my left eye on the 'miserable sinners' who are going by to church in very good clothes." Sand also touched a deeper current in Clover Adams. "Escape oblivion," Sand urged her readers, many of whom were peasants and laborers. "Write your own history, all of you who have understood your life and sounded your heart." Sand knew that their facts were facts, too.

With the spring of 1883 came an invitation to visit Clover's friend Anne Palmer in New York. Henry was close to finishing the first quarter of his history, covering Jefferson's first administration, and did not want to interrupt his work. In eleven years of marriage, the Adamses had never been apart, but Henry encouraged Clover to go to New York alone. She did, telling her hostess that she was making the trip to test his affection.

"How I did enjoy my outing!" she bubbled on her return. ". . . It has taken me one week to unpack my mental trunk—and set my new ideas in order." She and Anne had stayed out from early morning until late at night, visiting an exhibit of contemporary American art, dropping by the studio of Augustus Saint-Gaudens to see his sculptures, attending P. T. Barnum's "very fine" circus, and dining with Henry's friend E. L. Godkin, editor of the *Nation*. Clover also met with Clarence King's mother, who had come to New York from Newport to raise funds for a new art school in the South. Intending to stay for three days, Clover wired Henry that she would be gone for four. Even the train ride home was a lark, passed mostly in conversation with Washington acquaintances.

Henry was waiting at the station. As soon as he found Clover, he took her on a long drive. They stopped to pick wildflowers, and he sweetly said he was glad she had enjoyed herself, but he also made it clear that such a trip would never happen again. Next time he meant to go along rather than "stay behind in a big lonely house."

Finished with the first part of his history, Henry planned to have a few copies printed and send them to friends for comment. As usual, he and Clover would summer in the quiet of Beverly Farms, and while waiting for his critics, he planned to entertain himself by writing another novel in secret. Clover seemed not to mind that Henry preferred a solitary diversion to one they could enjoy together, perhaps because she had at last found a diversion of her own. "Am going to take a photo with my new machine this P.M. at Rock Creek," she reported to her father a few weeks after coming home from New York. She had taken photographs in the past but not with the fervor she now showed.

Photography in the 1880s demanded fathomless patience—not one of Clover's hallmarks—and for their patience practitioners were rewarded with one frustration after another. The expedition to Rock Creek Park, required a carriage as well as a servant to help with the heavy camera, the glass plates that served as negatives, and the requisite array of chemicals. In order to register an image, a plate had to be exposed to the light for several seconds, which limited photographers to stationary subjects; even a small motion, like the rustle of leaves in the wind, blurred the image. And with no accurate instrument for measuring light, overexposure and underexposure were constant hazards.

Since Clover said no more of her Rock Creek excursion, she may have been unhappy with the results. Certainly the starkness of black and white would have disappointed someone with her love of color. But whatever the discouragements of photographing nature, she was determined to succeed at portraiture. She sought advice from H. H. Richardson and from a friend and fellow amateur named Clifford Richardson. A chemist, Clifford Richardson helped Clover with the technical side of the craft and took her to a demonstration of a new process for printing photographs. She could not help noticing that she was the only woman present.

In a small notebook with a marbled cover, Clover kept instructions for various photographic processes and recorded the details of her experiments. "John Hay," a typical entry begins. " 'Democracy' in hand near window. *12* sec. Good." The portrait, which showed a mischievously solemn Hay holding the French edition, with *Démocratie* emblazoned on the cover, was one more Five of Hearts jape about the authorship of Henry's first novel. In the months that followed, Clover photographed H. H. Richardson, the painter John La Farge, the historian Francis Parkman, Oliver Wendell Holmes, Jr., the Hay children, generals, and senators. Henry sat for her, as did his parents, her father, and the family terriers.

"[M]y wife does nothing except take photographs," Henry wrote Lizzie Cameron from Beverly Farms in the summer of 1883. Lugging her camera to every corner of their twenty-five acres, Clover framed their house with trees and sky, posed Henry's cousins against outcroppings of granite, and arranged visitors before the sea. Indoors, she caught the sunny comfort of the parlor and ventured into Henry's study to photograph him, pen poised above a manuscript, his soft hand manacled by a stiffly starched cuff. Clover also made notes on a self-portrait: "Marian Adams in study—*15* sec—hideous but good photo." (Unfortunately, it has not survived.)

With the practiced eye of the connoisseur, Clover was quick to master the art of composition, and a pair of portraits taken on porches show her command of the subtleties of point of view. To photograph Betsy Wilder, the housekeeper who had helped to raise Clover and her brother and sister after their mother's death, Clover placed the eye of the camera slightly below Betsy and asked her to concentrate on the knitting in her lap. The relationship of camera to subject

One of Clover Adams's portraits of her father, Robert Hooper, M.D.
MASSACHUSETTS HISTORICAL SOCIETY

conveys deep respect. But when Clover photographed Henry's parents, she positioned herself steeply below them. Mr. and Mrs. Charles Francis Adams gaze sternly into the lens, looking down on Clover in the photograph as the Adams family did in life.

In the fall of 1883, Clover captured the elderly historian George Bancroft in half-profile, his white hair and long white beard glowing against a dark background. Struck by the incandescent beauty of the picture, John Hay took it upon himself to get it published. Writing to his friend R. W. Gilder, editor of the *Century* magazine, Hay noted that Bancroft was eighty-three and "one of these days will be gone. I suggest that you get a copy of it and put it in the hand of your engraver—in time." As an afterthought, Hay told Adams what he had done. If "Our Lady of Lafayette Square . . . be angered at my blabbing of her Bancroft, tell her I did not do it, or some such fiction," he begged, afraid that he had overstepped his bounds. The *Century* wanted Henry to write an essay on Bancroft to accompany

As a photographer, Clover Adams mastered the subtleties of point of view. By placing the camera slightly below Betsy Wilder, the housekeeper who helped to raise Clover and her siblings after their mother's death, Clover puts herself in a position of respect, but the sleeping dog and Betsy's knitting imbue the scene with a sense of warmth and comfort. By positioning herself steeply below Henry's parents, Mr. and Mrs. Charles Francis Adams, Sr., Clover forced them to look down upon her, which she felt they in fact did.
MASSACHUSETTS HISTORICAL SOCIETY

George Bancroft, one of America's most popular historians, photographed by Clover Adams in 1883. Captivated by the portrait, John Hay thought it should be published. Henry vetoed the idea. MASSACHUSETTS HISTORICAL SOCIETY

the photograph, and Hay hoped the Adamses would "think it worthwhile to comply with Gilder's prayer."

They did not. "As for flaunting our photographs in the 'Century,' we should expect to experience the curses of all our unphotographed friends," Henry told Hay, sounding a strangely proprietary note considering that he had expressed no interest in Clover's photography before Gilder's offer. Henry added that he despised the practice of praising one's friends in print, as Howells and Hay had done in their *Tribune* reviews of *The Prince and the Pauper* and *The Portrait of a Lady*. "Between ourselves, there is in it always an air of fatuous self-satisfaction fatal to the most grovelling genius." Clover, convinced that Henry was right, willingly suppressed whatever desire she might have felt to see one of her photographs in the pages of a national magazine. "The mutual admiration game is about played out or ought to be," she told her father.

Henry concealed a deeper motive for refusing the *Century*: as much as he liked Bancroft personally, he was not a wholehearted admirer of the historian's work. He had pummeled the final volume of Bancroft's popular *History of the United States* in the *North American Review,* and when Bancroft wrote a book about the Constitution,

Henry confessed to a friend that he had found it unreadable. By declining Gilder's proposition, Henry spared himself the squirms of writing false praise.

Henry's decision, however correct and comfortable from his point of view, robbed Clover's art of a chance for public acclaim. Having seconded his opinion, Clover was hardly blameless in the matter, and there is little to be gained by speculating on the fame she might have won if Henry had agreed to the *Century*'s request. But there can be no doubt that she relished the idea of public recognition. When a newspaper review of an exhibit of works by several amateur photographers described her pictures as "very skillful," she beamed. The mention was brief, but she considered it important enough to clip and send to her father. "Save this," the gesture meant. Her art was art, too.

9

Vagrant Hearts

*T*he Clarence King who sailed from New York to Liverpool in the spring of 1882 was a boy of forty—the owner of a thickening middle, thinning hair, and an impish delight in his own charms. Prancing about the first-class decks of the *Britannic,* he flipped twenty-dollar gold pieces high into the air and invited one and all to admire the huge letters of credit in his wallet. Pointing out one draft for $5,000, he earnestly explained that he meant to spend the entire sum on a single work of art.

Perhaps because he seemed astonished by his good fortune, King managed these high jinks without giving off the least odor of bad form. A fellow passenger would remember him not as a boor but a pilgrim, a man questing after beauty "as gravely as if he were a Knight of the Grail."

Ecstatic to be launched on the first long holiday of his life, King abandoned all thought of the business hurdles waiting abroad, where he needed to find new investors for the Yedras silver mine in Mexico. Nor did he trouble himself over the confusion he had left in his wake, where his friends the Hays had the distinct impression that he would travel to Europe with them—in July. "Did you ever hear of a more characteristic performance than that of our gorgeous Rex?" Hay marveled to Adams on learning that King had sailed May 6.

"He went away—just as I knew he wouldn't—and did not give up his room for the 15th of July nor say a word to me about it. . . . He is more trouble to me than all my money." Hay wondered whether King meant for his mother to use the stateroom, and hoped the Adamses knew Mrs. Howland's full name and address. They did not. Henry puckishly advised writing "several thousand copies, to all possible initials, as to Mrs. A. B. Howland, Mrs. B. A. Howland and the like."

Addressing Florence King Howland as plain "Mrs. Howland, Newport," Hay learned that she would not be going to Europe. In the cloying cadences of the veteran martyr, she explained that in spite of a deep yearning to share her "first impressions of the old world" with Clarence, "I believed that my child's rest of mind would be more complete if he knew I held the family helm." Mrs. Howland's mother, at eighty-three, was "liable to the changes of nature," and her own delicate stepson, George Howland, was "like an exquisite vessel of cracked glass which a rough touch might shiver in atoms." For Hay's sake, she regretted her ignorance of King's whereabouts, but mother and son had agreed that Clarence should be free from the burden of letter writing.

From Liverpool, King sped to London, determined to take care of business. The Boston entrepreneurs who controlled the Yedras were willing to part with their interest for $1 million, but King's high spirits led him to think he could do even better. He upped the asking price by half, hired an agent to look for buyers in London, and crossed the Channel to meet with the financiers of Paris. After a week of appointments, nothing was settled, but seeds had been sown. The geologist felt entitled to a little spree.

Decked out in a large beret and a green velvet suit with knee breeches, King headed for Spain. Henry and Clover had scorned Madrid as a "hole" and John Hay had dismissed the Spanish as incurable liars, but to King, the land below the Pyrenees overflowed with enchantments. He loved the "rich, vigorous odor of onions and garlic," the "dusty leather" look of the mountains, the sight of owls sailing through crumbled church walls. A devotee of Cervantes, King hunted up a Spanish barber's basin of the sort Don Quixote had worn as a helmet. He recorded this adventure in an essay called "The Helmet of Mambrino," bound it in a piece of fabric dating from the

*Clarence King in the green velvet touring costume he often wore during his two-year
European holiday.* HUNTINGTON LIBRARY, SAN MARINO, CALIFORNIA

days of Cervantes, and bundled the package off to an old friend in
San Francisco.

By July he was back in Paris, cabling promises to meet Hay in
Britain. "Of course he will not," Hay moaned to Adams, "but I am
glad he is alive, for general reasons, though I may never see him
more." In September, when King materialized at the Bristol Hotel in
London, Hay forgave him on sight. "He is the same delightful and
irrational creature as of yore—if possible, more amiable than ever,"
Hay told the Adamses of the "vagrant Heart." King had shed his
drab American wardrobe for the plumage of Savile Row—
impeccably tailored suits, elegant shirts with stand-up collars, and a
pair of yellow shoes shaped, he noted fondly, like Italian daggers.
The sartorial masterpiece had little to impart of the Yedras, but he
bubbled over about the land of Cervantes and showed off his $30,000
trove of art and bric-a-brac: a spangled matador's costume, brocades,
silks, scarves, rugs, porcelain, ecclesiastical oddments, and several

paintings by Mariano Fortuny, whose small and meticulous pictures commanded princely sums.

London in the autumn of 1882 teemed with famous Americans. W. D. Howells was there, as were Charles Dudley Warner, who had written *The Gilded Age* with Mark Twain, and J. R. Osgood, the Bostonian who published Twain, Howells, Hay, and King. Bret Harte was also in town, a perennial truant from the Glasgow consulship Hay had laboriously secured during his tenure as assistant secretary of state. Harte did not seem compelled to account for his delinquency, and Hay, practiced diplomat, held his tongue. The expatriate Henry James was a regular at the Americans' dinner parties, waving their invitations as proof that he did not despise his native land. "You see I am very national," he wrote an American friend; "do insist on that to people when you hear them abuse me."

With his unbounded *joie de vivre,* King struck James as "a kind of fairy-godmother," an impression undoubtedly fortified by King's extravagant generosity. When Howells waxed envious over the Fortunys, King insisted he have one. Howells and the rest of King's entourage watched with amusement as the geologist waged an unsuccessful struggle to tear himself away from the merriment of London. Expected at a country house in Scotland, King resolutely purchased a railroad ticket every day, and every day telegraphed his host that he would come tomorrow.

The novel *Democracy* had recently appeared in England, and Prime Minister William Gladstone's admiration of the work made it the talk of London. During a stroll among the great oaks and elms of Kensington Park, Hay and King listened with poker faces as Howells announced that he and a friend had identified the author: John W. De Forest of Hartford, Connecticut. It was not a bad guess since De Forest had written two novels about corruption in Washington during the Grant years.

Even Henry Adams, who had forsaken the Old World, wished he were part of the London scene. "My dear Hay-oh," he wrote in October from Beverly Farms. "Your name naturally prolongs itself into a sigh as I think what fun I should have had I been with you in England." Noting that a "brace of baronets"—his friends Sir John Clark and Sir Robert Cunliffe—had sent glowing reports of their encounters with the Hays, Adams rejoiced in the wonder of friendship. "The universe hitherto has existed in order to produce a dozen people to amuse the five of hearts," he mused. "Among us we know all mankind. We or our friends have canvassed creation, and there are but a dozen or two companions in it;—men and women, I mean, whom you like to have about you, and whose society is an active pleasure."

The only sour note in London was struck by Charles Dudley Warner, who confessed in King's presence that he had disliked Spain. Warner traveled like a typical Yankee, King fulminated, "his dull eye agreeably *frappé* by the red and yellow novelties of the warmer world, but his heart (burglar-proof with its hereditary chilled iron doors) beyond the reach of the southern spirit." A few days later, laid low by a cold, King was overcome with remorse. "It is low and mean to grumble and find fault with blind and deaf men," he told Hay. Begging him to forget the outburst, King explained that normal human obtuseness often puffed him up with pride in his own superior sensitivity. To cure his arrogance, he thought he should learn to mind his "commonplace business" and "pick out a decent woman and marry her and taste the cup of human joy which certain, ahem! aspiring, nose in the air, young men of my acquaintance don't seem to have the power to do."

Toward the end of October, Hay moved his wife and three children to Paris. Clara headed for the Rue de la Paix to consult Charles Worth about cashmere. John, once again in dreadful, mysterious health, paid a visit to Jean Charcot, the Continent's leading neurologist. Hay's gait and pulse were unsteady, he suffered from dizziness, and late afternoon regularly brought on deep depression. Most discouraging of all was his "invincible sense of something worse waiting just around the corner." Unable to diagnose his condition, the best American physicians had advised him to "brace up and not think about it." Hay had tried, to no effect, finally deciding to come abroad for a year of rest and medical consultations.

Charcot had little to offer but a label—*Neurasthenie Cephalique,* or weak nerves. It was the malady of the age. George M. Beard, an American physician and author of two books on nervousness, blamed modern civilization: steam engines, the rapid spread of information by press and telegraph, science, and "the mental activity

4 March. 1883.
Washington.

My dear

    Two letters of yours are in my drawer. As my wife wrote lately, I postponed doing so; not because I was without material for a letter — far from it; but that you might have your little amusements at intervals. Your letters are very well except in saying nothing of your health. This is an anxious subject with us, because the writer has hit right and left at everyone, and we would gladly know that you at least have escaped. Be not mad at my calling King mad,

A letter from Henry Adams to John Hay on the official Five of Hearts stationery, which was furnished by Hay. Hay called Clover "First Heart" and assigned her the pip at the upper left. Henry was at her right, Clarence King in the middle, and Clara and John Hay became, in Henry's words, "the nether Hearts."

MASSACHUSETTS HISTORICAL SOCIETY

of women." Railroads were unyielding in their demands for human punctuality, cities were noisy, stock speculation created unbearable tension. The victims of nervousness endured a plethora of symptoms, most of them familiar to Hay: insomnia, fatigue, noises in the ears, irritability, and phobias ranging from "fear of fears" to "fear of everything."

Whatever the merits of Charcot's diagnosis and Beard's theories, it remained for Whitelaw Reid of the New York *Tribune* to detect what the doctors could not. Writing to Hay in Europe in the hope of luring him back to the paper, Reid pointed out that Hay thrived in New York and Washington but fell ill in Cleveland. Why not give up Euclid Avenue and move to Manhattan? Reid asked. Anticipating that Hay's father-in-law might object, Reid noted that Hay's presence in New York would give Amasa Stone's financial affairs a firmer footing in the capital of capitalism.

Reid's timing was as uncanny as his insight. Clara's father, who no longer felt well enough to manage his business, wanted Hay to come home from Europe but could not quite bring himself to insist upon it. "I am some better in health than I was, but now have not much confidence in my health," one typical letter reported. "I can only say that I wish you were here now—It may be best you should not come—I fully appreciate the disturbance it would make were you to come here now." The old man asked Hay to carry this burden alone; he did not want to alarm Clara with news of his deterioration.

The only light spilling into the gloom of this Paris autumn was a rendezvous with Clarence King and Henry James, who joined the Hays for a few weeks at the Grand Hotel. In French that was as self-assured as it was eccentric, King informed the city's finest dealers in antiques that their wares were trash. To Hay's amazement, they responded by posting themselves outside his hotel-room door for hours, promising him Van Eycks and other treasures, and begging him to return to their galleries.

Eager to find King the wife he said he wanted, Hay arranged an evening at the Opéra Comique in the company of an American novelist named Constance Fenimore Woolson. King said only a few words during the outing, Hay gossiped to Lafayette Square, but Fenimore, "that very clever person, to whom men are a vain show—loved him at sight and talks of nothing else." A grandniece of James

Henry James knew the Five of Hearts well. John Hay admired James greatly, Clarence King found him a bit too fastidious, and Clover Adams thought his prose overstuffed. For his part, James was charmed by King's devil-may-care nature, valued Hay's friendship, and gently mocked the Adamses in a short story. LIBRARY OF CONGRESS

Fenimore Cooper and distantly related to the Hays, Fenimore was slim and quietly pretty, with a high forehead and regular features set in an oval face. She also possessed intelligence, sensitivity, and a comfortable income of her own. None of it stirred Clarence King.

Hay also misunderstood Fenimore's interest. King was an intriguing sprite, but the real object of her affection was Henry James. She had moved abroad in 1879 bearing a letter of introduction from one of his cousins, and when she met him the following year in Florence, she was immediately taken with his "beautiful regular profile" and his large light gray eyes, which took in everything and revealed nothing. James reveled in her praise of his work, and Fenimore interpreted his pleasure as a sign of mutual attraction. She did not perceive, nor did he think to mention, that he would have no bride but literature.

If Hay felt any disappointment as a matchmaker, it mattered little

*American expatriate novelist Constance Fenimore Woolson. John Hay hoped for a match
between Woolson and King, but she loved Henry James, who had no interest in marriage.*
HOUGHTON LIBRARY, HARVARD UNIVERSITY

next to his gratitude for the distractions of King's company. Beaming at the exploits of the gorgeous Rex, Hay reported that King was
"run after by princes, dukes and millionaires, whom he treats with
amiable disdain." His most fervent admirer was the flamboyant Ferdinand de Rothschild, intimate of the Prince of Wales and creator of
Waddesdon Manor, a 222-room palace on grounds measured not in
acres but miles. By exposing the great diamond hoax in 1872, King
had rescued several million Rothschild dollars, and when the geologist arrived in England, the baron rushed to embrace him. He
showered King with invitations, sought his approval of Waddesdon
Manor's Gainsboroughs and Beauvais tapestries and Bourbon furniture, and despaired whenever King left his side. The baron followed
him to Paris, dining one evening on artichokes and Belgian oysters
with King, Hay, and James. Highly amused by the baron's pursuit,
Hay reported it to Howells, who in turn told Mark Twain that
Rothschild "all but sleeps with [King]; chases him round and wants
him to come and spend the rest of his life with him."

For all his adoration, however, neither the baron nor his influential
friends showed an interest in Mexican silver. As 1883 began, King
complained that "not even the geological processes are so slow as a

London company." Again he thought the Yedras sale was imminent, and again he was braced for defeat. "Oh how I hate it all," he told Hay. Planning to sit for a portrait, he said he would not pose "in the dignified costume of a mountaineer but with my nose to a grindstone and fate holding me down."

The portrait was to be done by a young Swedish artist named Anders Zorn. Waiting for the money men in Lombard Street to make up their minds, King sat for two portraits and dreamed of making Zorn famous in Paris. But when two more Yedras deals collapsed, Zorn caught the brunt of King's wrath. Declaring both portraits complete failures, King refused to accept either. Zorn, with no money to show for months of work, turned in desperation to King's friends. Rothschild bought one of the paintings, and Hay cheerfully agreed to take the other. King, convinced that he would never sell the mine, fell into despair. "Soon I shall give it all up," he told Hay, "and go home with my tail between my legs whupped for the first time."

In Boston, King's financial backers were nearing the end of their patience. They had had no word from him since he had sailed with a vow to sell the Yedras in two months. Instead they heard endless rumors of his return: In October 1882, he said he would sail in November; in January 1883 he promised February. When Adams heard rumblings of their displeasure, he thoughtfully passed the word to Hay. Hay was incensed. King had "worked like a Turk for their interests all the time he was in Paris," Hay insisted. The fault lay not with King but with the "vacillation and treachery of French-men in business matters," obstacles which Hay felt the "square and serious" Bostonians could not fully appreciate.

But Adams was less swayed by Hay's stoutness of heart than his own sense that King had pushed Alexander Agassiz and his fellow financiers to their limit. "Is King insane or not?" Adams asked Hay. "Agassiz seems seriously to think he is, and I myself sometimes suspect it. He acts most strangely to the eye of a bystander. In Boston they talk pretty freely about him." The talk, Adams was too delicate to say, was gossip about King's capers in the slums of London. If Hay had not yet heard such stories, he soon would, through colorful dispatches from an American diplomat named Frank Mason. King, said Mason, goes down to the lowest dive at Seven Dials, chirps to the pretty bar maid of a thieves' gin mill, gives her a guinea for a glass of "bittah," gets the frail simple thing clean gone on him. Then whips out his notebook and with a smile that would charm a duchess asks her to tell her story. Naturally she is pleased and fires away in dialect that never saw print which the wily ex-geologist nails on the spot. Of course she is a poor pitiful wronged thing who would have been an angel if she had been kindly treated and taken to Sunday school when she was a child.—They are all so, you know. Think, Hay, of ten such girls, with their plump red cheeks, their picturesque slang . . . corralled in one book written for a good moral purpose. . . . I suppose, rather let us say we *hope,* that King is walking through all these narrow, slippery places upright and unstained as an archangel.

The archangel also befriended a group of girls who canned pickles for Crosse and Blackwell. Each week they convened for what King called "Sunday school," during which he claimed to instruct them in a fashion "not quite orthodox, but not so awfully heterodox either." When he discovered how little they knew of trees and flowers, the-ology gave way to botany, with outings to Windsor Castle, where they picnicked in the park. On one of these afternoons they poured a cup of their tea for no less a personage than Queen Victoria.

Or so King said when he boasted of his subterranean forays to the ladies of Belgravia and the gentlemen in the clubs of Pall Mall. Unlike Clover Adams and Henry James, who contemplated the vast-ness of London poverty and wondered how long the aristocracy could hold out, King did not raise the subject of barmaids and pickle girls because he burned to discuss social reform. He meant to shock, as he had in the days when he told coarse Western stories to the prigs of Washington. The English, however, were not so easily offended, and since King tended to blush as he narrated his adventures, his listeners had trouble believing that he was the rake he made himself out to be. Listening to his stories, the Adamses' friend Lady Char-lotte Clark concluded that King's "taste for the borders of the demi-monde" was pure affectation.

What Lady Charlotte did not know was that the tales King carried from the murkiest quarters of London were given a good scrubbing before they reached respectable ears. With Frank Mason, King pre-tended to woo barmaids for the lofty purpose of writing a book. The Crosse and Blackwell girls were mere backdrop for the heroism of a shining knight who carried light and beauty to the darkness of the slums. Such embroideries helped King disguise an uncomfortable truth: he frequented such places because he could not feel sexually attracted to women unless they were, by nineteenth-century bourgeois standards, his social inferiors. Dark skins aroused him, as did servants, laborers, and prostitutes.

King had come to his predilections by a tortuous route. Growing up without a father, he had been very close to his mother. While his choice of geology as a profession gave him an escape from her physical presence, her economic dependency and emotional fragility enabled her to cling to him. King grumbled that duty to her came between him and "every good thing," but his conscious resentment did not begin to encompass the complications of their relationship. Discussing peignoirs with Clover Adams, he had had no idea of what was revealed in his wish to clothe his mother in the image of the adventuress he had met on the Overland Express.

Since 1869, when maternal pressure forced him to break his engagement to Miss Dean, he had stayed away from women of the sort his mother would see as rivals—Constance Fenimore Woolson, for instance. The most telling aspect of Fenimore's first meeting with King was not her delight but King's uncharacteristic silence. Fenimore was yet another forbidden woman, declared off-limits by the most forbidden woman of all, his mother. And since King's upper-class social life offered him nothing but these forbidden women, it was almost inevitable that he would come to loathe them. Rather than confront his mother, he sought sexual satisfaction in secret, among barmaids and servants. They too were proscribed, but they were unlikely to make demands for marriage.

King's appetites were hardly unknown among the gentlemen of his day, and like King, many of the gentlemen who took their pleasures in unrefined purlieus imagined that the underclasses enjoyed freer, richer sex. "You burly lovers on the village green, Yours is a lower, and a happier star!" sang George Meredith, the Victorian novelist and poet. But that was a fantasy of minds rebelling against bourgeois notions of propriety; the pleasures of those who looked for love among the lower classes often exacted a terrible price. On one side were the wrongs committed against the powerless—masters who forced themselves upon servants being the prime example.

("Gentlemen is much greater blackguards than what blackguards is," noted a girl who sold oranges in the streets of London.) On the other side, those who moved secretly between two worlds carried an immense burden. Clarence King, fearing the opprobrium of his friends, had condemned himself to a life of concealment and half-truths of the sort he told at Lady Charlotte's dinner table.

December in Paris was "sour and nasty," Hay thought, and just before Christmas of 1882 he moved his family south to Cannes. Lonely for King, unimproved by the mineral-spring baths Charcot had prescribed, Hay found Cannes "a madness of toad-eating gaiety." The one redeeming feature was the presence of His Royal Highness the Prince of Wales, who was loudly singing the praises of a novel called *Democracy.* "[H]e says it is the first American book he has read which seems true all round," Hay reported to Adams. Hay himself, who had just reread it, considered it "far better than these *sacres rosbifs* Englishmen can possibly know," though he disputed Henry's belief that corruption was the deepest evil in American politics. In Hay's view, the American congressman was "not an especially strong or wicked man. He is—nine times out of ten, simply very ignorant and incapable of wise legislative action." Even more debilitating to the national good was the requirement that a congressman live in the district he represented. "We have 321 districts," Hay said. "In 200 of them there is nobody fit for Congress."

Inspired by the success of *Democracy,* Hay had dashed off an anonymous political novel of his own before sailing to Europe. A tale of the conflict between capital and labor, *The Bread-Winners* had its origins in a wave of railroad strikes that swept the United States in the summer of 1877. In Cleveland Hay had watched with alarm as mobs of "foreign workingmen, mostly Irish" intimidated federal troops, state militias, and politicians, who would not stand up to the strikers for fear of losing their votes.

Hay set his novel in Buffland, an industrial city not unlike Buffalo or Cleveland, and he populated the town with a host of unappealing characters, including a carpenter's daughter who spent her days in the library reading about Rothschilds, Astors, and the Polo Club—and went home "loathing her lineage." Poor Maud Matchin had no way to attract the millionaires she read about and no interest in the common laborers who called on her. "I can't put my hand in a hand that smells so strong of sawdust," she said of Sam Sleeny, a would-be suitor who worked for her father.

A good-hearted dolt, Sam Sleeny was easy prey for Hay's chief villain, Andrew Jackson Offitt, head of a unionlike brotherhood called the Bread-Winners. When Sam asked how the Bread-Winners would spend his two-dollar initiation fee, Offitt told him it went for "room rent and lights" and for "propagatin' our ideas, and especially for influencin' the press." Even the slow-witted Sleeny suspected that Offitt pocketed the money.

While Sleeny puzzled over the Bread-Winners, Maud fixed her sights on Captain Arthur Farnham, owner of a new house on Algonquin Avenue, the most elegant thoroughfare in Buffland. Maud went to Farnham for help in winning a job at the library, after which she planned to win Farnham himself. Guessing as much, Farnham tested her with a kiss. Her obvious pleasure led to accusations of larger ambitions, and Maud fled in humiliation. The unprincipled Offitt had been calling on her, and she confided that she would "owe a good deal" to the man who gave Farnham a beating.

Farnham is beaten but survives, a strike breaks out but stops short of violence, Offitt is murdered, Farnham proposes to the girl next door, and Maud Matchin begins to see the virtues of Sam Sleeny.

But all this happiness was misleading, the author lectured. Buffland, which refused to engage itself with the issues raised by the strike, was headed for doom. "The rich and prosperous people, as their manner is, congratulated themselves on their escape, and gave no thought to the questions which had come so near to an issue of fire and blood." They "kept on making money and bringing up children to hate politics as they did, and in fine to fatten themselves as sheep which should be mutton whenever the butcher was ready. There was hardly a millionaire on Algonquin Avenue who knew where the ward meetings of his party were held. There was not an Irish laborer in the city but knew his way to his ward club as well as to mass."

By design, *Democracy* had appeared while Henry and Clover Adams were abroad, and Hay undoubtedly intended to pursue the same strategy with *The Bread-Winners*. But by February 1883, when the

Hays left Cannes for Florence, publication was still months away. *The Bread-Winners* would run as a serial in the *Century* magazine, with the first installment to appear in August.

Florence was wet and gray. Sending a "cordial throb" to Lafayette Square, Hay grumbled that Clara worked him "rather hard," dragging him to "churches by the dozen." Hay much preferred the railroad stations, where he invariably spotted the Italian edition of *Democracy* on the newsstands. In low spirits and uncertain health, Hay was further depressed by word of another blow to the fortunes of his father-in-law. Years before, Amasa Stone had lent his brother $800,000 to start an iron and steel mill, which was now on the verge of collapse. "I cannot say what is best for you to do," the old man wrote to Hay; "while I am well enough to attend to business all is well but should I get sick it would be well if you were here." In early March, Stone forwarded $2,000, which he thought might help if Hay decided to come home early. Surrounded by his family but isolated by the need to conceal Stone's troubles from Clara, Hay felt miserably alone.

Between churches, he distracted himself with the company of W. D. Howells and the peripatetic Constance Fenimore Woolson. She had reread *Mountaineering in the Sierra Nevada* after meeting King and now suspected that he and Hay had jointly written *Democracy*. By writing the book together, clever scamps, they had hit upon a strategy that allowed each of them to claim innocence when the question of authorship arose. Hay's denials failed to persuade her otherwise.

Hay's Florentine afternoons with Fenimore were passed mainly in conversation about Henry James. Fenimore, whose novels and stories of the Great Lakes and the American South underwent one painstaking revision after another, had felt awe and despair in equal measure when she learned that the Master did not rewrite. Hay delighted Fenimore by saying that he had as little patience with James's detractors as with the Boston financiers who dared to question the honor of Clarence King. When American readers complained that James's short story "The Point of View" was anti-American, Hay acidly noted that no eyebrows would have been raised if James made his home in Chicago instead of London. "Of all vices I hold patriotism the worst when it meddles with matters of taste," Hay fumed.

All of this was music to Fenimore, who could hardly wait to share it with the Master. Did he know the depth of Hay's feelings? she asked James. "I did not, until one day in the Boboli Gardens, when he said—among other things—'If anyone speaks against James' writings in my presence, I consign him to contempt. And if anyone speaks against James himself, I immediately *hate* him.' " And when the lonely Hay confided that wherever King was, "there is my true country, my real home," Fenimore quickly appropriated the remark to advance her cause with James. "Well," she wrote him, "that is my feeling with regard to your writings; they are my true country, my real home."

Once Clara finished with the churches of Florence, the Hays returned to Cannes, drifting north to Paris and London in the spring. When Henry Adams inquired after Hay's health, Hay gamely replied that since he had none, he did not talk about it. The Hays would sail home May 10 on the White Star liner *Germanic*. King talked of going with them, and Hay hoped Henry and Clover would seize the moment for a Five of Hearts reunion at Delmonico's.

The Adamses sent their regrets. Henry had no faith that King would come home with the Hays just because he had said he would.

"[Y]our prophetic soul was right," Hay admitted at the end of April. Once more the mining negotiations had stopped short of a sale. The geologist had been "harassed beyond measure" and was "far from well," Hay told Adams. "I am sorry to leave him."

Ten months in Europe had done nothing to cure Hay, and he worried deeply about King, but he no longer felt concerned about Amasa Stone. As Clara staged one last raid on the shops of London, Hay paid a visit to the house where Thomas Carlyle had lived. "At your age he suffered precisely as you do—deep nervous depression, persistent indigestion and loss of sleep," Hay wrote his father-in-law. "Yet he lived to be 86 years of age and the last 25 years of his life were comparatively healthy and free from pain." Hay had also chanced to meet a hardy octogenarian with a similar history, the misery of his sixties followed by robust health and gay spirits. Sharing these stories with Stone, Hay predicted that his father-in-law's case would run the same course. "You have so much to live for," Hay added, "to enjoy the result of good you have done and to continue your career of usefulness and honor."

Hay's encouragement came too late. The day after the *Germanic* slipped her moorings in Liverpool, Amasa Stone locked himself in his bathroom, climbed into the tub, and fired a bullet into his heart. John and Clara Hay would not get the news until they landed in New York. Imagining their shock, Mark Twain marveled at how "odd and strange and weird all this is. Apparently nothing pleases the Almighty like the picturesque."

Henry and Clover read the newspaper accounts of Stone's sad end but saw no reason to be on the pier when their friends came down the gangway. Perhaps the Adamses concluded that their presence would do more to delay than comfort, or perhaps they shrank from offering the inevitably paltry gift of consolation. The Hays hurried home alone to bury Amasa Stone.

With family and friends, Henry Adams had always fled from grief, and Stone's death was no exception. Hastening through his condolences in his next letter to Hay, he made nervous small talk about the manuscript of his history, plans for the summer at Beverly Farms, and Don and Lizzie Cameron. Hay did not seem to mind, probably because he too was feeling evasive. "[I]nexpressible" was the most he would tell the Adamses of his and Clara's feelings. Nor did he wish to discuss the painful matter of Stone's ambivalent letters to Europe, cries for help that the proud old man had muffled and Hay had not heard.

Hay managed to bear the strain for a few weeks, long enough to help the lawyers start sorting through Stone's affairs. But after a summer of feeling alternately exhausted and inebriated "without hilarity or rum," he headed to the Colorado Rockies with his old friend George Nicolay. The brisk air at nine thousand feet and the prospect of resuming work on the Lincoln biography filled Hay with a sense of well-being he had not enjoyed for years. He jauntily carved the Five of Hearts emblem on a sandstone boulder beside the names of his "thousand brother idiots," and he looked forward to entertaining the Adamses when he returned to Cleveland in the fall. Euclid Avenue was not Lafayette Square, but they could wear their new enamel Five of Hearts pins, keepsakes Hay had brought from Europe. Perhaps the gorgeous Rex would be home in time to join them.

On August 23, 1883, the newly chartered Anglo-Mexican Mining Company of London purchased the Yedras for $1.4 million. Elated, Clarence King decided to postpone his return to America. As managing director of the new enterprise, King would earn $3,000 a year—more than he needed to support his mother's household. With his profits from the sale and his shares in the new company, King believed that he had at last secured his fortune. The long years in the blistering sun and merciless rains of Mexico were behind him. He could enjoy the "first long dream" of his life, he said, and surrender at last to the impulses of his "art-loving mind." King treated himself to German and Italian primitives, Dutch oils, and English watercolors. Like Henry and Clover Adams, King particularly admired the rich color and shimmering light of J. M. W. Turner, whose works he had known since his youthful reading of John Ruskin's *Modern Painters*. Prowling art galleries in 1883, King happened across the elderly Ruskin, who was selling his own collection of Turners in order to raise money for social causes. As Hay told Howells, King "poured lyric toffey all over him," and the old man extended an invitation to his home in the Lake District. Two Turners still hung on Ruskin's walls. When the critic offered his guest a choice, King allowed that "One good Turner deserves another" and bought them both.

King's art-loving mind also entertained fancies of writing political fictions in the manner of Henry Adams and John Hay. With mounting impatience, King had listened to the swells of London laugh at the vulgarity and corruption of the society portrayed by *Democracy*. Whatever the flaws of the New World, King felt that they were dwarfed by the inequalities of England, where society was "sharply divided into a little heaven of exclusive people" and "a big hopeless hell of common people to whom all doors are shut save the grave and America." King conceded that *Democracy* was clever but thought its moral "untrue." In his eyes, the protagonist, Madeleine Lee, was even more provincial than the Midwestern politicians whom she and her creator deplored. "The real moral," King told Hay, "is that in a Democracy, *all* good, bad, and indifferent are thrown together in the circling eddy of political society and the person within the whole field of view who has the least perception, who most sadly flaunts her lack of instinct, her inability to judge of people without the labels of old society" was Madeleine Lee.

Proposing to write a sequel called *Monarchy* or *Aristocracy,* King envisioned sending Mrs. Lee to London "in search of the fine old English code of society, morals, and statesmanship." His cast would include a member of Parliament as corrupt as Henry's Senator Ratcliffe; a married lord who poured vast sums into a theater for his mistress, a ballerina; and the Prince of Sharks, whose title was a labored pun on a labored pun—the Prince of "Whales." Mrs. Lee would find London as disillusioning as Washington.

A week after laying out this grand scheme, King retreated. "I take back all I said about writing a pendant for Democracy," he told Hay. "I won't do it. I am not clever enough, and I feel too deeply to write well on a national novel." The harp of Henry Adams, King seemed to suggest, was not so finely tuned. Months later, talking about the book as if he had never dropped it, King reported that he had not yet written a line of *Aristocracy,* but it was "getting into fair shape."

The same could not be said of the Anglo-Mexican Mining Company. To sell the Yedras, King and his American partners had accepted $400,000 in stock and the promise of $1 million in cash. But when a plunge in London stock prices left the new investors short of money, they asked to stretch out their payments. King granted the extension without consulting his Boston partners, once more taxing their patience. He considered making a trip to Mexico in the spring of 1884 (probably as a show of penance since his presence at the Yedras would not alter the realities of London), but he soon changed his mind. John Hay was coming to England, once more in need of tranquility for his jangled nerves.

This time Hay's symptoms could be traced to the raging national debate over *The Bread-Winners.* Recently published in book form, the novel was attributed to both Hay and Adams, and many readers concluded that the author of *The Bread-Winners* had also written *Democracy.* ("What an unspeakable idiot the Public is!" cried Clover Adams, who thought *Democracy* much superior.) No one relished the comparisons and wrong guesses more than Henry Adams, who, like Clover, was party to the secret. "I am glad to hear that you are publishing another novel," Adams had written Hay while *The Bread-Winners* ran in the *Century*. "I was so frank in telling you my unfavorable opinion of 'Democracy,' that I will try to read the new one in hopes that I may be able to speak well of it." With mock concern for Hay's anonymity, Adams asked, "Is it not a little risky . . . to lay the scene at Cleveland after laying the scene of 'Democracy' at Washington? Two such straws must be fatal."

Hay had played merrily along, blaming *The Bread-Winners* on Adams. "To think that while Mrs. Hay and I, and Mrs. Don Cameron, sat guilelessly by your fireside and bragged about Cleveland, you were taking down our artless prattle for the use of future satire—it is too much, 75 percent too much."

Outside the Five of Hearts *The Bread-Winners* was no joke. Dozens of *Century* readers protested Hay's treatment of unions and laborers, and numerous journals of opinion, including the *Atlantic,* excoriated the author for libeling the workingman while making no mention of abuses by monopolies and corporations. Hay stood the criticism for as long as he could, then climbed into the *Century* pulpit for a counterattack. "For several months I have listened in silence to a chorus of vituperation which seems to me unjust and unfounded," his anonymous letter began. In the past he had dismissed his work for his father-in-law as a sinecure, but now he told the world that he had always earned his own living. Skirting the question of whether he had treated labor unions too harshly, Hay claimed that he had not dealt with unions at all: the Bread-Winners was "a little society," run by a criminal who expropriated the language and methods of union organizers in order to swindle poor workmen. Defending his anonymity, Hay denied any cowardice or nefarious purpose. "I am engaged in a business in which my standing would be seriously compromised if it were known that I had written a novel," he said. "I could never recover from the injury it would occasion me if known among my own colleagues." Hay did not specify the injury he feared, and it is hard to imagine that *The Bread-Winners* would have ruffled the placid gentlemen of Euclid Avenue. Their problem, as he himself had observed, was apathy. With perfect ease Hay could

urge W. D. Howells to "come to Cleveland and get in a buggy with
me and see a novel in our neighborhood." But he did not want
curious strangers asking for the same tour.

In a "noice clean floy" rented from a Cockney liveryman, Hay and
King trotted through green woods, listened to the song of the
cuckoo, and inspected ancient churches. Mark Twain had found the
English countryside "too absolutely beautiful to be left out of doors,"
and after one excursion with King, Hay shared Twain's reverence.
"It was like a fairy scene," he wrote to Clara. Taken with the idea of
spending summers in Britain, Hay looked into the purchase of a
country estate. Between Amasa Stone's bequests and the riches Hay
had accumulated under Stone's tutelage, he and Clara were now
what Clover called "tri-millionaires"—worth some $3 million. But
Scottish castles and English manors, Hay decided, were still beyond
his means.

Tenderly devoting himself to Hay's care, King rowed him on the
Thames, took him to dine with Bret Harte and Henry James, and
indulged him in a visit with Constance Fenimore Woolson, who had
moved onto James's turf in 1883. Although James often called on
her, Fenimore had begun to sense that his ardor did not match hers.
"I am terribly alone in my literary work," she confessed to Hay.
"There seems to be no one for me to turn to." She wanted to believe
the rumors that Hay had written *The Bread-Winners* because she
longed to have him as a colleague. As with *Democracy,* she thought
she detected signs of a collaboration with King.

Over tea, Fenimore pleased Hay by telling him that she found
King "superlative," but this time Hay refrained from matchmaking.
Whether or not he guessed her attachment to James, he could see that
King was in no mood for talk of marriage. He was, in fact, "cross as
a bear," Hay told Clara. Financially pressed, the geologist had traded
his luxurious suite at the Bristol Hotel for modest lodgings in Bolton
Street, two doors from James. In Washington the Adamses and Hays
had recently purchased a piece of property on Lafayette Square and
had commissioned H. H. Richardson to build a pair of houses. Hay
hoped to send word from London that the fifth Heart would join
their colony. Still waiting for the Anglo–Mexican investors to honor
their promises, King was forced to decline.

★   ★   ★

King stayed in England until September 1884, then left as suddenly as he had sailed from America two years before. "Yes I am really back in America!" he wrote Hay on his arrival in New York. But as he sat in the oak-paneled hush of the Union League Club and asked himself how he felt about being home, he said, "there is but one answer which comes up from the very depths of my being. Save for my family and you and yours I am hopelessly 'out of it' and 'out of it' forever. I would not have believed so great a change possible. Everything but food seems to be so inferior, so crude, so banale. This first sensation is one long black regret that I must stay here and make the best of it." To King's distress, his stepbrother, George Howland, had been pronounced "too delicate" for college, and his mother was "more nervous and broken" than ever. "Were it not for the hope and confidence that I shall see you from time to time I would take an October steamer back again."

At every turn, King was overwhelmed by feelings of alienation and disconnection. Leaving his card with old acquaintances produced an avalanche of invitations, but dinners and parties only served to remind him of how far he had drifted from his old life. His precious hoard of paintings and bric-a-brac, put into storage because of his small quarters at the Brevoort House, underscored the rootlessness of his existence. While he envied the other Hearts their plan to live side by side on Lafayette Square, he knew that he could not join them even if he had the money. "If I were married, how I should delight in buying the house you are now living in and remaking it a little to suit my needs," he told Adams. "But I am human and could not bear the exasperating spectacle of your and Hay's domestic happiness." On a trip to Boston a few weeks later, King stayed away from the Adamses at Beverly Farms. After explaining that he had not had time for a visit, he made the curious observation that he had enjoyed Henry's friends Sir John Clark and Sir Robert Cunliffe more for their distance than their intimacy. They had, he said, "what I never saw in America, the easy habit of moderate friendship. Here one either hates or adores one's acquaintances. The sort of cordial mellow indifference of which the best English are capable was most charming and new to me." King cherished the Hearts, but he had come to fear their closeness even more than he needed it.

10

In Mid-Ocean

*F*or all that Clarence King left out of his letters, he confided more in his fellow Hearts than they did in him. In 1884 at least, the "spectacle of domestic happiness" that he envied his friends was largely an illusion, preserved by careful silences. The death of Amasa Stone had left the normally imperturbable Clara Hay feeling vulnerable and apprehensive. Throughout their marriage, John had kept up the graceful pretense that his relationship with Clara's father was a one-sided affair, with all the benefits flowing in the direction of John and Clara Hay. Believing this fiction, Clara worried that John would not know how to manage their finances without her father's guidance, when in fact he had handled the responsibility very ably for years.

In the spring of 1884, while Hay and King gamboled in the English countryside, Clara chanced to read a letter to John concerning a purchase of high-interest bonds that entailed more than the usual amount of risk. When Clara served notice that she wanted no part of such speculations, Hay rushed to soothe her anxieties. "You are the dearest, sweetest, truest woman that ever lived," he told her. "You make me love you more and more." Assuring her that their holdings were safe, he promised that henceforth he would avoid such propositions and "turn all of our property that I can into the securest form I can find."

Although there is no evidence of friction over the Hays' decision to ask H. H. Richardson to design a house for them in Lafayette Square, the move from Euclid Avenue surely unleashed a tempest. It seems unlikely that Clara would have wanted to leave her mother, who had not recovered from the shock of Amasa Stone's suicide, and even without that sorrow, Mrs. Stone would not have welcomed the Washington plan. It was she who had delayed Clara's wedding, putting off for as long as she could the unhappy day when her daughter moved away. While Hay claimed that the move to the capital was essential to his collaboration with Nicolay on the Lincoln biography, the truth was that they had worked successfully by mail for several years. Perhaps John prevailed by persuading Clara that Whitelaw Reid was right: Cleveland was ruinous to his health.

King's impression to the contrary, Henry and Clover Adams also had more tribulations than domestic bliss in 1884. The exclusivity of their H Street salon had the perverse if predictable effect of attracting swarms of unwanted guests. "Hardly a day passes that someone doesn't bring a letter of introduction," Clover complained to her father early in the year. To spare herself the parvenus, she instructed the servants not to admit anyone who inquired whether she was receiving—the standard approach of a stranger seeking entry without an invitation. Even Henry, who enjoyed parties and guests, lamented that Washington society was becoming "a mob almost as uninteresting and quite as crowded as in any other city." Faced with sheaves of invitations from newcomers longing to penetrate the innermost sanctum of social Washington, the Adamses adopted a policy of saying no to everyone. The strategy was awkward but efficacious, Henry explained to an English friend: "people begin by taking offence at it; then they cool down, and end by leaving us alone."

Apart from Clover's new passion for photography, little had changed in the lives of the Adamses. They rode in the morning, Henry worked in the afternoon, and they passed most evenings with friends. "Nothing could be pleasanter or less heroic," Henry told Sir John Clark. He never felt an urge to travel, he said, and Clover was even more immovable: "Nothing will induce her to contemplate any change except final cremation, which has a certain interest of new experience."

Still, they were both aware of the ennui creeping over their existence, especially since the departure of their vivacious young neighbor, Lizzie Cameron, who had gone to Europe in hopes of finding a cure for her husband's alcoholism. "We miss you—miss you—miss you," Clover wrote her. Confessing that she and Henry were "not as happy as we once were," Clover said they now wondered "how any man or woman dares to take the plunge." She closed with a heartfelt imperative: *"Come home."* Henry told John Hay that he and Clover were "becoming green with mould. We are bored to death with ourselves, and see no one else. At long intervals we chirp feebly to each other; then sleep and dream sad dreams. Don't quote this of us. We try to be cheerful at times when we meet a native."

Childlessness may have supplied the text for some of those dreams, but the Adamses also suffered from a less definable malaise: a gnawing sense that something, some larger sense of purpose, was missing. Part of their yearning appeared to be spiritual. Like most of their friends, they had long since divorced themselves from conventional religion. Dr. Hooper had not imbued his children with much Christian piety, and Clover was as irreverent about religion as everything else. Writing to a friend on a Sunday morning many years before, she noted that the church bells had "rung the white sheep into their respective folds and left the naughty black ones to outer sunshine and quiet. I'm so happy sitting on the floor with my back against the window and hot sun going through me bringing a prophecy of springs and summers and green things." She had twice gone to Trinity Church to hear Phillips Brooks, the most charismatic preacher in Boston, but, she said, "neither heart nor brain got any food."

Henry's rebellion against religion was one more aspect of his flight from the world of the Adamses. In his twenties, he had been thrilled by Charles Darwin's challenge to the biblical account of creation. Late in life he liked to say that he had been a Darwinist for fun, and he joked that the succession of presidents from Washington to Grant was all the evidence one needed to disprove Darwin's theory that life evolved from lower to higher forms. But as a young man, he befriended geologists and paleontologists and wrote admiringly of their work. He was also intrigued by the fledgling science of anthropology, with its investigations of culture and mythology. By treating Christianity as a set of myths, the anthropologists implied that it was no "truer" than Buddhism, Islam, or any other creed.

Henry Adams in his study at Beverly Farms, photographed by his wife, Clover, in 1883. The manuscript in the photograph may be part of Adams's history of the United States in the early nineteenth century, or the photograph may be a coy flaunting of his second secret novel, Esther, *which explored Clover's spiritual crisis.*
MASSACHUSETTS HISTORICAL SOCIETY

Some clerics, like Phillips Brooks, tried to ease the tension between science and religion by emphasizing that truth was the aim of both. While that may have reassured the communicants of Trinity Church, tougher minds saw that it dodged the fundamental conflict between the faith required by religion and the skepticism intrinsic to science.

In the summer of 1883, taking a break from his history, Henry decided to write a novel about the tug of war between faith and doubt. He called the book *Esther,* after his protagonist, who was in turn named for the central character in "Old Esther Dudley," a Nathaniel Hawthorne story set in Massachusetts after the American Revolution. No longer of sound mind, the aged Mistress Dudley did not understand that the British, whose cause she supported, had left for good. In vain she watched for the royal governor and the return of the old order. As a symbol of the rift between fact and wish, Old Esther Dudley made a convenient peg on which to hang a tale of the split between science and religion.

As with *Democracy,* Henry wrote in secret. And once again, he entrusted his dilemma to a female protagonist whose keen intelligence and emotional intensity were inspired by Clover Adams. Like Clover before her marriage, Esther Dudley lived at home with her father, a man who strongly resembled Dr. Hooper. William Dudley had been a widower for years, had inherited enough money to lead a life of leisure, and was not a pious man. At twenty-five, Esther was "absolute mistress" of her father's house. Observing that she was "not used to harness," a perspicacious uncle worried that she would rebel, "and a woman who rebels is lost."

Esther possessed all of the physical and intellectual shortcomings Henry had pointed out in Clover before their marriage. She was too slight, dressed badly, and owned a face composed of "imperfect" features. "Except her ears, her voice, and her eyes which have a sort of brown depth like a trout brook, she has no very good points." Her undisciplined mind, "as irregular as her face," suggested "a lightly-sparred yacht in mid-ocean; unexpected; you ask yourself what the devil she is doing there. She sails gaily along, though there is no land in sight and plenty of rough weather coming." She painted, much as Clover pursued photography. Henry declined to give his opinion of Clover's art, but Esther would never be more than "a second-rate amateur."

During their life in Boston in the 1870s, Henry and Clover had often visited the construction site of Trinity Church. Phillips Brooks and Henry Adams were second cousins, and the Adamses eagerly followed the minister's collaboration with their friends H. H. Richardson, who designed the church, and John La Farge, who decorated the interior. Henry built his novel around the construction of the fictional St. John's Cathedral in New York. Phillips Brooks became the Reverend Stephen Hazard, his name perhaps chosen to suggest Henry's ambivalence about his subject. Hazard would indeed prove a danger to Esther, and in a sense he would also be martyred, like St. Stephen. The temperamental John La Farge was cast as Wharton, a vain, opinionated, domineering artist.

Esther came to know Wharton and Hazard through her cousin George Strong, a geologist as footloose as Clarence King and as rigorously intellectual as Henry Adams. Wharton had belittled Esther's painting, but because she had more skill than some of his artisans, he invited her to take part in the decoration of St. John's. High up in the north transept of the church, she was to paint a figure of the blind St. Cecilia, patroness of music. For a model, she would use their new friend Catherine Brooke, a beautiful ingenue reminiscent of Lizzie Cameron. Not yet twenty-one, fresh from Colorado, Catherine delighted George Strong and his male friends. "Her innocent eagerness to submit was charming, and the tyrants gloated over the fresh and radiant victim who was eager to be their slave." By feigning gentleness, they lured her on.

Esther wanted to capture Catherine's radiance, but Wharton insisted that she pour her own soul into the painting. When Catherine accused Wharton of forcing Esther to paint like a man, Wharton snapped, "An artist must be man, woman and demi-god. . . . Put heaven in Miss Brooke's eyes!" he commanded. "I want to make St. Cecilia glow with your soul, not with Miss Brooke's." The celestial fire in the saint's eyes, Henry Adams wanted readers to know, was blindness.

As the painting reached completion and Esther returned to her own small studio, she missed "the space, the echoes, the company, and above all, the sense of purpose, which she felt on her scaffolding. She complained to Wharton of her feminine want of motive in life. 'I wish I earned my living,' she said. 'You don't know what it is to work without an object.'" Wharton replied that some of the world's greatest work had been done "with no motive of gain." Esther did not disagree but simply bewailed the fate of her sex: "Men can do so many things that women can't."

Esther's discontent swelled to anguish with the death of her father, an episode in which Henry Adams tried to imagine how Clover might react to the death of Dr. Hooper, then in his seventies. Listless and unable to sleep, Esther busied herself with trifles. The Reverend Stephen Hazard called every day, partly to offer solace and partly because of his growing attraction to Esther. When he declared himself and asked her to marry him, she agreed, grateful for his kindness and eager to fill the void left by the death of her father. To her concerns about the gap between his faith and her skepticism, he offered sublime comfort: "Love is the great magnet of life, and Religion is Love."

But as Esther listened to Hazard's sermons, she felt the same emptiness Clover had known in the Trinity Church of Phillips Brooks. And the more Hazard urged Esther to trust that his faith would conquer her doubt, the more agitated she grew. Sounding much like Madeleine Lee of *Democracy,* who wanted to know whether America was right or wrong, Esther asked George Strong, "Is science true?" Strong gave her a resounding negative. In that case, Esther inquired, why believe in it? He denied that he did. "Then why do you belong to it?" she pressed. "Because I want to help in making it truer," Strong replied.

Convinced that Esther was on the wrong track, Strong tried to dissuade her from using logic to acquire faith: "Faith is a state of mind, like love or jealousy. You can never reason yourself into it." But since she believed in Hazard, Strong thought there was no reason that she could not believe in his church. "Faith means submission," he said. "Submit!"

Cornered at last, Esther cried, "I want to submit. Why can't some of you make me?"

Finally Strong understood the force of Esther's will. Where he had once feared that Hazard would "turn her into a candlestick of the church," he now worried that Esther would destroy Hazard by destroying his faith. But with the cool detachment of the scientist, Strong chose not to interfere. He would stand by, as unblinking as Henry Adams, and wait for the inevitable collision.

Wrung out by her religious debates with Hazard, Esther allowed her aunt and uncle to take her away to Niagara Falls. Tears rolled down her cheeks as she watched the thundering cataract and listened to "the voice of the waters," which told her "a different secret from any that Hazard would ever hear." Face to face with the raw power of the falls, she realized that she could give to Nature what she could not give Hazard or his religion: submission.

Hazard came to Niagara to plead his case once more. Esther, wanting none of it, confessed that she could not enter his church without a feeling of hostility: "I never saw you conduct a service without feeling as though you were a priest in a Pagan temple, centuries apart from me."

Hazard calmly answered that he had heard these objections before. Since Esther was particularly repelled by the doctrine of the resurrection of the body, he asked her to imagine an afterlife in which she would *not* meet her loved ones. Surely, he argued, "the natural instincts of your sex must save you from such a creed!"

"Why must the church always appeal to my weakness and never to my strength!" Esther cried. "I ask for spiritual life and you send me back to my flesh and blood as though I were a tigress you were sending back to her cubs. . . . the atheists at least show me respect enough not to do that."

When Strong appeared, Hazard accused him of turning Esther against religion and fled in defeat. Esther, alone with Strong, struggled against tears. Strong consoled her with his judgment that she had waged a valiant fight. He offered to marry her. The novel ends with Esther's reply: "But George, I don't love you, I love him."

Taking their cue from Henry Adams, who set the conflict between Hazard and Esther in religious terms, many critics and biographers have seen *Esther* as the author's investigation of the paradox of faith in an age made skeptical by science. But the novel reveals less of the author's concern for the relation of man and God than his lifelong perplexity over the relation of man and woman. As a student at Harvard, Henry had read the tracts handed out by radical Boston women who wanted the right to vote. He found their arguments unconvincing, but as he reflected on the spirited, perceptive women in his own family—from his great-grandmother Abigail Adams to his rebellious sister Louisa—he realized that the inferior status of women was a result of history, not a fact of biology.

In 1876, when Professor Henry Adams was invited to deliver the prestigious Lowell Institute lecture in Boston, he used the occasion to attack the widely held notion that Christianity had rescued women from slavery. He began his talk, "The Primitive Rights of Women," by granting that the institution of marriage probably had evolved from notions of ownership. But he did not believe that primitive wives were property in any conventional sense. Among American Indians, wives retained their status as free members of their clans no matter how their marital status changed. The Egyptians were equally enlightened, inspired by the example of Osiris and Isis, the god and goddess who reigned as peers. In ancient Greece, wives were free-women, with rights their husbands were legally bound to respect.

Christianity had turned the tables, Adams argued. The church had risen to power on the ruins of the Roman Empire, "and of all the corruptions of the Empire none had been more scandalous than the corruption of the women!" In the new Christian order, a woman's submission—the act Esther Dudley found impossible—came to be prized more highly than her rights. Out of this demand for surrender arose the new feminine ideal: "the meek and patient, the silent and tender sufferer, the pale reflection of the Mater Dolorosa, submissive to every torture that her husband could invent." The professor did not think the inequity called for legislative redress of the sort sought by women's-rights advocates (who were, he believed, "a vile gang"). He preferred to trust in male common sense: Out of love for his wife and regard for his property, a man would instinctively seek equality with his mate.

This conservatism plus Henry's unsparing frankness about Clover's flaws have made it easy to accuse Adams of misogyny, and detractors have not lacked other evidence for their case. In an 1883 letter to John Hay, Adams said he struck out of his writing whatever Clover criticized "on the theory that she is the average reader, and that her decisions are, in fact if not in reason, absolute." The patronizing tone is unmistakable. But however intellectually superior Henry thought himself, he would not have sought Clover's opinion, much less acted upon it, unless he had respected it.

In another widely quoted letter, Henry told an English friend that the young women of America were "haunted by the idea that they ought to read, to draw, or to labor in some way, not for any such frivolous object as making themselves agreeable to society, nor for simple amusement, but to 'improve their minds.' They are utterly unconscious of the pathetic impossibility of improving those poor little hard thin, wiry, one-stringed instruments which they call their minds, and which haven't range enough to master one big emotion, much less to express it in words or figures." But that indictment is followed by an equally damning (though rarely cited) judgment of the male of the species: "Our men in the same devoted temper talk 'culture' till the word makes me foam at the mouth. They cram themselves with second-hand facts and theories till they bust, and then they lecture at Harvard College and think they are the aristocracy of intellect and are doing true heroic work by exploding themselves all over a younger generation, and forcing up a new set of simple-minded, honest, harmless intellectual prigs as like to themselves as two dried peas in a bladder."

Without denying Henry's condescension, it is possible to see his attitudes as part of his larger bafflement over the eternal battle of the sexes. In *Esther,* he clearly despised his male characters' treatment of women. He berated them for exploiting the young Catherine Brooke's eagerness to submit, and the idea that Hazard's will should dominate Esther's struck him as indefensible. He also saw the hollowness of Wharton's claim that his aesthetics were superior to Esther's. But when Henry tried to imagine how the sexual scales might be balanced, he saw no happy solutions. The contest between Hazard and Esther, which pitted one strong will against another, had had no winner. They ended with the dismal realization that not even love could bridge the gulf between them. In his own life, Henry had chosen a partner who was as much his equal as the times permitted. He never would have been satisfied with the benign docility of a Clara Hay. But in spite of the Adamses' closeness and compatibility, there remained a gap they longed to close. In writing *Esther,* Adams discovered that he, like Clover, like Esther Dudley, was alone in mid-ocean.

11

Seeking Shelter

*H*iding behind the feminine pseudonym of Frances Snow Compton, Henry Adams sent his gloomy *Esther* into the world in March 1884. In a mood to experiment, he persuaded Henry Holt, the publisher of *Democracy,* to issue the book with no advertising or publicity. The object of this furtive exercise (which Adams underwrote) was to see how the novel would fare on its own: what would the public make of a book unheralded by the ruffles and flourishes of the press agent?

The public paid virtually no attention. *Esther* attracted a perfunctory notice in *Publishers Weekly,* the journal of the book trade, and a passing mention in the *Nation,* which merely remarked that the *Literary World* had not received a copy for review. Nor had anyone else. In June, the frustrated Holt asked Adams for permission to "whoop up" the novel. Adams refused on the grounds that their experiment had just begun. With a touch of grandiosity, he had promised that if he died before he was ready to admit his connection with *Esther,* Holt could make the most of the Adams name. As he reminded the publisher, that was "a sure card."

Six months later, Adams conceded defeat. "So far as I know, no man, woman or child has ever read or heard of *Esther,*" he wrote to Holt. Clearly hoping for a triumph on the order of *Democracy,* Adams proposed that they run their experiment again, on the other side of the Atlantic. "I want to test English criticism and see whether it amounts to more than our own," he said. Holt obliged, and after three reviews—two of them negative—the novel sank in silence. Not even Clarence King and the Hays were let in on the secret.

Happily, life offered other diversions. Early in 1883, a sizable piece of property on the northwest corner of Sixteenth and H Streets had changed hands. It was rumored that the new owner planned a seven-story apartment building for the site, which was immediately east of the house occupied by Henry and Clover Adams. Upset by the prospect of "darkness and smoky chimneys" and the inevitable loss of neighborhood trees, the Adamses invited John and Clara Hay to join them in buying out the proprietor with the idea of building houses of their own. "I need not say how eager I am to spend your money to have you next door," Henry told John. "I would sacrifice your last dollar for such an object."

Henry's proposition caught Hay in a receptive frame of mind. A few months earlier, he had scouted the lakes of New Hampshire in search of a spot for a Five of Hearts summer colony, and he had entertained similar fantasies during his Colorado camping trip with George Nicolay. He had also imagined himself on Lafayette Square. "Do you think I could buy St. John's Church?" he once asked the Adamses. "I would not want to be out of an invalid's walk from your door." The price Henry projected for the corner of Sixteenth and H, over $70,000, seemed exorbitant to Hay, and he questioned the wisdom of undertaking so vast a project in his current state of "maladeimaginairity," but Henry's proposition was irresistible. He asked only that Henry make him a silent bidder, perhaps fearing that the steep price would reflect badly on his financial sagacity.

The Hays and the Adamses made their purchase in December for just under $75,000. For $25,000, the Adamses acquired about a third of the land, fronting on H Street. The Hays took the rest, on the corner of H and Sixteenth. Henry and Clover's windows would look south across Lafayette Square to the White House while the Hays' house, facing east, would stand opposite the pillared portico of St. John's on Sixteenth Street. Henry suggested that Hay could recoup part of his $50,000 by selling the northernmost chunk of his lot, along Sixteenth. Still dreaming of a Five of Hearts enclave, Hay offered the slice to King. When the geologist declined on account of his finances and his envy of his friends' married bliss, Hay decided not to look for another buyer.

To Hay's chagrin, and despite Adams's vow that no one would ever learn the extent of their profligacy, the price was soon the talk of Washington. Their $75,000 worked out to six dollars per square foot—twelve times the going rate in the local land market. Hay shrewdly guessed that the seller had leaked the news in an effort to drive up the value of his other real-estate holdings. Writing to Lizzie Cameron, Henry declared himself ruined by his extravagance, and Clover predicted that their spendthrift habits would force them to build cramped and squalid quarters. "We shall pad the tops of our heads so that the ceilings may not hurt them," she joked to Anne Palmer.

Pleas of hardship notwithstanding, the Adamses immediately hired the country's most celebrated architect, Henry Hobson Richardson, and the Hays quickly followed their lead. Although Clover disparaged Richardson's massive Romanesque style as "Neo-Agnostic" and objected to his penchant for such ornamental falsehoods as fireplaces that did not work, Henry considered one of Richardson's recent Washington houses the "handsomest and most ultimate" home in America.

Enchanted with the idea of inserting the architect's stone hulks among the trim, clean Federal-style houses of Lafayette Square, Henry was unfazed by the prospect of coping with Richardson's eccentricities, which seemed to have swelled with his size. Richardson, weighed 345 pounds, and drew attention to his girth by wearing brilliant yellow waistcoats. When he traveled on business, he liked to stay with clients and blithely expected their households to dance to his rhythms. He slept until noon then demanded breakfast in his room. His abnormal bulk was the consequence of a kidney ailment and demanded a spartan diet to which he paid almost no heed. Servants, he seemed to think, were meant to be bullied and nagged, and since he found walking a strain, he insisted upon being driven everywhere. Adams professed not to care and dared to imagine that by giving "vigorous instructions," he and Hay would succeed where Richardson's clients always failed—with the budget. Swept along by Henry's enthusiasm, Clover overcame both her reservations about

Henry Hobson Richardson, the greatest architect of his day, by Clover Adams. Richardson's houses for the Hays and Adamses, completed in 1886, stood side by side on Lafayette Square until the 1920s. The Hay-Adams Hotel now occupies the site.
MASSACHUSETTS HISTORICAL SOCIETY

Richardson's work and her long-standing aversion to building a house. At a loss to explain herself, she told Lizzie Cameron, "I like to change my mind all of a sudden."

The honeymoon between architect and clients lasted until the end of February. Looking at sketches of both houses, the Adamses thought the Hays' decidedly superior to theirs, and when Henry ventured to say so, back came a splenetic reply in a dark, heavy scrawl: "Did I trust too much to your knowing how to regard an unfinished drawing?" asked Richardson. "Your liking Hay's house better than your own is accounted for easily I think by the fact that in designing the former I was left entirely untramelled by restrictions wise or otherwise. (How's that old boy—couldn't help it—too good to pass.)" The architect promised to make Adams's house "*at least* as attractive as Hay's" and to incorporate all of Henry's "pet notions" as well.

Hay could afford to be tractable, and since he was far away in Cleveland, he cheerfully handed himself over to Richardson. The architect's ideas were bound to be better than his own, Hay told Adams, and besides, he joshed, there was a noble principle at stake: "As a means of moral discipline, it is not best for us to have our own way in everything; hence, architects."

The spat over the sketches cost Adams dearly. Henceforth Richardson would regard Hay as the enlightened patron of genius and Adams as the prickly, meddlesome fussbudget. The Hays could do no wrong, the Adamses no right—an egregiously unfair twist in view of Henry and Clover's artistic sophistication. When the Adamses passed along a sample of the ironwork they wanted for the grilles to be installed on the ground floor, the architect scoffed that "a designer of cast iron fences for a Western foundry could not do worse."

In some matters, Richardson's charm could be as expansive as his girth. Felled by a case of the mumps in the summer of 1884, he focused on Clover's passion for riding and spent hours writing her an erudite disquisition on the architecture of stables. After consulting the definitive English work on the subject, he was convinced he had hit on the perfect design for the Adamses' horse barn—spacious, properly lighted, and pleasing to the eye. "Really it is good," he told Clover. "Not a bad thing to look at from your back windows."

When the exteriors were finally decided upon, the two façades had little in common apart from their red brick and their height of four stories. The Adams house, with the Hay house on one side and Henry and Clover's rented house on the other, had a decidedly modern look. Its roof showed only one simple upward slope while the Hays' was a jumble of turrets, gables, and chimneys. The Adamses' windows were grouped symmetrically, the Hays' set off-center. The Hays' front door, on Sixteenth Street, lay deep in the recesses of a porte cochere, while the Adamses' main entrance was set back a few feet from the sidewalk, behind a pair of low stone arches.

By midsummer, even Hay was nervous about Richardson's visions of grandeur. "I fear I approach my Waterloo," he moaned to Adams. His estimate had jumped from $50,000 to $61,000 and seemed to include only "a wall and a roof." The newspapers had just revealed that the Democratic nominee for president, Grover Cleve-

land, had long ago fathered a child out of wedlock, and Hay playfully regretted that his architectural follies on Lafayette Square ruled
out the possibility of supporting "one of Cleveland's families."

The Adamses' price had soared, too, from $35,000 to $50,000.
Richardson, Henry told Hay, was "an ogre. He devours men crude,
and shows the effects of inevitable indigestion in his size." Hay
concurred with a sigh: "Any naturalist, looking at us, would say he
was born devourer and we devourees." Resistance proved futile, and
in the space of a few weeks, Hay's estimate shot up again, to $80,000.

Construction began in July, while Henry and Clover were at Beverly Farms. Returning to H Street at the end of October, they were
cheered by the sight of bricklayers, the perfume of fresh sawdust,
and the industrious din of hammer and saw. The Adamses sent
progress reports and photographs to the Hays, and Henry imagined
the moment when the Hearts would sip Chateau Latour '64 in the
mahogany splendor of the Hays' dining room. But once the wall
studs were up, Adams was assailed by a new worry: size. "Perhaps
my wife and I may squeeze into our stye, small as it is," he told Hay,
"but how you and the new baby can live in your confined quarters,
I don't know."

The new baby, named Clarence in honor of the fifth Heart, had
arrived a few days before Christmas. Too kind to shout his joy to
childless friends, Hay settled for telling the Adamses he had been
thinking of Henry's remark that bringing a child into the world
entailed even more responsibility than committing a murder. "And
lo!" said Hay, "here am I staggering under a fourfold responsibility." The new father saved his exultation for a letter to W. D. Howells, whose new novel, *The Rise of Silas Lapham,* had been running as
a serial in the *Century.* Hay had just finished reading the last installment to Clara, who was "in bed of a fine boy—a *fine* boy, mind you.
11-pound Boy, if you please." As for the novel, the Hays agreed that
it was "equal to the very best you had done—which is superlative
speech with us."

In Washington, snowstorms and squabbles with Richardson delayed construction, but numerous visits from John La Farge during
January and February of 1885 seemed to calm Henry's architectural
jitters. Bolstered by La Farge's confidence in Richardson, Henry
began planning embellishments. He envisioned "playful brickwork"

for his own house and La Farge stained glass for Hay's staircase windows.

Hay had his doubts, having commissioned La Farge to do a window for his church in Ohio. Although the glass had been "solemnly promised" for the previous fall, Hay told Adams, it had not yet been delivered. The building was now completed except for La Farge's window, "which makes me ashamed to go to Church, and I am consequently fast relapsing into heathendom."

On March 4, 1885, resting a beefy hand on a small Bible that had belonged to his mother, Grover Cleveland was sworn in as the twenty-second president of the United States. Against all predictions, voters had forgiven his youthful liaison with an older woman, a widow who had borne him a son. ("Ma! Ma! Where's my pa?" Republicans had taunted. Once the ballots were counted, Democrats had their riposte: "Gone to the White House. Ha! Ha! Ha!") As soon as the scandal broke, Cleveland had manfully confessed his part and quietly pointed out that he had supported mother and child for years. The clergy railed against Cleveland's morals, but much of the public sided with Mark Twain, who felt that there was no sane argument against a bachelor's relationship with a consenting widow. Those who contended otherwise, Twain tartly observed, knew perfectly well "what the bachelor's alternative was—and tacitly they seemed to prefer that to the widow."

Short, fat, and homely, Cleveland made a comical Romeo, and Henry Adams had laughed himself red over the campaign gossip. But he and Clover were delighted when Cleveland squeaked past their nemesis, James G. Blaine, to become the first Democratic president in twenty-eight years. A few nights after the election, rows of celebratory candles flickered in the Adamses' H Street windows, sending an unmistakable message across Lafayette Square to Chester Arthur's White House.

The unswervingly Republican Hay had campaigned for Blaine in Ohio, and Clarence King, just home from Europe, had also hoped for a Blaine victory. "I have always maintained that America was an utter and absolute failure socially, but a considerable success politically," he told Hay after the election. "It looks as if that last saving feature might break down too and then there would be left only cooking and personal friendship to cheer us up. . . . I wonder how dear Mrs. Adams will enjoy her Grover?"

On Inauguration Day, dear Mrs. Adams enjoyed her Grover immensely. Four years before, when Garfield took the oath of office, Henry and Clover had stayed home by the fire. This time they went to the parade and watched Robert E. Lee's son, a Harvard classmate of Henry's, riding at the head of a Virginia regiment in rebel gray. Close behind marched a corps of Freedmen, bayonets glinting in the sun. One band played "Dixie," the next rendered "The Union Forever." As Clover told her father, "everyone looked gay and happy— and as if they thought it was a big country and they owned it." In the evening, the Adamses eschewed the inaugural ball but posted themselves at an upstairs window to watch the fireworks bursting over the White House.

Cleveland's inauguration was to be the last festive occasion in Clover's life. A day or two later, word came from Boston that her father had suffered a serious attack of angina pectoris. Clover and Henry hurried to Cambridge, where Dr. Hooper was being nursed by her brother Ned and sister Ellen. The scene could have been lifted from the pages of *Esther*. Like Esther Dudley's father, Dr. Hooper was dying, and there was nothing for his daughter to do but watch and wait.

After a brief stay, Henry went back to Washington. He visited Clover three times during the next several weeks, and from Lafayette Square he wrote her almost daily. "Madam," his first letter began. "As it is now thirteen years since my last letter to you, possibly you may have forgotten my name. If so, please try and recall it. For a time we were somewhat intimate." Striking a cadence more like Clover's than his own, he described the scene he had found on his return: "Peace filled my mind when I heard the busy hammer resounding under our snow-covered roof, and saw that our topmost floor was going ahead just as fast as though the sun was out and birds began to sing." He sent his love to the Hoopers, adding, "There remains at the bottom of the page just a little crumb of love for you, but you must not eat it all at once. The dogs need so much!"

Since the Adamses were rarely apart and since the letters they wrote each other before their marriage no longer exist, Henry's missives to Cambridge in March and April of 1885 are the only record of the way in which he expressed his feelings for his wife. His omissions are telling. Perhaps fearing that Clover's deep attachment to her father would set loose a grief too great for either of them to manage, he carefully avoided any subject likely to trigger a thought of her impending loss. Nor could he bring himself to declare his love with the relaxed, unabashed sentimentality John Hay used in writing to Clara. Henry's letters often close with love to Clover and her family, and once he mustered a shout of "Love, love, love!" But it was a month before he dared to express the depth of his feelings, and he could not do it without resorting to a metaphor memorable less for its passion than its stiff intellectuality. His "solitary struggle with platitudinous atoms, called men and women by courtesy," he said, had led him to wonder: "How did I ever hit on the only woman in the world who fits my cravings and never sounds hollow anywhere? Social chemistry—the mutual attraction of equivalent human molecules—is a science yet to be created, for the fact is my daily study and only satisfaction in life."

For the most part, Henry kept up a cheerful patter, filling sheet after sheet of his creamy stationery with a mix of progress reports on their house, political gossip, news of friends, and notes on the flowers of spring. "The dogs and I have just come in from picking some violets for you, which we have put in your little Hizan tea-pot on our desk," he reported after one outing. Home from a long afternoon ride on April 9, he filed a dispatch filled with botanical minutiae of the sort she appreciated: "A few maples show a faint flush here and there, but not a sign of leaf is to be seen, and even the blood-root and hepatica hid themselves from my eyes. A few frogs sang in the sun, and birds sang in the trees; but no sign of a peach-blossom yet, and not even the magnolias and *Pyrus Japonica* have started. In 1878 the magnolias were in full flower and killed by frost on March 25, and in 1882 the frost killed them on April 10. . . . So you have not yet lost much spring."

As the new houses moved along, he described water pipes and furnaces and consulted her on "the great bell question"—the matter of where to put the electric bells for summoning the servants. He also sought and received her approval for a fireplace faced with a sea-green Mexican onyx, a stone he had discovered during a visit to the Smithsonian. Hay, he reported, was unhappy with his low, cave-like front entrance and protested that it would turn his children into troglodytes. Unconvinced by Henry's reassurances, Hay had fretted until someone else dropped by and raved about the house. "At this the dear Hay cheered up amazingly," Henry told Clover. It was Henry's opinion that the Adamses' house was handsomer than its companion piece, but he confidently predicted to Clover that the pair would create "a sensation."

Politics, with the change of administrations, was a source of endless anecdotes, including a baseless newspaper story that Henry Adams of Massachusetts had been appointed minister to Chile. Henry told Clover that the new president was greatly admired for staying on his feet when he received callers, a tactic that kept their visits wondrously short. As for the old president, Chester Arthur, he had pained a Washington hostess by walking off with an irreplaceable porcelain menu-card holder, mistaking it for a souvenir. Sharing the gaffe with Clover, Henry asked, "Does not this give an exquisite measure of the great booby's *savoir vivre?*"

In the company of H. H. Richardson, Henry paid a call at the White House—his first in almost a decade. They went over at nine o'clock on a Saturday night in late March, making the block-long journey by carriage, undoubtedly at Richardson's insistence. Miss Rose Elizabeth Cleveland, the sister and official hostess of the bachelor president, ushered them into the Red Room. Under a ceiling of copper and bronze stars flickering in the gaslight, they found the chief executive surrounded by a small group of female visitors. Although Cleveland was not as gargantuan as Richardson, it was easy to believe the newspaper reporter who reckoned that a line drawn from the outermost point of his paunch to the small of his back would measure at least two feet. Like the architect, the president believed that one should never walk if one could ride.

Richardson lumbered off with Miss Rose to inspect the White House conservatory while Henry stayed to chat with the president and his guests. The Pompeiian red walls intensified Cleveland's pallor, and the mouth under the dark mustache rarely voiced a thought or framed a smile. Faced with this silence, Henry gathered only one impression to send to Clover: "We must admit that, like Abraham Lincoln, the Lord made a mighty common-looking man in him."

Miss Rose was another matter. Thirty-nine and unmarried, she had been a professor in Buffalo. In the White House, she spent most of her time in her study, which looked north across Lafayette Square to the windows of Henry's library. A fervent champion of temperance, she had once written an article exhorting young women to frown at young men who joked about the cause. Once the male was made to feel that no lady would tolerate such behavior, she wrote, "alcohol will tremble on its throne, and the liquor traffic will hide its cancerous face." The amused John Hay had forwarded Miss Rose's sermon to Adams with the instruction, "Read and tremble!"

Back from the conservatory, Miss Rose deposited Richardson with her brother and fastened upon Adams, managing to arouse all of his ambivalence about women with intellectual ambitions. It was vastly entertaining to find a "sister professor" playing first lady, and as she talked about her new book on George Eliot, he was surprised to see how seriously she took her work. Miss Rose carried "an atmosphere of female college about her thicker than the snow storm outside my window," Henry wrote to Clover the next day. In spite of his condescension, Henry concluded that he liked Miss Rose. She had expressed a wish to meet Clover, and Henry hoped they would see more of her.

Around Lafayette Square, the Adamses' friends responded to Dr. Hooper's illness and Clover's absence with cascades of affection. "Please tell your father that I have become quite a dog's-tail of interest on his account," Henry wrote to Cambridge. "Lovely women, senators and cabinet ministers invade my privacy to ask about him, and hail me on the street to know the latest advices from you." For future conclaves of the Five of Hearts, Clarence King sent the Adamses a porcelain tea service with tray, pot, sugar bowl, creamer, and five cups and saucers. "All are prettily decorated with little bunches of roses," Henry told Clover, "and each has on it a rose clock-face with the hands pointing to five o'clock." He neglected to mention that all of the pieces except the tray were shaped like hearts.

John Hay came to town to check on his house and to see George Nicolay about their life of Lincoln, and he prolonged his stay to keep Henry company. Lizzie and Don Cameron, who were planning a summer in Los Angeles in hopes of clearing up an ailment in Don's lungs, suggested that the Adamses pay an extended visit. Sensing that Beverly Farms would overflow with painful associations after Dr. Hooper's death, Henry forwarded the invitation. "Don is to have horses for riding, and to live in the open air," he said, dangling a temptation he thought Clover would not be able to resist.

On a wet afternoon at the end of March, Clarence King stopped off for a few hours with Adams on his way to the Sombrerete mine in Mexico. They shared a pot of tea and ventured out in the rain to look at the new houses, which King warmly approved. King also inspected the Adamses' bric-a-brac and pronounced one of their Turners as good as the pair he owned. "Little was said of politics," Henry told Clover, "but you will be relieved to hear that he said he could not vote and had not voted for Blaine." That would have come as news to John Hay, with whom King had commiserated after Blaine's defeat. But after five years of close friendship, it is unlikely that either Hay or Adams would have been surprised by King's inconsistency. As Henry told Clover after King's brief stop, the geologist was as "sympathetic" as ever. Writing to Hay after the election, it was natural for King to share the disappointment of his Republican friend. Four months later, visiting with Adams across from Grover Cleveland's White House, he found it equally easy to identify with Henry's pleasure in the Democratic victory.

In his letters to Cambridge, Henry never flagged in his cheerfulness, but after a month of shuttling between Dr. Hooper's sickbed and Lafayette Square, he was out of sorts. "I bolt forward and back like a brown monkey," he complained to a friend. "Nobody wants me in either place. They won't take me for a nurse, and I can't live all alone in a big, solitary house when it rains and I can't ride. Even the gold-fish are bored, and the dogs fight to pass the time."

On April 9, Dr. Hooper slipped into unconsciousness. Four days later, Clover said, "he went to sleep like a tired traveller." Hastening to Cambridge, Henry was surprised to find Clover in good spirits.

So it seemed. A week after returning to Washington, Clover composed a dry-eyed account of her father's death, emphasizing his stoicism more than her own feelings. "He was unselfish and brave and full of fun until he lost consciousness, and he kept us all up, as he did not fancy hired nurses we had enough to do all those weeks to keep us sound," she told Anne Palmer. Of herself, Clover merely re-marked that she was "tired out in mind and body." She described the loss of her father in geographical rather than personal terms: "No one fills any part of his place to me but Henry so that my connection with New England is fairly severed as far as interest goes." She and Henry planned to stay in Washington until June, then camp out in Yellowstone, "taking our own outfit—horses, tents etc." If a suit-able tenant turned up, they would rent out their house at Beverly Farms.

H. H. Richardson ardently hoped that they would leave soon. Having just discovered that Henry's pronounced opinions came from his reading of Eugene Viollet-le-Duc, a French architect and critic famed for his restorations of medieval buildings, Richardson was eager to quash the influence. "It is a common saying in Paris that 'even well-bred horses shy at his buildings,' " Richardson scolded. "Really Henry in your present unnatural state of semi-artistic exal-tation my only hope of finishing your house successfully and pleas-ing you is to get your consent to a few things I have written for and then God-speed you to the Yellowstone."

To miss the black flies and mosquitoes, Henry and Clover post-poned their Yellowstone excursion until the end of July. But neither of them had much tolerance for the thick, wet heat of a Washington summer, and on June 10, they and their horses boarded a train for the mountains of West Virginia. They stayed a few days at Sulphur Springs, then moved on to Sweet Springs, settling into a wooden cottage nestled under an enormous oak. They wrote letters, read, rode through hills blazing with laurel and azaleas, and swam in the warm, effervescent waters of the mineral spring next to their cabin.

After a month in the mountains, they made a radical change of plans. Thinking about the death of Dr. Hooper, Henry concluded that he did not want to venture too far from his own father, who had been in failing health for most of the year. To his surprise, Clover was willing to go to Beverly Farms, which put him within easy reach of his parents in Quincy.

The summer passed with agonizing slowness, and Clover, despite her determination not to mourn, slid deeper into depression. She was having "a wretched summer, in the gloomiest state of mind," her brother-in-law Whitman Gurney told a friend. He was touched to see that her "general depression has been accompanied by the greatest sweetness towards us." Henry told one of his English friends that Clover had been "out of sorts for some time past, and, until she gets quite well again, can do nothing." To John Hay, Henry confided that his hands were "full," but he offered no details.

Henry and Clover's new house had become a torment to them, and the North Shore of Boston furnished little relief since Whitman and Ellen Gurney had commissioned Richardson to build them a house nearby in Pride's Crossing. Henry thought it looked like a cave and wondered whether his did, too. On edge, he hounded Richardson.

"If it was any other fellow I couldn't think anything about it," the architect growled in return. "I'd know I was right but I always feel when I am with you or writing to you about the house that there's something that might 'go off' and the tendency is to muddle me." A day later, receiving yet another Adams fusillade, Richardson escalated his sarcasm. "For God sake excuse my pleasant letter of yesterday," he roared. He also volunteered that whatever Henry's qualms, he himself had been feeling "quite easy about the houses since I heard that your brother Charles had seen them and didn't like 'em."

Hay's reports of the cost of furnishings filled Henry with anxiety. In New York, Richardson had taken the Hays to what Hay called a "$1,000 store" since there seemed to be nothing for sale for less than that. Clover seemed unable to engage herself with the decisions she and Henry needed to make, and when Henry tried to think about wallpaper, curtains, and carpets, his mind went blank.

The Adamses also found themselves at odds over an ornamental detail for their façade. The two low arches and their supporting capitals, all made of stone, were to be accented with carvings of birds, mythological creatures, leaves, and flowers. From the beginning, they had planned to add to the carving over the years, and Henry had even promised, only half in jest, to include Lizzie Cameron's likeness in the stonework. Soon after Henry and Clover arrived at Beverly Farms in July, Henry asked their friend Theodore Dwight of the State Department library to look after their new house. "[I]f you see the workmen carving a Christian emblem, remonstrate with them like a father," he ordered. Henry wanted a

The cross in the carved stonework of the Adamses' facade was Clover's idea. Henry considered it "bad art and bad taste." LIBRARY OF CONGRESS

peacock, and Richardson had favored a lion. Apparently Clover told Richardson she wanted a cross. When Dwight reported that a cross had indeed made its appearance, Henry felt he had no choice but to accept defeat. "Your account of the cross and the carving fills my heart with sadness and steeps my lips in cocaine," he told Dwight. Earlier he had vowed to "plaster it over with cement," but now, he felt, "I can neither revolt nor complain, though the whole thing seems to me bad art and bad taste. I have protested in vain and must henceforth hold my tongue." He asked Dwight to say nothing about it since their "dear Washingtonians chatter so much that one is forced to deny them food for gossip."

The cross rose between the two arches and served as a backdrop for a carved medallion of a winged beast. The motive for Clover's insistence on it remains a mystery, as does the reason behind Henry's declaration that it was "prophetic of the future" and filled him "with terror." If Clover was suffering through a religious crisis akin to the one described in *Esther,* neither she nor Henry breathed a word of it. But Henry's novel had foreseen another aspect of Clover's emotional breakdown with uncanny accuracy. "Everything seems unreal," Esther had said to the minister after she learned that her father was dying. "Your voice sounds far-off, as though you were calling to me out of distance and darkness. I hardly know what we are saying, or why we are here. I never felt so before." In the long, excruciating summer at Beverly Farms, Clover was overpowered by the same sense of unreality. "Ellen I'm not real," she often cried to her sister. "Oh make me real—you are all of you real!"

Back on H Street at the beginning of November, Henry and Clover found their new house nearing completion. Floors were varnished, wallpaper was hung, and dogwood blossoms were being chiseled into the stone fireplace in the dining room. Taking a walk through Hay's house, Henry estimated that John and Clara and their four "heartlets" would be able to take possession by New Year's Day if they didn't mind living upstairs while the workmen put the last touches on the library and the foyer.

To Henry's disappointment, the newspapers had not yet reviewed Richardson's Lafayette Square duet. He and Hay were left with no public reaction but "grim silence" until mid-November, when Frank Carpenter, the capital correspondent of the Cleveland *Leader,* filed a breathless account of the mansion soon to be inhabited by Colonel and Mrs. John Hay of Euclid Avenue. Touring the house for his Ohio readers, Carpenter began with the price tag: an eye-popping $100,000. The bricks were custom-made, wider and longer than common brick. The cavernous foyer, paneled with South American mahogany, gleamed like a new piano. Above the wainscoting, walls of terra-cotta red reached to a high ceiling crisscrossed with great rafters of mahogany. The grand stairway was "so wide that ten persons could walk up abreast without jostling." Carpenter gaped at the dining room, which was larger and more elegant than the state dining room of the White House. Nearly every room boasted an ornately sculpted fireplace. Throughout the house the floors were laid double, Carpenter marveled, "and you cannot see a crack any-where. A footfall hardly sounds on them." The house was graced by three bathrooms, one tiled in porcelain. "There is a big bathtub in this room, a set of marble wash basins with silver spigots having hot and cold water, and the cute little bath in which to wash your feet. This last is stationary, and the idea seems [to be] that one should sit on the corners of the wash basin and dip his feet into it." The bath-rooms, like the other rooms of the house, were equipped with elec-tric bells. Carpenter concluded that the cost was "not much in

The Hay house, facing Sixteenth Street. Abutting it, with two stone arches fronting on H Street, is the Adams house. The white-pillared dwelling just beyond was the home of Henry and Clover Adams from 1880 through 1885. LIBRARY OF CONGRESS

comparison with several millions, and a man of John Hay's money can afford to own and run a house like this."

"The shy reserve with which this writer goes into my bathtubs is very winning," Hay said when he sent the item to the Adamses. "Since this thing was printed, every charity sharp and confidence man in Cleveland has been after me, trying to get his share before the fool and *all* his money were parted." On a more somber note, Hay said he and Clara hoped the cool weather of autumn would make Clover feel "more robust."

The change of seasons did nothing to lift Clover's spirits. Numb with depression, she could barely speak, much less join in the laughter over Hay's new celebrity in Cleveland. When she tried to talk, she often broke off and rubbed her hand against her forehead, as if she had lost the point of her thought. "I see little or no one, and my doors are tight shut," Henry told Hay. At the end of November, when the English elections forced his old friend Robert Cunliffe out of Parliament, Henry sent his consolations and observed that the defeat would give Cunliffe time to travel. But, he hastened to add, "I hardly want you to come here just now, for my own plans and prospects are a little unsettled and I could not enjoy your visit as I would like." He explained that Clover had been "as it were, a good deal off her feed this summer" and showed "no such fancy for mending as I could wish."

One of the few friends they saw was Rebecca Dodge, whom Clover had befriended after seeing her out walking in Lafayette Square. Miss Dodge called every day, and during one visit managed to coax a smile from Clover. Profoundly grateful, Henry followed Miss Dodge to the door and told her he would never forget it.

On Friday, December 4, the Adamses paid an evening visit to Lizzie Cameron, who was not feeling well. Although Clover had sent her a large bouquet of roses and had come several times with Henry to ask after her, these kindnesses did nothing to alleviate Clover's overwhelming sense of unworthiness. In vain she struggled to find "one single point of character or goodness" on which to stand and "grow back to life." Henry was the soul of tenderness—"more patient and loving than words can express," Clover wrote her sister in a letter that would never be mailed. "God might envy him—he bears and hopes and despairs hour after hour."

On Sunday morning, December 6, the Adamses had their customary late breakfast. In response to Henry's questions, Clover said she felt somewhat better. Henry, bothered by a toothache, had made arrangements to see his dentist. As he left the house, he met a caller, probably Rebecca Dodge, who asked whether Clover wanted company. Henry went up to her room to inquire and found Clover slumped on the floor before the fire. Unable to revive her, he carried her to a sofa and ran for a doctor. It was too late. The potassium cyanide, a chemical for retouching photographs, had done its work in an instant.

Rebecca Dodge wanted to help. Henry, stunned, could make only one request: "Don't let *any one* come near me."

12

Hearts That Ache

*T*he details of the next twenty-four hours are scant. An undertaker, summoned from Pennsylvania Avenue, laid out Clover's body in the bedroom she had shared with Henry. Telegrams were dispatched to the Hoopers and the Adamses. Nicholas Anderson tried to call and was turned away. Some discreet person—Rebecca Dodge, perhaps, or the physician—told newspaper reporters that Clover had died of "paralysis of the heart."

Since nothing is known of the first night Henry spent in the house with his dead wife, one can do no more than guess at his feelings. If only he had put the potassium cyanide out of reach. If only he had not left Clover alone, particularly on a Sunday morning, the time she had always reserved for writing to her father. If only he had sought the help of a specialist in nervous disorders. If only he had not written the merciless, *Esther.*

In the morning the Washington *Post* carried the news of Mrs. Adams's "heart paralysis" on the front page. Friends hastened to Henry's door but were denied entry. Worried, they watched his house, and word soon spread through the neighborhood that Henry Adams could be seen at an upstairs window, staring forlornly at the bare trees of Lafayette Park.

At noon the door was opened to Ned Hooper and Ellen and Whitman Gurney, just arrived from Boston. To the Gurneys, who had spent the summer near the Adamses, Clover's suicide seemed almost inevitable. "It has been a terrible summer . . . for poor Clover, and one can hardly wish her otherwise than at rest," Whitman told one of his friends. Ellen, writing to their summer neighbor Mrs. James Elliot Cabot, remarked that the shock was "largely for you outside— we had been consumed with anxiety—and probably others think that if we had only done this or that and have shown feeling! We did the best we knew how—and we know no better now. I think any other course would have been cruelty."

The most obvious "other course"—one that Ellen apparently considered cruel—would have been a mental hospital. Dr. Hooper's children had often gone with him when he volunteered his medical services at an asylum near Boston, and the family appreciated the value of such institutions, but Clover and her siblings lived in terror of the emotional ills that stalked their maternal relatives. In Clover's eyes, suicide was preferable to madness. When an artist of her acquaintance killed himself in 1879, she mused that the act might have "saved him years of insanity, which his temperament pointed to."

Apart from mental hospitals, the Adamses could have consulted S. Weir Mitchell, a Philadelphia physician and man of letters who specialized in anxiety, hysteria, depression, and other nervous afflictions. Mitchell had treated John Hay and frequently joined the Adamses for tea when he came to Washington. He once charmed Clover by presenting a volume of his poems with the advice that she thank him before reading it in case she found it wanting. But if the Adamses knew much about Mitchell's "rest cure" for women (which Sigmund Freud later used in combination with psychoanalysis), it is unlikely that they would have considered it for Clover. The cure consisted of four to six weeks in bed accompanied by a strong dose of what the doctor called "moral medication." Self-control was the secret, he lectured; neurosis, like a bad temper, could be held in check. Mitchell made his patients promise to "fight every desire to cry, or twitch, or grow excited." After weeks of confinement they were eager to rejoin the world, and if they had learned their lesson well, they thought less about changing their circumstances than accepting them. Neither Henry nor Clover would have tolerated a

point of view that assigned so little value to the patient's feelings.★
Whatever the reasons for deciding that Clover's situation precluded
outside help, Henry had the full support of Ellen and Ned when he
entrusted Clover's recovery to his own tenderness and the restorative
powers of time. When months passed with no sign of a cure, he
resolved to wait years.

Now the waiting was over. With Ned and the Gurneys, whose
sadness was tinged with relief that Clover's ordeal had ended, Henry
tried valiantly to rise above his misery. From the moment of their
arrival, Ellen found him "as steady and sweet and thoughtful as
possible." But later in the day, after his brother Charles appeared,
Henry gave vent to a powerful anger. At dinner, to which he defi-
antly wore a scarlet necktie, Henry ripped the black mourning band
from the sleeve of his jacket and hurled it to the floor. To the surprise
of family and friends, he decided that Clover would not be buried
with Dr. Hooper in Massachusetts. She would lie on a slope in Rock
Creek Church Cemetery, a sunny churchyard where they had often
gone on horseback in search of the first wildflowers of spring. In life
Henry had been unable to separate Clover from her father; in death
he could.

Henry implored his fellow Hearts to stay away. Hay and King,
who were together in New York, had little choice but to honor their
friend's request. "I hoped all day yesterday and this morning to hear
from you, and thought it possible you might summon King and me
to be with you at the last," Hay wrote from the Brunswick Hotel on
December 9.

> I can neither talk to you nor keep silent. The darkness in which you
> walk has its shadow for me also. You and your wife were more to me
> than any other two. I came to Washington because you were there.

★ While Mitchell assumed that his rest cure would work for all high-strung women, he
believed that their male counterparts could be helped only by highly individualized treatment.
"The mental attitudes of the nervous man demand of his physician the most careful attention,
nor can we afford to disregard anything in his ways of life or his habits of thought and action,"
he wrote in the December 1877 issue of *Medical News*. "We must determine for him how far
and how much he shall use his mind, whether or not it is well for him to continue his work,
whatever it be, what his amusements should be. The careful student of such cases will find in
the individuality of his cases the need for the most minute of such studies." (Quoted in David
Rein, *S. Weir Mitchell as a Psychiatric Novelist,* 35-36.)

And now this goodly fellowship is broken up forever. I cannot force on a man like you the commonplaces of condolence. In the presence of a sorrow like yours, it is little for your friends to say they love you and sympathize with you—but it is all anybody can say. Everything else is mere words.

Is it any consolation to remember her as she was? that bright intrepid spirit, that keen fine intellect, that lofty scorn of all that was mean, that social charm which made your house such a one as Washington never knew before, and made hundreds of people love her as much as they admired her. No, that makes it all so much the harder to bear.

Neither Hay nor King knew that December 9 was the day Henry had set for Clover's funeral. The brief service, conducted at home by a clergyman who was a friend of the Hoopers, was as private as the Adamses' wedding at Beverly Farms thirteen years before.

Like Hay, King assumed that the burial would be in Massachusetts. "I had confidently expected that you would have passed through New York en route to lay the form of your wife near Boston and that I should meet you and lay these few words of heartfelt condolence which seem every moment on my lips," King wrote from the Wall Street office of his mining company. "I think of you all the time and lament that such great sorrow as yours cannot be more evidently and practically shared by those who love you."

King included no tribute to Clover in his letter, perhaps because he could not think what to say in view of the news in that morning's papers. A curious journalist had looked up Clover's death certificate and discovered that her "heart paralysis" had been induced by a self-administered dose of potassium cyanide. The newspapers showed their annoyance with the deception by taking revenge on the deceased. The Washington *Critic* rekindled the old rumor that Clover had written *Democracy*. While her talk was considered "entertaining," the paper added, she had a reputation for saying "bitter things," was "generally distrusted," and had "failed to become popular." Other papers quickly followed the *Critic*'s lead, and the legions who had been excluded from the Adamses' drawing room had the malignant joy of seeing their suspicions confirmed in print. The sniping even undermined the compassion of one of Clover's oldest friends, Eleanor Shattuck Whiteside. "How often we have spoken of Clover as having all she wanted, all this world could give, except children—and not having any was a greater grief to Mr. Adams than to her," she wrote. "And now . . . down comes a black curtain, and all is over. Yet in my unorthodox mind I can't help hoping that hers was invincible ignorance, and that somehow and somewhere she is learning better things."

It remained for the Boston *Transcript* to give Clover her due. Calling her one of Washington's "most brilliant and accomplished women," the paper noted that her house "was the pleasantest resort of the cleverest men and women who live in and who visit the capital. She came nearer being the head of an intellectual coterie than any woman there, and to be asked to her home was a privilege which comparatively few obtained, and to which many aspired. [Mr. and Mrs. Adams] took Presidents, and Cabinet officers and senators at their worth, and high rank of itself gave no one a passport to their house."

The vibrant Clover of old would have been pleased—and vastly amused. She had never liked the *Transcript*. It was too Irish, she had complained to her father—so preoccupied with the doings of O'Haras and Flanagans that it overlooked her Beacon Hill friends.

With public scandal heaped upon private humiliation, Henry vowed to survive by pushing straight on without looking back. "I feel like a volunteer in his first battle," he told Hay. "If I don't run ahead at full speed, I shall run away." Even as he urged Hay to expedite the family's move to Washington, he stoutly insisted there was no cause for alarm. "Never fear for me," he declared. "I shall come out all right from this—what shall I call it?—Hell!"

H. H. Richardson realized at once how much it would mean to Henry to have the Cleveland Hearts installed next door. "I am driving your house with all my might and main," he wrote to John, "and do earnestly hope you and Mrs. Hay will decide to move in this year, even if it does necessitate some little picnicking and even discomfort in the beginning."

True to his word, the architect stopped only once, for an umbilical hernia. Painting a comic picture of his dilapidation, Richardson told Hay that his massive frame was now "so covered and held together with pads, buckles, straps etc. that when I stretch real hard I'm not quite certain that I'll come together in the same place again."

The trusses were the only light moment in a grim season. In spite of Henry's resolve to focus on the future, he soon found himself thrust into the past. Each day brought a flood of letters from friends, forcing him to think about his wife. Though he destroyed most of them, he welcomed the task of responding, which passed the time and asked of him no more than he was able to give.

To Lizzie Cameron, who was still in bed with an undiagnosed ailment, he wished a quick recovery for his own sake. "All Clover's friends have now infinite value for me," he told her. "I have got to live henceforward on what I can save from the wreck of her life, and it is lucky for me that she had no friends but the best and truest." Sending her one of Clover's favorite pieces of jewelry as a keepsake, he asked, "Will you keep it and sometimes wear it to remind you of her?"

In a letter to Mrs. Samuel Gray Ward, whom the Adamses had befriended during their honeymoon trip on the Nile, Henry touchingly recalled Clover's affection for her. "You were closely associated with the heaviest trials and the keenest pleasures of our life. The peace that you have reached in this world was a delight to her, and the memory of our twelve years of perfect happiness will always bring back to me the thought of you." Having witnessed Clover's unhappiness in Egypt, Mrs. Ward understood what Henry meant by "heaviest trials," but she probably did not catch the subtlety of his arithmetic. The Adamses had been married for thirteen and one-half years, not twelve. The calculation was not a mistake. For the rest of his life, Henry would date his tragedy from the beginning of Clover's breakdown in the spring of 1885, nearly eight months before the horrific, unthinkable day of her death.

Again and again Henry expressed surprise and regret at finding that he did not stand alone in his anguish. As he told Mrs. Ward, "My table was instantly covered with messages from men and women whose own hearts were still aching with the same wounds, and who received me, with a new burst of their own sorrows, into their sad fraternity. My pain seemed lost in the immensity of human distress." To his publisher, Henry Holt, Adams observed, "What a vast fraternity it is,—that of 'Hearts that Ache.' With Mrs. Ward, Adams spoke from his heart, but with Holt, who shared the uneasy secret of *Esther,* Adams fell into self-conscious bitterness: "How we do suffer! And we go on laughing; for, as a practical joke at our expense, life is a success.''

Across the Atlantic, Henry James had been stunned to hear of Clover's suicide, which he obliquely described as her "solution of the knottiness of existence.'' Sharing the news with a friend, he voiced his sympathy for Henry Adams and mourned the loss of "that intensely lively Washington *salon*.'' If James wrote to Adams—and he almost certainly would have wanted to pay tribute to his "Voltaire in petticoats''—the letter has not survived. A few years later, James would write "The Modern Warning," a short story about a woman who poisoned herself. Like Clover, the protagonist was intelligent, outspoken, and sharply critical of things English.

James also sent word of Clover's death to his friend Constance Fenimore Woolson. Though Fenimore did not know the Adamses, she instinctively understood the loss to the Hays. On the day after Christmas, seated before a velvet-framed triptych with photographs of James and Hay and Howells, Fenimore sent her condolences to Hay. Picturing the new houses on Lafayette Square, she imagined that Clover's absence would make the beginning of their new life together "particularly desolate and sad.'' As for suicide, she said, "I have never been able to think that a sudden death is to be deplored for the one who is taken,—I should like to die without warning myself; but for those who are left, it is very terrible.''

By the middle of January, Henry was sufficiently settled in his new house at 1603 H Street to offer the Hays a place to stay until the carpetlayers and paperhangers finished their work next door. Theodore Dwight, the State Department librarian, had moved in to keep Henry company, and the two of them were soon able to take their meals in the second-floor dining room, near the pretty stone fireplace carved with dogwood blossoms.

Henry passed most of his days on the second floor. In his study overlooking the snowy lawns of Lafayette Park and the White House, he answered letters, and in the adjoining large library, he spent hours hanging pictures. "You have no conception what a vast resource this offers," he told Hay. Intended to serve as a drawing room, the library, dominated by a fireplace of sea-green onyx, would show off the best of the Adamses' art collection. Turners and Constables were hung on the walls, and jades and porcelains were arranged atop the bookcases. With their fresh varnish, the new wooden floors made gleaming frames for the Oriental rugs. Conspicuously absent were Clover's great treasures, the portraits of Mr. and Mrs. Grove by Sir Joshua Reynolds. They would soon be donated to the nearby Corcoran Gallery of Art, which promised to hang them in a spot of Henry's choosing.

Before the month was out, the Hays took possession of 800 Sixteenth Street and made the dismaying discovery that Henry was planning to desert them. Thinking ahead to summer, he knew he did not want to subject himself to the heat and desolation of Washington, but he could not face a return to Beverly Farms, the scene of Clover's disintegration. Europe was also out of the question—"full of ghosts," he felt. Ultimately he settled on Japan, hoping, he said, that "where everything is upside-down, I shall find myself in keeping with the rest." To his pleasure, John La Farge had agreed to come as his guest.

As May drew to a close, Henry said good-bye to the Hays, left his checkbook in the care of Theodore Dwight, and set off for New York hoping to "get out of the rest of life every new flavor it has." At the Brunswick he found Clarence King in fine form, buoyed by new financing for his Mexican silver mines and confidently predicting that they would pay off at last. Henry worked up enough courage to leave a copy of *Esther* in King's care.

Before leaving the city, Adams asked La Farge to take him to the studio of his close friend Augustus Saint-Gaudens. As a memorial to Clover, Adams wanted Saint-Gaudens to sculpt a human figure expressing acceptance of the inevitable. The best model Adams could suggest was the Buddhist Kwannon, the calm, contemplative goddess of compassion. He also mentioned his attraction to two maternal images he and Clover had admired in the frescoes of the Sistine Chapel—the mother of Jesse and the Sistine Madonna.

Saint-Gaudens listened attentively, then struck pose after pose. When he hit on one that pleased his visitor, he put his young assistant in the same position, pulled a cloth from a nearby clay figure, and improvised a hood that left the boy's face in deep shadow. The fabric, damp with clay, fell into thick, rich folds. Fully satisfied, Adams left Saint-Gaudens with one instruction: "I don't want to see the statue until it's finished." Henry's injunction was a belated but

Augustus Saint-Gaudens in his studio, painted by Kenyon Cox. When Saint-Gaudens shaved off his beard, Clarence King was surprised to find the artist's chin "as hard and sharp as his sculptor's chisel." METROPOLITAN MUSEUM OF ART. GIFT OF FRIENDS OF THE SCULPTOR, THROUGH AUGUST F. JACCACI, 1908. ALL RIGHTS RESERVED.

touching tribute to his friend H. H. Richardson, who had died of kidney failure a few weeks before. Artists, Adams now knew, were better left alone.

The travelers went off on June 3, 1886, "in high spirits," King wrote to Hay, "La Farge dodging creditors and sheriffs all day and trying to borrow a few thou' right and left wherewith to paint Japan red." In Albany they headed west aboard a luxurious private railway car supplied by Henry's brother Charles, president of the Union Pacific. While La Farge sketched the scenes rolling past their windows, Adams napped and read Buddhism. During a stop in Omaha, a young reporter spotted the special car and inquired about their plans. La Farge, his gray-green eyes twinkling through his thick spectacles, soberly declared that they were in search of Nirvana. "It's out of season!" the lad shot back.

Beyond a love of cigars and good conversation, Adams and La Farge had little in common. Adams had admired the artist's stained glass since the early 1870s, when Richardson, La Farge, and Saint-Gaudens collaborated on Trinity Church in Boston, but La Farge was bored to stupefaction by Henry's passion for American diplomacy in the early nineteenth century. In La Farge's view, the War of 1812 was "the very dullest affair [Adams] could find! but that is what it means to be an Adams; puritanism must come out in seeking the disagreeable somehow." At six feet, La Farge towered over his friend. Adams's sense of fashion extended only to wearing black suits in winter and white in summer. La Farge wore nothing but fine silks and linens next to his skin and had been known to spend an hour donning and shedding shirts and ties before arriving at a combination that met his fastidious standards. Intellectually, both men were extravagantly endowed, but their styles of mind sprang from opposing instincts. La Farge was a sponge, soaking up philosophy, mythology, and literature as eagerly as he absorbed art. Adams was a distiller, a seeker of essences who cared less for particulars than large truths.

As a moralist, La Farge could be as severe and high-minded as his friend, but he was rarely troubled by the conscience that tyrannized Adams. The artist had long since left his wife and nine children in Newport, claiming that the climate disagreed with him and that his atelier would enjoy more prosperity amid the tycoons of New York. He never lacked for commissions, but his finances were in perpetual disarray. The artist meant well, his wife explained to their children, but sometimes he "forgot" them. On these occasions, which were not infrequent, she had no one to turn to but the Almighty. It was an ironic fate. Margaret La Farge owed her deep faith to her husband, who had insisted that she convert to Catholicism despite his own unwillingness to practice the creed in any remotely conventional manner.

Whatever Henry Adams's shortcomings as a husband, they paled beside the *droit de seigneur* of John La Farge. During his courtship of the beautiful Margie Perry in 1859 and 1860, La Farge unashamedly announced that he craved "inequality." "[Y]ou *must* love me the most," he said. "I will exact it from you to the last drop, Margaret." She must also promise to love him forever, "even if my love for you were to die." These edicts, issued incessantly, were accompanied by orders to learn to ride and read French and promises to direct her reading for life. As for Catholicism, there was no point in quarreling, he said. "Please yield—as I feel that I am right."

Eternally at odds with life's intrusions on art, La Farge in 1883 joined two acquaintances in forming a company designed to free him from business worries. Two years later, the enterprise collapsed in a storm of lawsuits when La Farge discovered that his chief financial partner had put up only half the amount he had promised and had then proceeded to borrow heavily against the company's assets. In addition to warring over money, La Farge had the delicate mission of retrieving from his erstwhile partners a number of life-size photographs of women who had posed for him in various states of undress. To imbue his church windows with "high character," La Farge explained to the court, he used models who were "ladies of social standing and refinement." His partners argued that the photographs were the property of the company while La Farge insisted that to surrender the pictures would violate the "sacred pledge" he had made to protect the ladies' privacy.

La Farge responded to such distractions by decrying the materialistic spirit of the age. Fuming about the austerity of the budgets for murals and stained glass in churches and public buildings, he said, "You can hardly imagine how absurd it is to realize that you cannot give certain extra folds to a cloak because they will cost so many dollars more, or that an extra angel's head is worth seventy-two dollars and must be cut out." But when a generous patron like William C. Whitney gave him carte blanche to do his "damnedest," La Farge bristled with contempt. The millionaire was acidly informed that "he had not money enough to pay for what I *could* do," La Farge told a friend; Whitney would get only what the artist considered "fairly fitting."

Adams and La Farge were a few days out from San Francisco, gnashing their teeth at rough seas and the hymn-singing missionaries who shared their mail boat, when Clarence King tied up a parcel and hastily penned a note to John Hay. "I send you a novel I have just read called 'Esther,'" he began. "It has given me a strange, painful interest and I await with some palpitations to hear what you say of it and who you conclude wrote it." When the book arrived in Lafayette Square, Clara read a few pages and told John that she thought it sounded like him or Adams or King. Hay asked her to read it aloud. When she finished, he immediately wrote King to ask why none of Henry's friends had ever heard of the book.

From the Sagamore Hotel on New York's Lake George, where he was passing the Fourth of July, King explained Henry's "quaint, archaic project" of issuing the book without publicity to see if "a dull world" would notice.

> Later came to his mind a second reason why he should let the volume lie where it had fallen in the silent depths of American stupidity and that was a feeling of regret at having exposed his wife's religious experiences and as it were made of her a clinical subject *vis-a-vis* of religion as in Democracy he had shown her in contact with politics. Later when Dr. Hooper died of heart failure as the old man in Esther died he felt that it was too personal and private a book to have brought into its due prominence so he has let it die.

Adams had given King leave to share the book with the Hays provided they told no one else. King found *Esther* "far more compact and vivid" than *Democracy* "but one of the most painful things imaginable. I had the hardihood to say to him that he ought to have made Esther jump into Niagara as that was what she would have done. He said 'certainly she would but I could not suggest it.' "

Writing to Adams on Five of Hearts stationery, Hay said that he would "owe gratitude to King for making me read such a masterpiece of thought and style—and a little grudge to you for not telling me. It is the first New York story I have ever read in which there is real human talk and feeling—of a grade above that of shop-girls and reporters." Baffled by the silence that had greeted the book, Hay supposed that critics "read nothing unless they are told: otherwise how could they have helped seeing the best thing that has been printed in ten years." Lacking King's fortitude, Hay avoided the subjects of Niagara and Esther's hysteria.

Weeks later, when Hay's praise reached Adams, the author was pleased that his "melancholy little Esther" had found a friend. "Perhaps I made a mistake even to tell King about it," he mused to Hay, "but having told him, I could not leave you out. Now let it die! To admit the public to it would be almost unendurable to me. I will not pretend that the book is not precious to me, but its value has nothing

Painter, muralist, and stained-glass artist John La Farge, by Clover Adams.
MASSACHUSETTS HISTORICAL SOCIETY

to do with the public who could never understand that such a book
might be written in one's heart's blood.''

Adams and La Farge steamed into the great bay of Yokohama on
July 2. Behind the city, soft green hills rose up to a silver sky.
Inundated by new smells and sounds, the travelers watched from the
deck as muscular Japanese sailors, their open blue-and-white robes
fluttering behind them like scarves, transferred the ship's cargo to a
flotilla of sampans. On the quay, a ricksha sped the newcomers to a
hotel overlooking the harbor and the vast, smooth sea, which reminded La Farge of the blank expanses in Japanese prints. Late in the
afternoon he and Adams ventured out into the crowded streets to
dicker with curio peddlers, watch sumo wrestlers, and glimpse a bit
of theater with a dwarf acting the part of a spider trapped in a web.
    Based in Yokohama, they would explore Tokyo in the company
of two former Bostonians. At thirty-three, Ernest Fenollosa was an
authority on the art and architecture of Japan. He had come to Tokyo
in 1878 to teach philosophy and political science at the Imperial
University, and he stayed on to devote himself to art. William
Sturgis Bigelow, a first cousin of Clover Adams, had arrived in
1882. Like Clover's father, he had studied medicine but felt neither

the desire nor the need to practice. Drawn to Buddhism, he transplanted himself to Japan to build a life around Oriental philosophy and art. Together Bigelow and Fenollosa had collected thousands of paintings, prints, and ceramics for the Museum of Fine Arts in Boston.

From the beginning, La Farge was a happier tourist than his companion. He noted every flower, delighted in the smooth roadbed of the local railway, and rejoiced in the "passionate delicacy and care" of Buddhist paintings. Adams recoiled from the "oily, sickish, slightly fetid odor" he smelled everywhere, and throughout his trip would complain that Japanese women were like cheap dolls—wooden, jerky, mechanical. They were "badly made and repulsive," he told Hay. Tokyo he found remarkable only for "the stench of several hundred thousand open privies." He also chafed at the tutelage of Bigelow and Fenollosa, who opined rather strenuously on what should and should not be admired. "I was myself a Buddhist when I left America," Adams grumbled, "but [Bigelow] has converted me to Calvinism." Impatient with Bigelow's determination to reason his way to Nirvana, Adams decided that "the only Paradise possible in this world is concentrated in the three little words which the *ewig* [eternal] Man says to the *ewige* Woman."

In spite of his own dissatisfactions, Henry took pleasure in La Farge's enjoyment. La Farge could linger in a museum for hours, oblivious of itineraries and train schedules. Through vile smells, dismal accommodations, indigestible food, and a touch of cholera, the artist maintained "the neatest humor, the nicest observation, and the evenest temper you can imagine," Henry marveled, wishing the same for himself. But his mood had only begun to blacken.

In mid-July, when Adams and La Farge took up residence amid the shrines of Nikko, Henry scoffed that Nikko's celebrated temples looked like toys and sarcastically noted that the only thing Japan took seriously was its tea ceremony, a long, complicated ritual that ended with the presentation of a brew he found undrinkable. Anticipating as much, he had brought his own tea from Washington, along with bedsheets, flea powder, tins of Mulligatawny soup, and acid phosphate for stomach upsets. The last, he told Theodore Dwight, "is now my steady tipple." Adams and La Farge planned to spend a month at Nikko, where La Farge wanted to sketch the landscape in search of inspiration for a major mural he had contracted to paint in New York. With no such occupation for himself, Henry grimly pledged to "make excursions and kill time."

Adams scraped bottom a few days later. In need of a confidant, he turned not to one of his fellow Hearts but to an old friend far from the gossipy drawing rooms of Washington and New York. "I do not know whether you heard that I ran away from America," he wrote Sir Robert Cunliffe in Wales. "Life there had become intolerable. My own existence was knocked to pieces, and I could do nothing with it. My father and mother were suffering under a variety of trials, very different from mine, but not easier to bear. Add to this that my brother-in-law Gurney had broken down, and that the greatest anxiety was felt on his account; and that I could do absolutely nothing for any of them, while I was in a fair way to break down myself. You will see from all this, why I am now writing to you from Nikko . . . where I see as little as possible to remind me of myself, and can gain three or four months of hardening to my difficulties." After reciting his long list of grievances against Japan, Henry volunteered that he no longer cared about the political questions he had once passionately debated with Cunliffe. "The world seems to me to have suddenly changed, and to have left me an old man, pretty well stranded and very indifferent to situations which another generation must deal with. . . . I have been thrown out of the procession, and can't catch up again."

The letter proved a wonderful purgative. Three days later, writing to Hay at eight o'clock "of a sweet morning," Henry sang the joys of Nikko. While he could not yet appreciate the art of tomb and temple, he was captivated by the meticulous gardens and the natural beauty of towering evergreens and steep mountainsides. As La Farge sketched, Adams photographed. In all, he decided, Nikko could be classed "very high among the sights of the world."

La Farge was feeling "delightfully lazy." Everything in Nikko "exists for a painter's delight, everything composes or makes pleasant arrangements, and the little odds and ends are charming, so that I sometimes feel as if I liked the small things I have discovered better than the greater which I am forced to recognize." He reveled in the little waterfall outside their house, the fringe of purple iris around the pool at the base of the falls, the moss-carpeted stone stairways in the forest.

La Farge had been an aficionado of Oriental art since the 1850s, when he bought his first Japanese woodcuts. One of the earliest American artists to use Japanese techniques, he was particularly attracted to the works of Katsushika Hokusai, who signed himself "The Old Man Crazy about Painting." Bigelow and Fenollosa considered Hokusai pedestrian, but La Farge admired his passion for perfection, and he was ecstatic on discovering the same "secret beauty" in the architecture of Japan. From the most ornate temple to the plainest house, exquisite care had been taken with finish and detail. The Japanese insistence on simplicity sometimes resulted in interiors that were overly severe, La Farge felt, but on the whole he preferred this "civilized bareness" to the clutter of American homes.

Reflecting on all that he had seen, La Farge felt himself in a "strange nearness" to the feelings of Japanese artists. He had the sensation that he had always known Japan; it was America that seemed "queer, strange, and often unreasonable." But when he tried to paint from his feeling of kinship with the Japanese, he failed. His pictures of fountains and statues emitted a stale, documentary air. In the clouds and rugged hills of Nikko he thought he had found an appropriately mystical background for the mural of Christ's ascension he was to paint in New York, but the ethereal delicacies he savored with his eye eluded his hand.

Part of La Farge's trouble was the heat, which Henry estimated to be somewhere "between 90° and 200°." Even under a parasol La Farge dripped with perspiration and could not keep his spectacles from fogging. Shedding his Western suit for a light Japanese robe, Henry spent the scorching afternoons stretched out on their shady veranda, reading Dante's *Paradiso* and writing letters. "Shall I bring you an embroidered *kimono* for a dressing-gown, or would you rather have a piece of lacquer? or a sword?" he asked Lizzie Cameron, his comely young neighbor on Lafayette Square. "I am puzzled to know what to bring home to please myself. If I knew what would please you, I would load the steamer with it."

The unknown ailment Lizzie had suffered during the winter turned out to be pregnancy, and the baby, a girl, was born a few weeks after

Adams left for Japan. Adams learned of the birth from John Hay, who forwarded a letter Lizzie had written to Clara. On a sheet of her husband's U.S. Senate notepaper, Lizzie explained that she and Don had wanted to call the baby by Clover's given name, Marian. But "Mr. Adams was so far away there was no means of knowing whether he would like it or not. So Mr. Cameron, to gratify his father, gave her the old fashioned name of his grandmother,— Martha Cameron—which I like very well, but which has no association such as the other would have had." Declaring himself "rather upset" by this news, Henry informed Hay that he had no intention of discussing the matter with Lizzie. Apart from his comments on *Esther,* Henry made no references to Clover in his letters from Japan. The act of photographing gardens and temples must have filled him with thoughts of his wife, but he did not voice them, and he expected his friends to observe the same silence.

On the eve of Henry's departure for Japan, Clarence King had talked knowingly of the transports to be found in the arms of Oriental women, whom he considered gloriously free of the inhibitions of their American sisters. But it was Henry's opinion that sex did not exist in Japan, "except as a scientific classification." Not even the geishas he and La Farge twice engaged would change his mind. As he told Hay, "I am lost in astonishment at this flower of eastern culture. . . . Absolutely the women's joints clacked audibly, and their voices were metallic." Henry's intense aversion may well have been a sign of the sexual turmoil of a forty-eight-year-old man who saw himself as "too young to die and too old to take up existence afresh." Caught in this limbo, with his natural self-consciousness painfully exaggerated by the circumstances of Clover's death, Henry might have found it easier to reject the exotic, submissive women of Japan than to entertain desires that seemed to dishonor the memory of his decidedly unsubmissive wife. The most congenial female Adams encountered in his travels was the wife of Ernest Fenollosa, whose ministrations delivered him from the "oily nastiness" of the local cuisine and spared him the labor of negotiating with innkeepers and ricksha drivers.

La Farge expressed no strong attraction to the women of Japan but did not share Henry's antipathy. Fascinated by the diminutive bodies of the Japanese, male and female, he sketched appreciatively as a group of working girls sponged the day's sweat from their bare arms and breasts, and he admired the ruddy glow of female flesh on hot afternoons, when villagers slept nude in the shade.

At the end of August the travelers left Nikko and headed south. "We have worked conscientiously as mere sightseers until all is confused," La Farge reported from Kyoto. From a blur of temples, tombs, and gardens, he could summon up no vivid scenes but that of the soft dawn. "Before the city wakes and the air clears, the crows fly from near the temples toward us, as the great bell of the temple sounds, and we hear the call of the gongs and indefinite waves of prayer." The sight inspired one of his finest watercolors, *Sunrise in Fog over Kiyoto*. With its dreamy streaks of pale pinks and blues and greens, it owed less to his Japanese travels than to the Impressionist-style experiments of his youth.

As their October 2 sailing date approached, both Adams and La Farge were overcome by a sense that they had not made the most of their three months in Japan. La Farge felt "perpetually harassed" by the obligation to sketch the superabundance of artistic details he wanted to remember. Adams's disappointment centered on bric-a-brac. In the three decades since Commodore Matthew Perry had opened Japan, much of the country's art had been carried off by foreigners like Bigelow and Fenollosa. After examining uncountable bronzes, lacquers, screens, fans, kimonos, scrolls, swords, chests, ivories, paintings, prints, and porcelains, Adams managed to spend $2,000, but he doubted that he wanted a tenth of his purchases. To Hay, who had put up $1,000 and charged Adams with the mission of shopping on his behalf, Adams wrote that he had acquired "some good small bits of lacquer and any quantity of *duds* to encumber your tables and mantles; but nothing creditable to our joint genius."

The travelers ended their stay in Japan with a pilgrimage to Mount Fuji. Gazing at the violet cone, La Farge confessed that he could think of no words to express "the simple splendor of the divine mountain. As [Adams] remarked, it was worth coming to Japan for this single day." Adams himself did not bother to note this enthusiasm.

Crossing the Pacific in the company of the Fenollosas, Adams and La Farge arrived in San Francisco on October 20. Henry's brother Charles was waiting on the wharf, the bearer of bad news. Whitman

Gurney had died of pernicious anemia on September 12, and Charles Francis Adams, Sr., was not expected to live out the year. In the velvet opulence of the Union Pacific directors' car, Henry and Charles tried vainly to cheer themselves with a trip down the California coast, then swung east to their gloomy errands in Boston.

For La Farge, Japan had been a long, delicious bath of sensation. He wished he might have it all again, this time without the pressure to sketch. Adams was eager to sum up the experience and move on. "Japan and its art are only a sort of antechamber to China," he told Hay. "China is the only mystery left to penetrate." Dreading the return to Lafayette Square, he vowed that once he finished writing his history, he would go to China for good. "You will hear of me then only as of a false pig-tail pendant over eighteen colored suits of clothes; which, I am told, is the swell winter dress of a Chinese gentleman. . . . Five years hence, I expect to enter the celestial kingdom by that road, if not sooner by a shorter one, as seems more likely to judge from the ways of most of my acquaintances at home."

PART THREE
———

INTIMACIES

13

Rebellious Ore

With the suicide of Clover Adams, the Five of Hearts was reduced to four, and no one would ever replace "First Heart," as John Hay had called her. In a year or two, the notepaper with the embossed red hearts would disappear from their correspondence, and they would cease to speak of their quintet. One of the last references to the group appeared in a May 1887 letter from Hay to Adams's old London intimate, Sir John Clark, who had befriended all of the Hearts during their travels abroad. "Once in a great while," Hay said of the nomadic Clarence King, "he gives us a day—never more than that—in Washington, and then there is Jubilee among the Four of Hearts—even the vacant chair seems less gloomy when he is there."

But if the playful trappings of the Five of Hearts slipped away, their friendship did not. In 1886, while Adams wandered in Japan, Hay and King dreamed of establishing a summer colony at Lake Sunapee in New Hampshire, where the Hearts and a few choice friends such as W. D. Howells could vacation together. Explaining the scheme to Adams, Hay encouraged him to sell his Beverly Farms house to Don and Lizzie Cameron, who were spending the summer there at Henry's invitation. "[C]ome and take your pick of all the land on Sunapee," Hay urged. "We hold any amount from one to one hundred acres at your disposition."

King was even more insistent: "We shall not give anyone a chance to colonize with us till you come home and look over the tract and say if you should like to join us." He felt sure that Adams would be enchanted by their twelve hundred acres, which rolled down the slope of Mount Sunapee to the wooded shore of the lake. His imagination racing, King asked Adams to "look over the Japan houses and pick out a jewel of artistic design and find out what it could be duplicated for, shipped to Boston and put up." He had already selected a spot for it—a "dignified grove of aged maples with log docks and shadowy vistas of ferny darkness behind." While Clara presided over the children, King and Hay and Adams would spend their days in the Japanese house, writing history together. Because of their love of questions with no answers, they could publish their works jointly as "The Impasse Series."

Adams, convinced that his life was over, could muster no more enthusiasm for Sunapee than for anything else. Reading King's architectural dictates, he heaved a weary sigh. "Will nothing short of a house content him?" he asked Hay. What Adams thought of the suggestion to sell the Beverly Farms place, he declined to say. On occasion he would confess that his wife's death had broken his life in two, but he was not ready to put their past up for sale.

By the end of 1886, the realities of King's Mexican silver mines had punctured his dreams of Sunapee. Although the mine at Prietas was running at a profit, operations at Sombrerete and Yedras were beset by labor quarrels and a problem known to mining engineers as "rebellious ore"—rock that could not be refined by the standard process. More expensive methods proved successful, but at Sombrerete, where the ore was of middling quality, the higher costs pared profits to nil. While King predicted handsome returns for the high-grade ore at Yedras once the refining obstacles were overcome, he had begun having serious trouble raising capital. The millionaires he knew at the Union League and Metropolitan clubs in New York still considered him a charming dinner partner, but after years of hearing about the promise of the lost treasures of the conquistadors, they had begun to doubt that he would ever deliver. A few days before Christmas, King turned to Adams for a loan, which he secured with a painting by J. S. Cotman, an English landscape artist whom Adams admired. He was also $45,000 in debt to his boyhood friend James Gardiner and John Hay, who together held King's mining shares as collateral.

The difficulties could not have caught King by surprise. His own ore had turned rebellious during his sybaritic idyll in Europe, and the discipline, stamina, and sound judgment he had brought to his work on the Fortieth Parallel survey had given way to heedlessness and an optimism that bordered on the fantastic. Whenever his neglect created a crisis, he drove himself to near-exhaustion to resolve it, but he ceased to pay attention the moment the storm passed. Hay wished he would forswear mining, take one of the "roomy, well padded" academic chairs he had been offered, and concentrate on pure science.

King was not about to give up. Like Mark Twain and Henry Adams's brother Charles, he despised the rich yet longed for wealth. E. L. Godkin, the editor of the *Nation,* might have been speaking for all of them when he lamented the "gaudy stream of bespangled, belaced and beruffled barbarians" flooding New York. Plenty of people knew how to get money, Godkin observed, but to be rich properly required "culture, imagination and character." King, who fancied himself in ample possession of these noble traits, regularly indulged his artistic side in the company of John La Farge. When the Century Club closed for the night and other men went home to their wives, the painter often invited the geologist to his studio on West 10th Street. Over candlelight suppers prepared by La Farge's Japanese servant or a steak grilled in a sauce concocted by King, they spun dreams of a higher life, an existence devoted to art and devoid of Godkin's barbarians. Sometimes they ventured a few doors down 10th Street to the dingy storeroom where King kept his art collection. La Farge marveled at trunkful after trunkful of paintings, drawings, and bibelots fit for museums. "By the bye I have a Turner or a Millet somewhere here," King would say, and with a little rummaging the masterpiece would turn up. When the Yedras mine paid off, King planned to build a mansion around his treasures. For the largest room, King wanted a frieze encircling "a large space filled with the most beautiful of stained glass." La Farge, of course, would do the glass, and each panel would be based on a story from *The Divine Comedy*.

As their financial affairs slid into ruin, King and La Farge amused

themselves for hours with elaborate artistic schemes, including one
for Grant's Tomb. After a million mourners thronged the streets of
New York for Grant's funeral procession in 1885, a committee of
civic notables was appointed to select a design for a memorial to the
greatest hero of the Civil War. Ideas poured forth from every quarter. Appalled by the "confused gropings" of the public, King took
matters into his own tasteful hands with an unsigned essay in the
North American Review. The mask of anonymity gave him the mischievous fun that Adams and Hay had had with *Democracy* and *The
Bread-Winners* and allowed him to propose a monument uniquely
suited to the talents of John La Farge.

In King's view, the popular notion that the design should be
"strictly American" was absurd since the only monuments fitting
that description were Indian earth mounds and the stone tombs of
the Mayans. But he was also wary of American efforts to adapt the
styles and customs of other civilizations, which seemed to him to
have produced only mutilation and burlesque. As proof he offered
the Fourth of July. "There were a hundred ways, graceful and grave,
in which Independence Day might have been commemorated," he
wrote, but Americans chose the "senseless pandemonium" of *"a
Chinese jollification by fire-crackers."* The newly completed Washington Monument he found equally preposterous—an Egyptian phallus.
The standard European complaint that Americans had talent but no
genius was "most unfair," King scoffed, since it overlooked our
"positive and unrivaled genius for the inappropriate."

Pondering styles for Grant's monument, King ruled out Egyptian
and Greek models on the grounds that America had little in common
with either civilization. Renaissance styles struck him as better suited
to sumptuous palaces than memorials, modern French architecture as
"too gay and bright" for a tomb, and Gothic motifs as too easily
abused in translation. The correct model, he felt, was classical Rome.
"The chief experiences of the Roman people were what ours have
been—war, trade, and sudden expansion into national greatness."
Both Romans and Americans "loved luxury and pomp" and "adored
quantity," he wrote. "Size, brute mass, the big figures of the census
are our pride." King also detected parallels between General Grant
and the captains of the Caesars. "Simple and direct, uncomplicated
by the high-strung self-consciousness of the present age," Grant had

gone to battle "with the absorbed directness of a soldier of the second century."

Since the monument would crown a bluff above the Hudson River and be visible from all sides, King suggested a domed drum akin to the Tomb of Hadrian. In place of the emperor's masonry, King proposed the use of as much stained glass as the structure would support. Illuminated from within, it would gleam like a jewel in the night.

Remembering the plan years later, La Farge said the design had proved "too poetic and ideal" for the likes of a committee. The stained-glass jewel lost out to a stubby Greco-Roman pastiche that undoubtedly confirmed King's low estimate of American taste.

Long before, in one of his mountaineering sketches for the *Atlantic*, King had catalogued the crudities of the West and then paused to reflect that what a man was mattered less than what he might become. Holding forth on Grant's Tomb, King revealed more than he knew of what he himself had become in the years since his adventures in the Sierra Nevada. In aesthetic matters, he was surer than ever of his superior delicacy and refinement. Like La Farge, who believed the world was "stuffed with sawdust," King saw himself a lonely standard-bearer in a vulgar wasteland.

The essay also hinted at King's increasingly troubled relations with women. Among the philistines he excoriated were a bevy of "bediamonded women" he had once encountered in a Fifth Avenue drawing room. He admired the room, but his companions declared it inferior to the boudoir of one of their fashionable friends. Safely anonymous, the author gave full rein to his scorn. The boudoir in question was "nothing but the *disjecta membra* of a once important bank account," he wrote; "it reeks money, it exudes costliness—very likely the chairs are stuffed with curled coupons—but to an art-loving mind it is a dreary, poverty-smitten waste." Turning to New England's crimes against the architecture of classical Greece, King sneered at the imitation Parthenon found in every village—executed in pine and typically inhabited, he suspected, by a "prim little Puritan maiden, sharp as a stock-broker, and with an unabridged dictionary of a mind."

At the time King composed his sermon on style, he despaired of ever finding a wife. Writing to John Hay on Five of Hearts stationery in May 1885, he confessed to feeling "very sulky" as the result of one of his "conscientious efforts . . . to find the sixth heart." The young women who had flanked him at dinner the night before, he said, "were in fine form (as the hostess afterwards told me) and screamed scraps of subjects at me in their macaw voices till they left my slow faculties in a state of irritated daze. The New York girl is certainly a phenomenon. What she would doubtless call her mind is a mere crazy quilt of bright odds and ends. Bits of second-hand opinion cut bias, snips of polite error patched in with remnants of truth which don't show the whole pattern, little rags of scandal &c &c all deftly sewed together in a pretty chromatic chaos well calculated to please a congenital dude but fatiguing to a lover of natural women, such as I am."

At forty-three, King was as defensive about his bachelorhood as Henry and Clover Adams had been about their lack of children. If a conversation turned to marriage, King snuffed it at once with an outlandish pronouncement. He explained his unmarried state by taking a coin from his pocket, flipping it, and declaring, "Woman is too one-sided—like a tossed-up penny—and I want both sides or none." On another occasion he insisted he would never marry a woman just because he had said he would: "People who marry without any better reason than that must surely come to grief." His friends shrugged off his bravado and joked that Clarence King had never married because he was so complete he did not need a second half.

By 1886, indictments of womankind had become a staple of King's letters to Hay. Meeting a Mrs. Davis at Lake George, he complained that her mind was "crammed full of remnants" picked up "at Macy's when they were selling off, for below cost, a world of snips of unreasonable information. She has something quite a propos but utterly mistaken about everything." On a trip to Lake Sunapee, he was stunned by a kiss from Sarah Durgin, wife of the man who tended the property which Hay and King hoped to buy. "It was a revelation; so thin and cold, so dreary and colorless," King said. ". . . I am capable of walking up to the cannon's mouth but I refuse to ever again march up to the mouth of a New Hampshire woman." Poor Sarah, he moaned. Her kiss "seemed like the only one she had, the little pittance she had saved for heaven knows how long." Thoroughly depressed, King vowed to go "far up on the side of [Mount Sunapee] out of human hearing and fetch two or three long drawn howls, by way of relief. I have seen this work well with wolves: they scream away their griefs and then brace up in capital form."

The visit to New Hampshire also produced a specimen of Boston femininity for his vivisection. "You know the type," he told Hay, "caramels, matinees . . . the last slang, a good dress and a bad hat." When she displayed "a charmingly pretty little pink blister on her plump white palm," acquired while rowing on the lake, King mused that it was the sort of detail W. D. Howells would invent. King prescribed resin and gallantly volunteered to show her how to feather the oars. A few days later he reported that he had indeed taught her to row and had offered further counsel on blister prevention: henceforth she was not to wear her "huge diamonds" while working the oars.

Reading the Sunapee letters, Hay thought his friend "in delicious vein" and wished he would write the novel he had long promised. Hay did not perceive that King's disdain of women masked enormous fears. An account of a visit with Miss Gail Hamilton, a writer who had also been one of his schoolteachers, spoke volumes of the dangers King felt in the presence of women. Having known Miss Hamilton for most of his life, he told Hay he had watched her pass from "the sweetness of natural womanhood . . . through the acetous fermentation of belated virginity into the hard cider of middle age." At fifty-five, she had "like some old Madeira passed into the flavorless rainwater stage. She is pellucid and harmless, amiably neutral, unintoxicating. She buzzes pleasantly and like certain bees has left her sting in some victim or other. I liked her more than ever before."

Though King's anxieties did not turn him against all women, he abominated the ones deemed most acceptable for a man in his position—the spirited, thoroughly modern types who populated the fiction of Henry James. Like others who felt misplaced in the Gilded Age, King liked to maintain that civilization was a nervous disease, and he lodged numerous complaints against his overcivilized male contemporaries, including the fastidious Henry James. King accused the novelist of looking "a little askance" at his fictional characters unless they belonged to his own class, and he suspected that before James ventured into the darker quarters of London, he "gathered up a few unmistakably good invitations and buttoned them in his inner pocket so that there should be no mistaking the social position of his corpse if violence befell him." But King reserved his most savage attacks for the modern female, whom he saw as badly educated, overly talkative, and sexually inhibited. Unable to abide her, he idealized her primitive sister. "Paradise, for me, is still a garden and a primaeval woman," he told Hay. "I have a feeling that I should not have eaten the forbidden fruit, but somehow I would have fenced with the two edged sword and defended my Eden, and to-day there would have been much less sorrow and fewer mugwumps."

In Newport for a visit with his mother, King waxed lyrical about a "grandly barbaric Congo woman" and her "tribe," who had come to work in the house. "They are all very black and very silent, all have teeth like glistening ivory," he told Hay. "We are living with the hordes of the Congo and you taste mysterious spices and poke your fork into incredible ragouts, and hear songs of the Guinea Coast and see faces gay and loose with a heredity of sweetly dissolute centuries." Reveling in the new sensations the blacks had brought to the "grim calvinistic scotch propriety" of his mother's house, King could not help contrasting the naturalness of the servants with the life that modern men and women were expected to lead. "Civilization so narrows the gamut! Respectability lets the human pendulum swing over such a pitiful little arc that it is worthwhile now and again to see human beings whose feelings have no inflexible bar of metal restraining their swing to the limits set by civilized experience and moral law."

During his European holiday, King had boasted to lords and ladies of his escapades in the slums, but in America he felt obliged to temper his conversation. Perhaps he feared that word of his special tastes would reach his mother or that his business partners would read his sexual predilections as one more sign of flawed judgment. His fellow clubmen had heard him proclaim that miscegenation was the only hope of the white race, and his intimates knew, in a general way, of his attraction to dark-skinned women. But he was reluctant to share the particulars with anyone except John Hay. In the spring of 1887, King went out west on mining business, and somewhere in California he fell in love with an Indian woman named Luciana. She was "as near Eve as can be," he told Hay. Riding with Luciana in the mountains, King said, the "world was all flowers and Luciana's face the most tender and grave image of Indian womanhood within human conception. . . . We came upon a spring high up in the mountains, where the oaks were dewy with sea fog and the orange poppies all aflame in the grass; and there we dismounted and looked out on the silver sea, and I came as near it as I ever shall."

As grieved as King was to part with Luciana, he had no intention of forging a permanent bond. Like the girls of the London slums, she was supposed to be material for a novel. But after the icy kiss at Lake Sunapee, so unlike the "oceanic fullness of blood and warmth" he had tasted among the poppies, King moaned that his efforts to reduce Luciana to "a mere literary figure, a lay woman draped with rich emotions and posed as model for my book" were dismally unsuccessful: "she will not down." With a flash of grim humor, he remarked that his situation was not without hope. "Business troubles I am told have a way of grinding off the fairest pictures from the soul and I have always enough of them to erode the bloom off anything."

Luciana faded from his letters, but as his financial woes deepened, King felt himself increasingly attracted to the forbidden world of dark skins. In 1887, forced out of the management of the Yedras mine and faced with expensive delays at Sombrerete, King traded his Savile Row suits for rough clothes and prowled the black neighborhoods of New York, registering at hotels under an alias. He also undertook a secret mission on behalf of a seventy-year-old quadroon who was said to be the illegitimate daughter of a leading Southern politician. She and King had chatted briefly years before during a chance meeting in a lawyer's office, and they had charmed each other instantly. Despite her age and white hair, King found himself taken with "an eye like incandescent lava." The lawyer, now in failing health, asked King to act as guardian of her affairs, which had been left in "the trusteeship (not with legal form of course) of a gentleman of the old school who with his wife have been true and faithful to her." His own finances in shambles, King nevertheless hastened to New Orleans on her behalf. This much he reported to an old mining colleague, Samuel Barlow, in hopes that Barlow could recommend a discreet attorney in New Orleans—an older man, a Creole perhaps, "who knows about such histories and has outgrown idle curiosity."

Here the matter dropped. King's letters never revealed the identity of the old quadroon or her celebrated father. The episode would not warrant mention were it not for another secret that soon overwhelmed King's life.

Sometime during 1887, at the home of a friend in New York, a young black nursemaid named Ada Copeland caught the geologist's eye, and they struck up a covert romance. He was forty-five, she was twenty-six. This time King would conceal his passion even from John Hay. It was one thing to own up to an exotic liaison in far-off California, quite another to do it amid the proprieties of home. But the most startling aspect of King's secrecy was his unwillingness to reveal his real identity to Ada. For fourteen years she would know him as James Todd. And somehow James Todd managed to persuade her to become his bride in a ceremony that included everything but a marriage license.

The unorthodox wedding took place in September 1888, at the home of the bride's aunt on West 24th Street in Manhattan. An organ and a Bible were installed for the occasion, and a black Methodist minister was invited down from his 85th Street church to perform the rites. The groom, in a dress suit, put a ring on the bride's finger, and the Reverend Mr. Cook pronounced them Mr. and Mrs. James Todd. Chocolates and a cake with white icing were shared with her friends and family. Their impressions of the mysterious, well-spoken stranger with the deep-blue eyes and the receding blond hair went unrecorded.

What explanation would have persuaded Ada to wed King without a license? What account of himself did he give her family? Why, after a succession of subterranean affairs with dark-skinned women, did he seek a permanent attachment? These questions and dozens more remain unanswered. Apart from the wedding details, all that is known is that the groom soon rented a house for the bride on Hudson Street in Brooklyn. Afraid of being found out, he decided to keep rooms at the Brunswick Hotel or one of his clubs. The gentlemen of the Union League and the Metropolitan, long accustomed to his comings and goings, would think nothing of his frequent absences. In Brooklyn, he told curious neighbors what he had told Ada and her family: he was a railroad porter from Baltimore.

In the house on Hudson Street, Ada gave birth to a son. In yet another deception, King named the baby after himself, calling him Leroy, from the French *le roi*—the king. Over the next several years, Ada would bear two more sons and two daughters. However King viewed the obligations of fatherhood, his experience with the ancient quadroon had taught him that such affairs could be managed honorably without the formalities of legal documents.

Despite their sketchiness, the facts of King's relationship with Ada do much to explain the escalating tension between his private and public selves in 1887 and 1888. Publicly, he balanced his Mexican mining defeats with high hopes for new business ventures—banks in El Paso and San Diego as well as a coal partnership with Henry Adams's brother Charles, president of the Union Pacific. Their enterprise mined anthracite for locomotive fuel, and they soon hit on the lucrative idea of selling most of their stock to one of their largest customers, the Erie Railroad.

After hours, King divided his time between Hudson Street and dinners with such friends as John La Farge. On occasion they were joined by the architect Stanford White and Augustus Saint-Gaudens, who was as dilatory in business matters as King and La Farge. A year had passed since Henry Adams had commissioned the sculpture for Clover's grave, and Saint-Gaudens had given it almost no thought. In the summer of 1887, the quartet dined amid some rather pungent horses at the Riding Club, an experience King found "a curious mixture of art and hippodrome: some very good talk, but I confess I don't like an ammoniacal flavor to my iced lemonade." King's chief delight that evening was Saint-Gaudens, who had just shaved his beard and "laid bare the most extraordinary chin—long, pointed, equine. . . . I had no idea that beneath that peaked beard was a chin as severe and hard and sharp as his sculptor's chisel."

La Farge was working on the church mural he had planned during his Japanese travels with Henry Adams. In a single day, he told King, he had "whacked in a whole Apostle." He was also painting two decorative panels for the music room of Whitelaw Reid's new mansion. Hay had recommended La Farge for the job, advising his old *Tribune* colleague to give the artist a free hand. Reid took the counsel, and La Farge was working with rare contentment. King, however, was not enthusiastic about the results. One female figure was "as nude as Eve," he told Hay, but "so entirely without temperamental charms, that I do not want her." To Adams, King wrote that La Farge's nudes were "beautifully executed but not archaic enough to suit my grovelling mind."

Neither King's secret pleasures in Brooklyn nor his male friendships sufficed to ward off restlessness and despair. From time to time he thought about moving himself and his mother's Newport household to Washington, ostensibly to be near Hay and Adams. He also may have meant to move Ada and the children, who could blend easily into the life of the capital, which Henry James had described as "a Negro village liberally sprinkled with whites."

Rebelling against the knowledge that his relationship with Ada would rule out summers at Lake Sunapee, King bombarded John Hay with confusing letters and wild plans. Hay relished King's discourses on "comparative gynaecology," with their description of Sarah Durgin's glacial kiss and the volcanic warmth of Luciana, but King had neglected to mention whether the land purchase had been consummated or not. With a good-natured sigh, Hay said he supposed he would find out when his bills arrived.

Sunapee also inspired King to new flights of financial fancy. Expecting that he would soon be able to repay a $12,500 loan from Hay, he offered his friend a novel alternative: "I have wondered whether it would be perfectly agreeable to you if I put that into my part of the purchase and into a cottage which should be ready for my occupation next summer. As the title to the land will be [yours] and the house insured, it will be good security." While he acknowledged that there was no reason for Hay to grant such an indulgence, he said he offered the suggestion in case "it would amuse you to do it." Certain that Hay would consent, King had already sketched the house he wanted. Stanford White estimated the cost at $8,000. King urged Hay to hurry to Sunapee with an architect of his own and "cover in a cottage by snowfly."

The would-be summer colonists were soon having second—and third—thoughts. Recounting a trip he and Clara took to New Hampshire with King in the spring of 1887, Hay told Adams, "Ten minutes before we got there, we looked each other in the three faces,—we had been making conversation for an hour to keep from saying the things that beset us,—and all at once we said in chorus:—"We don't want the place!" and each begged pardon of the other for changing our minds. We got off at old Durgin's, feeling like murderers, and kept up a ghastly chatter to throw dust in his eyes. He harnessed up his machine and took us to see the farm—and lo! we fell in love with it over again." King, undoubtedly because of his deepening involvement with Ada, decided not to join in the purchase.

The Hearts came close to a reunion in September 1887, when King tried to organize a group expedition to Mexico. But the Hays, just home from Queen Victoria's Golden Jubilee, quickly bowed out. "We both feel we need rest and recreation, after our arduous summer drinking tea with them there Kings," Hay joshed. Hay faced several weeks of business chores in Cleveland as well as a deadline on the Lincoln biography; he had promised Nicolay a first draft by spring. Adams was still game, and King promised that they would travel by way of New Orleans, where, he said, he would "be entranced to pour gumbo over your soul." From that cheery prospect King tumbled deep into gloom. Freed from family obligations, he said, he would gladly rove forever in search of "the Garden of Eden or the Fountain of Eternal Wit or any other thing we were sure not to find. But fate has rivetted the chains of prosaic labor and dull duty forever on my legs and I shall never in time or space get beyond their tether and their clank. I am told that self sacrifice and the stabbing to death of one's heart's desires are most desirable and that if I am duly meek and lay low I shall derive much advantage in the line of noble qualities but when I look over the rather parched surface of my soul I don't find the promised spiritual herbage sprouting up as yet."

At the last minute, floods in Mexico forced them to cancel the trip. During the next year, the vagrant Heart would drop out of another Mexican excursion as well as a voyage to Cuba with his friends, and his whereabouts would become increasingly uncertain. In the autumn of 1888, when the second Mexican trip was still pending, Hay joked to Adams, "Won't you join us in this twice-told imaginary journey which will not be made?" A few months earlier, Hay had gone to King's Wall Street office and learned that the geologist was in California. When Hay returned to his New York hotel, however, there sat King, surrounded by the four little Hays. Frustrated by the

The peripatetic Clarence King. FROM *CLARENCE KING MEMOIRS*, COURTESY OF THE
JOHN HAY COLLECTION, JOHN HAY LIBRARY, BROWN UNIVERSITY LIBRARY

geologist's errant ways and "the Silence of the King, which passeth
the power of profanity to do justice unto," Hay suspected his friend
had joined "some oath-bound order which pledged him, under fearful sanctions, never to tell anybody anything."

King blamed his unpredictability on his health. Years of camping
out and working in damp mines had left him vulnerable to throat and
lung infections. The problem was real, but it also enabled him to
disguise his disappearances as periods of convalescence.

Ultimately the strains of secrecy and business reverses exacted
their toll. In July 1888, two months before the sham wedding, King's
health collapsed. His doctor prescribed a year's rest beginning with
a long stay at Hot Springs, Arkansas. King was in no position to
heed the advice. "I am awfully poor now and must work hard," he
confided to Adams. Desperate for money, he even stooped to consulting on a platinum mine that he suspected did not exist. "The
central figure is an alchemist of eighty years who had devoted 45
years to this ore in as quaint a hocus pocus laboratory as ever was,"
he wrote Hay from a Pennsylvania backwater. "I spend all my time
in wondering that I listened to the story and came."

★   ★   ★

Determined to ignore the demands pressing in on all sides, King once more sought refuge in the world of letters. "Artium Magister," an essay in the October 1888 *North American Review,* scolded institutions of higher learning for their "joyless" methods of teaching the classics, which forced a boy to "parse instead of feel Aeschylus, and scan rather than discuss Virgil." Better that the youth should be "a cowboy, with the Bible and Shakespeare in his saddle-bags, the constellations his tent, the horse his brother, than to have life, originality, and the bounding spirit of youthful imagination stamped out of him by a competent and conscientious corps of badgering grammarians." The issue was crucial, King argued, because classical ideals could offset the deleterious effects of life in an age of "sodden materialism." Once instruction moved beyond "the mechanics of dialects" and "dry pedantic torture," the classics could have "inestimable value in the creation of American character," King concluded. "Then a university parchment may cease to add irony to ignorance. Then will come some man whom the world will recognize as Artium Magister."

Like his pronouncements on Grant's Tomb, King's opinions on pedagogy mattered less for their intellectual content than for what they showed of his character, and the most telling passages of "Artium Magister" had nothing to do with education. On the brink of committing himself to Ada, King was obsessed by what he saw as the utter failure of nineteenth-century womanhood. Woman per se lay beyond the scope of his essay, but he managed to work in a diatribe on the shortcomings of heroines in modern fiction, who were, he assumed, "more or less true to the human model."

Think of the stunted and petty women and their incredible meanness; of the primeval, monkey-scale of their average intelligence; remember how few wholesome, sweet, strong women are found in that army of distorted, diseased creatures who march between the covers of English fiction, laden down as they go with all the tragicomic foibles flesh is heir to, and all the conceivable deviations from noble and normal womanhood; and then reflect how French realism has flung woman naked in the ditch and left her there scorned of men, and grinning in cynical and shameless levity over her own dishonor. Or to come nearer home, recall the pretty, brightish, smug little people who are made with inimitable skill to illustrate the sawdust stuffing of middle-class democratic society.

Out of it all is there one figure for weary eyes to linger upon: one type of large and satisfying womanhood; natural in the rare and ravishing charm of a perfect body; sweet with the endowment of a warm, quick, sympathetic temperament; sound and bright in intellect; pure and spiritual, with a soul in whose pellucid depths fixed stars of the moral heaven reflect themselves, undimmed by mists of earth, untrembling from the jar of modern conflict? Is there any more womanhood in them all, English, French, and American put together and fused into one, than can be learned in a single hour before that Greek Venus in the Louvre, who is only perfect goddess because she is perfect woman? Is there not in this one ideal, with her rich femininity, her Doric strength, the calm warmth of her countenance, the supple pose of her vital body, and that irradiating aura of love which enfolds her with its mysterious veil, more of human nature than one can patch together out of all the thousands of photographic portraits of actual, but distorted and incomplete characters that crowd modern fiction?

Among the women King saw in society during 1888, the only ones he could tolerate were the self-effacing and the harmless, such as Clara Hay and his old teacher, Gail Hamilton. Twice during the summer he felt moved to express his admiration for Clara, not realizing that her very blankness allowed him to see in her precisely what he needed to see. Writing to Henry Adams, King praised Clara in terms he might have used to describe the statue of the Greek Venus: "her Archaic Grace is Doric as ever in the indisturbable balance of her rooted repose." Women who were "not covered deep with a luxuriant growth of juicy temperament" made him "miserable," he added. "To kiss a woman and feel teeth through her thin lips paralises me for a week." Apologizing for his "snarl," he explained that it had been set off by a recent social gathering, where he had had to kiss a number of young women whom he did not want to kiss. "Their little minds squirm and contract under the irrita of light conversation as a dead frog curls up his wiry toes at the galvanic touch but I am not deceived by their involuntary simulation of life. I know they are dead."

King insisted to Hay that the "calm and grand" Clara was unique among her sex. If other women possessed her heart and mind and the "strength of nature too, I don't know where they live." Then he lapsed into a self-defense that must have left his friend wondering what was wrong: "I have a sort of grim muttering sound in my ear that seems to me as if you were taking me to task for not writing literature, but if you saw my life you would not. If you knew the difficulties of my situation in all its respects and phases, you would not blame me for consenting to sink into a quiet drudgery from which I frankly see that I may never emerge."

A more despairing bridegroom would be hard to find. And whatever happiness King knew in his stolen hours with Ada was soon interrupted. Early in November, he left for Hot Springs. Sending Hay a "thousand thanks" and a receipt for yet another loan, he asked that his destination be kept secret. "I have told no one except Mother where I have gone as people think one only goes to Arkansas for malign influence of the planet Venus."

While it is tempting to speculate that King wanted the secrecy because Ada went with him, the darkness of his mood suggests that he was alone in Arkansas. Sentenced to sixty days of mineral baths and "farcical" meals, affronted by a physician "who thinks my sorrows are a form of deep muscular rheumatism," King wondered whether he had "the pluck to stand it with all the visible horrors of human wrecks surrounding me on every side and no human being to talk to." He seethed when he learned that local officials routinely solved racial disputes simply by posting notices requiring Negroes to leave town. Arkansas, he told Hay, "is to me the most barbarous and terrible place I ever was in."

A few months later, back on the East Coast, King stopped off in Washington for a brief visit. As he and Henry Adams strolled in the spring sunshine of Lafayette Square, Adams was surprised to see that King's hair had grown almost as gray as his own.

14

Passions and Tensions

*H*enry Adams had returned from Japan at the end of 1886 certain that his life in Washington was over. As much as he treasured John Hay, the friendship was not enough to keep him in Lafayette Square. Like Madeleine Lee in *Democracy,* he longed to burrow into a remote corner of the world, perhaps never to return. He preferred China to Mrs. Lee's Egypt, and all that stood in the way was the task of finishing his massive *History of the United States of America during the Administrations of Thomas Jefferson and James Madison.* To hasten the end of the work, he persuaded Theodore Dwight, who had lived at 1603 H Street during his absence, to stay on and help with research.

But little by little, without realizing it, Henry began to piece together a new life on H Street. Agonizingly unsure of himself in the beginning, he issued no invitations and could barely respond when friends took the initiative. To Lizzie Cameron, who urged him and Dwight to dine with her until they found a cook of their own, he stammered, "I—or we, if you prefer it—should of course delight in taking you—and your cuisine—at your word to its full extent; but if we did, we should never get a cook; the inducements to delay would be irresistible, and Dwight would see untold blemishes in every new candidate. On the other hand, we—or I—or he—are, am or is delighted to accept any invitation you will send us."

Two of Henry Adams's favorite visitors were Elizabeth Sherman Cameron, his beautiful young neighbor on Lafayette Square, and her daughter, Martha. FRANCES BENJAMIN JOHNSTON, FROM THE COLLECTIONS OF THE LIBRARY OF CONGRESS

Part of Henry's shyness sprang from his attraction to the attentive slate-blue eyes and the vivacity that endeared tall, slender "Mrs. Don" to Washington. But beyond the fear of making a spectacle of himself by falling in love with a married woman twenty years his junior, Henry was having difficulty conceiving of his place in society without Clover at his side. He had not gone to a dinner party in the capital since the spring of 1885, when Clover's breakdown began, and he did not relish the picture of himself as the extra guest for whom a dinner partner had to be found. Nor did he wish to preside over afternoon tea. Tea had been Clover's glory. Henceforth Henry would pass his five o'clocks with the Hays.

For all this self-consciousness and timidity, Henry saw no need to bar his own door, and it did not take long for his breakfast table to gain the notoriety his drawing room had once had. Served at twelve-thirty, a Henry Adams breakfast was governed by only one rule: guests must invite themselves. "When his colored major-domo answered your ring, you never inquired, 'Is Mr. Adams in?' " one frequent guest remembered. "He was always in, and the right number of seats were ready." Friends were encouraged to bring new faces; without being told, they understood that the host would tolerate anyone but a bore. Adams soon boasted that his house was "the haunt of all the most charming women going," including Mrs. Cam-

eron, and he was equally proud to note, as a testament to his pop-
ularity, that his grocery bill had ballooned to $500 a month. Recalling
his own youthful pleasure at the London breakfasts of Monckton
Milnes, Adams made young visitors especially welcome. "Uncle
Henry," they called him, and he regarded them as nieces and nephews "in wish."

Among the young men who found their way to his table in 1887,
his pride was Cecil Spring Rice, a twenty-eight-year-old junior secretary newly posted to the British legation. Women adored his span-
iel face, his unfailing good nature, and a sartorial ineptitude that
made him, as one of his biographers kindly put it, "untidy to ex-
cess." Lizzie and her friends "elder-sistered him," insisting that he
"bring his socks and linen to be revised and corrected." They also
fretted over Springy's absentmindedness about eating, a worry Uncle Henry soon put to rest. Once introduced to Adams, Springy
proved willing to come for dinner as well as breakfast, and since the
British legation was only a block east on H Street, he often dropped
by between meals.

Springy's sunny wit was keen enough to hold its own against
Adams's dark humor, and his observations on American life were
sufficiently wry to appeal to the historian's rarefied tastes. When the
New York Harbor Board was caught paying large sums to a company that dredged by day and dumped the dredgings back into place
by night, Springy and Adams could greet the news with more laughter than indignation. To Springy, American politics was "all dullness
relieved by rascality"—a sentiment congenial to the jaded Adams.

The young man, who considered Uncle Henry "rather an interesting sort of cynic," needed only slight acquaintance to discern that
the descendants of John and John Quincy Adams were "as odd as can
be." There was no denying the cleverness of Henry Adams and his
brothers, he told an English friend, "but they all make a sort of
profession of eccentricity. One of them wrote a book of which a
review appeared so bitter and strong that he wrote the Editor to ask
who had done it. He was told, his brother.—Two of them were
arguing. One said, 'It seems to me I am the only one of the family
who inherits anything of our grandfather's manners.' 'But you dis-
sipated your inheritance young,' answered the other."

With Uncle Henry's tutelage, Springy soon endorsed the idea that

mediocrity and corruption were inescapable in a political system
wholly dependent on funds raised by party machines. He saw at once
that the Senate, which had come to be known as the Millionaires'
Club, cared less for voters than for the titans of copper and railroads,
and that the House of Representatives was little more than a collection of errand boys hand-picked by senators. Washington had no
room for a cultivated intellectual like Secretary of State Thomas
Bayard, Springy observed: "That sort of thing doesn't go down
among a lot of politicians and business men like the Senators. They
don't like to call him their superior and so say he is a pompous ass."

Springy also adopted his mentor's disdain for White House public
receptions. Sounding uncannily like the author of *Democracy,* he reported that visitors to Grover Cleveland's White House were herded
into a large drawing room "with a ghastly picture of Lincoln opposite Mrs. Washington, as if they were married." There the crowd
waited until "the fat short President" appeared. "You form a line and
move past as hard as you can, shaking hands. The children get their
heads patted." No matter what Cleveland said, Springy noticed,
everyone agreed—"like people on the stage, all at once."

Much as Spring Rice revered the opinions of his Uncle Henry,
they parted company on the merits of the first lady. Frances Folsom Cleveland, who had married the president in 1886, had made
no impression on Adams apart from her "splendid vigor in handshaking." Springy, accustomed to the reserve of royalty, was delighted by Mrs. Cleveland's informality. To his amazement, she
thought nothing of telling him about a spat with her husband. In
the middle of a heat wave, Cleveland had "gone on the loose and
bought himself an orange tawny linen suit," Springy wrote home
to England, explaining that the President was "5 feet high and 4
feet wide" and had "no neck and six chins." Mrs. Cleveland's predicament was plain. "What would he look like in it, think?" she
had asked Spring Rice. Using one ruse after another, the first lady
managed to keep the president away from the suit, but the mercury
continued to rise, and finally he said he *had* to wear it because all
his other suits were too warm. He capitulated only when Mrs.
Cleveland insisted that no self-respecting son of Erin could vote for
a man wearing orange.

★   ★   ★

Washington in 1887 oscillated between the pretentious and the primitive. Sewers were in short supply, but a surprising number of the carriages clattering along the streets of Lafayette Square sported silver fittings and liveried footmen as members of the Millionaires' Club competed in the new game of conspicuous consumption. Spring Rice's instinct for the comedy between these poles made him entertaining company for Henry Adams, whose self-imposed seclusion had not quelled his interest in society or his appetite for gossip. But the greatest value of Springy's companionship was the distraction it gave Henry from Lizzie Cameron. What had begun as infatuation had ripened, with her encouragement, into a deep, vexing love. Lizzie did not consider divorce an option, and she and Henry seem to have agreed not to have a sexual relationship.* Acutely sensitive to the damage that even the most scrupulous attentions might inflict on Mrs. Cameron's reputation, Adams calculated his every move. To keep tongues from wagging, he made a point of seeing her in the company of others, often at his breakfasts. In March, when he sent her a decorative Japanese screen, he imagined her awkwardness in explaining the present and offered to let her pay for it. "I would rather you should take it as a gift," he told her, "but if you are tired of gifts, I am willing you should take it on what terms you like."

The breakfast establishment closed for the summer of 1887, when Henry went up to Quincy to work on his history and watch over his mother, who at seventy-nine possessed a full complement of the infirmities of old age. The Camerons were only thirty miles away, in Henry's house at Beverly Farms. Lizzie invited him for a visit, but he could not face a return to the scene of Clover's collapse. Separated from Lizzie, he nonetheless managed to shower her with discreet signs of affection. Fresh fruits and vegetables could be had by send-

* At least no biographer to date has turned up evidence of a physical liaison, and many have tried. In an age when divorce was difficult, scandalous, *declassé,* and a sure road to social ostracism, some lovers found it nobler—and perhaps even erotic—not to act on their sexual impulses. As the connoisseur Bernard Berenson once explained to a friend, "After all, it is a delightful thing to keep one's self in hand. I have enjoyed the effort not to possess, no less than the delight in possession. Think of the hundreds of women one has desired without love, and refrained from, even when one could have had them. Such suppressed desire immensely enriches life—and so it should." (Quoted in Ernest Samuels, *Bernard Berenson: The Making of a Connoisseur,* 65.)

Cecil Spring Rice, an amusing young Englishman assigned to the British legation in Washington. He quickly became a regular at Henry Adams's breakfast table.
REPRODUCED FROM *ROMAN SPRING*, BY MRS. WINTHROP CHANLER

ing express to Quincy Market, he informed her. She was to watch the sea for signs of his Adams nephews, who had been instructed to take her for a ride in their new boat. Toward autumn, when the Atlantic air turned chill, he exhorted her to use the furnace. When Senator Cameron arrived in Beverly after devoting much of the summer to politics, Henry sent his best regards and inquired, "Can I do anything for him?"

In September, Lizzie, chaperoned by their mutual friend Rebecca Dodge, paid a call on Henry at his mother's house. "You are, of course, the nearest reasonable approach to an angel—assuming angels to be like you," he wrote Lizzie two days later. But expressions of tenderness alternated with darker outbursts, welling up from the hurts of their covert, incomplete love. Knowing that Lizzie dreaded his departure for China, he could not stifle a malicious impulse to tell her about the typist who had come to Quincy to speed his work: "I am victim to a female called a caligraphess, or some such classical title . . . whom I am slowly killing with five hours a day of type-writing, in order to hurry my journey to the Celestial Empire. Hu-man victims should always be sacrificed before beginning a journey."

Henry's last weeks in Quincy were so filled with yearning for Lizzie that he fastened on an absurd plot for seeing her before they returned to Lafayette Square. At his request, Lizzie had shipped the Beverly Farms table linens to Washington for his breakfast table, which meant he would have to replenish the stock at Beverly. Both he and Lizzie would pass through New York en route to Washington in October, and he hoped Lizzie would help him shop in Manhattan. When the Camerons left New York just as Adams arrived, Henry sank into a gloom he had not felt in months. "I am sorry," he wrote to Lizzie, "for time does not seem to clear away the wreckage of life, or to show how to climb over it."

A plan to dine in New York with La Farge also fell through, spurring a tirade against the heap of "might-have-beens which make life an incessant delusion." Back on H Street, Henry soon had one more might-have-been to blacken his mood: La Farge refused a com-mission to paint Lizzie's portrait. "I am too sensitive to my sitter's influence," the artist explained. "I am not incapable of making a likeness—every painter can do that—but everything affects me to the extent of a paralyzing result." Lizzie's constantly shifting expressions presented "all sorts of difficulties," he said. "There is a distinct in-terior which contradicts the exterior at moments—or rather there are changes which make one wonder whether they are not really most important. All this is stupid as an explanation—but I wish I were a portrait painter who learns to be very cool as he is most interested."

November brought a much more serious blow. Clover's sister, Ellen Gurney, unable to recover from her husband's death a year before, hurled herself in front of a train. Full of apprehension for Clover and Ellen's brother Ned, who was prostrate with grief, Ad-ams endured the calamity without a word. He knew too well the unnerving lesson that Ellen's friend Alice James had just discovered in the violent death: "what paralytics we all are, so remote from our nearest and dearest that we are helpless to save them from such a desecration of their personal sanctity."

Clarence King and John Hay promised to cheer Adams up with a jaunt to Cuba, but on the eve of the journey King bowed out. Between a mining setback and a "long surgical struggle" with his throat, King said he could not get away. Hay, who was also besieged by throat troubles, decided to accompany Adams only as far as Florida. He was disinclined to expose his inflamed vocal cords to Havana, where a smallpox epidemic was in full bloom. Knowing Adams's apocalyptic frame of mind, King guessed that Henry would find the pox an added attraction—"a spice of horror and danger."

The amiable Theodore Dwight allowed himself to be pressed into service as Henry's traveling companion, and in early March, after leaving Hay in Winter Park, they steamed south from Tampa. "Havana is just my affair," Henry reported to Hay. "I swagger about in a big straw hat, and wallow in Cuban dirt." He conceded that the palm trees were more handsome than he had imagined and that the ancient women in black mantillas were "just lovely." But the gore of the bullfight repelled him, the shops sold nothing he wished to buy, and he soon fell prey to the "jim-jams"—his name for vile moods that he felt powerless to control. In one bleak moment, he could not stop himself from reminding Lizzie of the bitter predicament posed by his love. "I am, of course, eager to return," he told her, "but probably should come back by way of Panama and New Zealand."

By the time Adams and Dwight returned to Washington in late March, the mornings were warm enough for rides among the forsythia and bloodroot of Rock Creek Park. Ned Hooper's nerves had begun to mend. The breakfast table was rarely deserted, Spring Rice kept Adams well stocked with political gossip, and the jim-jams vanished.

Henry also hit upon a satisfying new medium for expressing his secret love. Senator and Mrs. Cameron's daughter Martha, almost two years old, became a constant caller at 1603 H Street. Sometimes she came in the company of her mother, but just as often a servant carried her over from the cream-colored house at 21 Lafayette Place and left her alone with Adams. In his somber black suits, he crawled on the floor with Martha and showed her how to open the secret panel in his library, which hid a dollhouse. When they tired of playing indoors, they visited his horse in the stable or went around the corner to see the pigeons kept by the Hays' twelve-year-old son Del. By "incessant bribery and attentions," Henry boasted to his diary,

"[I have] quite won her attachment so that she will come to me from anyone. . . . Her drawer of chocolate drops and ginger-snaps; her dolls and picture-books, turn my study into a nursery." The child signaled her affection for her bald, gray-bearded playmate by conferring a pair of pet names: Dordy and Dobbit. Dordy was Martha's approximation of Georgie (which, for reasons of her own, she preferred to Henry), and a Dobbit, she would later explain, was someone who took care of little girls when their mothers were busy.

Martha also became the recipient of numerous playful love letters intended for her mother. In the summer of 1888, when Adams returned to Quincy and the Camerons again went to Beverly Farms, Henry wrote Martha, "I love you very much, and think of you a great deal, and want you all the time." But such bliss was not to be, he said, because "I've grown too stout for the beautiful clothes I used to wear when I was a young prince in the fairy-stories, and I've lost the feathers out of my hat, and the hat too, and I find that some naughty man has stolen my gold sword and silk-stockings and silver knee-buckles. So I can't come after you, and feel very sad about it." Explaining that he was taking care of his mother, he urged Martha to do likewise "for poor mamma does not know very well how to take care of herself, and needs you to look after her, and keep her out of mischief." Dobbit suspected Martha's mamma of misbehavior, he said, "because she has not written to me for a month, and I have always noticed that when ladies do not write to me, they are in mischief of some kind."

Lizzie's silence probably owed less to mischief than bewilderment. Henry himself seemed not to know what he wanted from her. After receiving her last letter, he had told her, "I hardly know which is worse,—to hear, or not to hear, from you; for when I do not hear, I am uneasy, and when I do hear, I am homesick." He longed to see Lizzie but could not face the house at Beverly Farms. Pondering his mother's approaching death and thinking that for three years he had been "sad, sad, sad," he told his diary, "I would certainly be quite willing to go with her." Unable to alleviate his mother's pain or his own, Henry shut himself up in the Adams library and worked on his history. "The frenzy of finishing the big book has seized me until, as the end comes nigh, I hurry off the chapters as though they were letters to you," he told Hay in July. In August, he left his desk only to exercise the horses. Finally, on September 10, 1888, he wrote the last page of his narrative. Like his idol Edward Gibbon, chronicler of the fall of Rome, Adams marked the completion of his great labor out of doors. "I walked in the garden among the yellow and red autumn flowers, blazing in sunshine, and meditated," he told his diary. "My meditations were too painful to last. The contrast between my beginning and end is something Gibbon never conceived." Elation, triumph, relief—he seemed to feel none. Writing to Lizzie, he merely noted that he would return to Washington with the "last volume of my history, finished; and I begin at once to print the whole affair. China looms in the distance."

China might loom in the distance, but that was all Adams knew about it. Apart from learning a few Chinese ideographs, he had done nothing to further his plans. Lizzie loomed in the foreground, as uncertainly as ever. His future in her life promised nothing. Still, Henry found it easier to look forward than back. The act of remembering had become a torture. As soon as he finished his history, he began destroying the diary he had kept since adolescence. (Whether by accident or ingeniously spiteful design, all that remain are entries from 1888 and 1889, which contain several mentions of the destruction.) His past would lie buried until he began remodeling it in *The Education of Henry Adams*.

Restless after months of hard work and bored by the prospect of correcting and proofing nine volumes for publication, Henry tried to lure Clarence King into joining him for a trip to Fiji. King demurred, and when Henry persisted, King confessed that he could not go because he was "in the deepest water."

One of the family situations which with frightful certainty avalanche themselves down upon me is now at its height and as my grave is my only escape from them, I must as I have so many *many* times before, stand by and struggle.

I found myself at 24 years of age with eleven people dependent on me alone. . . . Not merely their maintenance but their whole affairs have rested on my shoulders ever since. As a consequence the quarter of a million I have earned professionally has gone to them, I had to refrain from marrying the woman I wanted to, and now in middle age I am poor and what is worse so absorbed in the hand to mouth struggle

for income that I see the effective literary and scientific years drifting
by empty and blank when I am painfully conscious of the power to do
something had I the chance. . . .

I often think you must feel as if you were mistaken in my capacities,
that you had blundered in fancying me enough above the great democratic level to bother with.

With all the sense of disappointment and the anger at fate there has
grown a sense of shyness about being much with the only friends I care
for—you and Hay; for in spite of his health and your sorrows you both
succeed in your work. I alone seem to fail!

But when King told Hay of his decision not to go to the Pacific,
he said nothing of his tribulations: "Henry Adams wants to go to Fiji
this autumn and with that tragic way he has of jesting, whets my
appetite for the voyage with the promise that we shall drink our
enemies' blood from their empty skulls. He does not seem to know
that enemies are impossible to me among archaic peoples." King
vowed that if he were ever overcome by a thirst for blood, he would
seek out an American female of the Lizzie Cameron type, whose
"liquor sanguine would be thin and cool enough for an August
beverage."

Hay and a few others in the breakfast coterie understood the bond
between Henry and Lizzie, but King knew no more about it than
Adams knew about King's life with the "archaic" Ada Todd. King,
predictably, had never liked Lizzie, and the disdain was mutual.
Aware of King's taste in women, she icily asked why he didn't marry
his cook. King shot back, "Why this had never occurred to me I
cannot conceive, but thank you fervently for the suggestion." Irked
by his broken promises and his habit of bobbing in and out of Washington without notice, Lizzie could not fathom the claims he had on
the affections of John Hay and Henry Adams. "If he were my friend,
I should hate him," she once exploded to Adams.

The Fiji adventure gave way to a less ambitious excursion when
Henry's old friend Sir Robert Cunliffe, the Welsh baronet, decided
to come to the United States in the autumn of 1888. Courtesy of
Henry's brother Charles, they traveled much of the West in the
comfort of the Union Pacific directors' car, taking in the Great Salt
Lake, the Columbia River, and Mount Shasta, whose glaciers King
had charted in his youth. In San Francisco, watching a golden sunset,

Henry pointed to the rolling Pacific and dared Cunliffe to run away with him to China. "Ignominiously he turned his back on all that glory, and set his face eastward for his dear fogs," Henry wrote home to Lizzie.

The travelers passed election day among the big trees of Yosemite. Adams preferred President Grover Cleveland to the Republican challenger, Benjamin Harrison, but did not care enough about either of them to cast a ballot. Since America had prospered under Cleveland's stewardship, the populace was little roused by debates over tariffs and Treasury surpluses. The lower orders of the Republican Party launched an attack on Cleveland's morals, spreading rumors that he beat his wife. An astonished Cecil Spring Rice described the situation for his friends in England: "[Mrs. Cleveland] is said to have fled from Washington in the summer because he became unsupportable and also to have been obliged by him to send away a maid who interfered in her behalf and got a cut on the head with a broomstick. The fact is that, as anyone can see, they are a most devoted couple." Springy concluded that no other country in the world had "such a base system of politics and politicians."

Squinting at the world through steely blue eyes, Benjamin Harrison, lawyer and Sunday school teacher, radiated all the warmth of Mount Shasta's glaciers. A campaign joke had it that everyone who shook his hand went away a Democrat. Not even a partisan as devout as John Hay could work up enthusiasm for him. "Benjamin Harrison got there, and I suppose I must vote for him," he sighed to Adams after the GOP convention. In the end Cleveland captured almost one hundred thousand more popular votes than Harrison, but Harrison carried the electoral college by a wide margin.

Back home on Lafayette Square after his nine-thousand-mile ramble with the baronet, Henry gazed across Lafayette Square to the White House and penned a bitter valediction to the business of his forefathers. "My heart still reproaches me for being so unsympathetic to you about your political interests," he wrote to Cunliffe, "but you ought to reflect that I am positively brutal to my own people about ours. . . . To me, politics have been the single uncompensated disappointment of life—pure waste."

March 4, 1889, the raw and windy day when Harrison took office, found Henry sequestered in his study, where he had been for weeks. He proofed pages of his history as they came from the printer, re-wrote his final chapters, and bombarded his publisher, Charles Scrib-ner, with instructions reminiscent of the edicts he had issued to H. H. Richardson when his house was under construction. Scribner was to use a particular printer and a paper selected with the advice of John La Farge. He was also told not to mark the chapters with Roman numerals, which struck the author as "rather clumsy."

As a master of irony, Henry must have savored the joke played by the gods who sent a new generation of politicians flocking to his breakfast table at the very moment he announced his wish to be shut of them. Henry Cabot Lodge had come to the capital in 1887, a freshman congressman from Massachusetts. Tall and spare, Lodge carried himself with the hauteur of the Cabots, who had grown rich trading rum and molasses in the early days of the Bay Colony. His patrician speech, his spike of a beard, and his close-fitting suits with the trouser pockets foppishly cut on the horizontal made an indelible impression on his House colleagues. They loathed "Lah-de-dah" Lodge on sight. Rigid and self-righteous, Lodge believed himself ruled by no passion but the national good. But with his old history professor Henry Adams and other friends, Lodge was known as a genial host, and, when political *bêtes noires* did not rear their fractious heads, he could work considerable charm as a guest.

The other newcomer, appointed to the U.S. Civil Service Com-mission by President Harrison, was Theodore Roosevelt, just turned thirty. He arrived in Washington on a Monday morning in May 1889, inspected the three offices set aside for the commissioners, and took the biggest one for himself. Before the week was out, Roosevelt had dined with the Lodges, where he encountered Henry Adams, whom he had met years before on the Nile, when Roosevelt was a boy and Adams was on his honeymoon. To Adams, the barrel-chested young dynamo from New York was an object of pity. At the *North American Review,* Adams had championed civil-service reform for years to no avail. Seeing the idealistic gleam in the eyes behind the pince-nez and listening as the innocent declared his determination to wipe out the evils of patronage, Henry had only one thought: "the poor wretch."

Though Roosevelt was no less sure of his godliness than Cabot Lodge, he had none of Lodge's remoteness. To grasp the difference between the two, one had only to ride with them in Rock Creek Park. Both were excellent horsemen, but Lodge moved with the grace of an English country squire while Roosevelt favored the thundering style he had acquired among the buffalo herds and cowboys of the Wild West.

Roosevelt's uninflected exuberance would eventually grate on Henry's nerves, but for the moment Adams was taken with the young commissioner and his "sympathetic little wife," Edith. The three quickly discovered their shared affinity for Cecil Spring Rice, who had been best man at the Roosevelts' wedding. When Adams learned that Theodore and Edith had not yet found a house in Washington, he tried to persuade them to move into 1603 H Street. They declined but soon joined the Lodges, Hays, and Camerons as part of the breakfast ensemble.

Bored by the political fulminations of Lodge and Roosevelt, Henry repeated scarcely a word of their doings in his letters. But he was instantly curious about their experiences as authors. Lodge's *Life of George Washington* and the first volume of Roosevelt's *Winning of the West* appeared to wide acclaim in 1889, and Adams marveled to discover that they *enjoyed* the hoopla. "[B]oth Cabot and Teddy Roosevelt are on the shop-counters in apparent self-satisfaction," he wrote to Hay, adding that he felt "sick" to think it would soon be his turn for "that disgusting and drivelling exhibition of fatuous condescension."

Henry's protest was sincere—to a point. He had concealed the authorship of *Democracy* and *Esther* for several reasons, including a wish to avoid publicity. But his complaint to Hay veiled deeper fears of rejection. Though he feigned indifference to public approval and dismissed the nine-volume *History of the United States of America during the Administrations of Thomas Jefferson and James Madison* as "my poor, stupid maunderings," he could hardly have felt apathetic about the appearance of a work that had consumed a decade of his life. Nonetheless, in the fall of 1889, when his first two volumes were greeted by virtually unanimous praise, he held his pose, stubbornly refusing to confess his pleasure.

★   ★   ★

While John La Farge moaned that Henry's history chronicled the
most tedious era of America's past, the fact was that Adams had set
out to probe an intriguing pair of questions: Who were these new
Americans, and what would become of them? To find out, he had
consulted periodicals, travel books, census figures, speeches, economic data, diplomatic and military archives, letters, diaries, memoirs, congressional records, and court proceedings. The result was a
saga as remarkable for its detail as its sweep. Introducing President
Thomas Jefferson, he focused on his clothing, noting that

> Jefferson, at moments of some interest in his career as President,
> seemed to regard his peculiar style of dress as a matter of political
> importance, while the Federalist newspapers never ceased ridiculing
> the corduroy small-clothes, red-plush waistcoat, and sharp-toed boots
> with which he expressed his contempt for fashion.
>
> For eight years this tall, loosely built, somewhat stiff figure, in red
> waistcoat and yarn stockings, slippers down at the heel, and clothes
> that seemed too small for him, may be imagined . . . sitting on one
> hip, with one shoulder high above the other, talking almost without
> ceasing to his visitors at the White House. His skin was thin, peeling
> from his face on exposure to the sun, and giving it a tettered appear-
> ance. This sandy face, with hazel eyes and sunny aspect; this loose,
> shackling person; this rambling and often brilliant conversation, be-
> longed to the controlling influences of American history, more nec-
> essary to the story than three-fourths of the official papers, which only
> hid the truth.

Contemplating Pierre L'Enfant's ambitious plans for the city of
Washington, Adams was struck by the "contrast between the immensity of the task and the paucity of means," a gap which led
visitors in 1800 to suspect that "the nation itself was a magnificent
scheme."

As a New Englander and an Adams, Henry could not bring himself to make heroes of Jefferson and Madison, both Virginians. Adams was willing to grant the success of Jefferson's first term, but
only because it allowed him to crow that the triumph owed less to
Jeffersonian ideals than to his embrace of such notions as a strong
central government. Madison was stingingly portrayed as the man
who mismanaged the War of 1812. Adams was swayed less by the

American victory than by the British burning of the White House, Madison's humiliating flight from the capital, and New England's threat to secede.

Closing his history with an essay on American character in 1817, Adams observed that the traits of "intelligence, rapidity, and mildness seemed fixed . . . and were likely to become more marked as time should pass." He still wondered what this new race would become. "They were intelligent, but what paths would their intelligence select? They were quick, but what solution of insoluble problems would quickness hurry? . . . They were mild, but what corruptions would their relaxations bring? . . . What interests were to vivify a society so vast and uniform? What ideals were to ennoble it? What object, besides physical content, must a democratic continent aspire to attain? For the treatment of such questions, history required another century of experience."

Adams had written a classic, and his fellow historian Francis Parkman was one of the first to tell him so. "If the public is not an ass, as it is apt to be, it will see that you have laid it under a great and lasting obligation," he predicted. John Hay pronounced Henry's style "perfect, if perfect is a proper word applied to anything so vivid, so flexible, and so powerful. I never expected to read anything which would give me so much pleasure."

The achievement seemed to delight everyone but the author. "It is evidently a horrible thing to finish one's magnum opus," King told Hay after hearing from Adams in the fall of 1889. "I who will never begin mine may always have the gentle tonic of perpetual gestation, the soft genial pride of an important bellyful, with none of the throes of printing and none of the ghastly hollowness of collapsing sides. . . . I wonder if after all my crippled life isn't well enough and if the peace of obscurity which gathers about me, isn't worth as much as anything I might achieve if fate were suddenly to undo my fettered hands." As unhappy as he was, King said, "I am a comic opera beside Henry Adams whose grim gray scorn of this universe seems to me very ashen and disembodied."

Although some of Henry's gloom could be traced to his self-consciousness in the face of publicity, his largest regrets sprang from a sense that the volumes written after Clover's death did not measure up to the ones written before: "the light has gone out," he told

Lizzie. "I am not to blame. As long as I could make life work, I stood by it, and swore by it as though it were my God, as indeed it was."

Once the first two volumes appeared, Adams announced that he was putting down his pen. "With the year 1890 I shall retire from authorship," he told Henry Holt, who had published *Democracy* and *Esther*. "As an occupation I can recommend it to the rich. It has cost me about a hundred thousand dollars, I calculate, in twenty years, and has given me that amount of amusement. In July I sail from San Francisco for new scenes and adventures."

China promised not only a change of scene but much-needed release from the growing tensions of clandestine love. Between Lizzie's determination not to divorce Don and Henry's resolve not to sully her reputation, there was little room for expression or growth. Their love was like some rootbound plant. Even the most innocuous encounters had to be arranged from the point of view of the tale bearers. In the summer of 1889, when Lizzie announced that she planned to visit Newport en route to Beverly Farms, he suggested she send Martha to him in Quincy. "You can pick her up in passing," he proposed. "We will give you quarters for a night, if it is proper." At fifty-two, he considered himself "much too dull, too solemn and too old to be suspected of impropriety," but he urged her to consult the matrons of Newport if she had any doubt on the point. She decided not to visit him. That fall, in order to escort Lizzie and Martha from Boston to New York, where he would hand them over to Don, he felt obliged to cast himself as gallant friend of the family. He managed to steal a few hours with Lizzie among the Rembrandts of the Metropolitan Museum, but he was careful to include John La Farge in the excursion.

The long separations imposed by Henry's three summers in Quincy and the Camerons' sojourns in Beverly Farms and elsewhere provided at least one consolation: the gossip mills were left without grist. Perhaps during Henry's long stay in China they would cease to churn altogether.

Limitations and frustrations notwithstanding, Henry was too much in love with Lizzie to stand by his original plan of passing the rest of his days in the Celestial Empire. By the spring of 1890 he had made up his mind to visit the South Seas first then travel to India.

From there he would retrace Marco Polo's route to Peking. He reserved the right to come home if boredom set in, and his breakfast circle understood that "boredom" meant loneliness for Mrs. Cameron.

As his departure approached, Henry grew wistful and tense. "Our little family of Hays, Lodges, Camerons and Roosevelts, has been absolutely devoted to each other, and as I was the one to be lost, I came in for most of the baa-lamb treatment," he wrote to a friend. For the first time since Clover's death he found himself among intimates "so closely connected as to see each other every day, and even two or three times a day, yet surrounded by so many outside influences and pressures that they are never stagnant or dull." Gamely he declared himself "glad to close up my literary existence so cheerily. In Washington nothing lasts; and one should, like a man-of-the-world, bid good-night before the other guests are gone and the hosts are tired."

Hay saw no profit in Henry's defection. "That pleasant gang which made all the joy of life in easy, irresponsible Washington, will fall to pieces in your absence," he mourned. "You were the only principle of cohesion in it. All its elements will seek other combinations except me, and I will be left at the ghost-haunted corner of 16th and H."

Once again John La Farge would accompany Adams in his wanderings, and once again La Farge's chaotic business affairs would delay their departure. Henry whiled away the days indexing his history. In the evening he strolled across the square to 21 Lafayette Place for a julep with Lizzie and Don. Chastely they sat on the veranda, watching fireflies and listening to the spirituals that floated through the summer night.

At the end of July, when the heat forced the Camerons to retreat to the mountains of Maryland, Henry paid them a brief visit. Coming home, he found the city "luridly solitary." The Hays were at Lake Sunapee, the Roosevelts at Oyster Bay. The Lodges were on Boston's North Shore, near Beverly Farms, as were Spring Rice and the entire British legation.

With La Farge's promise that they could leave New York on August 16, Henry headed north to Boston, ostensibly to bid farewell to his family. His brother Brooks was using the house at Beverly Farms, which displaced the Camerons, who had settled in a hotel nearby, on

the rocky coast at Manchester. A short meeting with Lizzie filled
Henry with unappeasable longing. Desperate for one more encounter, he rose at dawn to send her a telegram. Could she see him before
he boarded the afternoon train to New York? There was no reply. "I
felt that it would not reach you," he admitted in a note written a few
minutes before his train left. "The mere hope of seeing you again
made me try the experiment, but it was foolish, for the disappointment is worse than the regret."

A week later, Adams and La Farge went down to the piers of San
Francisco and boarded their steamer for Honolulu. In his last letter
before sailing, Henry made no declaration of love except for a restrained "you know in advance all that I have to say." The night
before, descending the hotel staircase, he had been seized by a desire
to see Martha, he said, knowing that Lizzie would read herself into
the scene. Nor would she miss his presence in the sonnet he enclosed.
His subject was Eagle Head, a rocky point near Manchester, where
the "flashing sea," which longed to embrace the cliff, was "Most
beautiful flinging itself away."

15

An American Gentleman

*A*s California slipped into the fog banks behind Adams and La Farge, John Hay sat on the dark green slope of Mount Sunapee and took stock of his life. He had a wife and four children who adored him. His bank accounts ran into the millions. For three years he had known immense literary celebrity while the *Century* magazine serialized the life of Lincoln he had written with John George Nicolay. The figure in his mirror was still trim, the hair still dark brown, the smile as quick and warm as a boy's. Even age seemed to weigh in his favor: he would soon be fifty-two, the point at which a man's charms reached their peak—or so he had read in Balzac.

Hay could not taste the joy of any of it. Staring into the black stillness of Lake Sunapee, he saw his life as a failure—the sum total of a long column of blunders, accidents, and missed opportunities. "I cannot tell you how my heart sinks at the thought of your going away without me," he wrote to Adams. "I recognize it as the last ringing of the bell. I now feel that I shall never go west, and thence east. I shall never see California nor the Isles of the Sea." Clarence King tried to console him with the promise that they would make their own Pacific odyssey someday, but Hay knew better: "King will never be ready, nor will I."

Obliged to pass up the trip in order to oversee the construction of a house at Lake Sunapee, Hay gradually surrendered to the pleasures of rowing and swimming with his children and of watching them climb trees, play Indians, and explore the uninhabited islands of the lake. He bandaged their cuts and caressed their bruises and at night sang them Civil War songs in his clear, sweet voice. "Mrs. Hay has once more proved her superiority to me in practical sagacity," he admitted to Adams. "This sojourn which I regarded with horror has turned out rather agreeable."

The children seemed as exotic to him as any cannibal Henry Adams might meet in the South Seas. Alice, ten and fearless, plucked green snakes from the hillsides and curled them around her arms as bracelets. Five-year-old Clarence whistled and sang for anyone who would listen, and his sense of humor could not have failed to delight his father. Ill with the chicken pox, he announced that he did not like the name and commanded the family to refer to his affliction as the "Yabbit Pox."

"Poor old Del," as his father referred to him, was a bit of a disappointment. Soon to turn fourteen, he was heavyset and sluggish and seemed to be scowling even when he was not. Knowing that he would never distinguish himself as a student, the boy's parents prayed only that he might learn enough to escape being a dunce. Father and son ventured down to Boston to shop for fishing tackle, but Del enjoyed neither the expedition nor the prospect of Sunapee bass tugging at the line.

Hay's favorite was Helen, a beguiling, dark-eyed imp of fifteen. She was "useless and incapable as a Sultana," he told Adams, "but so bright and cheery that she is well worth her keep. I do not think I would like her better if she had the moral worth of a regiment of Cordelias." As far as a father could tell, Helen's chief fault lay in her attractiveness to "the measliest set of pinfeather boys" he had ever seen. During a summer visit with her friend Constance Lodge, a dozen boys vied for the honor of taking Helen for a walk along the cliffs on her last night in Nahant. She said yes to all of them. When Cabot and Nannie Lodge found out, they insisted that she entertain the boys at the house. On the appointed evening, the youths assembled on the deep porches facing the sea and filled the night with song. Cabot did not realize until very late that the music was intended to camouflage Helen's comings and goings. She had been taking the boys, one by one, for the promised walk on the cliffs. Amused to find himself outmaneuvered, Cabot contented himself with eavesdropping, and his worries about Helen's ability to fend for herself must have melted when he heard her explain to an admirer, "I am a tough, and I come from a tough place, and I live in a tough street, and the farther you go the tougher it gets, and I live in the last house."

Pondering architect's drawings and negotiating with contractors in the summer of 1890, John Hay often found his thoughts drifting to the Lodges' cavernous wooden house on the crags of Nahant. Only Henry Adams and Lizzie Cameron knew it, but John Hay and Nannie Lodge had fallen in love. In 1887, when Cabot took his seat in Congress, Hay needed only a glimpse to see that Nannie at thirty-seven was easily the peer of Henry Adams's beloved Lizzie Cameron. Her dark hair was swept into a loose knot at the back of her head, her skin was a pale, pure ivory, and her eyes, according to John Singer Sargent, were an "unforgettable blue"—verging on violet. Mesmerized by "the kindness and intelligence of her expression," Sargent would always regret that he had not painted her. With her elegant silk gowns, perfect carriage, and aquiline nose, Nannie looked as queens ought to look but never did, said Theodore Roosevelt.

Intellectually, none of the women of Lafayette Square was a match for Nannie Lodge. Growing up in the erudition of Cambridge, Anna Cabot Mills Davis read voraciously and could toss off classical quotes with as much aplomb as a university man. The daughter of a rear admiral, she could also hold her own when the talk turned to naval affairs. Cabot, her distant cousin and childhood sweetheart, routinely asked her to pass judgment on his speeches. Whatever she thought inferior he tossed into the fire and rewrote. Sensing—correctly—that the cure for Cabot's arrogance lay beyond her powers, Nannie settled for undercutting his ferocity at strategic moments by addressing him as "Pinky."

By the summer of 1890, Hay and Nannie were deeply in love. Taking a cue from Henry Adams and Lizzie Cameron, Hay was careful not to see Mrs. Lodge alone. In Washington, Professor Adams and Colonel Hay escorted Mrs. Cameron and Mrs. Lodge to

John Hay in his prime. WESTERN RESERVE HISTORICAL SOCIETY, CLEVELAND, OHIO

concerts and museums while their husbands toiled nobly on Capitol
Hill. After their outings, the quartet frequently retired to Adams's
house, where, as far as anyone else knew, they comported themselves with perfect respectability.

But the story that unfolds in Lizzie's letters to Henry in the South
Seas is not a tale of innocence. At the end of August, as Adams and
La Farge steamed into Oahu, the Hay family descended from their
New Hampshire mountain and boarded a train for Nahant. "John
and Nanny got a little walk together but on the whole behaved
extremely well," Lizzie reported. In October, the Camerons journeyed to Cleveland to visit Lizzie's family and found the Hays in
residence on Euclid Avenue. They had come to Ohio to enroll poor
old Del in a new boarding school. Clara, handsome and uncharac-
teristically chatty, seemed not to have guessed at her husband's infidelity, but Lizzie was troubled to find that everyone else in
Cleveland appeared to know about it. "I hate to hear it here in Mrs.
Hay's home," she told Henry. Hay, just back from duck hunting and

looking "brown and well," was eagerly anticipating a trip to New York for a banquet in honor of Henry Morton Stanley, the great explorer of Africa. Nannie and Cabot would also be in New York. "It *is* rather a coincidence that Mr. Hay must start on the same day," Lizzie remarked. Hay and the Lodges planned to stay on for the horse show, which opened the following week. Cabot was an avid equestrian, but Hay had never displayed an interest in horses.

There had been a similar rendezvous in New York the year before, when Hay gave a dinner at the Knickerbocker Club for three American artists who had won medals at the Paris Exposition. Nannie had gone to New York at the same time, "leaving Cabot to run Congress," as Adams discreetly put it.

Returning to Lafayette Square after the horse show, Hay dismantled a crate from Italy and gingerly lifted out a painting in a circular gilt frame. "My big Botticelli has come and is hanging on the stairs," he informed Adams. "It is a beautiful thing—a picture of the first importance. I lie awake nights fearing it will warp and get up in the morning to see if the convexity has become critical during the night." Roosevelts and Camerons were summoned to view the Madonna and Child, which glowed against the rich paneling of the foyer. Hay arranged to sit by Lizzie at dinner, and they spent the evening talking of Adams. "He says that there is a big hole in his life where you dropped out of it," Lizzie wrote. "I understand that."

By going away, Adams created a labyrinth of complications in the romance of Colonel Hay and Mrs. Lodge. At the end of January 1891, Hay took Lizzie aside at a party to confide that Clara was about to leave for Cleveland. He had planned a series of lunches, concerts, and plays with Nannie, and he wanted Lizzie and someone else to go with them. "But we cannot decide upon the fourth man," Lizzie told Henry, "and Mr. Hay and Nanny seem to think it very stupid of me not to like anyone well enough to spend long hours with him alone. Oh, how I miss you!" For a breakfast at the country club, they exasperated Lizzie by turning to Ward Thoron, a young man she considered a fuddy-duddy. "Have I come to that?" Lizzie asked. "You *must* come home! *When* are you coming? I cannot endure it forever." Before leaving town, Clara Hay had introduced another obstacle by accepting an invitation for John on one of the evenings he

*Mrs. Henry Cabot Lodge (known as Nannie), one of the most popular women in Wash-
ington and a particular favorite of John Hay.* REPRODUCED FROM THE LETTERS AND
FRIENDSHIPS OF SIR CECIL SPRING-RICE, EDITED BY STEPHEN GWYNN

had planned to spend with Nannie. "I cannot get out of it without a
disagreeable squirm," he told Lizzie. "I can only curse the day I was
born and give up trying to be happy." Ultimately, the lovers and
their accessory were forced to the most dire extreme—inviting the
cuckold himself. "Cabot has to be the fourth man in all these parties,
and it is a little fatiguing for me," Lizzie reported. Though Lizzie did
not appreciate the farce, the high-pitched cackle of Henry Adams
must have been audible from one end of Tahiti to the other.

Two political imbroglios made Cabot even more contentious than
usual in the winter of 1890–91. The first was a consequence of a high
tariff, which had begun to have a paradoxical, and wholly unintended, effect on national life. As Cecil Spring Rice noted, America's
steep duties on imports had accelerated "the pauper emigration from
Europe, as a number of industries have been seriously hurt there and
the workmen are flocking over. The feeling against immigration is
very strong indeed here." Cabot, declaring that the country was
being overrun by "undesirables"—namely Slavs and Italians—

announced that he did not intend to stand by and watch "the quality of American citizenship decline." Nor would he tolerate "a system which is continually dragging down the wages of American labor by the introduction or the importation of the cheapest, lowest, and most ignorant labor of other countries." To staunch the flow he introduced a bill requiring newcomers to be literate in their native language. The measure met a well-deserved death on the desk of President Cleveland, who vetoed it, but the notion of racial purity endured as one of Cabot's most infuriating obsessions.

Lodge was also smarting from the defeat of a nobler effort, a bill to provide federal supervision of polling places in order to assure that Southern Negroes cast their ballots unmolested. As a member of the party which had freed the slaves and a proud heir of Boston's anti-slavery movement, Cabot was genuinely appalled by the harassment of Negro voters—and astonished to find that almost no one in Congress shared his views. White Southerners felt they had nothing to gain by broadening the Negro franchise. Northern Democrats feared the bias of election officials appointed by a Republican administration. And Northern Republicans darkly forecast economic upheaval. As Don Cameron bluntly put it on the floor of the Senate, "Northern capital has been flowing into the South in great quantities, manufacturing establishments have been created and are now in full operation, and a community of commercial interest is fast obliterating sectional lines. . . . The Election Law would disturb this desirable condition." Pinky in high dudgeon struck Nannie as "pretty amusing," but Lizzie came home from an evening of his righteous company feeling tense and drained.

Whatever Clara Hay's suspicions of her husband's infidelity, they did not show in her appearance. "Mrs. Hay is looking too stunning this winter," Lizzie told Henry. "She is really superb." In seventeen years of marriage Clara had barely changed. At forty-one, she was still quiet, docile, pious, and dull. Hay had grown as bored with her tranquility as he was with the rest of his existence. She still refused to go out on Sundays, even for a sedate meal with such intimates as the Roosevelts. Her robust figure, which Hay had once seen as the bloom of beauty and health, had turned irrevocably to fat. Giving up potatoes and bread did not seem to help. During a stay in New York,

Clara Hay with her children Del, standing, *and,* from left, *Helen, Clarence, and*
Alice. JOHN HAY COLLECTION, JOHN HAY LIBRARY, BROWN UNIVERSITY LIBRARY

Hay could not help remarking on how much she enjoyed "a whack
at the vittles of the Hotel Brunswick." In short, Clara was the opposite of the slim, witty, sparkling Mrs. Lodge.

To John it seemed that no matter where Clara was, most of her
time was spent packing to go somewhere else. On Lafayette Square
she pined for Cleveland, in Cleveland she craved the refinements of
Europe, and in English ballrooms she longed for the rusticity of Lake
Sunapee. For years the Hays had gone round and round, a pair of
prosperous gypsies trailing children, servants, and an Everest of luggage. In 1887 they watched Queen Victoria parade through Picca-
dilly for her Golden Jubilee and called on the Andrew Carnegies at
their castle in Scotland. Hay stocked up on Old Master drawings in
London and joked to Adams that he had spent "the last cent I got for
'Democracy' in minerals for Mrs. Hay." The summer of 1888 was
passed in the Colorado Rockies, where Hay had once carved the Five
of Hearts emblem into a boulder. The children learned to ride, they
climbed Pike's Peak, and Hay struggled against another outbreak of
baffling medical symptoms.

After a winter on Lafayette Square, the Hays dove once more into London society, where they met a woman who delighted Hay by announcing that *Democracy* and *The Bread-Winners* were the only American novels worth reading. "I tried to make her believe I wrote them, but it was n.g.," Hay reported to his literary accomplice in Lafayette Square. With his poise and self-possession, Hay impressed a London *Star* reporter as "the embodiment of that perfection of manner which the American gentleman can show even better than the cultivated man of any other nationality."

The Hays visited the Camerons, who were summering in a rented castle near Birmingham, and they renewed their friendship with Cecil Spring Rice. Now attached to the Foreign Office in London, Springy took every opportunity to tell his American friends about the burdens borne by those who managed affairs of state for Her Majesty. One June day had been devoted to a case of jam newly arrived by diplomatic pouch from Russia. The jam jars had burst in transit, Springy told his friends, "and all our despatches together with various silks which the royal family were smuggling in according to their wont arrived dyed a sanguinary red—The messenger thought he was conveying the mangled remains of a nihilist."

Springy was amusing, society was amusing, the *Star* was amusing, but Hay was not amused. Writing to Adams from London, he asked, as if he himself wondered, "What are we doing? Nothing in particular;—we dine somewhere every night; we go to a few big jams where we know nobody, and moralize on the passing show." He reserved his most astringent moralizing for earls and baronets who chattered about social reform while gorging on champagne and truffles. There was, he told Adams, "a touch of comic-pathetic in an aristocrat who thinks he is a radical, sitting gaily on the bough and sawing away at it, between himself and the trunk."

Hay's favorite Londoner was Henry James. Forty-five in the summer of Victoria's jubilee, James had just returned from Florence and his first encounter with the perils of intimacy. For several months he had rented an apartment in the Villa Brichieri, a crumbling mansion leased by his friend and fellow novelist Constance Fenimore Woolson. Before going to Italy, he had written a friend about Fenimore's "immense power of devotion" to him, but he did not seem to realize she was in love.

Both James and Fenimore worried what the gossips would make of their living under the same roof. James's letters emphasized the separateness of their lives and often gave the impression that Fenimore was more of a duty than a pleasure—someone to be "worked in," as he put it. But in a letter to their old friend John Hay, James made no secret of his contact with Fenimore: "I see her every day or two—indeed often dine with her." Fenimore was more concealing. When she wrote Hay, she was full of praise for his Lincoln biography, which was serialized by the *Century*, but said almost nothing about James.

Soon after James settled into the Villa Brichieri, he reviewed Fenimore's new collection of stories, *Rodman the Keeper,* for *Harper's Weekly*. After a few courtly compliments on her "remarkable minuteness of observation and tenderness of feeling," he noticed that she was particularly fond of "cases of heroic sacrifice—sacrifice sometimes unsuspected and always unappreciated" and of "irretrievable personal failures, of people who have had to give up even the memory of happiness, who love and suffer in silence, and minister in secret to the happiness of those who look over their heads." He also detected a fascination with "secret histories" and "the 'inner life' of the weak, the superfluous, the disappointed, the bereaved, the unmarried. She believes in personal renunciation, in its frequency as well as its beauty." James the critic was as perceptive as ever, but in his letters and notebooks he gave no sign of recognizing Fenimore's self-renunciation as the theme of their relationship.

When James went back to London, Hay found him "in good looks and good spirits and full of new schemes of work." But the Tuscan interlude with Fenimore clearly left him unsettled. Shortly after his return, James wrote "The Lesson of the Master," in which a distinguished writer lectures a novice on the sacrifices demanded by the gods of art. It was the Master's conviction that wife and family blocked the path to greatness. The price of immortality was celibacy.

As much as Hay disliked the vagabond life, he had neither the will to refuse his wife's requests nor the ambition to shape their lives along some other line. Throughout their marriage, his career had traced the path of least resistance. As custodian of the fortune left by Clara's father, he felt no urge to strive for the riches of a Carnegie or a Vanderbilt. What he called "the greasy details of money-making" demanded his attention for only a few weeks a year. Enviably free to do as he chose, he let himself be carried along by the designs of others. He had moved to Cleveland at Amasa Stone's bidding, he went to Washington as assistant secretary of state purely from a sense of duty, and he stood in for Whitelaw Reid as editor of the *Tribune* only because he could not summon the force to decline. Without the spur of a collaborator, it is difficult to imagine how Hay would have persevered for the two decades it took to complete the forty-seven hundred pages of *Abraham Lincoln: A History*.

In 1885, five years before the book appeared in print, the *Century* magazine agreed to pay the unprecedented sum of $50,000 for the right to serialize it. The first installment appeared in November 1886, a month after the *Century* allowed a giddy Clarence King to insist that Hay and Nicolay had outdone Boswell and Carlyle. "A Boswell may crawl along at the heel of mediocrity and amuse whole generations with his twaddle and tattle," King proclaimed. "Carlyle could scream his hero-worship in forced, fantastic phrase, and still leave you an utter stranger to his demi-god." But John Hay, master realist, possessed both "poetic vision enough to truthfully discern . . . the whole hidden framework of society" and the ability to "keep his feet always on the solid bottom while wading deepest into the foaming river of life."

At *Harper's*, W. D. Howells refrained from reviewing the biography during its three-and-a-half-year run in the rival *Century*, but when the ten-volume edition finally appeared in the summer of 1890, Howells admired it at length. He lauded the evenhanded treatment of Lincoln's political rivals and the authors' decision to base accounts of certain events entirely on Confederate sources. For Howells, the glory of Hay and Nicolay was that they had captured the glory of Lincoln, who had grown inexorably, Howells said, "to a national proportion, until at his death he stood so completely for his country that without him it may be said that his country would have had no adequate expression."

After fourteen years of writing and four of publishing, Hay was pleased to have the praise of his old friend, particularly since he had warned him that the material had grown "musty and dry." Tired of Lincoln and of writing, Hay cared little about the book's reception elsewhere. "It is out, and out of my thoughts," he wrote to Adams in the Pacific.

Adams never sent Hay a word about the book, but behind the scenes he dropped hints that it deserved serious recognition as well as popular acclaim. When Harvard tried to award Adams an honorary degree for his *History of the United States of America during the Administrations of Thomas Jefferson and James Madison,* he urged the university to bestow the laurels on Hay and Nicolay instead. "Nothing that I have ever done, or ever shall do, will hold its own beside portions of the Lincoln," he insisted to Harvard's president, Charles W. Eliot. As far as Adams knew, "no great man of any time in any country has ever had from his contemporaries a biography that will compare with this whether in scope, taste or literary execution."

"Those gentlemen did not write history," Eliot countered. "They were actors in many of the scenes they described, and therefore, could not be historians. They have prepared invaluable materials for the subsequent historian, and done an admirable piece of literary work; but I submit that they have not written history."

Adams must have known that *Abraham Lincoln,* for all its mass, lacked the grandeur of his own history. Hay and Nicolay had done less to interpret events than reconstruct them, and the style Adams claimed to see was lucid but mundane. Although Hay and Nicolay were both agile writers, they had deliberately muted their natural voices because they did not want readers to sense where one of them left off and the other began. As Hay saw it, the task was to "put facts together without a word of ornament or fancy." The result was seamless—and bloodless.

In the spring of 1890, as Hay slogged through the last sheaves of *Lincoln* proof, he decided to join Adams in retiring from authorship. "I can write no more, I sincerely believe," he told Howells. But as much as he longed to be shut of Lincoln, he dreaded the emptiness of his future. Adams had the South Seas and China to explore. Hay had nothing—no dreams, no ambitions, no plans. As he confessed to Adams, "I envy you many things, but, most of all, that power of making up your mind to do things, and then doing them without any fuss." At Adams's suggestion, Nannie Lodge had been enlisted to try to persuade Hay to dash off a short biography of William Seward, Lincoln's secretary of state. Hay refused. Nor was he tempted by the princely $12,000 annual retainer Whitelaw Reid offered in exchange for casting an occasional eye on the *Tribune* political coverage. "I am growing old and irritable and I hate controversy," he explained to his brother. "A mean personal attack, sent by some sneak in an envelope, makes me uncomfortable for all day." The Lincoln biographer was not as easily incensed as the author of *The Bread-Winners,* but he had had his fill of critics and grievance-bearers while *Abraham Lincoln* ran in the *Century*. Each day's mail brought new annoyances, such as the query from a New England parson who suspected that Lincoln's assassination had been masterminded by the Jesuits. "The whole thing is growing very ridiculous," he grumbled to Nicolay. "Every old deadbeat politician in the country is coming forward to protest that he was the depositary of Lincoln's inmost secrets and the engineer of his campaigns."

Hay was mildly interested in the noisy political passions of Lodge and Roosevelt, but unlike them he was content to stand on the sidelines until someone asked his help. In 1889, soon after Benjamin Harrison's inauguration, Hay had been dispatched to smooth the feathers of Whitelaw Reid, who felt that Harrison owed him an appointment as minister to London in exchange for the *Tribune*'s support during the campaign. Working quietly in the background, Hay persuaded Reid to settle for the ministry in Paris. In the gloomy summer of 1890, when Adams deserted Hay for the South Pacific, the idea that Hay himself would one day represent America in London would have struck him as preposterous.

The following spring, after his winter of thwarted assignations with Nannie Lodge, Hay sailed for Europe alone. "His love for Nannie does not wane," Lizzie wrote Henry. "I am awfully sorry for him." Lizzie was to follow a few weeks later, and she and Hay had made a pact to see each other as soon as she arrived. "I'll talk of you and he of Nannie!" she told Adams. In London, Hay hosted a dinner in her honor, seating her between himself and the silver-haired Bret Harte, who had been dismissed from the Glasgow consulate in 1885 after President Cleveland chanced upon one of his short stories. All but forgotten in the United States, Harte scratched out a living by re-working his tales of the Wild West for English magazines.

From France, Lizzie reported to Adams that she and Hay had gone on "a real Parisian spree. I hope that you are jealous? Please don't tell him I told you, but we dined in *cabinet particulier,* and went in a lower loge to a ballet. I actually felt wicked and improper. He did too, for he felt obliged to follow up the precedent and to tell me how much he loved me. I feel as if we'll always have this delicious secret be-tween us—only I have to take you in."

Back in London at the end of May, Hay suffered a series of fainting spells and what he described as a heart attack. His doctor diagnosed the malady as "nerves" and assured him there was no cause for alarm. Weak and frightened, Hay told Lizzie he expected to die within the year. Lizzie agonized over how much to reveal to Henry, who was half a world away. "I am really afraid that he will die before he gets started home," she wrote. She crossed out "die" and inserted "be ill" but did not obliterate her first choice of words. Adams would have to draw his own conclusions.

Waiting for his ship, which sailed July 1, Hay went to a few parties, rested, took the iron pills prescribed by his doctor, and wrote his wife a letter she would be sure to cherish if he did not survive the voyage home.

I want the days to pass and bring the 1st, so that I can feel that every hour brings me nearer to my beloved ones. I am so weak and good for nothing. I hope your presence and your love will be the medicine that will make me well again. I feel stricken with remorse some times to think how much you have done for me and how little I have done for you. And yet I know it will continue so until the end. I shall bear the ever increasing load of obligation and shall do nothing to lighten it. Yet, after all, you would never have met with a man who could love you more or appreciate more fully your sweet and noble qualities. But that does not make my obligation less. It merely increases it. For seventeen years your true heart, your rich and noble nature, your beauty, has been mine, and have made me happier than it is possible for most men ever to be. And I cannot think what I have done, more than anybody might have done, to make you happier, my darling. If Heaven grants me a return to health and to life, it shall be my study in the future to try to find some way of adding to your happiness. I am

The Hay summer house, Lake Sunapee, New Hampshire. JOHN HAY COLLECTION, JOHN HAY LIBRARY, BROWN UNIVERSITY LIBRARY

not half good enough for you—but I do love you with all my heart and nobody could love you more. God bless and guard you and bring us together again.

Three weeks after arriving home, Hay arranged to go up to Lake Sunapee alone, ostensibly to put an end to the dawdling of carpenters, painters, and paperhangers. He also found time for an excursion to Boston. Writing to Adams, Hay would admit to no more than the extraordinary coincidence of meeting Nannie and a friend in the street. The trio then proceeded to the Somerset Club, where the ubiquitous Cabot joined them for lunch. Firmly in control of the Republican Party in Massachusetts, Pinky was feeling "pretty gay," Hay reported, "and rather enjoys kicking his enemies." Mrs. Lodge was also "in high spirits," which Hay attributed to the news that Adams had decided not to go to China.

But not even the engaging Mrs. Lodge could coax Hay out of his melancholy as 1891 wound to a close. Sitting by the fire on a snowy December day, with Clara embroidering handkerchiefs at his side, Hay asked her what to write to Henry. "Tell him to come home!"

she said. Lizzie Cameron and Nannie Lodge felt likewise, he added. "But what can I do? I can say I hunger and thirst for the sight of you, but that is all. If you are happy where you are, I would be sorry to see you change your habitat. For I feel myself just now the worst company in the world and as if I should not cumber the earth much longer."

16

Tame Cat

On August 30, 1890, Henry Adams and John La Farge and their mountain of luggage ascended a Honolulu hillside to a spacious, comfortable house with a sweeping view of the city and the vast blue Pacific. While La Farge explored their new quarters, fingering mosquito nets in the bedrooms and inhaling the perfume of sandalwood and roses wafting through the house, Adams sulked on the veranda. Hawaii, he feared, would prove nothing more than "a case of Japan aggravated to final dissolution." The streets of Honolulu had been clogged with Japanese, readily identifiable by their blue-and-white kimonos and the infernal clack of their wooden sandals. Nor did he care for palms, he decided. To his ear, they did not rustle or beckon, as the poets insisted, they moaned, like humans in distress.

But Henry's misgivings proved no match for La Farge's enthusiasm. Ignoring his temperamental stomach, La Farge eagerly sampled squid, spooned guava from the rind, and persuaded Adams to surrender to the luscious pleasures of the mango. With the artist as a guide, Henry also learned to savor the infinity of violets in the clouds above the luminous sea (which was "butterfly blue," according to La Farge), the purplish-rose of bougainvillaea blossoms, the brilliance of the lemons, and the "fiercely green" acacia.

La Farge set up his easel on the terrace and quickly discovered the

futility of trying to catch the fleeting light and chaos of color in the
tropics. As Adams watched one watercolor after another turn to
thick purple soup, he deduced that Hawaiian "skies and seas and
mountains are not to be caught by throwing paint on their tails with
ever so accurate an aim. The painter is only maddened by their
evanescence when he tries to fix them." La Farge's sartorial exacti-
tude compounded the challenge. One morning as he waited for his
servant to fetch trousers and slippers, the sunrise he yearned to capture changed into a scene that meant nothing to him. Undaunted, La
Farge went to his easel every day, and with his encouragement,
Henry painted too—stiff little watercolors that reminded him of
young ladies' embroidery.

In a month of climbing, riding, and sailing around the islands of
Hawaii, the only real surprise encountered by the travelers was the
"old-gold girl" who had sent Clarence King into ecstasy years before. Seeking out the spot where King had watched bare-breasted
young goddesses glide down a waterfall, Adams and La Farge found
that the franchise had passed to a troupe of sullen young men who
performed only for money. "The old-gold girl, and all King's illu-
sions of 1872, belong to a region of youth and poetry which no
longer exists in 1890," Adams reported to Hay. "The native is rather
sympathetic and rather pathetic, but is no longer archaic and as yet
affects me little. What is more to the point, I notice that La Farge, in
spite of excellent intentions, evidently fails to feel a yearn towards
them."

So surfaced the first signs of Henry's fear of the fabled sexual
powers of Polynesian women: his relief at finding himself unstirred
and the validation implicit in La Farge's indifference. With Hay,
Adams pretended that his feelings might change, but a letter he
wrote to Lizzie Cameron as he waited for the steamer from Hawaii
to Samoa made it plain why the South Seas female held so little
appeal. "I still cling to you," he confessed. Then, as if worried that
he had gone too far, he reminded her that he would be "wholly
white-haired" when he returned. If she threw him over, he added, "I
shall not struggle."

Lizzie professed not to understand. "You are bound to me in no
way," she insisted. "You went your way free as air and I have no
claim on you but the claim of the weak on the strong. It is for you

to throw me over, not I you. The dependence is wholly one-sided as proved by your going away."

Squeezed between Lizzie's refusal to divorce and Henry's unwillingness to have a sexual tie to a married woman, their relationship had had little room to flourish in the four years since Henry's return from Japan. At most, they offered each other safe haven, Lizzie prying Henry loose from his endless introspection and self-doubt, Henry soothing the hurts of her life with a bourbon-soaked tyrant. Now, with thousands of miles and the possibility of years between them, they were inclined to scrutinize their complicated bond. Both of them were afraid—Henry of being dismissed, Lizzie of being loved with an ardor she could not return. Composing her first letter after Henry's departure, she felt obliged to acknowledge his farewell sonnet on the vain struggle of the waves to embrace the rocks of Eagle Head, but the intensity of the poem made her uneasy. "It isn't every day that one receives lovely sonnets from distinguished writers!" she chirped. Perhaps feeling that she owed him more, she turned deftly to a subject that was certain to please him. Even without sonnets, she said, she considered him a poet of high order. "*Esther* makes me doubt if I shall ever find your limitation." Like Henry's other intimates, she knew that he cared more for the novel than for the entire nine volumes of his history.

Early in October, after ten days on the heaving Pacific, Adams and La Farge transferred from their steamer to a small schooner for the final leg of the voyage to the Samoan village of Pago-Pago. The boat dropped anchor close to shore, and an ebony giant wearing little but an ivory nose-ring bundled La Farge into a waterproof tarp, slung him over a shoulder, and carried him—flailing and protesting—to the beach. When the giant splashed back to the schooner for his second passenger, the diminutive Adams climbed obediently into his arms and held fast to his neck.

With elaborate courtesy the travelers were escorted to the village guesthouse, where a young girl began grating pepper roots for *kava,* the traditional drink of Samoa. Coal oil, Adams thought as he drank, and no amount of coconut milk seemed to wash away the taste. La Farge bravely downed his bowl, but only once. For the rest of their stay he would politely accept the *kava* and leave it undrunk.

In the evening, sitting cross-legged before a kerosene lamp, they witnessed their first *siva*. Out of the darkness sprang five girls naked to the waist, their bronze skin gleaming with coconut oil. Seated in a row facing their guests, the girls began singing and swaying, clapping their hands and extending their arms in all directions. "La Farge's spectacles quivered with emotion," Adams noted. After the performance Henry's cigars and La Farge's pipe were fetched from their lodgings, more *kava* was brewed, and, Henry told Lizzie, "soon we were all sprawling over the mats, smoking, laughing, trying to talk, with a sense of shoulders, arms, legs, cocoa-nut oil, and general nudeness most strangely mixed with a sense of propriety. Anyone would naturally suppose such a scene to be an orgy of savage license. I don't pretend to know what it was, but I give you my affidavit that we could see nothing in the songs or dances that suggested impropriety. . . . Unusual as the experience is of half-dressed or undressed women lying about the floor, in all sorts of attitudes, and as likely as not throwing their arms or their shoulders across one as one lies or sits near them, as far as we could see the girls were perfectly good." At the end of the evening, Adams and La Farge, still in their suits and ties, were commanded to lie on the floor of the guesthouse. The girls covered them with a large mosquito net, left a lamp burning to keep away the evil spirits, and retired to their own well-lighted huts.

When Adams and La Farge moved on to Apia, the capital of Samoa, they sat through *siva* after *siva* without seeing any sign of the lewdness that led the missionaries to threaten the dancers with excommunication. For one performance the dancers deferred to the clergy by covering themselves with banana leaves, a gesture that succeeded only in reminding onlookers of "the world and the devil," Henry thought. Sometimes a dancer favored one of the visitors with a kiss at the end of the performance, an act of boldness invariably followed by an embarrassed flight into the darkness. One evening after the village elders retired, the dancers slipped off their waist-cloths for a moment, but even that struck La Farge as "innocent and childish." Writing to Lizzie about this dance, known as the *pai-pai,* Henry said only that he had been unaroused. For Hay's eyes he furnished more detail. After the usual beginning, the *pai-pai* dancers soon pretended that their waistcloths were about to fall off. "The dancer pretends to tighten it," Henry said, "but only opens it so as

John La Farge struggled valiantly to do the impossible: Capture the grace of Samoan dancers on paper. ISABELLA STEWART GARDNER MUSEUM, BOSTON

to show a little more thigh, and fastens it again so low as to show a little more hip. Always turning about and moving with the chorus, she repeats this process again and again, showing more legs and hips every time, until the *siapa* [waistcloth] barely hangs on her, and would fall except that she holds it. At last it falls; she turns once or twice more, in full view; then snatches up the *siapa* and runs away." Though Henry admitted that the *pai-pai* gave him joy, lust seemed out of place. "The audience is far less moved by it than a French audience is by a good ballet. Any European suddenly taken to such a show would assume that the girl was licentious, and if he were a Frenchman he would probably ask for her. The chief would be scandalised at European want of decency."

For La Farge, the graceful dancers furnished as many frustrations as delights. Over and over he tried to sketch the *siva,* but the lines changed as fast as he could see them. Nor could he capture the shimmering glow of the coconut-palm fire, which bathed the dancers in a "perpetual ripple of light." Looking at his sketches he decided that the effort to freeze exquisite motion on paper was nothing short of "stupid."

Adams and La Farge passed most of their days in the village guesthouse, an oval chamber forty feet long with a high thatched roof. Coral gravel covered the earthen floor, and finely woven straw mats covered the coral. The straw panels that served as walls could be raised and lowered as the weather required. Food was as close as the roof posts, which were hung with oranges and bananas. Eggs were plentiful but elusive: Samoan hens ran free and laid their eggs where they pleased, exhibiting a decided preference for the thick under-brush of the forest at the edge of the village.

The visitors were soon known to everyone in Apia. Young girls came calling, enchanted by such Western appurtenances as the hand-kerchief and the teaball. As soon as the young women understood that La Farge was not a *misonari,* they eagerly bared their chests to pose for him, though they seemed constitutionally incapable of sit-ting still for more than a minute before curiosity compelled them to jump up and admire themselves on the sketch pad. When Adams and La Farge donned the native loincloth, the *lava-lava,* and headed for the beach, children trailed behind in the hope of glimpsing the exotic Caucasian body parts concealed beneath. Their curiosity amused Ad-ams, but the impeccable La Farge was much troubled by his *lava-lava,* which kept slipping its knot and floating away.

Thanks to the natives' familiarity with the *John Adams,* an Amer-ican frigate that had once called regularly at Apia, John Adams's great-grandson and his friend were accorded all the courtesies shown to visiting potentates. The king brought them a large sea turtle, a gift reserved for royalty. But since custom dictated that each present be returned with a more expensive item, the generosity of Samoan chieftains was a mixed blessing. "If I increase my presents, they double theirs," Henry sighed. "They are ruinously extravagant in such matters and of course expect the same style from me."

Adams had come to the South Seas hoping to indulge his interest in anthropology, and the villagers cheerfully allowed him to wrap his tape measure around their heads, arms, chests, waists, hips, calves, and ankles. As he recorded his findings, he was surprised to discover that the women's heads, with a circumference of twenty-three inches, were as large as his own. He was struck by the strength of the women as well as the similarities between male and female phy-siques. "Often in walking behind them I puzzle myself to decide from their backs whether they are men or women, and I am never sure," he told Hay. The gestures of the women were "free and masculine," and they went into battle with the men. As physical specimens, Henry concluded, the people of Samoa were the ultimate aristocracy, and aristocracy was their highest art. They had done "what in theory every scientific society would like to do,—they have bred themselves systematically," he explained to Lizzie. "Love-marriages are unknown. The old chiefs select the wives for the young chiefs, and choose for strength and form rather than beauty of face. . . . The consequence is that the chiefs are the handsomest men you can imagine, physically Apollos, and the women can all carry me in their arms as though I were a baby."

La Farge watched in admiration as the amateur anthropologist diligently probed Samoan laws and rituals. "Web after web I have seen him weave around interpreter and explainer, to get to some point looked for, which may connect with something we have already acquired," he wrote to his family in Newport. "As many times as the spider is brushed away, so many times he returns." After several weeks of fruitless questioning, Henry was convinced the Samoans had "an entire intellectual world of their own, and never admit outsiders into it. I feel sure that they have a secret priesthood more powerful than the political chiefs, with supernatural powers, invocations, prophecy, charms, and the whole paraphernalia of paganism. . . . I never imagined a race so docile and gentle, yet so obstinately secret." Henry accepted his defeat, but he did not like it. "They've no business to exist unless they mean something, and they won't let me know what they mean," he grumbled to Hay. "One cannot live permanently on purple mist and *soufflé*."

Adams and La Farge were also puzzled to find that the voluptuous bodies and perfect climate stirred so few signs of emotion. To La Farge it seemed that the Samoans had facts but no thoughts, and as far as Adams could tell, they possessed "no longings and very brief passions." Nor could La Farge understand why their idyllic existence had inspired no art apart from their exquisite straw weaving. Searching for an explanation, he wondered whether the development of art required oppression and rebellion: perhaps before the artist felt driven to create a new world, he had to feel himself in opposition to the machinations of priests and kings. In their Eden, only recently invaded by the white man, the Samoans had had little to rebel against. *"Après nous les artistes,"* Adams wryly assured his friend.

Hay was thrilled by Adams's letters from Samoa, particularly with his observations on the guileless sexuality of the islanders. Writing to Adams, he recalled a moment when King had said, "in one of his exquisite tirades against women, as a climax of contempt, 'Sex is such a modern affair, after all.' You seem to have come upon it at a moment when it is purely a matter of structure. What a parallax you have got upon it—seeing it as a wholesome fact in Polynesia, as an instrument of mere perversity in Paris, as a sentimental reminiscence in the etiolated society of Washington. A man would need two or three lifetimes to do justice to the impressions you have received."

But Henry's decorum among the old-gold girls filled Clarence King with exasperation. "How detached from this world Henry's letter sounds; the ravelled sleeve of care knitted up into a garment of quieted nerves and softened temper," he wrote to Hay after reading the first Samoan dispatch: "It is too late for him to get a rise from his solar plexus—The girls stir only his gray matter. It is no envy which makes me so assured, it is one of the most startling pieces of apposition I ever heard of—Henry a mere cerebral ganglion *vis-a-vis* with one of the initial centres of human heat. I know these women well enough to realize [their] puzzled wonder as to where the rest of him has gone. When the ganglion has done a-gangling he loves to lie a-writing in the sun and how well he does it—a new response to all fresh stimuli, an art which has become nature, a nature which has become art."

A true anthropologist would investigate with his heart as well as his mind, King said. The cerebral approach would lead to an appreciation of differences between two peoples, but only through emotion could one grasp similarities. "Now Henry is most impressed by the *differences* just as he is in history or politics. The interesting limitations of the natives are his theme just as in all probability if there were a philosophical Samoan he would lie under a coconut tree and spend the cool of the afternoon cerebrating over Henry's limitations, wondering why H. didn't avail himself of the glorious privilege of drifting with the ebb and flow of his emotions, why he had so slender an equipment of feeling, so very dry a light."

Nor did King approve of the watercolors La Farge mailed home to his studio in New York. As he told Hay, he found La Farge's renditions of Samoan femininity memorable only for the "primeval glow" of old-gold flesh.

> All in all I don't care for them and await with feverish impatience the lovely truth Henry's Kodak will not fail to record. How I sympathize with that Kodak! Somewhere in the sacred coil of its umbilical centre, at this hour lies the faint potentiality of a face waiting to be developed by reagents more sensitive than the vision of either of our friends. A face which will touch and enchant me. Its very barbaric indefiniteness will speak a language to me which Henry's letters and La Farge's *too* counterfeit presentments show they have not begun to learn the first low inarticulate sounds of. The results of their trip will in general only illustrate themselves. I hug this belief for I love primal woman so madly that I should have acted with jealousy had they discerned her.

Unwilling to act out King's fantasies, Adams impishly sent him long inquiries about Polynesian geology and saved his most sensuous adventures—tepid as they were—for others. To Hay went the details of the *pai-pai,* and to Lizzie Cameron he told the story of a memorable expedition to a spot known as Sliding Rock. Escorted by a group of young people, Adams and La Farge crossed a mangrove swamp and entered a forest. The horses moved slowly up a steep path, nosing through vines and banana leaves. After an hour of climbing in silence—except for the shrieks and barks of the birds—they heard the rush and felt the swirling cool air of a waterfall. They tethered their horses and followed their hosts to the rim of a cascade that descended in a series of steps, a smooth lava staircase carpeted in green. By the time Adams set up his camera at the base of the falls, the girls were already tumbling over the rocks. Some were barebreasted, others wore necklaces of banana leaves, and others were clad in the shapeless calico gowns prescribed by the missionaries. As Adams quickly saw, the wet dresses emphasized every mound and declivity they were meant to obscure. He fired away with his Kodak even though the rapid motion and patchy sunlight meant certain failure. La Farge planted himself beside the stream and sketched as fast as he could, hoping to capture enough to make a painting later.

For lunch the girls had prepared Samoa's greatest delicacy, *pollolo,*

John La Farge's sketch of young Samoan women playing in a waterfall.
MRS. HENRY ADAMS LA FARGE

a long, thin seaworm that appeared only once a year, at dawn, at a
certain coral reef near Apia. Aficionados took their *pollolo* raw, but
for the visitors it had been mashed and cooked with coconut meat.
Adams gamely spread the dark-green paste on bread, tried a bite, and
swore to La Farge that it tasted like *foie gras*. La Farge, whose stomach had not been the same since his epicurean binge in Hawaii,
confined his repast to fruit and the shrimp the girls plucked from the
pool. After lunch, when a soft rain began to fall, Adams and La Farge
settled under their umbrellas for a smoke. The rain stopped, the sun
streamed through the trees, and the golden swimmers resumed their
games. Sliding Rock was as close to paradise as these two pilgrims
would come.

Paradise preyed on Henry's mind for weeks after the excursion to
Sliding Rock. His nerves were never steady as the calendar moved
toward the anniversary of Clover's death, and after a sleepless night
at the end of November, he rose at dawn to compose a poem for
Lizzie. He began by describing the sunrise and musing on the activities of his friends in far-off Lafayette Square, saving his anguish for
the last quatrain:

Death is not hard when once you feel its measure;
One learns to know that Paradise is gain;
One bids farewell to all that gave one pleasure;
One bids farewell to all that gave one pain.

Adding to the letter on December 6, his "haunting anniversary," he told Lizzie that he had slept little the night before and was "not positively hilarious. I rarely am so on this day; but if five years can pass, I suppose I can stand ten."

As touched as she was by the verses, Lizzie disputed his dismal point of view. "You are not dead, but very alive,—a living presence by my side in many long hours, and I think, I *have* to think, that you will come back," she replied. "Oh, how I wish that it might be soon!" To her immense relief, Don had been reelected to the Senate in November 1890, which meant that they would stay on in Washington, but without Adams and his breakfast table, she rarely saw the Hays or the Roosevelts. Torn between her loneliness for Henry and her sense that she must not burden him with it, she struggled to have it both ways.

> I dared not write to you yesterday. It was one of those days when I felt that you *must* come back. That I could stand it no longer. If I had written I should have said *Come,* I know. Even Martha felt it in sympathy for she talked of you all day, and at tea wanted you "so bad!" I do miss you more and more, and have horrible revolts now and then when I think how the days are passing by, and our lives drawing nearer their end, and all these months are wasted, lost. It isn't life without you. And yet not for worlds would I bid you return if you must return to restlessness and unhappiness. . . . If I could feel that you were happy over there, I would be happy here,—or [happy] alone at least. I must not write in this way, I know. . . . If you let me unsettle you I shall never forgive myself. Now back to trivialities. . . .

The trivialities of her unhappy winter included country club dances for the new crop of debutantes, the botched assignations with Nannie Lodge and John Hay, and several evenings of theater starring Sarah Bernhardt. Inspecting the legendary actress backstage, Lizzie found "a very much dyed, painted smallish woman, very vivacious, very French, and very common." After the meeting, Lizzie was flattered to hear that Madame Sarah always asked whether Mrs. Cameron was present and where she sat, but the pleasure was short-lived. To distract herself, she experimented with photography. Though she had neither the gifted eye nor the perseverance that had enabled Clover Adams to triumph over the limitations of the nineteenth-century camera, she managed, with the help of Theodore Dwight and many sessions in Henry's darkroom on H Street, to make a few prints she considered good enough to send to the South Seas.

If Lizzie meant to please Henry by taking up photography, she need not have bothered. In spite of her interest in the pictures he sent from Samoa, and in spite of Clarence King's hope that Henry's Kodak would capture the essence of Polynesia, Henry had decided that "the photograph takes all the color, life and charm out of the tropics, and leaves nothing but a conventional hardness that might as well be Scotch or Yankee for all the truth it has." Turning violently against the camera—in words that betrayed his fury with Clover for her suicide—he ranted that photographs "kill as dead as their chemicals."

Still, Lizzie's photographs and letters filled him with hope. "Perhaps you may cure me after all, and I shall come back contented and in repose of mind, to be your tame cat, after the manner of Chateaubriand, and various elderly English gentlemen, once my amusement to watch," he told her. "Is it worth your while? Please say yes." Henry drew the image of the tame cat from a celebrated nineteenth-century French love affair between François-Auguste-René de Chateaubriand and Juliette Récamier. In his old age, Chateaubriand, a diplomat and author known as "the cat," was satisfied to be the devoted friend of his former lover.

With his heart in Lafayette Square, Henry could give little thought to the politics and history of Samoa. While he vaguely wished that its archaic condition could be preserved and prayed that the islands would escape "the frantic barbarism of the sugar-planter," he had seen enough to conclude that the old ways would soon disappear. "Gunpowder and missionaries have destroyed the life of the nobles," he told Hay. In the old days, chiefs had battled only with other chiefs. "The idea of being killed by a common man was sacrilege.

The introduction of fire-arms has changed all this, and now, as one of the chiefs said with a voice of horror, any hunchback, behind a tree, can kill the greatest chief of Samoa."

La Farge was more moved than Adams by their talks with the king, who persuaded the artist that the fate of Samoa lay in the hands of the world's most powerful nations, including the United States. "One must go abroad and far away to realize that whenever we wish we are one of the main powers of the world," La Farge wrote in one of his most impassioned letters from the South Seas. "It is on our sleeping that grasping nations like England and Germany depend." Since the western coast of the United States bordered a long stretch of the Pacific, La Farge considered the ocean the "natural property" of the United States. "We must either give up Hawaii, which will inevitably then go over to England, or take it willingly, if we need to keep the passage open to eastern Asia, the future battleground of commerce." Most worrisome were the Germans, whose coconut plantations dominated Samoa's economy. The former German consul had boasted to his American counterpart that Germany feared nothing from the United States because democracies always frittered away their energy in petty domestic squabbles, and because America had neither the army nor the navy to carry out its wishes abroad. "Before you can make up your mind to anything, we shall have taken Samoa for ourselves," the Kaiser's envoy predicted.

Of all the white men in Samoa in 1890, none was more famous than Robert Louis Stevenson. In 1887, after the successes of *Treasure Island, Kidnapped,* and *Dr. Jekyll and Mr. Hyde,* Stevenson and his wife, Fanny, had said good-bye to Henry James and their other London friends and sailed for America. In New York Stevenson befriended La Farge's good friend Augustus Saint-Gaudens, who sculpted a medallion of the writer at work—in bed, propped against pillows, notebook on knee, cigarette in hand. After touring the United States, the Stevensons moved on to the South Seas and in 1889 decided to carve out a small plantation near Apia.

Venturing up Stevenson's mountainside in mid-October, Adams and La Farge were wholly unprepared for the sight that greeted them. The illustrious immigrant's yard was a tangle of burned stumps, the plantation house a mere shanty with an iron roof. The great man was "so thin and emaciated that he looked like a bundle of sticks in a bag, with a head and eyes morbidly intelligent and restless," Henry wrote home to Lizzie. "He was costumed in very dirty striped cotton pyjamas, the baggy legs tucked into coarse knit woollen stockings, one of which was bright brown in color, the other a purplish dark tone." Fanny Stevenson, barefoot, had darted into the house as soon as she spied the visitors in the clearing. She had returned a moment later in shoes but no stockings. "She wore the usual missionary nightgown which was no cleaner than her husband's shirt and drawers," Adams said. Both husband and wife had wild masses of dark hair, and both were sorely in arrears in the matter of baths. Stevenson recognized La Farge's name, probably from conversations with James and Saint-Gaudens, but he seemed unacquainted with the house of Adams. (Learning of this gap in Stevenson's knowledge, Hay urged Adams to be of stout heart: "Bear up under this, like a man, in the interest of science.")

Stevenson, who had long suffered from consumption, bore all the visible symptoms of his disease—eyes gleaming with fever, overly ruddy cheeks, a frantic restlessness. He "perches like a parrot on every available projection, jumping from one to another, and talking incessantly," Adams told Hay. Fanny was also in broken health, afflicted with rheumatism and the effects of poverty, hunger, and the hard labor of clearing three hundred acres of jungle. The immaculately groomed John La Farge was bound to disapprove of the Stevensons' haberdashery, but in Fanny's case, he claimed that his judgment was strictly medical: a woman with rheumatism should not go about without shoes and stockings.

Once they saw beyond the squalor, however, Adams and La Farge were deeply impressed by Stevenson's energy and his devotion to literature. "For months he has sailed about the islands in wretched trading schooners and stray steamers almost worse than sailing vessels, with such food as he could get, or lived on coral atolls eating bread-fruit and yams, all the time working hard with his pen," Henry told Lizzie. Stevenson had "seen more of the islands than any literary or scientific man ever did before, and knows all he has seen." Wondering how the wasted Stevenson could work so tirelessly, La Farge decided he must be an *aitu,* a Samoan devil spirit not bound by the laws of the flesh.

Stevenson eagerly accepted the Americans' invitation to call on them in Apia, but afterward he fretted that too many obstacles stood in the way of real friendship. As he wrote to his friend Henry James in London, Adams and La Farge's guesthouse in Apia was difficult to reach from his mountaintop: "I had to swim my horse the last time I went to dinner; and as I have not yet returned the clothes I had to borrow, I dare not return in the same plight." He also guessed that the Americans would be reluctant to venture up his mountain again because they suspected "the horrid doubt that weighs upon our commissariat department; we have *often* almost nothing to eat; a guest would simply break the bank; my wife and I have dined on one avocado pear; I have several times dined on hard bread and onions. What would you do with a guest at such narrow seasons? eat him? or serve up a labour boy fricasseed?"

While James wrung his hands and wished that the English mails permitted him to send a crate of foodstuffs from Fortnum and Mason, Adams and La Farge gracefully solved the problem by sending food in advance of their next visit. And to La Farge's delight, they discovered on arriving that although the Stevenson larder was empty, the wine cellar was not: Louis and Fanny considered Bordeaux an essential of everyday life. La Farge and Stevenson talked shop for hours and found that they shared the pleasure of regarding themselves as craftsmen rather than artists—men with a healthy tolerance for the compromises one had to make in the course of earning a living. Reflecting on Stevenson's kindness, Adams regretted the shabby portraits he had sent to Lafayette Square and asked his friends not to repeat his remarks. "I never met a man with less judgment," Adams wrote to King, "and on a venture I would damn in advance any opinion he should express, but he is excessively intelligent, amusing, and, to us, friendly, not to say more. Don't abuse him."

Bearing letters of introduction from Stevenson, La Farge and Adams boarded a small steamer for Tahiti on January 29, 1891. As they tossed in the swells of the trade winds, Adams lay on deck in a kimono and tried, without success, to ward off seasickness by reading his way through the stack of novels he had saved for the voyage. Six days and thirteen hundred miles later, he gratefully set foot on the tidy stone quay of Papeete. La Farge was charmed to overhear snippets of French conversation and to see that the shady streets bore names like Rue des Beaux-Arts and Rue de la Cathédrale. To Adams, Papeete seemed "sweetly pretty," but in the blend of Tahitian and French colonial strains he sniffed "a South Sea melancholy, a little sense of hopelessness and premature decay." Compared to the open, good-natured Samoans, the Tahitians struck him as lifeless and sad.

Henry's greatest joy on arriving in Papeete was finding two letters from Lizzie. "You must imagine what I can't write, and be sure you imagine it strong as it is," he told her. She wished he had been in Washington for Christmas, and he shared the feeling. "You can have no doubts on that subject, or, if you have, they must be queer ones. I get no sort of satisfaction from the consciousness that you are much better off to be rid of me." Though he dreaded the prospect of several idle months in Tahiti, he saw no alternative. Since La Farge felt that he had just begun to work well, Henry thought it only fair "to sit still for months at a time to give him a chance."

It was a generous decision in light of the doubts Adams had about La Farge's Polynesian work. La Farge was extremely suggestible, Adams told Hay, and his struggles to capture the scenery usually netted more prose than poetry. As a result of his own mechanical dabbling, Henry could appreciate his companion's finesse, and he willingly entertained the possibility that La Farge's paintings might be the best ever done in the South Seas, but he also believed that an artist was doomed to defeat amid the swiftly changing lights and shadows of the tropics. Each day the natives came to study the visiting painters at work, and to Henry's immense amusement, they saw no difference between his labored watercolors and the work on La Farge's easel.

In the evenings, the guests were usually invited to hear a *himene,* a sort of *siva* with singing but no dancing. Henry thought the hymns more polished than the music of Samoa, but he missed the accompanying movements, which the missionaries had banned. While La Farge hoped to see a secret performance of the old dances, which were said to be more erotic than the *pai-pai,* Adams was convinced that such practices had long since died out. Looking at the dolorous women in their missionary nightgowns, he could not believe that they knew how to dance. The talk of Tahitian lasciviousness was one more Polynesian hoax, he told Lizzie. Noting that he and La Farge were still waiting for their first sexual proposition, he joked that he was "disgusted, for I expected to be quite besieged by splendid young female savages. They are a fraud."

The only bigger fraud was the missionaries' insistence that they had wrought an improvement by introducing Western morality. "I see no use in talking about morals here," Henry declared. "Morals must be a European invention, for no sooner were they introduced here by three English and French ships only about a century ago, than they swept away the entire population in fifteen or twenty years." Tahiti's population had withered from two hundred fifty thousand to ten thousand, and Henry had grave doubts about the survival of the species. Though Clarence King liked to tweak the gentlemen of the Century Club by arguing that miscegenation was the only hope of the white race, the half-breeds Henry saw in Tahiti inspired no such optimism. To his eye, their "whitey-brown" complexions suggested weakness and disease, and Tahitians were in fact susceptible to consumption, rheumatism, and alcoholism. "Rum is the only amusement which civilisation and religion have left them, and they drink—drink—drink," he told Lizzie.

At least part of the melancholy Henry saw in Tahiti was his own. He knew it was perverse to feel restless among silver waterfalls and velvet mountains and the most vibrant colors in the world, but he felt powerless to stop himself. "My mind has given way," he confessed to Lizzie in mid-March. "I have horrors. No human being ever saw life more lovely than here, and I actually sit, hour after hour, doing nothing but look out at the sky and sea, because it is exquisitely lovely and makes me so desperately homesick; and I cannot understand either why it is so beautiful or why it makes me so frantic to escape."

Henry's moods proved as changeable as tropical light, and within a week he had found the cure for his ennui. Courtesy of a letter from Stevenson, Adams and La Farge were presented to Tati Salmon, the thirty-eight-year-old ruling chief of Tahiti. They were instantly smitten. Son of a female chief and Alexandre Salmon, a Jewish merchant from London, Tati had the girth and great rolling laugh of H. H. Richardson. Tati prized Henry James above all other writers, and with his keen intelligence and English education, he had managed to retain considerable power over political affairs in spite of the fact that the French flag had flown over Tahiti for fifty years. "Hebrew and Polynesian," Adams decided, "mix rather well."

Adams was even more taken with Tati's mother, Ariitaimai, hereditary chiefess of Tahiti's oldest and most powerful clan, the Tevas. In deference to Western custom, Tati served Adams and La Farge at table when they came for a meal, but Henry was pleased to see that Ariitaimai, as stately and ladylike as Clara Hay, eschewed this barbarism and sat on the floor. At Adams's request, she recounted Tahitian legends and crooned ancient melodies. Flattered by the attentions of the Americans, Ariitaimai convened a family council and expressed a wish to adopt them. When the family consented, she bestowed the honor in a solemn ceremony conducted in Tahitian and translated by one of Tati's sisters. Adams became Tauraatua (Bird-Perch of God), and La Farge was christened Teraaitua (Prince of the Deep). While Henry knew that his Tahitian duchy was not much larger than the *lava-lava* he now wore every day, the honor was unmistakable. As he explained to Lizzie, the title was "a very real thing, and was borne by Tati's ancestors, and is actually borne now by his second son."

La Farge teased that Henry was becoming "more Teva than the Tevas," and it was true. Having been officially adopted, he now had an occupation: helping the family write its history. "I have at last got them into a condition of wild interest in history," he bragged to Lizzie. "My interest appears to have captured the old lady, who astonished her children by telling me things she would never tell them; and as they had to act as interpreters, they caught the disease one by one, till at length they have all got out their pens and paper, and are hard at work, making out the family genealogy for a thousand years back." Before leaving Tahiti, Adams worked sheaves of notes into a lengthy genealogical discourse interspersed with legends and love songs. One of Tati's sisters was to finish the rest and send it to him for polishing and a private printing. But he doubted that he would ever see the manuscript again. As he told Lizzie, "Energy in Tahiti is a very brief affair." Whether the book was finished or not, Henry wrote Hay that he loved Ariitaimai "with all my heart, and quite admit King's estimate of the archaic woman, if she is the standard."

After eight months of annoying King with letters about everything but the women of the South Seas, Adams was ready to render a definitive opinion for his friend. As far as Henry could discern, the Polynesian woman owned a capacity for "vices and nice impulses" but no real intellect or emotion. She was a creature of whim, as happy to run away from a man as to run away with him. Adams said he had found it amusing to make her acquaintance, but she did not inflame him with desire, and he saw no reason to proclaim her superior to her modern sisters. The irritation King must have felt on reading Henry's appraisal he tactfully kept to himself.

In the spring of 1891 came news that Henry had awaited for months: the Saint-Gaudens sculpture had finally been installed at Clover's grave. Lizzie Cameron thought the pose of the seated bronze figure "strong and calm," and Hay confidently proclaimed it Saint-Gaudens's masterpiece. "It is full of poetry and suggestion. Infinite wisdom, a past without beginning and a future without end, a repose, after limitless experience, a peace to which nothing matters—all are embodied in this austere and beautiful face and form." Stanford White's pink granite stonework for the site—a setting and pedestal for the figure and a long, curved bench for visitors—was equally "splendid in dignity and simplicity," Hay said.

Clarence King considered the statue "far above" any other modern sculpture he had seen, but in the hooded head and downcast eyes he saw bottomless despair. "Would it were not so appropriate, alas, that there is not a ray of faith, not a throb of hope in that gaze," he told Hay. "The tangled complexity of modern emotions, of unillumined doubt, of icy courage play over its nervous features. It is utter restlessness in complete repose. As if the poor woman was sitting there sheltering herself in the folds of her own shroud, trembling perplexed and tortured over the fate of her own soul."

Eager for Adams to see the statue, Lizzie Cameron and Theodore Dwight photographed it, and Dwight rushed off a parcel of pictures. "I could knock his head off," Saint-Gaudens wrote to Adams when he discovered that the pictures were on their way to Tahiti. Upset that Adams would get his first impression of the work from photographs, Saint-Gaudens had hoped to limit the damage by selecting the pictures to be sent, but Dwight, who enthusiastically admired the sculpture, had seen no cause for worry.

As soon as Saint-Gaudens made his vexation known, Lizzie and Henry's brother Charles wrote Henry that the photographs expressed neither the power nor the majesty of the sculpture. Charles had seen the photos first and was horrified. Reduced to paper and deprived of color, the figure looked like "a discouraged and disappointed mendicant, wrapped in a horse-blanket," Charles told Henry. But the "instant I saw the figure a great sense of relief came over me; and it grew upon me during the half hour I sat before it. . . . It is rest,—complete, sudden, painless rest,—after weariness, trial and suffering."

Henry hastened to tell Saint-Gaudens that the photos had not prejudiced him against the work. He had great confidence in Hay's judgment, he added, and "if your work approaches Hay's description, you cannot fear criticism from me." Grateful for Lizzie's assurances, Henry told her that he felt as if he had shed his last anxiety. "If the statue is half what you describe it, I can be quite contented to lie down under it, and sleep quietly with her. At the end of all philosophy, silence is the only true God."

Early in June 1891, as Adams and La Farge prepared to leave Tahiti, Henry faced up to the fact that nine months of separation from Lizzie had given him no clearer understanding of their relationship or their future. For months she had flashed conflicting signals, crying out with loneliness in one sentence and disqualifying her claims upon him in the next. Henry parried adroitly with promises to return—if she thought he should. Unable to lure him back to Washington, Lizzie dangled another temptation. She was spending the summer in Europe and would not sail home until November. Would Henry meet her in Paris?

Aching to see her, Henry decided not to wait for the scheduled steamer from Papeete to Fiji, the next destination on his itinerary. He found a sea captain willing to change course for $2,500 and readily submitted to the extortion. "I am actually starting on a ten-thousand-mile journey to see—you!" the tame cat purred in a last note from Tahiti.

Henry could dredge up little enthusiasm for Fiji, and as soon as he could, he coaxed La Farge aboard a ship bound from Fiji to Australia. In early August they reached Sydney—and winter. Shivering before

By the time Henry Adams and John La Farge reached Fiji in 1891, Adams wanted only to push on for Paris, where Lizzie Cameron awaited him. La Farge had little time to use the sketch pad in his lap. MASSACHUSETTS HISTORICAL SOCIETY

a coal fire and listening to the din of trams and hansoms beneath his hotel window, La Farge framed a wistful conclusion: "Our South Seas days are over."

Adams pronounced the trip a huge success. "To have escaped a year of Congress and high-thinking, by bagging a year of solid Polynesian garlands and materialism, is as sweet a joy as to run away with another man's wife," he told Hay, who was sure to appreciate the analogy. But he pretended that the odyssey had come to an end because La Farge was needed in New York. "[He] is no more eager to come home than I am, and we would both gladly give another year to doing the Malay Archipelago and India; but my conscience says that La Farge ought to go, so I have imposed on myself the contract of taking him to England and shipping him home in October." Nothing was said of the tryst with Mrs. Cameron in Paris.

For two months, as Adams and La Farge hopped westward from island to island, Henry thought of little except Paris, but on his last day at sea, the joy of anticipation turned to anxiety and paralysis. "For the first time I am beginning to feel that the long journey, which seemed interminable, is really ended, and that all the old perplexities, with plenty of new ones, are going to revive," he told Lizzie. "The pleasure of seeing you once more overbalances everything else; but in the depths of my cowardice I feel more than ever the conviction that you cannot care to see one who is so intolerably dead as I am, and that the more you see of such a being, the more sorry you will be that you ever tried to bring him back to life. . . . Men are certainly the most successful invention the devil ever made, and when they arrive at a certain age, and have to be constantly amused, they are even harder to manage than when they are young, mischievous and tormenting."

Landing in Marseilles on Friday, October 9, Henry found several letters from Lizzie, one of which announced that she was enjoying Paris for the first time in her life and another expressing the hope that he would not arrive on Saturday night, when she would be out. "I *had* to go or to boldly say the reason," she explained.

Adams and La Farge reached Paris late Saturday night. For a man who was said to be needed in New York, La Farge showed little desire to go there. Quickly sensing that he was not wanted in Paris, he said farewell and headed for the French countryside.

When Mr. Adams presented himself to Mrs. Cameron in her apartment near the Champs-Elysées on Sunday, October 11, 1891, he was, as he had promised at the start of his voyage, "wholly white-haired." He was also gaunt after fourteen months of living on fish and breadfruit, and his travels had cost him several teeth. Standing before her in his ill-fitting suit, he looked much older than his fifty-three years.

Lizzie, not quite thirty-four, radiated excitement and self-confidence. She had spent the summer whirling from salon to salon, enchanting counts and duchesses, intoxicated by her conquests. With half the world between her and Henry Adams, she had dared to flirt and caress and beg him to come home. He had been wary, but he was not invulnerable, and the idea of her distress was a form of seduction he could not resist. Here he was—impeccable in his conduct but unable to hide the depths of his adoration. Now what?

Neither of them knew. For the next two weeks, Lizzie kept to her round of parties and dinners, paying little attention to the man who had raced ten thousand miles to be with her. Henry played with five-year-old Martha and tried to distract himself with evenings at the theater. At the end of October they moved on to London, where they saw more of each other but quarreled bitterly. "You took me so by surprise the other night," Lizzie wrote from the *Teutonic,* which sailed for America on November 4. "I had no idea *that* was to be our goodbye. I was furious!"

Henry responded in kind. "I am really annoyed that you thought my good-bye abrupt, and had no idea it was to come then. I thought I had told you in the afternoon that my good-bye was intended to be our last words in your rooms, for, later, I should have no chance for more than a mere word of farewell." Pondering the confusion, he decided it was "of a piece with my whole visit,—fragmentary, interrupted and unsatisfactory." He and La Farge had hoped to see each other in London before La Farge sailed on November 11, but Henry was too distraught. After Lizzie's departure he had gone straight to his old friend Charles Milnes Gaskell at Wenlock Abbey, the ancient manor where he and Clover had spent part of their honeymoon. Shut up in his room on a stormy afternoon, he poured out his hurt.

I ought to spare you the doubtful joy of sharing my pleasures in this form; but you, being a woman and quick to see everything that men hide, probably know my thoughts better than I do myself, and would trust me the less if I concealed them. You saw and said that my Paris experiment was not so successful as you had meant it to be. Perhaps I should have done better not to have tried it, for the result of my six months desperate chase to obey your bidding has not been wholly happy. . . .

More than once today I have reflected seriously whether I ought not at once to turn round and go back to Ceylon. As I am much the older and presumably the one of us two who is responsible for whatever mischief can happen, I feel as though I had led you into the mistake of bringing me here, and am about to lead you into the worse mistake of bringing me home. Not that I take a French view of the matter, or imagine you to be in the least peril of falling into the conventional dilemmas of the French heroines; but because, no matter how much I may efface myself or how little I may ask, I must always make more demand on you than you can gratify, and you must always have the consciousness that, whatever I may profess, I want more than I can have. Sooner or later the end of such a situation is estrangement, with more or less disappointment and bitterness. I am not old enough to be a tame cat; you are too old to accept me in any other character. You were right last year in sending me away, and if I had the strength of mind of an average monkey, and valued your regard at anything near its true price, I should guard myself well from running so fatal a risk as that of losing it by returning to take a position which cannot fail to tire out your patience . . . but . . . as I have learned to follow fate with docility surprising to myself, I shall come back gaily, with a heart as sick as ever a man had who knew that he should lose the only object he loved because he loved too much. I am quite prepared to have you laugh at all this, and think it one of my morbid ideas. So it is; all my ideas are morbid, and that is going to be your worst trouble, as I have always told you. Yet I would give you gladly as many opal and diamond necklaces as Mr Cameron would let you wear if I could only for once look clear down to the bottom of your mind and understand the whole of it. I lie for hours wondering whether you, out on the dark ocean, in surroundings which are certainly less cheerful than mine, sometimes think of me, and divine or suspect that you have undertaken a task too hard for you; whether you feel that the last month has proved to be—not wholly a success, and that the fault is mine for wanting more than I had a right to expect; whether you are almost on the verge of regretting a little that you tried the experiment; . . . whether you are fretting, as I am, over what you can and what you cannot do; whether you are not already a little impatient with me for not being satisfied, and for not accepting in secret, as I do accept in pretence, whatever is given me, as more than enough for any deserts or claims of mine; and whether in your most serious thoughts, you have an idea what to do with me when I am again on your hands. . . . French novels are not the only possible dramas. One may be innocent as the angels, yet as unhappy as the wicked; and I, who would lie down and die rather than give you a day's pain, am going to pain you the more, the more I love.

After a week of brooding among the crumbled walls of the medieval abbey, Henry told Lizzie that he wished he had been born in the Middle Ages. "Progress has much to answer for in depriving weary and broken men and women of their natural end and happiness; but even now I can fancy myself contented in the cloister, and happy in the daily round of duties, if only I still knew a God to pray to, or better yet, a Goddess; for as I grow older I see that all the human interest and power that religion ever had, was in the mother and child, and I would have nothing to do with a church that did not offer both. There you are again! you see how the thought always turns back to you."

17

House of Madness

Reluctant to subject himself to the emotional predicaments of Washington, Henry wandered from Wenlock Abbey to the Scottish castle of his friend Sir John Clark, back to Wenlock and London, and on to Paris, where he dined alone on Christmas Eve. His *cri de coeur* had drawn no response, and when he reported, with some amusement, that Sir John thought he should take a wife, Lizzie delivered a second blow by rushing to agree. "You ought to marry," she declared in her first letter from Lafayette Square. "And it is I who say it to you! But I have never thought otherwise, not for one moment. Women are not so cheap and worthless as you think them and fine noble characters do exist who could become that other self about which you used to talk."

La Farge's reacquaintance with reality was less crushing but no more triumphant. For fifteen blissful months, with Adams underwriting their travels, the artist had been spared the indignities of earning a living. He returned to a desk piled high with unpaid bills and menacing letters from creditors. To stave off the fiercest threats, he was forced to sell one of his favorite sketches of the *siva* to Isabella Stewart Gardner, the Boston collector, for $2,000.

Clarence King was thrilled to see La Farge again, gloom and all. The artist was "more and more an interesting phase of humanity,"

255

King wrote to Hay from the Century Club in January 1892. "In Polynesia he evidently did not fully realize the sex side of the great problem of primitive culture. Once back here the women begin to grate on his relaxed and comforted nerves and he reacts instantly by hating them. They annoy and irritate him beyond words, and he begins to reflect and cry out that the brown sister of the palm grove didn't exasperate him at all, and he turns and rends the blizzards that blow into his studio door and then comes up to the Century and talks as I have for years." Though it seemed to King that the South Seas had heightened La Farge's sensitivity (and left him "more unfitted than ever for the practical side of his work"), King still felt that the essence of Polynesia had eluded La Farge: "it is the droll germs of civilization not the full stature of naturalism which have captivated him. I could see with Henry that what delighted him were the things he could be sure the Doña [Lizzie Cameron] would appreciate and enjoy—in short the primitive *culture*. With La Farge it is the gay naif's faltering first steps in social matters that tickle his sense of humor just as a very clever man is charmed with the little ways of children."

Months later, when Tati Salmon came to the United States, King could not resist quizzing him on the Tahitian view of Adams and La Farge. "It is just what I outlined to you when they were in the islands," King told Hay, delighted to have his suspicions confirmed. "They classed them as either angels or demigods without passions or sentiments. . . . Other white men wanted women and didn't care a damn for legends and ghosts. They wanted legends and ghosts and didn't care a damn for women. The like was never seen before and all the old women came to the front and the gamy ones kept in the dark. But, said Tati, coiling his huge anaconda-like arm around me and making my ribs crack, 'If either of them had given me the wink I would have shown them a world they never dreamed of.' "

The Tahiti of Paul Gauguin, who arrived three days after the departure of Adams and La Farge, would have been much more to King's liking. Gauguin soon shared his hut with a thirteen-year-old girl, easily persuading his conscience that she was "the equivalent of eighteen or twenty in Europe." He admired the Salmon family and apparently gave Tati the wink, for he had no difficulty in seeing the erotic entertainments that Adams preferred to think ancient history. Putting the matter as delicately as possible in his South Seas memoir,

Noa-Noa, Gauguin told of nude dancers who whirled round and round the king, aiming to "touch certain parts of his body with certain parts of theirs. . . . The peaceful island vibrates with frightful cries. The falling evening shows the fantastic spectacle of a multitude in ecstatic madness." (La Farge had little use for Gauguin's words or his pictures. *Noa-Noa* was "foolish," he told Adams when he read it in 1906, and the paintings seemed "driven to do something to attract attention. Even their own attention.")

For King, Tati and the South Seas represented a dream not only of uninhibited sex but of escape—from the conflicts of his secret life with Ada, from a seemingly endless string of business failures, from the demands of his hypersensitive mother and her stormy household, from scientific disappointment, and from civilization in general, which he regarded as an assault on human nerves. Since 1889, King's financial affairs had been locked in a downward spiral. Profits at the Sombrerete mine in Mexico, never robust, disappeared entirely as a result of a long, steady decline in the price of silver. In the spring of 1890 King raced to England in search of new capital, but before he could succeed, his partners sold control of the mine to investors in Kansas City.

A partnership with Charles Adams fared no better. As president of the Union Pacific, Charles retained the geologist to evaluate coal deposits and had promised a commission whenever the railroad made a purchase. But when a stock market crash in 1890 forced a reorganization of the Union Pacific, Charles was cashiered and King's services were no longer required. "[T]hat coal arrangement which he had cooked up with your brother Charles, and which he looked forward to as a provision for his declining years, has gone to Hades," Hay told Henry. So, apparently, had five of King's business associates. The "tornado of falling stocks" carried off three of them, a fourth perished in a train wreck. The last suffered a fate unknown, but, said Hay, "each in his agony kicked over a full pail of milk which King had been a year in drawing."

A Clarence King defeat always seemed to trace the same arc: just as he prepared to harvest his riches, they were snatched away. By King's account, the Sombrerete had been sold at the very moment he had reached an understanding with European financiers. Now five unexpected deaths had obliterated a year of hard work. Fortune kept one step ahead no matter how swiftly he ran. Not for him the self-flagellation of Charles Adams, who willingly shouldered the blame for the Union Pacific debacle. "I lack combativeness," Charles admitted. "I get into a fight easily enough; but, being in it, I lack desperate courage. Neither am I alert and ready. I fail because I cannot make up my mind on the instant and my reserves are not at my command." King preferred to fault the malign hand of destiny.

Hay knew that hedonism and distractability contributed heavily to King's bad luck, but he was inclined to explain his friend's troubles in kinder terms. "He handles vast interests but cares so little for money that he gains very little," Hay wrote W. D. Howells in 1890, when King went to Cuba to scout minerals for American investors. "A touch of avarice would have made him a Vanderbilt. A touch of plodding industry would have made him anything he chose. Yet I fear he will die without anything except to be a great scientist and the sweetest-natured creature the Lord ever made,—but, come to think of it, that's something."

As the year drew to a close, King seemed as chipper as ever, though Hay worried that his ruin was permanent. Hay had cheerfully advanced him more than $100,000, which King secured with his art collection, scientific books, and stock in the El Paso National Bank. The bank had been organized by King and some friends a few years before in the hope of catching a boom as El Paso grew into a railroad hub. Hay had also done what he could to shore up King's professional reputation, using his influence as an alumnus of Brown University to arrange an honorary LL.D. for the geologist in 1890. But neither loans nor laurels seemed to help. "Every struggle he makes in his world of finance gets him deeper in the mire, costs him something of life as well as of money," Hay had fretted in a letter to the South Seas. "It would be an advantage to his pocket as well as his immortal soul to drop everything and go sailing away to you and happiness. I *think* I would have the inertia to go with him, if he and my wife gave me a good shove. But he will not go."

Ostensibly King refused because of a fresh crisis at his mother's house in Newport. His half-sister Marian Howland was about to marry a young artillery officer against Florence King Howland's wishes. As Mrs. Howland had told Clara Hay in a letter announcing the engagement, she held the lieutenant in the highest regard but deplored a career that "dooms my daughter to poverty and homelessness. . . . The grim realities of arithmetic are veiled by the rosy mists of joyful hope." King felt he ought to be on hand after Marian's wedding in case their mother broke down. True to form, Mrs. Howland suffered from insomnia and frayed nerves for months, forcing Clarence to divide his time between New York and Newport.

But there were deeper reasons for passing up a trip to the South Seas in 1891. On January 24 King became a father for the second time, when a daughter was born to James and Ada Todd of 291 Hudson Street in Brooklyn. King named the baby Grace, probably in memory of the infant sister who had died when he was six.

In the year before Grace Todd's birth, King had taken lengthy business trips to Colorado, Cuba, Europe, and the Mother Lode country of California. Ada, believing him to be a Pullman porter, did not doubt the necessity of his long absences, but she could not help wishing that he spent more time with her. In one of the few letters to survive their relationship, King tried to assuage her disappointment with a reminder of their need for caution. "My darling, I know all your feelings," he told her. "I know just how you love me and how you miss me and how you long for the days and nights to come again when we can lie together and let our love flow out to each other and full hearts have their way. Your letter gave me true joy. I read it over and over and felt like a new man." He had stayed away, he explained, for fear of being seen by people who might do them harm. "The most important thing to us of all others is that the property which will one day come to me shall not be torn away from us by some foolish, idle person talking about us and some word getting to my old aunt. For the sake of your darling babies we must keep this secret of our love and our lives from the world." James Todd's old aunt, like James Todd himself, was a convenient fiction: if a mining bonanza ever did materialize for Clarence King, James Todd could claim that he had finally come into his inheritance.

Except for the vigils at his mother's bedside, King stayed closer to home in 1891, leaving New York only for short jaunts to Boston, Lake Sunapee, and Washington. His Mexican mining failures and devil-may-care reputation hampered new business prospects, and red ink continued to stream into his ledgers. Embarrassed that he had not yet squared his account with Hay, he blamed the problem on his obligations to his mother, "who had four times previously in her life seen everything swept away and who is, I know, incapable of standing another great shock in life. She has suspected that I have been in trouble but I have been forced to keep up appearances with her." Mulling the alternatives, King thought he could auction his art and his geology books, but he feared that that "would be an open advertisement of my ruin and hence enormously decrease the opportunities for further business." A better tack might be to sell the El Paso National Bank stock, which would cover his debts without creating untoward publicity. "I think I shall decide that way but will consider details and act soon," he promised Hay.

The strains of supporting two families on borrowed money drove King from one geological consulting assignment to another, and with no hope of a rest in the South Pacific or anywhere else, he burrowed into an old refuge: intellectual endeavor. Four years earlier, just before his sham wedding to Ada, he had kept up his nerve by composing "Artium Magister," a critique of higher learning. This time he threw himself into the task of writing "The Education of the Future" for the March 1892 issue of *Forum*.

In a single generation, America had progressed from barbarism to "Philistine vulgarity," King observed. As soon as modern men understood the value of science, they made the error of leaving the classics behind. "Science found education blundering peacefully along, cultivating half of the mind with charming results and letting the other die of disuse: it worked the startling miracle of electrifying this dead half into life and bringing it to perfect activity; and straightaway, satisfied with this remarkable achievement, it proceeded to neglect the ideal half which the classics had made so much of, drove it into disuse, and caused it to perish. It has substituted a new sort of half-man for the old one."

Marveling at the speed with which the discoveries of physics were converted to practical use, King predicted, "Energy will be made cheap. Flight through the upper air will be a daily matter of course." But he bewailed the lack of similar progress in the biological sciences. "We have been quick to adopt railways, but we cannot realize heredity; we have eagerly put our ear to the telephone, and been wilfully deaf to the voice of science which is offering to tell us how to make our own children strong and fair. . . . We accept the army of incompetence, of insanity and disease, as a burden from Providence, and think ourselves very virtuous for liberally wasting the pound of cure when the ounce of prevention is utterly neglected. This is the age of energy; next will be the age of biology."

King rambled from one abstraction to another, pointed out the flaws in classical and Renaissance precepts of education, and abruptly concluded that "science will do with education whatever it sees fit." Educators themselves would be the last to devise a remedy for the present deficiencies. The answer, whatever it was, would come "out of biology and psychology. It will be the magnificent gift of science."

As in the past, King's essay mattered less as social comment than as a source of clues to the author's tempestuous life. His hopes for advances in biology and psychology undoubtedly sprang from the disordered nerves he saw in his mother's family, and the death of his young son Leroy, which probably occurred in 1891, may have inspired his wish to know how to "make our own children strong and fair." The essay also offered a revealing glimpse of King's struggle, in the face of mounting odds, to persuade himself not to abandon his first mistress, science. There was no "truer hero," he said, "than an investigator who never loses heart in a life-long grapple with the powers of the universe. It requires courage of the highest order to stand for years face to face with one of the enigmas of nature; to interrogate patiently, and hear no answer; to try all known methods and weapons of attack, and yet see the lips of the sphinx compressed in stony immobility; to invoke the uttermost powers of imagination; to fuse the very soul in the fire of effort, and still press the listening ear against a wall of silence. It is easier to die in the breach."

The financial disasters of 1890 rekindled King's old ambition to join the ranks of these true heroes by making a lasting contribution to geology. In the late 1870s, as the Fortieth Parallel crew finished writing up the results of its pioneering survey, King, at his own expense, had outfitted a sophisticated laboratory to gather the data he needed to test a hypothesis on the upheaval and subsidence of the earth's surface. If he succeeded, he thought he would be able to determine the age of the earth. A British scientist, Lord Kelvin, speculated that the earth had begun in a molten state and was still in the process of cooling. Lord Kelvin theorized that the earth's temperature was hottest at the core and cooled gradually toward the surface. King began where Lord Kelvin left off, imagining a thick *couche,* or bed, forty or fifty miles beneath the earth's surface. As molten substances flowed along the underside of the *couche,* they forced it to expand, which ultimately pushed new mountains through the earth's crust.

To verify his hypothesis, King needed extensive data on such phenomena as viscosity, elasticity, and the effects of temperature and pressure on rocks. Using laboratory equipment purchased by King, scientists had been conducting the requisite experiments for years, and at the end of 1891, King believed that he finally had enough information for a scientific paper on the subject. Availing himself of Adams's invitation to use his empty house, King went to Lafayette Square in December intending to spend ten days hard at work on his essay.

Hay was delighted. For years King had been discussing his ideas with other scientists, and Hay worried that if King did not publish soon, someone else would—robbing him of one more triumph. But King abandoned his essay a day after he started, claiming that he needed to know more about the effects of physical stress on the chemical structure of molecules. Science was perverse, he explained to Hay in a long letter from the Century Club. "When I got hold of the pillars of the temple of geology I pulled down the whole structure. Every previous theory since included goes down in the crash." Whatever its failings, he still believed that his theory was "the nearest to an adequate idea yet evolved, but to fail in one job is to fail in all." His fellow geologists were "like men who aim at a deer and shoot with just enough powder to roll the bullet out of the gun. I make the dust fly right under the deer's feet but I am just as harmless as they. . . . To start as I did to build a structure and come out as a general destroyer is one of the curiosities of investigation."

" 'Viscosity' has gone to the bowwows for the present," Hay reported to Adams on January 6, 1892, King's fiftieth birthday. Noting that King's finances continued to deteriorate, Hay wished he would give up mining and devote himself to science. "He owes nobody but those who will never bother him. But he *patauges* [wallows] in the mire as if his life depended on his getting out—and gets deeper in all the time. I have just written him a letter and talked to him like a Dutch uncle. . . . I am in despair about him. I cannot make him do what he ought, even though I offer to stand the racket.''

Hay hesitated to say so, even to Adams, but he was standing the racket already. King often asked Hay for money, usually $2,000 to tide him through some unforeseen exigency, and just as often explained his failures to repay (on occasion signing himself "Unremittingly yours"). His prospects seemed perpetually rosy, and he never doubted that he would one day make good on his IOUs. But the evidence, had he been able to see it, pointed toward catastrophe.

Among the smaller signs was the shabby state of his once-elegant wardrobe. During a visit to Newport in the summer of 1892, he had had to decline an invitation to the opulent villa of Whitelaw Reid because he no longer owned the proper clothes. "I haven't a coat to my back," he confided to Hay. The languid, simple Newport of his youth had been overtaken by hordes of vulgarians, many of whom had amassed great fortunes with no talent King could discern. Even more offensive than the doltish millionaires were their ostentatious wives. What a pity, he scoffed, that couturiers invented fashions faster than society provided occasions for wearing them. The women, "with boxes and boxes of undisplayed frippery," had been forced to divide tennis days at the Newport Casino into three periods so that a new gown could be worn to each. If Columbus had known it would come to this, King moaned to Adams, he "never would have discovered us."

October 12, 1892, marked the four-hundredth anniversary of Columbus's landing in the new world, but the United States was not quite ready to celebrate. There was a president to be elected, and the summer and fall of 1892 were given over to one of the gloomiest campaigns on record. Benjamin Harrison had been nominated to run for a second term, and the Democrats turned once more to Grover Cleveland. "The two candidates were 'singular persons,'" Henry Adams recalled years later, "of whom it was the common saying that one of them had no friends; the other only enemies." As a heat wave and a cholera epidemic swept along the Eastern seaboard in August, Clarence King, himself a victim of sunstroke, contemplated the presidential choices and wondered to Adams, "What if cholera should decide the election: as between Harrison and Grover which would you attack if you were a conscientious cholera germ?"

When Harrison lost, many Republicans fixed the blame on one of their own: Civil Service Commissioner Theodore Roosevelt. In his crusade against corruption, Roosevelt had noisily exposed the fact that the postmaster and the U.S. marshal in Baltimore, both of whom owed their appointments to Harrison, were extorting campaign contributions from employees. Harrison's postmaster general tarried when the matter was brought to his attention, and a congressional probe bitingly concluded that such inaction revealed either an arrogant disdain for the law or negligence "to the last degree." Roosevelt, glowing with rectitude and cocky enough to think that he could undo the political damage, dashed off a magazine article in praise of Harrison's foreign policy. It seems not to have entered his sublimely focused mind that the affairs of the State Department lay beyond the purview of a mere Civil Service commissioner.

For Harrison, the scandal and the campaign passed in a blur. His wife, long ill with tuberculosis, died two weeks before the election. Cleveland won, Harrison went home to Indiana to grieve, and Commissioner Roosevelt began to seek other employment.

And so it fell upon Grover Cleveland to press the gold telegraph key signaling that the Chicago World's Columbian Exposition had officially begun. The pudgy presidential digit executed its duty at a few minutes past noon on the first of May 1893. Steamboats blew their whistles, fountains shot white jets high into the air, the crowd cheered, a battleship fired salute, and the "Hallelujah Chorus" confirmed, for any remaining skeptics, that this was America in full glory.

With their glittering white palaces and ambitious waterways, the exposition grounds were the product of "the greatest meeting of artists since the fifteenth century!" said Augustus Saint-Gaudens, one of the participants. His Diana, goddess of the hunt, aimed an arrow into infinity from her perch atop the agricultural hall designed by McKim, Mead & White. There were temples by the dozen, paying homage to electricity, machinery, manufactures, fisheries, mining, horticulture, transportation, the arts, and women. Daniel Chester

French's sixty-five-foot-high female figure of the Republic presided over a lagoon stretching on for half a mile. America had even reinvented the wheel for the occasion: night and day, throngs waited to ride in the glass cars of George Washington Gale Ferris's magnificent contraption, which transported them, 1,440 at a time, to the dizzying height of twenty-five stories, where they gasped at the gleaming city spread out below.

Henry Adams had his first look at the fair two weeks after it opened, making a hurried trip with Lizzie and Don Cameron. Years before, after he and Clover returned from the centennial exhibition in Philadelphia, Henry "registered an oath never to visit another of these vile displays." The prospect of spending several days in the company of Mrs. Cameron gave him ample reason to break the vow, but he did not expect Chicago to be an improvement on Philadelphia. Alighting from the senator's private railroad car, he was enchanted to find himself wrong. The exposition was more beautiful than Paris, he averred. He had never dreamed that his vulgar age would "rise to the creation of new art, or the appreciation of the old." He deeply regretted the need to scurry back to Washington to prepare for a summer abroad.

Adams sailed on June 3, and the Camerons soon followed. In mid-July, they all met in Zermatt and headed for Lucerne, unaware, in the serenity of the Alps, of the economic avalanche taking place at home.

The trouble had been brewing for more than a year. Gold had flowed steadily out of the U.S. Treasury, the result of a rise in imports and an unintended consequence of the Sherman Silver Purchase Act passed three years before. To halt the slide in silver prices that had ruined Clarence King and uncountable other mining entrepreneurs, the law had authorized the government to purchase and mint fifty million ounces of silver a year. It also provided that greenbacks could be redeemed for silver or gold. Wall Street preferred gold, and in the summer of 1892, as labor unrest and farm protests spread across the country, nervous financiers began cashing in their dollar bills for gold, accelerating the drain from the Treasury. Early in 1893 came the news that several of the nation's largest corporations had grossly overstated their earnings and declared dividends they could not possibly pay. Stock prices sank sharply and crashed entirely when European bankers, who had financed much of America's industrial growth, dumped their American securities. Six hundred banks were forced to close their doors, taking thousands of small businesses and farms along with them.

Arriving in Lucerne on July 23, Henry Adams found a frantic letter from his brother Charles. The Adams family trust, managed by their brother John, had been hard hit, and John had cracked under the strain. Charles urged Henry to come home at once. Henry hurried to England and sailed July 29.

In Boston, he found everyone "in a blue fit of terror, and each individual thinks himself more ruined than his neighbor," he wrote Lizzie in August. "Until they recover their reason, I see no hope of getting on sound bottom." Henry owed no one, no one owed him, and he had prudently tucked away enough money to meet expenses for a year. He saw little cause for alarm save a temporary—albeit frightful—decline in the value of financial assets. The panic would end soon, he predicted, "as all panics do, in general exhaustion. Then we shall be all right. We have only to stand up and go on."

John Hay was equally sanguine. He and his family had gone to Europe in July, intending to stay for a year, and he saw no reason to change plans. Though his mail from Cleveland and New York was "full of dolor and profanity," he told Adams that he was convinced that "seedtime and harvest will follow each other." He would pay his debts when his debtors paid him.

Bored in Quincy, Henry organized a family expedition to the Chicago world's fair, taking Charles, his wife and daughter, and one of Clover's nieces. This time he meant to stay for two weeks. They rode the Ferris wheel, watched fireworks, and reveled in "the lowest fakes of the Midway," Henry reported. He studied the contents of the great exhibition halls and told Hay that he stared "like an owl at the dynamos and steam engines," which he saw as "an appeal to the human animal, the superstitious and ignorant savage within us, that has instincts and no reason, against the world as money has made it."

In Washington an emergency session of Congress repealed the Sherman Silver Purchase Act and restored a measure of confidence in American credit. But fifteen thousand businesses had failed, dozens of railroads were insolvent, and unemployment was on its way to the unthinkable high of four million. Clearly shaken on his return to H Street in October, Adams wrote Hay, "My dear democracy is all in pieces; not a rag of decency is left." He foresaw "universal bankruptcy" and felt his toes "getting cold with a very familiar sensation of being shut out-doors in the blizzard." He had had no word from King but knew that he was in trouble. His bank in Texas had "busted with the rest," Adams glumly told Hay, "and I fear he has gone under."

The El Paso National Bank collapsed as much because of fraud as panic. Two officers of the bank, one a friend of King's since the Fortieth Parallel survey, had diverted funds to their own purposes. When bank examiners uncovered the irregularities, King requested time to raise new capital, but the panic had rendered the point academic.

With the bank collapse, the stock market crash, and the birth of another child in July 1893, the pressures on King intensified, but the agony that finally broke him was physical—the flare-up of an old spinal injury. For weeks he could not sleep, and he often found himself wandering through neighborhoods with no idea how he had got there. At the end of October, after a visit to his mother, he came back to New York in excruciating pain. Among his errands was a favor for Frank Emmons, his Fortieth Parallel colleague, who had introduced him to Adams two decades before. Emmons, also a casualty of the panic, was having difficulty joining the Century Club, and King promised to help.

On Sunday afternoon, October 29, King stood before the caged lions of the Central Park zoo. Shabbily dressed and long overdue for a haircut, he bore no resemblance to the dandy whose immaculate suits and silk hose had graced the evening campfires along the Fortieth Parallel. What happened next is unclear, but it appears that someone bumped him and, perhaps because of the pain in his back, he turned suddenly violent. He himself later claimed to have been "jostled" against a black butler from a house on Madison Avenue. King was arrested, hauled to the nearest police station, and booked on charges of disorderly conduct.

Terrified that another lapse in judgment might expose his black family in Brooklyn, King avoided his rooms at the Union League Club, where newspaper reporters lay in wait. He handed himself over to his physician and meekly consented to be committed to Bloomingdale Asylum, a mental hospital in the northern reaches of Manhattan.

IS CLARENCE KING INSANE? the New York *Sun* asked in a front-page headline on November 3. No, replied his doctor in the next day's *Tribune*. King's spinal inflammation, the national financial crisis, and his "extreme sensitiveness over his professional obligations brought about the condition of his present nervous depression which at times assimilates melancholia. . . . [I]t seemed best to Mr. King himself, as well as to his friends, in view of the fact that he had no family, that he should go to some place where he could have good nursing and absolute freedom from care. Under such circumstances, there is little doubt that he will recover his aforetime health and vigor."

In Washington, Henry Adams read the papers and immediately deduced that "something remains untold." He supposed he could learn the details by going to New York, but as he told Hay, "I don't care to ask." In Henry's remove there was a suggestion of defensiveness—armor, perhaps, against the haunting memories of Clover's breakdown. He would not go to see King unless someone asked him to.

From La Farge came word that it was best to stay away. For the moment King was seeing no one but his doctors and James Gardiner, his friend since childhood. "[W]hat he wants is to be alone and irresponsible for a little while," La Farge explained. King's collapse had come as a blow to La Farge, but the artist's concern was not without reservation. "[A]s you know," he told Henry, who knew precisely the opposite, "I have never been really intimate with him." La Farge seemed to fear that his association with King, whose erratic behavior had occasioned much gossip, would reflect badly on himself.

The worst of King's crisis passed in a week. As his spinal torment subsided, his spirits quickly revived. The Bloomingdale doctors assured him that he had not lost his sanity, an opinion confirmed by S. Weir Mitchell, the eminent Philadelphia neurologist who had ministered to John Hay. After examining King at Bloomingdale, Mitchell concluded that his derangement was not organic and that with care and rest, he would recover in a few months. The only medical dissent came from King's mother, a fervent homeopath, who had insisted on coming to New York against the advice of everyone involved. King's friends kept her away as much as possible, but they could not shake her conviction that the illness could be traced to one of the medicines prescribed by his physicians.

When Constance Fenimore Woolson sent news of King's breakdown to Henry James in London, the novelist was sympathetic but unsurprised. "It's miserable to think one may never see him as he delightfully was," said James. "In truth I never thought there was no madness at all in his sanity—and feel indeed as if there may be some sanity in his madness."

Adams, ready to be of help to King, stayed in Washington and busied himself with the final details of his memoir of the last queen of Tahiti. He had had ten copies printed in December and a few days before Christmas sent them off to Tahiti for corrections and additions. He told Hay that he knew little about King's situation "except that he is getting on well, and that his friend Gardiner is always with him. If anything can drive him to sanity, I think Gardiner can do it; he would drive me to a much further region."

Adams's low esteem for Gardiner undoubtedly came from King, who loathed Gardiner's second wife, the sedate daughter of an Episcopalian bishop. Resenting her influence on his old friend, King had taken particular delight in offending her. During one dinner at the Gardiner house, King had horrified his hostess by telling stories about Civil War rations covered with mold and fly eggs, and about Cuban cigars being rolled to exquisite smoothness on the bare thighs of beautiful young women. Mrs. Gardiner barred King from her house. But a bishop's daughter could scarcely object to Christian kindness, so her husband went daily to Bloomingdale.

On New Year's Eve, two months after the episode at the zoo, King finally felt well enough to write to Adams. "I refrained from boring you with the miseries of my months of torture here," he explained, "and I don't think I should ever have broken silence were I not at last convinced that the progress of recovery, though of geological slowness, is really going to arrive at a cure." The doctors would check his spine again but had already told him he was well enough to leave. "[N]ext week is to be my last in this house of madness." The doctors had laid down only one condition for his release: he must promise to head South for more rest. "What do you say to taking the Island trip with me?" King proposed. He had boned up on the Caribbees, "and if any trust can be put in human testimony they must be splendid for scenery and absorbing for geology. A light opera bouffe effect is evidently given by the extremely characteristic darkeys with their chatter and bandannas, with something serious and orchestral in the way of gumbo and pepperpot. Rum is the agent of erosion from all accounts. Antigua makes a celebrated dish of turtle and grows the finest pineapples in the solar system." There was no danger of "a recurrence of disability," King insisted, and in any event, his personal care would be the responsibility of his valet, James Alexander, who was "a monument of medical wisdom." King had only one reservation: "Common honesty demands that I confess that I am likely to be rather dull company for a little while but in a few days I will be gay enough."

The next mail at Bloomingdale delighted King with an almost identical traveling proposition from Adams. "Curious that the impulse should have seized us simultaneously," he wrote back at once. "I am overjoyed that you are minded to join forces with me, it was what I have been secretly longing for."

"Comfort him and jolly him up," Hay instructed Adams from Rome when he learned of the plan. "Saturate him with sunshine and sapodillas, and get him to come and live in Washington like a man and brother. Now that his affairs have gone to everlasting smash, we can set him up in a bijou of a house, and give him corn and wine and oil to educate us in viscosity." From King's stepbrother in Paris, Hay had heard that Mrs. Howland planned to take King to Nassau, a prospect that chilled Hay to the marrow. Happy to learn that Mrs. Howland had been outflanked, Hay felt free of all worries but one: King's silence. Hay had not heard from him for more than a year, he told Adams. "I have sent him money and securities sufficient, I hoped, to clear him, but have never been informed that he received them, much less what use he made of them. I am as much worried over him as if he were my child, but I do not know what to do to help him, in face of his obstinate silence."

Henry guessed the reason at once. "I never owed money to anyone," he answered, "but imagine how it must alter relations."

*   *   *

At the end of January, just before Adams and King started for Cuba, the Hays were drawn into a crisis that rivaled King's for tragedy and enigma. In Rome they received word that their old friend Constance Fenimore Woolson had died unexpectedly in Venice—by a fall from an upper-story window. She had been ill with influenza and had hired a nurse, but the nurse was elsewhere in the apartment when the fall occurred. An accident, some said. The Italian newspapers suspected *suicidio*.

Fenimore had returned to Italy in 1893 after three frustrating years in England, where she had gone to be near Henry James. James was courtly and attentive but could not—or would not—see that she hoped for more. Alone in Venice in December, she hired a gondola the day before Christmas and traveled out to the Lido, where she walked the beach for hours, gazing beyond red sails and the blue Adriatic to the snowy Alps in the distance. On Christmas, having turned down an invitation to dinner, she strolled in the Piazza San Marco and sat by her fire reading Milton's "Hymn on the Nativity" and *A Christmas Carol*. "I have taught myself to be calm and philosophic," she wrote to a niece, "and I feel perfectly sure that the next existence will make clear all the mysteries and riddles of this. In the meantime, one can do one's duty or try to do it." But, she added, "if at any time you should hear that I have gone, I want you to know beforehand that my end was peace, and even joy at release."

Nine years before, when she learned of the suicide of Clover Adams, Fenimore had remarked to John Hay that she would not mind a sudden death, "but for those who are left, it is very terrible." For Henry James, Fenimore's suicide was terrible indeed—so ghastly that he could not face going to Rome for her burial. "Before the horror and pity of it I have utterly collapsed," he wrote to Hay, who had been enlisted to oversee the interment. Claiming that his presence would add nothing, James promised to wire money for flowers and asked Hay to lay them at her grave.

Thoroughly traumatized, unable to admit that he had played any part in Fenimore's unhappiness, James immediately set about transforming her incomprehensible death into a private work of art, a work that would proceed, with the logic and order of fiction, from cause to inevitable effect. Writing to a friend the day after hearing the rumor of suicide, he ascribed the event to a physiological cause: "some sudden explosion of latent brain-disease." A day or two later, he still leaned toward a physical explanation but suggested that "the sadness of her lonely Venetian winter" combined with the fevers of influenza might "abruptly have deepened into suicidal mania." A few days afterward, writing to his friend W. W. Baldwin, an American physician who had known Fenimore well in Florence, James allowed himself a brief burst of anger and offered a wholly psychological explanation: "Miss Woolson's evident determination not to send for you seems to me insane—just as her silence to me does: in spite of letters which in a *normal* state she would infallibly have answered. She kept us both ignorant—with a perversity that was diseased."

By March 24, exactly two months after her death, the novelist had constructed the sad tale of Constance Fenimore Woolson from start to finish. Writing to his brother William, who had always found Fenimore happy and sociable, Henry described her gaiety as a "purely exterior manifestation." Because of her deafness, he explained, she was more isolated than anyone knew, and her deafness combined with "her tragically conscientious *politeness*" gave her an air of cheerfulness that belied "her whole general feeling about life, her intimate melancholy." The novelist claimed that Fenimore had been close to suicide once before and was stopped only by the kindness of two or three friends. To know Fenimore well was to be in a state of "constant vague anxiety" about her, he said. The "irresponsible delirium of fever" had caused her death, "but this delirium worked upon a predisposition unmistakable—a predisposition which sprang in its turn from a constitutional, an essentially, tragic and latently insane *difficulty in living*—; an element rendered unspeakably touching by her extraordinary consideration for others—those to whom she was attached." The narrator, full of sympathy, apparently never guessed that he might have played a role in the unhappy events he described.

At her own request, Fenimore was buried in the Protestant Cemetery in Rome, the resting place of another of James's great fictional creations, Daisy Miller.

On February 3, 1894, three days after the Hays stood in the bright Roman sunshine at Fenimore's grave, Adams met King in Tampa and dashed off a reassuring note to Hay. "He feels better and seems fat, bright and active. . . . He says he is writing to you now. Perhaps he is."

He was. Apologizing for his silence, King explained that during his illness he had found it impossible to write to "those for whom I have the most feeling—my mother and you. It seemed as if the stirring of a sentiment overcame me hopelessly." He had "a world" he wanted to say to Hay, but it would have to wait: "I have to avoid business and anything serious and keep in shallow water," he said. For the moment, he was grateful to have survived. "Looking back to last July when my spinal trouble with its reflex effect began, I cannot understand how I have ever lived through the merciless agony which crazed and nearly killed me. It seems as if the human organism could not survive such suffering. But here I am gradually but apparently surely recovering with the promise from the doctors of a new lease of life, and health as good as I ever had in my life. This I cannot believe but who am I that I should doubt Weir Mitchell?"

King and Adams posted their letters to Rome and boarded the evening steamer to Havana. King chatted excitedly of the voluptuous femininity awaiting them and vowed to introduce Adams to the tropical carnalities he had urged upon him for years. When King's "ideal negro woman" chose not to show herself in Havana, he was undaunted. If they headed east to Santiago de Cuba and stationed themselves in the center of town, King insisted, they were sure to find "five hundred exquisite females, lovely as mulatto lilies and graceful as the palm-tree." But Santiago also failed them, in spite of their rigorous adherence to King's plan. "We took meals at the Restaurant Venus on the Plaza, and sat there with lizards up our legs and down our necks, while the band played, and the five hundred women did not come," Adams told Hay with unconcealed glee. "Not a one! King was broke up. He had lived only on this dream of unfair women, and he could not believe it was thin air."

Adams undoubtedly was relieved not to find the women of King's fantasies, but he worried that the noisy hotels and vile meals they had endured for two weeks were working against King's recovery. After a sleepless night in Santiago, Henry proposed that they rent a house. With the help of the British consul, whom King knew from a business trip to Cuba, they came into possession of a country place in the hills of Dos Bocas, eight miles from Santiago. Airy and comfortable, the house overlooked a narrow valley brimming with trees and flowers. The silky breezes, sublime view, and the tranquility "were enough to make life what it ought to be," Henry thought. In white linen trousers and "baked in joy and sweat," according to King, Adams puttered in the garden, hiked the trails along the mountain ridges, and painted watercolors of their surroundings. He also helped himself to the books in the house, which included, he told Hay, "your detestable and ribald novel Democracy."

Sleep came easily in Dos Bocas, and King set off every morning at six with pickax and basket to collect specimens of the local geology. Courtesy of the British consul, the visitors passed a day studying rocks from a narrow-gauge railroad that carried freight along the coast. "We ran close along the seashore, under a cliff of coral rocks," Henry wrote to Lizzie, "and whenever King saw anything that amused him, he stopped the engine and we strolled among the stones."

In the evenings King and Adams sat down to "most complicated harmonies" arranged by their cook, Pepe, who had liberated them from a regimen of canned food fried in garlic. Pepe's culinary philosophy, which mandated the use of "a little of everything in every dish," enchanted King more than Adams. Unable to appreciate such exotica as beans with saffron, Adams cursed his Bostonian narrowness and fought Pepe's blazes by mixing sweet fried bananas into everything he ate.

After dinner, King could not be kept at home. Scrambling up and down the steep slopes of the valley during the day, he had met dozens of natives and was determined to study them as intently as he studied the geology. Within ten days he made the acquaintance of all the elderly blacks in the hills, unabashedly conversing in a Negro-Cuban variation of the Spanish he had concocted for dealing with Mexican miners. He learned their dances, grilled them about voodoo, and listened in fascination to their plans for an insurrection against the Spanish. The last major uprising, which dragged on for ten years, had ended in 1878 with promises of reform, but the promises had gone unfulfilled. The panic of 1893 created new tensions as thousands of workers lost their jobs on sugar and tobacco plantations. The plight of the Cubans—noble primitives crushed by the forces of civilization—was made to order for Clarence King, and he soon managed to talk his way into a prison to visit a Señor Guillermon, one of the rebel leaders. "When the sentinel paced into the dungeon toward us," King said, "Guillermon talked in ordinary tones of a recent coal discovery, but when the soldier retraced his steps, strode out of the room and across a wide corridor, the old fighter's eyes blazed and his lips poured into my ear the secret of the coming war."

As the intoxicated King narrated his adventures, Adams grew alarmed. If the Spanish found out, he and King could be jailed or deported. King laughed. If the governor arrested them, he told Adams, he would have to arrest the entire population of Santiago because "every man, woman, or child in the entire province was a rebel or a brigand or both."

No Spanish soldiers knocked at their door, and the only observable consequence of King's nocturnal prowlings was a flood of hospitality. For Señor King, friend of the revolution, the natives stopped at nothing. One Sunday morning the visitors found themselves in receipt of a brace of fighting cocks, thoughtfully provided to spare them the necessity of traveling all the way to the town plaza for blood and gore.

On April 10, after a brief jaunt to Nassau, King and Adams sailed into the green waters of Tampa Bay. "Whatever else our trip has been, it has certainly been good for King," Henry reported to Hay. King struck him as "more sane now . . . and if he would be obliged to stay quiet for half an hour, I think he might be quite reasonable. I tell him this every two or three minutes, but it doesn't affect him."

Back in New York, King filed his own dispatch with Hay. "That pessimistic angel Henry has been more kind and gentle and healing in his way with me than, as Ruskin expresses it, 'an eternity of clear grammatical speech would explain.' He was simply delightful, genial and tropical in his warmth, physically active as a chamois, and as for his talk there was only bitter enough to give a cocktail effect to his high-proof spirit." Henry talked of building a winter house at Dos Bocas, and King hoped he would. "I think the world-hate would perspire out of him and he might take hold of life and even of letters again." As for his own future, King said he had "resolved (and have

thus far succeeded) to smother and hide my pessimistic hate of civilization and be as straightlaced and wooden and fatuously American
as anybody. I shall go to the Metropolitan Club and make myself
beloved of all the stable boys whom fate has raised to the *n*th power
and chum with all the huxters *manquées* and carry off the role of a
good practical sensible American bourgeois cad, to the queen's
taste." Faulting himself for having let his "detestation of things New
Yorkean" stand in his way, he said he was now "going with a
singleness of purpose, an early and late devotion to the New York
struggle for money. No matter how much I hate the people and the
life no one shall see it or know it. . . . I have sinned, I own, in
allowing my nature to influence my life. I shall do it no more till I am
able to say to my nature, 'at last it is your turn, be free!' "

Adams too received word that King had developed "an undreamed
of power to hold back from expressing anything I really believe" and
an iron determination to "attend strictly to business." So far, though,
he had had little success. Fortunes, he noted astringently, were difficult to make when one had to devote the larger part of one's day to
rustling up enough money for dinner. But, he added, "I harbor
hopes."

PART FOUR

CULMINATIONS

18

A Splendid Little War

Banking on his hopes, King moved Ada and the children from Brooklyn to roomier quarters on North Prince Street in Queens. The neighborhood, once a nursery, boasted some of the most exotic foliage in New York City—ginkgos, Japanese maples, dwarf horse chestnuts, and Chinese cypresses. With eleven rooms, the new house easily accommodated a piano, and James Todd promised his little girls that when they were old enough, they would have music lessons. Though his work still kept him away from home for long intervals, he engaged a nurse, a cook, a laundress, and a gardener to help Ada run the household.

In the summer of 1894, when the strains of this new establishment proved more than King could manage, he took the drastic step of dismissing his mother's servants and installing her in a Newport boarding house. He would not "start her housekeeping again till the current of my affairs turns in a better direction," he wrote Hay from a silver mine near Spokane, where he hoped to earn enough to cover expenses for a few months. Frustrated, full of remorse, he was still determined to persevere. "The one great sin of my life is to have blindly got into such a miserable position with you who are the dearest friend I ever had or ever shall have on earth. I never should have recovered reason and dared to begin life again had there not been a germ of faith that refused to perish. That little mustard seed grows within me and its still small voice keeps me up with a promise of remaking my life and of righting myself so far as mere debit and credit goes with you." Ailing, he gamely vowed to "do without" his health, "as other invalids do." Heading East he intended to call on mining entrepreneurs in Denver and Chicago, and there was a hopeful glimmer from one of the old Mexican silver mines.

After a visit to his mother in October, King overcame the "almost painful hesitation" he felt to see old friends and went up to the Hays at Lake Sunapee. He stayed only a day before a telegram summoned him back to New York—to help "an exigent millionaire," Hay supposed—but Hay was pleased to inform Adams that their cherished vagrant was "in fine form, cheerier than I have seen him for several years,—full of schemes, all of them brilliant, not to say iridescent, in promise. I was glad to see him hopeful again, with, or without, reason."

The true state of King's affairs was soon made known to Hay by an unexpected source: Ferdinand de Rothschild, the English baron who had trailed King everywhere during his European holiday in the 1880s. King asked Rothschild for a loan early in 1895, and the baron, who knew of King's stay at Bloomingdale, wanted Hay's advice. "Personally," he said, "I have always had the greatest trust in the perfect honour of our friend, but should his mind be deranged I would consider it waste to send over the money." Hay undoubtedly put the best face on his friend's circumstances, but whatever he concealed from the baron mattered less than what the baron had revealed to him: King could no longer bear to ask Hay's assistance. Henceforth Hay would have to connive in secret to help him.

The first move in this new game came in the summer, when Hay learned that King's stepbrother, George Howland, wanted to return to Paris to continue his art studies. Hay considered George a third-rate Sargent and an imbecile to boot, but he seized the moment to write a generous check in order to relieve King of one dependent. A few months later Hay conspired with Adams in a convoluted plot whereby Adams offered to buy King's most valuable painting, *The Whale* by J. M. W. Turner, which had already been mortgaged to Hay. When King asked Hay's permission, Hay immediately wired his consent, then dashed off a triumphant note to Adams: "I feel as if I were giving King the money *and* the picture, giving you the picture and the chance of doing a good deed with the money, and saving myself the price of the picture, all at once."

The money from Adams, $2,500, did little more than clear up a swarm of bills. No matter what King tried, he always seemed to be in arrears. Though he still kept an office on Wall Street, it generated little business because so many financiers had lost faith in his grand mining schemes. After hours, when he went up to 43rd Street for dinner at the Century Club, he found that his Wild West yarns and rhapsodies on dark-skinned women no longer commanded an audience. Accounts of long evenings with John La Farge, once his closest companion at the Century, vanished from his letters. The collective timidity of New York provoked him "almost to homicide," he told Adams. "I go from my work to my little room and drug myself with wine and mine Cervantes." The long-suffering Cervantes had always been his hero, and King liked to fantasize that he, too, "after much petty misery," would have the force to write a *Don Quixote*.

King had not lost the habit of escaping with his pen, and as his business affairs floundered in 1895, he once more wrote himself into worlds free of insult to mind and spirit. He tried another scientific essay on the age of the earth, and when that failed, he gave himself to a crusade that had interested him since his Cuban excursion with Henry Adams. On lower Broadway, a few blocks from King's office on Wall Street, a band of exiled revolutionaries were trying to build American support for Cuban independence. Every afternoon over peanuts and beer they briefed newspaper reporters on the latest Spanish atrocities in Havana. Many of their stories were total fabrications, but the suffering in Cuba was genuine. The revolution King had heard about in the hills of Santiago had begun in February 1895. The Spanish retaliated by herding the Cubans into concentration camps, where miserable sanitary conditions and inadequate food would ultimately claim four hundred thousand lives. Those who escaped the fate of the *reconcentrados* were only marginally better off: a U.S. tariff on sugar imports had put many plantations out of business, spreading unemployment and hunger throughout the island.

Stirred by the plight of the Cubans, King took it upon himself to plead their case in two long articles for the *Forum*. In the first, which ran in September 1895, he traced the history of Spain in Cuba. From the outset, he argued, the Spanish had been bent on cruelty and despoliation. Execration was heaped upon execration, promises of reform went unkept, and a crushing burden of taxes and tariffs had left the island "bankrupt under the coarse heel of a despot too blind to see even his own advantage." As a result, King concluded, nothing remained to the Cubans save "ruin and rage. It is now too late. Spain can never win back the heart of Cuba."

A year later, for a blood-and-thunder tale of the rebels in combat, he drew on the campaign notes of their military leaders. Painting the Spanish army as a sneering Goliath, he recounted the reaction in Havana when summer rains forced the fighting to a halt. "Officers and soldiers kept the town smiling with camp jests and tales of the droll 'nigger bandits,' as they called them, whom they had fought in the field and were to finish off in the autumn," King wrote. Young officers and "gray generals, stiff with glory and armor-plated with orders and decorations, became centres of cheerful ostentation in every *sala*." As the sounds of Spanish marches drifted through the night, nothing seemed to be "more quaint and amusing than the 'mock-heroic' personage who stood four hundred miles away in the woods, waving his machete and publishing edicts which were in the style of epic poetry and savored strongly of Cervantes's invincible knight."

The Spanish soon learned that the Cubans "were capable of any sort of desperate onslaught," King continued. Every time General Antonio Maceo led his rebels in a charge, he squeezed the Spaniards between a pair of impossible choices: "If they stretched out a military net on either hand, wide and strong enough to catch him in case he swerved, the meteoric chieftain was quite capable of raising that horrid cry, 'Al machete,' and storming the weakened town. To be hacked to death in their own stronghold was far the worse of two evils, so every commander of them gathered his full force about him, shotted his guns, held his breath and—let the Cubans pass."

Compared to the "raggedness, hunger and privation" of the Cubans, King said, "Valley Forge was a garden party." But he had no doubt that the rebels would prevail if their neighbors in the United States gave them even the tiniest show of support. "They look for no gallant American Lafayette to draw sword for them and share the penury and hardships of their camps," King insisted. All they needed was America's official recognition of the Cuban belligerency. Such a move would legitimize the rebellion and, in accordance with international law, allow the United States to treat the rebels as a sovereign nation. Spain, King reminded his readers, had recognized the Confederate States of America only a few weeks after Fort Sumter. "We can return to her, in the interests of liberty, the compliment she then paid us on behalf of slavery," he wrote. "The justice will be poetic."

The revolutionaries of lower Broadway, thrilled to see such fervor in the influential pages of the *Forum,* presented King with a flag captured from the Spaniards in battle.

Adams was as deep into Cuba as King. Years later Henry would say that King had dragged *him* into the fray, but the truth was that Adams embraced the cause on his own after another trip to Cuba early in 1895. In the year since he and King had nested in the hills of Dos Bocas, the Cuban economy had buckled, and politics and society were hurtling toward chaos. Henry spent much of 1895 away from Washington, but when he returned in the fall and thought about the presidential contest of the coming year, it seemed to him that Cuba was "the only real issue."

With a political zest he had not displayed in twenty years, Henry began working behind the scenes for Cuban independence. The opposition was formidable, he knew. His neighbor in the White House, Grover Cleveland, wanted no part of the rebellion. Nor did bankers and industrialists, who believed that the expense of a war would only prolong the bad times ushered in by the Panic of 1893. Nothing could be accomplished, Henry told his brother Brooks, "till the great Trusts come over to our side. For we are now more than ever under the control of Capital." Convinced that capitalists would dismiss lofty arguments about the justice of the Cuban cause, Henry decided on another tack: he would persuade them that Cuba was "a great field for their greed."

On a Sunday morning in February 1896, Henry crossed H Street and walked east to 21 Lafayette Square, the home of Don and Lizzie Cameron. The three of them were joined by Henry Cabot Lodge, a U.S. Navy lieutenant, and two young Cubans who had opened an unofficial legation in Washington to lobby for their cause. The Senate Foreign Relations Committee had recently passed a resolution

In the Cameron house at 21 Lafayette Square (now Madison Place), senators J. Donald Cameron and Henry Cabot Lodge, along with Henry Adams, schemed with Cuban insurgents to build American support for a revolt against the Spanish colonial government at Havana. PATRICIA O'TOOLE

calling for American recognition of the belligerency, but the Cubans in the Cameron parlor wanted an official U.S. endorsement of their fight for independence.

A few days later, Senator Cameron did the Cubans' bidding, and Henry Cabot Lodge, the outspoken freshman senator from Massachusetts, shot up to add his support. A free Cuba would be "an opportunity for American capital," he said, sounding Adams's theme. After six weeks of debate, Senator Cameron's resolution sailed through both houses of Congress. A resolution did not carry the weight of law, but it sent an unmistakable signal to the White House.

Lizzie played a double role in the cabal. The Cubans addressed their letters to her rather than to Senator Cameron or Senator Lodge, who, despite their sentiments, were members of a government that

Senator J. Donald Cameron of Pennsylvania, husband of Elizabeth Sherman Cameron.
SENATE HISTORICAL OFFICE

did not recognize the revolution. And on behalf of Henry Adams, Lizzie strove to keep Don's wandering, alcoholic attentions firmly fixed on the cause. In the summer of 1896, when the Cubans explained their financial desperation to her, she proudly reported to Adams that she had Don "worked up . . . to try to get some money out of the Standard Oil people in return for concessions granted."

When Congress reconvened in the fall, the Cubans wanted Senator Cameron to carry his resolution one step further and push for active intervention by the United States. Adams wrote a paper citing the precedents for such a move in which he argued that the Monroe Doctrine gave Congress ample leeway for whatever action it deemed necessary to keep European powers from meddling in the affairs of the Western Hemisphere. In short, if the Cubans wished to be rid of Spain, there was nothing to stop the United States from helping them. Henry's report went to the Senate Foreign Relations Committee under Don Cameron's name and was adopted by a unanimous vote.

Lodge immediately pressed for a resolution in favor of intervention but was soon forced to abandon the fight. The business interests that had underwritten his run for the Senate refused to accept the argument that war would bring prosperity, and President Cleveland let it be known that he would not, under any circumstances, intervene in Cuba. He had no wish to be remembered as the president who committed his country to war on the eve of leaving office.

Grover Cleveland was the most unpopular man in America in 1896. His decision to restore the gold standard had cost him the support of his Democratic constituency, and the lingering effects of the Panic of 1893 had won him no friends among Republicans. When the Democrats assembled in Chicago to choose their candidate, they picked the most vociferous foe of the gold standard they could find— William Jennings Bryan. A charismatic thirty-six-year-old lawyer from Nebraska, Bryan whipped the conventioneers into a frenzy with his eagerness to slay their dragon. "You shall not press down upon the brow of labor this crown of thorns," he warned the money-changers, "you shall not crucify mankind upon a cross of gold."

Overnight Bryan became the hero and the hope of everyone who felt manipulated by what one impoverished farmer called "the plutocrats, the aristocrats, and all the other rats." Lashing out against the tiny band of capitalists who controlled America, Bryan exhorted his listeners to reject the premise that "if you will only legislate to make the well-to-do prosperous, their prosperity will leak through on those below." The truth was just the reverse, he said: "if you legislate to make the masses prosperous, their prosperity will find its way up through every class which rests upon them."

Brooks Adams remarked to his brother Henry that William Jennings Bryan was the "first great slap in the face the new aristocracy has ever had." But Henry saw no chance for a radical idealist and confidently predicted that the financiers who worked the strings would elect William McKinley.

They could hardly fail. Mark Hanna, a blunt-spoken shipping and mining magnate who represented himself and Ohio in the U.S. Senate, had been building McKinley's campaign exchequer for four years with contributions from his fellow millionaires, Andrew Carnegie, Henry Clay Frick, and John Hay among them. As a public speaker, mild-mannered Governor McKinley of Ohio was no match for the Boy Orator of the Platte, but as one McKinley enthusiast rejoiced to point out, the Platte was a river "six inches deep and six miles wide at the mouth." What McKinley lacked in voltage, he made up for in reassurance. Bryan stirred people, but he also frightened them with his talk of abolishing the Supreme Court and nationalizing the railroads. While Bryan barnstormed America, McKinley sat serenely on the front porch of his white clapboard house in Canton, Ohio, and let America come to him. Day after day, carefully chosen delegations of every conceivable interest group, from veterans and temperance societies to Negroes and Presbyterians, stood respectfully on McKinley's lawn as he dilated upon the necessity of the gold standard and high tariffs. When he finished, a select few were permitted to ask questions that had been prepared in advance by his staff.

Much as John Hay feared the radicalism of William Jennings Bryan, he was content to confine his politicking to his checkbook, sending Hanna $1,000 a month for the campaign. Hay spent most of the summer sightseeing in Europe with his children, but after a pilgrimage to Canton in October, he was sufficiently impressed with McKinley's independence from Hanna—and sufficiently unnerved by Bryan's popularity—to agree to help. For the last three weeks of the campaign Hay shouted himself hoarse carrying his party's warning to America. If the voters elected Bryan, factories would close. The dollar would cease to command respect. And the nation's precious liberties would be in the hands of a demagogue. On November 5, America sent McKinley to the White House with the largest majority won by any candidate since Ulysses S. Grant. Still, Bryan's sweep of the South and much of the West did not go unnoticed by the elitist author of *The Bread-Winners*. "The strain of universal suffrage on the virtue of the country is tremendous," he sighed to a friend.

Adams professed not to care who lived behind the pillars of the large white house on the south side of Lafayette Square, but the politics of the season carried the threat of a double loss. Senator Cameron, deserted by the Republicans of Pennsylvania, had not stood for re-election. To the horror of his wife and Henry Adams, he talked of retiring to his farm near Lancaster. Hay might also defect. There was talk of an embassy, perhaps London, an expression of gratitude for services rendered to the campaign.

Hay wanted the appointment, but before he could have it, he had to suffer the embarrassment of eliminating his chief rival. In a reprise of the Republican presidential victory of 1888, Whitelaw Reid decided that he deserved London as a reward for the *Tribune*'s support. McKinley had no more use for Reid than Benjamin Harrison had, and once again Hay was drafted to coax him into a quiet retreat. This time the situation was even more delicate because Reid knew that Hay was being considered for the post. His awkwardness painfully apparent, Hay tried to persuade Reid that the editor of the *Tribune* was "a bigger man than any Secretary or Ambassador. I implore you not to suffer yourself to be driven into a quarrel with McKinley. It will hurt one of you as much as the other and do absolutely no good to either. He is not to blame, as to you or me. It is circumstance and not altogether volition which decides these things."

Recognizing that he was beaten, Reid asked only for a face-saving letter to show to friends who expected him to hold a position in the new administration. Hay drafted a message from McKinley regretting that Reid's chronic chest ailment precluded an appointment.

Somewhere in the middle of this epistolary blizzard, Hay decided to make a pitch for his own candidacy. "There has been so much talk about my being sent to England that I presume you may have given some consideration to the matter," he wrote to McKinley in an unsigned, undated letter with no salutation. "I do not think it is altogether selfishness and vanity which has brought me to think that perhaps you might do worse than select me." Hay thought that his appointment would "please a good many people and so far as I know offend nobody" and noted that he had no wish to hold the office long, which would allow McKinley to name a new ambassador "in some critical time when it might serve a useful purpose."

On March 3, Hay hosted a stag dinner for McKinley at 800 Sixteenth Street. The next morning, as McKinley dressed for his inauguration, he slipped on a gold ring containing a few strands of hair from the head of George Washington. The ring—engraved with G.W. and W.M.—had been sent by Hay with a wish that President McKinley would attain the glory of the first president. A few days later, the newspapers announced that John Hay would represent the United States in the Court of St. James's.

Adams was heartbroken. "Apparently I am going to be left out of the next few years, and lost," he told a friend. Hay, in a moment of inspired tenderness, asked Henry to join him for the voyage to England, and Henry leaped at the invitation. But he could hardly bear to think of his future in Washington. "The poor old Square is shipwrecked," he wrote Lizzie, "and though you and Hay may someday recover your foothold, I am pretty effectually drowned."

On April 14, after a few days in New York with Cabot and Nannie Lodge and an interminable testimonial dinner that left the new ambassador feeling that he had had "gallons of melted butter" poured over his head, the Hays and Henry Adams sailed on the *St. Paul*. At sea Hay learned that a spectacle of "welcome and flapdoodle" awaited him on the pier in Southampton and promptly fell into a funk. When the ceremonial moment arrived, he yearned to be with Adams, who had fled to the bowels of the ship. Henry James, down from London to tender his own welcome, silently absorbed the pomp and fawning and then, as if shaping his observations for a novel, asked Hay, "What impression does it make on your mind to have these insects creeping about and saying things to you?"

Settling into the embassy left Hay little time for Adams, who soon moved on to Paris, telling his brother Brooks, "London does not need me. The more I come here, the more I feel that it has no use for me." Henry would not permit himself to say that it was Hay who didn't need him, but when the two friends parted in the spring of 1897, they headed in opposite directions. Hay was looking toward the new century and America's emergence as a world power. Adams, wanting no part of it, sought refuge in the soaring cathedrals of the Middle Ages. His heart would stay there for the rest of Hay's life.

By leaving Washington, Hay and Adams missed the return of their favorite rogue elephant. Since Harrison's defeat in 1892, Theodore Roosevelt had spent most of his time in New York City, serving as police commissioner. He had also read voraciously, and pondered the meaning of America, and when he came back to the capital as assistant secretary of the navy in the spring of 1897, there was much

The imperious Henry Cabot Lodge, by John Singer Sargent, 1890. NATIONAL PORTRAIT
GALLERY, SMITHSONIAN INSTITUTION. GIFT OF THE HONORABLE HENRY CABOT LODGE.

on his mind. His largest preoccupation was the end of the frontier
epoch of American life, noted a few years earlier by historian Frederick Jackson Turner. The so-called Turner thesis, officially titled
"The Significance of the Frontier in American History," had attracted wide attention since its appearance in 1893, and Roosevelt,
like others, was restlessly searching for new frontiers. For Roosevelt,
the key to the future lay in a book called *The Influence of Sea Power
on History,* by naval historian Alfred Thayer Mahan. Mahan held that
since great industrial nations produced more than they consumed,
they could grow only through foreign trade. World commerce depended upon shipping, and protection of a nation's merchant fleet
called for a well-muscled navy deployed at strategic points around
the globe.

Roosevelt's pastiche of Turner and Mahan added up to an idea
whose time had not yet come. A costly naval buildup clashed with
the mood of the country and with President McKinley's inaugural

pledge to avoid "the temptation of territorial aggression" presented by the unrest in Cuba. The new assistant secretary, never one to shirk a task on grounds of mere impossibility, set out to change the temper of his time. Without Henry Adams's breakfast table, he made the Metropolitan Club his noon-hour pulpit and energetically proselytized for overseas expansion and the requisite navy. He also let it be known that if he had his way, Spain would be ejected from the Caribbean tomorrow. Adams in Paris missed out on the details, but within three weeks of Roosevelt's return to the capital, one of the old breakfast circle passed along the essentials: "Theodore the Talkative is having a hard time trying to be reticent."

There was even less reticence to come. In June Roosevelt told an audience at the Naval War College in Newport that a powerful American fleet would mean peace, not war, because foreign navies would not dare to attack. But if they did—and he seemed to hope they would—the war that followed would be a just war. "All the great masterful races have been fighting races," he declared, "and the minute that a race loses the hard fighting virtues . . . it has lost its proud right to stand as the equal of the best." Fretting that education had made men soft, he implored his listeners to remember that there were "higher things in this life than the soft and easy enjoyment of material comfort. It is through strife, or the readiness for strife, that a nation must win greatness. We ask for a great navy, partly because we feel that no national life is worth having if the nation is not willing, when the need shall arise, to stake everything on the supreme arbitrament of war, and to pour out its blood, its treasure, and its tears like water, rather than submit to the loss of honor and renown."

Back in Washington, the perfervid assistant secretary came in for a sharp "wigging," but the private reproaches of his superior were lost in a thunder of public applause. Newspapers across the country reprinted his address and praised him for a job well done.

Ambassador John Hay needed only a week or two in his office at 5 Carlton House Terrace to remember why he had sworn off diplomacy. His calendar told a tale of appointments and disappointments, of streams of callers—American citizens, members of Parliament, arms merchants hoping for an American war with Spain. To Hay it seemed that everyone who came to see him wanted some favor beyond his power to grant.

The chief vexation of his first few months was the Diamond Jubilee of Queen Victoria. To console Whitelaw Reid, President McKinley asked him to head a special American delegation to the Jubilee without realizing that British protocol would exclude most of the contingent from the choicest balls and banquets. "Our special Embassy consists already of some dozens of whom only one will receive any special attention, and the rest will kick so hard as to be heard on the roof of the world," Hay moaned to Adams. "And your poor old friend, J. Makepeace Hay, will take all the kicking." London in the throes of Jubilee was abominable, he added. "Six miles of lumber deform the streets. The fellow-being pullules. How well you are out of it!"

Adams lolled in Paris and Henry James fled to the seaside resort of Bournemouth, but the American ambassador had no such options. He dutifully acquired a collapsible top hat, packed his wife and daughter Helen and the trains of their satin gowns into a rented brougham, and swam through oceans of ceremony. For all his elitism, the author of *The Bread-Winners* did not feel entirely at ease among English aristocrats, but he turned in a fine performance. "The Hays conduct themselves admirably," beamed Henry White, the ambassador's chief aide and a polished veteran of London society. They were "perfectly simple" but easily made the acquaintance of "the royalty and such people as they should talk to."

By early July, Hay could tell Adams that Jubilee was "gone like a Welsh-rabbit dream." The adulation of Queen Victoria filled him with amazement. "What a curious thing it is—that there has been no King in England since Elizabeth of special distinction—most of them far worse than mediocre—only the foreigner William III of any merit—and yet the monarchical religion has grown day by day, till the Queen is worshiped as more than mortal, and *The Prince* will be more popular still when he accedes. And to look at him as he waddles across the floor at a state ball! but I rap on wood and stop."

Apart from the jubilee, the embassy asked little of John Hay in 1897. The business pending between the United States and England was neither urgent nor critical. On behalf of Canada, Britain wanted

to settle a long-standing disagreement over the Alaskan boundary as
well as quarrels over fishing rights in Newfoundland and the hunting
of seals in the Bering Sea. Hay also organized a conference to explore
the possibility of an international pact on "bimetallism"—currency
based on silver as well as gold. Though McKinley had campaigned
as a goldbug, he had promised to investigate bimetallism. As he soon
learned from Hay, there was no point in pursuing the matter. London's financiers, the most powerful in the world, were wedded to
gold.

The autumn passed quietly, and the ambassador began to enjoy
himself. His workload was heavier but less difficult than he had
expected, and in December, when he finally had his own moment
with Queen Victoria, he came away as enchanted as the most ardent
royalist. Just before a dinner at Windsor Castle, Her Majesty had
examined the seating plan and advised the Lord Steward of a change:
she wanted Mr. Hay at her side. "I prepared myself for a silent
evening," Hay wrote to Clarence King. But the frail old queen
proved surprisingly "chatty and amiable. I was told the next day that
they had rarely seen or heard her talk so much."

With little of significance on his agenda, Hay threw himself into
planning a Nile cruise for his first official leave, set for mid-January.
"Mrs. Hay says you must go," he informed Adams. Henry replied
at once: "If Mrs. Hay says I am going to Egypt with you, you may
bet your life it is so." Hay also sent invitations to James and King,
but neither could come. Having just purchased Lamb House in Rye,
James felt pressed to stay home and work. King's excuses were
vague and pocked with contradictions. The Nile was out, he said,
because he could not leave his mother. But in the next breath he said
he expected to spend the winter working out West, and in the next
he admitted he had no assignment. "What an abject idiot he is not to
chuck it all and come over to us, as I am eternally begging him," Hay
fumed to Adams.

Between the anniversary of Clover's suicide and the prospect of
returning to the scene of her breakdown on the Nile, Henry passed
a turbulent December in Paris. He battled the demons by immersing
himself in medieval poetry, but a dinner with Augustus Saint-
Gaudens forced his thoughts to the peaceful bronze at Clover's grave.
For days he longed to join his wife in Rock Creek. Trying to describe

his gloom, he had told a niece, "When one has eaten one's dinner, one is bored at having to sit at the table. Do you know that I am sixty in six weeks and that I was only forty-seven when I finished my dinner?"

Though Cairo did not upset him, the moment he boarded the Hays' *dahabeah* he came undone. "I knew it would be a risky thing," he told Lizzie, "but it came so suddenly that before I could catch myself, I was unconsciously wringing my hands and the tears rolled down in the old way, and I had to get off by myself for a few minutes." Regaining his composure, he pronounced himself able to "stand anything." But he had to admit that no amount of will could diminish the intensity of this encounter with the past: "there is hardly a moment when some memory of twenty-five years ago is not brought to my mind."

For four weeks the steam-powered *dahabeah* chuffed along the green river, stopping to let the travelers stroll among sunbaked ruins or make dusty forays to distant temples and tombs. Clara Hay, too dignified to ride the donkeys supplied for these excursions, traveled "like Cleopatra," Henry reported, "on a throne borne by strong Nubians, and visible from miles across the plain." Self-conscious about the fragility of his nerves, Henry was piqued to find that the Hays never seemed to feel irritable, even when they had headaches. On the whole, however, he decided that Egypt was "better than opium. It soothes and smooths one's creases out."

On the last day of February the ambassador's party returned to Shepheard's Hotel in Cairo, where they found the American colony in a state of high excitement. While the Hays and Henry Adams were lazing on the Nile, an American battleship, the U.S.S. *Maine,* had blown up in Havana on February 15. When Adams asked for the precise time of the explosion and learned that it had happened after dark, at 9:40, he blurted out his awful conclusion: "Then the Spaniards did it."

Assistant Secretary of the Navy Theodore Roosevelt held the same opinion, but President McKinley desperately hoped otherwise. The *Maine*'s visit to Cuba, arranged in advance with the Spanish ambassador, had been intended as a sign of reduced tension between the

United States and Spain. Spanish naval officials in Havana had accorded the *Maine* all the requisite courtesies, and when the explosion occurred, they hurried to the rescue.

More than 250 sailors perished on the *Maine,* and the newspapers cried for vengeance. McKinley, pleading for calm, appointed a court of inquiry to determine whether the disaster was an affair of chance or malevolence.

Assured by the embassy that there was no need to shorten his vacation, Hay and his family moved on to Athens. Adams, refreshed by his encounter with the lost civilizations of Egypt, went off to study the antiquities of the Near East, wholly unperturbed by the prospect of war. "I lose my head when other people are calm," he wrote to Brooks. "For two years, the Cuban business drove me wild, because other people stupidly and brutally and wilfully refused to listen to its vital warnings. For two years, with the Senate to back me, we moved heaven and earth to get the people into a track. Now that the countries have pitched into the ditch, I've no more to do with it. . . . [M]y business is to look ahead."

Toward the end of March, while Hay sat at his desk in London and Adams haggled with antique-coin dealers in the bazaars of Smyrna, McKinley's court of inquiry concluded that the *Maine* had been sunk by an "external explosion." The report stopped short of blaming either the Spanish or Cuban rebels desperate for American intervention.

To the disgust of Theodore Roosevelt, McKinley was still "bent on peace." The president offered to let the Spanish pay an indemnity for the *Maine* and tried to persuade them to sell Cuba to the United States. "McKinley," seethed Roosevelt, "has no more backbone than a chocolate eclair."

Ambassador Hay canvassed London for opinion on the *Maine* affair and assured the President that no one in Britain opposed an American war with Spain: "The commonest phrase (from Liberals, Conservatives and Radicals) is 'We wish you would take Cuba and finish up the work.' "

By April 25, both countries had declared war, and a few days later the obstreperous assistant secretary of the navy resigned to join a cavalry regiment, a move deplored by all who knew him. "He has lost his head," said his superior, Secretary of the Navy John D. Long. To the secretary it seemed that Roosevelt was "deserting the post where he is of most service and running off to ride a horse and, probably, brush mosquitoes from his neck on the Florida sands. His heart is right, and he means well, but it is one of those cases of aberration—desertion—vainglory; of which he is utterly unaware. He thinks he is following his highest ideal, whereas, in fact, as without exception every one of his friends advises him, he is acting like a fool. And, yet, how absurd all this will sound if, by some turn of fortune, he should accomplish some great thing."

Hay was considerably more scornful. By joining "a cowboy regiment," Roosevelt was giving up a position "where he had the chance of his life," the ambassador wrote to Adams. Adams, reading the news in Constantinople and thinking of the economic and military decrepitude of Spain, predicted that the Spanish would be forced to surrender long before Theodore had a chance to prove his virility. John La Farge disapproved on more esoteric grounds. Seeming to forget that he had for all practical purposes abandoned his own wife and children, La Farge clucked that Roosevelt was "behaving very badly in leaving his family for a junket like this; he is going *because he wants to;*—that's what is so deplorable in a husband and father."

By August, the war was over, and it seemed to many that Theodore Roosevelt had won it. He had not only charged Kettle Hill with his Rough Riders, he had also set the stage, months before his resignation from the Navy Department, for Commodore George Dewey's conquest of Manila, where Filipino insurgents had been fighting the Spanish in a struggle much like the one in Cuba. A week or so after the sinking of the *Maine,* Secretary Long, bleary with fatigue, had taken a day off to get a massage and see his podiatrist about some painful corns. Roosevelt had seized the moment to fire off a cable ordering Dewey and most of the Asiatic squadron to Hong Kong:

> . . . KEEP FULL OF COAL. IN THE EVENT OF DECLARA-
> TION OF WAR SPAIN, YOUR DUTY WILL BE TO SEE THAT
> THE SPANISH SQUADRON DOES NOT LEAVE THE ASIATIC
> COAST, AND THEN OFFENSIVE OPERATIONS IN PHILIP-
> PINE ISLANDS . . .

Colonel Theodore Roosevelt of the Rough Riders, heroes of the Spanish-American War.
LIBRARY OF CONGRESS

"[T]he very devil seemed to possess him yesterday afternoon," Long moaned in his diary. He vowed never to leave his assistant in charge again, but he did not order Dewey to change course.

When the Spanish surrendered in Santiago, the town where rebels had once whispered their secrets to Clarence King, John Hay gracefully admitted that he had misjudged Roosevelt:

When the war began I was like the rest; I deplored your leaving your place in the navy where you were so useful and acceptable. But I knew it was idle to preach to a young man. You obeyed your own daemon, and I imagine we older fellows will all have to confess that you were in the right. As Sir Walter wrote, 'One crowded hour of glorious life, Is worth an age without a name.' You have written your name on several pages of your country's history, and they are all honorable to you and comfortable to your friends. It has been a splendid little war; begun with the highest motives, carried on with magnificent intelligence and spirit, favored by that Fortune which loves the brave. It is to be concluded, I hope, with that fine good nature which is, after all, the distinguishing trait of the American character.

Hay was beginning to sound like a statesman. From the start he had shared Henry Adams's vision of a short conflict, and both of them turned their thoughts to peace well before Roosevelt saw combat. At the end of May, Adams had offered the ambassador his terms for an armistice: Cuban independence, autonomy for Puerto Rico, withdrawal of Spanish troops from the Caribbean, and withdrawal of American forces from the Philippines "on condition of retaining a harbor of convenient use for a coaling station."

Hay had been thinking along the same lines but doubted that they would get their way. "The weak point in both of our schemes is the Senate," he told Adams. "I have told you many times that I did not believe another important treaty would ever pass the Senate. What is to be thought of a body which will not take Hawaii as a gift, and is clamoring to hold the Philippines? Yet that is the news we hear today. The man who makes the Treaty of Peace with Spain will be lucky if he escapes lynching."

From his London post, Hay had been sounding out Europeans on the peace, and he saw less reason to worry about Spain than Germany. Cecil Spring Rice, now second secretary at the British embassy in Berlin, sent alarming intelligence. "The jealousy and animosity felt toward us in Germany is something which can hardly be exaggerated," Hay warned Henry Cabot Lodge. According to Spring Rice, the Germans wanted "the Philippines, the Carolines, and Samoa—they want to get into our markets and keep us out of theirs." If the United States annexed Hawaii, as seemed likely, Spring Rice predicted that Germany would demand some Pacific outpost, perhaps Samoa, as compensation. Above all the Germans did not want the United States, in its eagerness to quit the Philippines, to turn them over to England or France.

To McKinley, who had little desire to preside over a Pacific empire, Hay reported that England hoped the United States would retain control of the Philippines. "[O]f course we can consider nothing but our own interests," he added, "and the more I hear about the state of the Tagalo population and their leaders the more I am convinced of the seriousness of the task which would devolve upon us if we made ourselves permanently responsible for them."

As Hay waded through the currents and crosscurrents of imperial politics, he was struck by a curious paradox: "the only power cordially friendly to us on this side of the water is England and England is the one power which has most to dread from our growing power and prosperity. We are her most formidable rival and the trade balances show a portentous leaning in our favor. But notwithstanding all this the feeling here is more sympathetic and cordial than it has ever been."

To Henry Adams, the new harmony between Britain and the United States was not in the least paradoxical. Germany, "the grizzly terror," had simply "frightened England into America's arms." How delicious of Fate, he thought. The Kaiser had achieved in a summer what Adamses had tried to do for generations.

Henry had thought about basing himself in London for the summer to watch the peacemaking, but a quick visit with the ambassador convinced him to move on. As he explained to a friend, "I might innocently annoy Hay by saying—or not saying—what nonsense is my habit to talk by way of holding my tongue. There are idiots enough of the amateur diplomate class without counting me." At the end of June, he joined the Camerons at Surrenden Dering, a grand Elizabethan manor that was, he said, "about the size of Versailles." Surrenden's baronial rooms overlooked the weald of Kent, a deer park, and an immensity of terraced lawn, where guests assembled daily for tea.

Don Cameron, who saw no reason to suffer either the ritual of tea or the hordes invited by his wife, spent whole days racing along leafy country lanes in a trap drawn by a pair of long-tailed trotters. Each evening as he sat down as head of a table of twenty, he waited on tenterhooks to see what crimes the kitchen staff had committed against the fruits and vegetables he was importing from America at ruinous expense. On one occasion the suspense lasted until dessert, when the cook crowned her feast with a pink mush that upon investigation, turned out to be boiled watermelon.

Surrenden was only a few miles from Rye, and Henry James came

In the summer of 1898, Don and Lizzie Cameron rented a mansion in the English coun-
tryside. Seated in front are Martha Cameron, left, and the Hays' daughter Alice. Seated
in back, from left, are Ambassador John Hay, his son Clarence, Edith Hoyt, and Hay's
daughter Helen. Standing left to right are Don Cameron, Henry Adams, Spencer Eddy,
and Hay's son Del. It was here that Ambassador Hay learned that President McKinley
wanted to appoint him Secretary of State. PRIVATE COLLECTION.

over to study the complicated dance of Henry Adams and Lizzie
Cameron. Their affair, unmentionable in the Adams family, was
"one of the longest and oddest American *liaisons* I've ever known,"
he told a friend. "Women have been hanged for less—and yet men
have been too, I judge, rewarded with more." Rumors of a Cameron
separation had been floating around Europe for a year, and James's
visits to Surrenden, where Adams was so much in evidence and Don
so pointedly absent, left him feeling "somehow haunted with the
American family, represented to me by Mrs. Cameron." There was
no denying her beauty and grace, but he could not bring himself to
like her. He found her a bit "hard" and thought she had "sucked the
lifeblood of poor Henry Adams and made him more 'snappish' than
nature intended."

James must have felt somewhat misplaced among the Americans
at Surrenden in the summer of 1898. Far from sharing their zeal for

the conquests in Cuba and the Philippines, he looked at the war and saw "nothing but the madness, the passions, the hideous clumsiness of rage." Like his psychologist brother William, who believed that Theodore Roosevelt was "still mentally in the Sturm and Drang period of early adolescence," Henry James was deeply suspicious of the brand of patriotism exalted by the most famous of the Rough Riders. The same week the United States declared war on Spain, the novelist had reviewed *American Ideals,* Roosevelt's collection of manifestoes on "The Manly Virtues," "True Americanism," and kindred matters. A hopeless puerility muddled Roosevelt's thinking, James said, and he frostily observed that in a task as momentous as the shaping of a national character, "stupidity is really the great danger to avoid."

Lizzie Cameron and Henry Adams had hoped to make Surrenden a sort of country house to the embassy, but John Hay, immersed in cables and dispatches, could not leave London until peace was in sight. Early in August, knowing that a preliminary armistice would soon be signed, Hay left the embassy in the hands of Henry White and headed off to his friends. For some time he had suffered from a painful kidney ailment, and he went to Surrenden with the firm intention of getting a rest. Surrounded by friends and family, he soon felt restored. "Don is the finest type of old Tory baronet you ever saw," he reported to Cabot. "His wife makes a lovely chatelaine, and Oom Hendrik has assumed the congenial functions of cellarer and chaplain."

Into this elegant tranquility on the evening of August 14 came Henry White with a cable for Hay from the president:

IT GIVES ME EXCEPTIONAL PLEASURE TO TENDER TO YOU THE OFFICE OF SECRETARY OF STATE. . . . IT IS IMPORTANT THAT YOU SHOULD ASSUME DUTIES HERE NOT LATER THAN THE FIRST OF SEPTEMBER.

William R. Day, the current secretary, was resigning at McKinley's request in order to negotiate the final peace treaty in Paris.

Hay was shocked and depressed. He felt certain that the State

Department would kill him in six months. His tumult is preserved in a trio of letters written the next day. In the first, he declined the appointment because of his health. But after discussing the situation with Adams, Hay decided that it was wrong for any member of a government to refuse his president's request. Nor did Hay think it proper, after the president had given him a post he wanted, to turn down one he did not. "Your despatch received," began his official acceptance. "I am entirely and most gratefully at your disposition. But I fear it is not possible to get to Washington by September first. I am suffering from an indisposition, not serious but painful, which will prevent my moving for some little time. I shall require several days to break up my establishment and get away. If about four weeks delay could be granted me I could be there by first of October. . . . If the need of a change is urgent and it would be inconvenient to wait for me, I hope you will act without reference to me."

Still dissatisfied, he wrote privately to McKinley to confess his conflict. "I cannot tell you with what emotion I received your telegram offering me the post of Secretary of State. The place is beyond my ambition. I cannot but feel it is beyond my strength and ability. My first impulse was to express my gratitude and affection and to decline an honor so conspicuous and so exacting. But I reflected that you must have had good reasons for your action and that possibly my declining might disturb other arrangements you had in mind; and that, finally, I had no right to refuse any duty you might think proper to assign me." Had McKinley not offered the State Department, Hay said, he would have retired from the ambassadorship the following year. "But you have chosen to confer on me this crowning mark of your favor and confidence and whatever may be my dread of the result I can only accept it with affectionate gratitude and a recurrent hope that Heaven may grant me the strength I so sorely need to make me not too unworthy of so great an honor."

Clarence King, wandering alone from mine to mine in his futile quest for wealth, had never felt as desolate as John Hay on his new pinnacle. The State Department was a bastion of patronage, which meant that Hay would have little chance to make appointments of his own. "He has no one to rely upon," Adams wrote to a friend. McKinley's cabinet was "a heavy load to carry," and neither Hay nor Adams could conceive of a foreign policy "likely to satisfy anybody." Hay wanted Adams to succeed him in London,★ but both of them knew he would not get his way. Adams was a Democrat, with no standing in McKinley's crowd. "Nothing short of a cataclysm in America could throw up men without political backing into offices of cabinet rank," he explained to an English friend. Still, Hay's idea pleased him. "All my life I have lived in the closest possible personal relations with men in high office. Hay is the first one of them who has ever expressed a wish to have me for an associate in his responsibilities. Evidently something is wrong with Hay—or with me."

On a soft September day, Hay came to Surrenden to take his leave. Henry James had welcomed him in Southampton, and with his exquisite sense of completion, traveled to Surrenden to say farewell. A year and a half later, walking his dog in the country, the novelist would recall Hay's pause "before the plunge, on that great Surrenden terrace," and he wondered how often the secretary wished he were back in Kent with the "kind old English air coaxing, and lovely women and distinguished men just respectfully hanging to your coattails."

★ On August 30, 1898, Hay wrote to Lizzie Cameron that when Queen Victoria asked him who the next ambassador would be, "I could not comfort her; I said she would dote on Whitelaw [Reid], that she could not see enough of [Joseph] Choate, that if she could get [Senator James] McMillan it would be the crown of her career, and if Mr. Adams came she would want to abdicate in his favor." The embassy went to Choate, a brilliant lawyer.

19

A Taste of Empire

On September 30, 1898, his first day as Secretary of State, John Hay spent the morning stewing about his wardrobe. His steamer trunks had arrived from England, but the keys were nowhere in evidence, and no amount of poking or prodding persuaded the locks to yield. Meticulously barbered and manicured, the secretary was annoyed to think that when he went to the White House for his induction into the third-highest office in the land, he would have nothing to wear but one of the two suits he had chanced to carry home in a valise.

John Marshall Harlan, associate justice of the Supreme Court, administered the oath to Hay in the presence of William McKinley and his cabinet, after which Hay took the secretary of state's seat, at the president's right, for a "talkative" cabinet meeting. In the afternoon he walked next door to the overgrown architectural bonbon that housed the State, War, and Navy departments, taking possession of a spacious, sunny suite looking out upon the green lawns of the Ellipse and his friend Clarence King's least favorite monument, the huge white phallus that paid tribute to George Washington, father of the country. Hay signed letters for an hour, shook hands with everyone in the department, and at five o'clock called for the carriage at his disposal. "The first drive I ever took deliberately, without you," he wrote his wife, who was at Lake Sunapee. He had promised to dine with Senator Mark Hanna, but there was time to ride out Connecticut Avenue as far as the zoo and back home to Lafayette Square, corner of Sixteenth and H.

Though Hay did not say what he thought about as he sat alone in the back of the victoria, his letters to Clara during the next two weeks showed how deeply he resented his new burdens. "I will not give up to the miserable habit of lunching at the Department," he told her. "I get an hour off, from one to two, and then go back till 4:30. I think that earns my salary." As for his colleagues at the State Department, he had not found one congenial soul: "I have never, not even in a foreign country, felt so absolutely alone."

The enormity of Hay's task undoubtedly sharpened his sense of isolation. The splendid little war, a mere ten weeks of scuffling over an impoverished Caribbean island and an obscure Pacific archipelago, had transformed the United States into a world power—the peer of England and France, a threat to Germany, the guardian of the Western hemisphere, and a potent new force in the Orient. Few people, he told a friend, "appreciate what an immense shop it is we have been put in charge of." As secretary of state, Hay had more responsibility for this sprawling new concern than anyone but the president.

The first order of business in the autumn of 1898 was the Philippines. In the rush to trounce the Spaniards, little thought had been given to the next chapter of Philippine history, and President McKinley had hoped that the United States would make a quick exit after the Spanish surrender. But war among rival native factions and the possibility of German intervention convinced him that the situation called for more. Anguishing over the proper course, McKinley paced the floor night after night and sometimes fell to his knees to ask "Almighty God for light and guidance," he later told a group of clergymen.

> And one night late it came to me this way—I don't know how it was, but it came: (1) that we could not give them back to Spain—that it would be cowardly and dishonorable; (2) that we could not turn them over to France or Germany—our commercial rivals in the Orient— that would be bad business and discreditable; (3) that we could not leave them to themselves—they were unfit for self-government—and they would soon have anarchy and misrule over there worse than

Spain was; and (4) that there was nothing left for us to do but take them all, and to educate the Filipinos, and uplift them and civilize and Christianize them, and by God's grace do the very best we could by them, as our fellow-men for whom Christ also died. And then I went to bed, and went to sleep and slept soundly, and the next morning I sent for the chief engineer of the War Department (our map-maker), and I told him to put the Philippines on the map of the United States, and there they are, and there they will stay while I am President!

Translating the Lord's wishes into temporal terms, McKinley paid Spain $20 million for official title to the islands. To Mark Twain, who believed that the Philippines belonged to the Filipinos, the very idea of such a bargain seemed "divinely humorous," but most Americans thought the sum of $20 million had a fine, generous ring. The fact that the United States had embarked on a war to free Cuba and had ended by imposing itself on the Philippines troubled no one but a few cranks.

Unhappily for the president and his new secretary of state, one of the malcontents was their rich and powerful friend Andrew Carnegie. A Scottish immigrant with a keen interest in the affairs of the British empire, Carnegie saw imperialism as a spectacularly bad investment. "That Britain 'possesses' her colonies is a mere figure of speech," he warned in the *North American Review;* "that her colonies possess her is nearer the truth. 'Our Colonial Empire' seems a big phrase, but, as far as material benefits are concerned, the balance is the other way. Thus, even loyal Canada trades more with us than with Britain. She buys her Union Jacks in New York. Trade does not follow the flag in our day; it scents the lowest price current." Totting up Spain's recent credits and debits in the Philippines, Carnegie found only minuscule gains. Even these, he reckoned, would be wiped out by the cost of the soldiers and sailors the United States would need to maintain order in the political chaos of the Philippines.

When Carnegie learned of the plan to pay Spain $20 million, he grandly offered to put up the money himself and give the Filipinos the independence he saw as their inalienable right. Rebuffed, he descended upon the White House in a wrath and told McKinley that he hoped the rebels would gun down any Americans who tried to take control. Awed by the fury of a man renowned for his self-possession, one newspaper correspondent guessed that Carnegie would not be "invited to call again in the near future."

His next target was the secretary of state. McKinley was being ill-served by his advisers, Carnegie told Hay. It was wrong for cabinet members to say that the president was doing his duty by acceding to the popular clamor for the Philippines. It was Carnegie's belief that a president's duty lay in telling Congress "not what any section of the people thinks, nor what all parties think, *but what he himself thinks best.*"

"Andrew Carnegie really seems to be off his head," Hay reported to a friend. "He writes me frantic letters signing them 'Your Bitterest Opponent.' He threatens the President, not only with the vengeance of the voters, but with practical punishment at the hands of the mob. He says henceforth the entire labor vote of America will be cast against us, and that he will see that it is done. He says the Administration will fall in irretrievable ruin the moment it shoots down one insurgent Filipino." In a caustic reference to a bloody uprising at a Carnegie steel mill several years before, Hay added, "He does not seem to reflect that the Government is in a somewhat robust condition even after shooting down several American citizens in his interest at Homestead."

Hay dealt with Carnegie's rage as he dealt with most conflict—he ignored it and hoped it would go away. For his part, Carnegie did his best to maintain his friendship with Hay despite their quarrel. Over the Christmas holidays he sent Hay a supply of Scotch for a cold. Hay responded with an invitation to dinner. The Philippines went unmentioned. But away from the civilities of Lafayette Square, the secretary lobbied the Senate for ratification of the peace treaty with Spain while Carnegie vigorously worked against it. On December 27, the same day he wrote Hay as a "staunch Republican" to warn that farmers and laborers would vote Democratic because they feared competition from cheap Philippine imports, he also volunteered to help spread such fears. Writing to Carl Schurz, the aging idealist who was fighting one of his last great crusades, Carnegie offered money to print and distribute one of Schurz's numerous anti-imperialist speeches. "I will be your banker," he said. "That is the way in which I can aid the good work. You have brains and I have dollars. I can devote some of my dollars to spreading your brains."

Carnegie, Schurz, and the other anti-imperialists (the "aunties," as Theodore Roosevelt called them) could be noisy and nettlesome, but their opposition merely inspired the president and his men to cloak their policies in terms even loftier than those used by the protesters. Self-government would come when the Filipinos were ready, McKinley promised. In the meantime, the United States was morally obliged to preserve order. To those who insisted that America had betrayed its highest principles by forcing itself upon an unwilling people, the secretary of state had a ready answer: "I cannot for the life of me see any contradiction between desiring liberty and peace here and desiring to establish them in the Philippines."

With the peace treaty moving toward ratification, it seemed to Henry Adams that the secretary of state's worst trouble at the beginning of 1899 was an overburdened social calendar. After ten cabinet dinners in six weeks, Hay swore he would expire from tedium. Beset by sore throats and headaches (which he blamed on overexposure to bores), the secretary occasionally managed to excuse himself from a dinner or a ball, but his absence rarely escaped notice. The first lady overflowed with indignation one night in January when she discovered that Clara Hay had come alone to a party. "I don't understand these wives who put their husbands to bed and then go out to dinners," she scolded. "When I put Mr. McKinley to bed, I go to bed with him." Forwarding this nugget to Lizzie Cameron in Paris, Henry added, "Certainly Mrs. McKinley's suggestion that Mrs. Hay was going to bed somewhere else was poetic and even lyric."

By February 4, Hay felt well enough so that he and Clara could host a dinner of their own, in celebration of their twenty-fifth wedding anniversary. It was a strange evening. Clara, whose waistline had followed an expansionist course for years, appeared in her bridal gown, leaving Henry Adams to wonder in tactful silence about the magnitude of the necessary alterations. Cabot and Nannie Lodge were present, which suggests that neither Clara nor Cabot fully apprehended the state of affairs between John and Nannie. "It was all

kind and cordial and genial, but one must not stop to think," Henry
told Lizzie.

Life on Lafayette Square had changed. Henry's breakfast establishment still did a brisk trade, and his afternoons still ended with a walk
and a cup of tea with Hay, but Hay's elevation to secretary of state
subtly altered their friendship. Hay, loyal and sensitive, tried to preserve the ease between them by insisting that his office meant
nothing—that it was, as Adams put it, "pure fungoid, and not a part
of his nature." Alone they talked little of politics, but as Hay's closest
friend, Adams inevitably found himself listening to more Washington shoptalk than he cared to hear. Though he knew how to evade
the questions of diplomats who flocked to his breakfast table in the
hope of catching some hint of the secretary's business, there seemed
to be no defense against the insufferable Henry Cabot Lodge. One
winter evening, after enduring an hour of "dreary Senatorial drivel"
between Hay and Lodge on the subject of the peace treaty with
Spain, Henry moaned to Lizzie, "I sit silent. What do I care whether
the Treaty is ratified, or whether we take the Philippines?" Henry
also sat silent as Cabot expressed "an earnest wish" that Hay "would
not look so exceedingly tired when approached on business at the
department" and Hay "with sobs in his voice assures me that the
Senator gives him more trouble, about less matter, than all the gov-
ernments of Europe, Asia and the Sulu Islands, and all the Senators
from the wild West and the Congressmen from the rebel confederacy. Tell me, does patriotism pay me to act as a buffer-state?"

Watching the political game at close range, Adams declared himself vastly relieved that Hay had not succeeded in getting him the
London embassy. The only detail that gnawed at him was a rumor
that he could have had the post if he had pressed for it. As Justice
Oliver Wendell Holmes told the story years later, Adams had "wanted it handed to him on a silver platter." Whatever Henry's unconscious desire for the power and position of Adamses past, he
regularly expressed the feeling that Fate had been kinder to him than
to his friend in the State Department. "I've managed to drag on a
degraded existence for the last thirty years without an office or an
honor to my family-back, as far as I can see, all the better for freedom," he told Lizzie early in 1899. But Henry was not sure that

spending twenty years in the shadow of the White House had had a salutary effect on his character. As he confessed to an English friend, "I have grown so used to playing the spider, and squatting in silence in the middle of this Washington web, and I have seen so many flies and other insects caught and devoured in its meshes, that I have now a little the sense of being a sort of ugly, bloated, purplish-blue, and highly venomous hairy tarantula which catches and devours Presidents, senators, diplomates, congressmen and cabinet-officers, and knows the flavor of every generation and every country in the civilized world. Just now my poor friend Hay is caught in the trap, and, to my infinite regret, I have to make a meal of him as of the rest."

In February, as soon as the peace treaty cleared the Senate, the secretary of state turned his attentions to the Orient. Expansionists such as Roosevelt and Hanna had encouraged American businessmen to view the Philippines as a stepping-stone to the huge, untapped markets of the Far East, particularly China. (No one but a few peevish "aunties" thought to ask how many American goods a nation of starving peasants was likely to buy.) As a newcomer in the Pacific, the United States was in a delicate position. Since 1895, when China lost a war with Japan, the weakened imperial dynasty had been exploited by Europeans demanding one economic concession after another. One by one, China's ports, mines, and railroads were falling into foreign hands. Hay's challenge was to gain a commercial foothold for the United States without engaging in what he called "the great game of spoliation."

Aware that his ignorance of the Far East was almost as vast as Asia itself, Hay longed for the guidance of W. W. Rockhill, a distinguished Orientalist assigned to the American consulate in Athens for want of a more suitable post. But the congressional grip on State Department appointments kept Hay from naming so much as a bootblack, and he had to bide his time. When a death created an unexpected vacancy early in 1899, Hay pounced. Byzantine as it seemed to the uninitiated, W. W. Rockhill, the chief architect of Hay's Far Eastern policies, would answer to the title of director, Bureau of American Republics.

By late summer, the new director had fashioned a simple and ingenious piece of statecraft. In a note to be sent to the major European powers, the United States would acknowledge their respective spheres of influence in China and ask each to guarantee that its domain would be free of commercial discrimination.

Rockhill's note, signed by the president, inspired reams of piety, but none of the powers was willing to endorse the plan unless all of the others did. After a few months of corresponding privately with ambassadors and foreign ministers, Hay allowed someone in the State Department to leak news of the plan and to spread the rumor of its imminent acceptance. Overnight John Hay became as famous as Theodore Roosevelt and his Rough Riders. Hay's "Open Door," as the newspapers dubbed it, was foreign policy of a sort that made Americans feel proud. It avoided the "permanent alliances" George Washington had warned against in his farewell address, it protected China from further rapacity, and it leveled the playing field of commerce. Once the American acclaim began, no one in Europe dared to veer from the noble trail blazed by Secretary Hay, and Hay, banking on his luck, audaciously decided to interpret the silence as consent. All six powers were informed that since everyone had agreed, the arrangement would be regarded as "final and definitive."

The Open Door was a splendid little coup. But a bitter humiliation that unfolded during that same period deprived Hay of most of his joy. The Spanish-American conflict had drawn new attention to the isthmus of Panama, where a canal had been under construction, in fits and starts, since 1881. Expansionists, who viewed the canal as critical to America's defense and foreign trade, believed that it was time for the United States to step in and complete the canal with American financing and supervision. But an old agreement with Great Britain stood in the way. Signed in 1850, the Clayton–Bulwer Treaty kept either country from acquiring exclusive use of the canal or asserting dominion over any part of Central America. In its day, Clayton–Bulwer was considered a triumph for the United States since it prevented Britain from gaining control of one of the most strategic strips of land in the Western Hemisphere. After the intoxications of the Spanish-American War, however, Americans newly aware of their muscle saw no point in subsidizing a canal they could not control. Shortly after Hay joined the State Department, President McKinley asked him to work out a cordial abrogation of Clayton-Bulwer and negotiate a new treaty.

In theory, Hay was the ideal man for the job. The most popular diplomat ever to represent the United States at the Court of St. James's, he had come home convinced that Anglo-American cooperation was the best guarantee of world peace and prosperity in the coming century. But in his grand dreams of partnership with England, Hay overlooked his partners in the U.S. Senate—with punishing results.

The negotiations began smoothly enough. Hay asked his trusted London colleague Henry White to raise the treaty question with Lord Salisbury, the prime minister. Lord Salisbury invited White to his estate for the weekend, and on Saturday morning after breakfast they retired to the library for a chat. The foreign secretary immediately agreed to consider a replacement for Clayton-Bulwer. He would authorize Sir Julian Pauncefote, the English ambassador to Washington, to negotiate with Hay and asked only that the new arrangement levy tolls on the ships of all nations. That understood, the lord and his sons treated White to an afternoon of shooting—"particularly pleasant," White thought. In the evening he cabled his satisfying news to Hay.

Hay's troubles started soon after he opened talks with Pauncefote. Although the secretary made no secret of the proceedings, he had not officially informed the Senate of his intention to work out a new treaty, which gave Democrats an opportunity to hint darkly of "secret alliances" with England. Hay understood the accusation for what it was—pandering to the anti-English sentiments of Irish and German voters—and he was so indignant he refused to respond. But silence has a way of persuading critics that they are right, and the attacks continued. Hay had been "educated in the English school," Senate Democrats sniffed. Irked by the unfairness of the jibe, McKinley asked his aides why no one had thought to say, "Yes, he was trained under Abraham Lincoln."

Though McKinley admired Hay for taking the high road, the secretary's motives were not entirely pure. With no appetite for the donnybrooks that exhilarated Theodore Roosevelt and Henry Cabot Lodge, Hay simply found it easier to hold his tongue than defend himself. And in spite of the claim that he acted only in the best interests of America, Hay cared more for the good opinion of his friends in England than for the U.S. Senate, a body which he regarded as the bane of American diplomacy. Like secretaries of state before and since, Hay was often sorely tried by the constitutional requirement that treaties be ratified by a two-thirds majority of the Senate. As Hay saw it, the arrangement was fatally flawed: by allowing a treaty to be defeated with only one-third plus one of the votes, the provision gave the upper hand to the minority.

Coupled with Hay's suspicion that senators were, at bottom, a swinish lot, his frustrations with the Constitution inclined him to leave the Senate out of his transactions whenever he could. In his mind, the Open Door was a tour de force not only for its effects in China but also as a display of what a State Department could accomplish without senatorial fetters. Ultimately the abrogation of Clayton-Bulwer and the new terms drawn up by Hay and Pauncefote would have to be approved by the Senate, but Hay did what he could do to disarm the opposition. Forwarding the papers to Henry White in London, Hay explained that he had "tried to avoid entering into unnecessary details. In fact my principal purpose in drawing up the treaty was to avoid any contested points or anything which would cause acrimonious discussion in the Senate. I hope the Foreign Office will see with what sincere friendly purpose the treaty has been drawn, and will refrain from any changes or amendments, which, however meritorious in themselves, might cause the rejection of the treaty by exciting the opposition of one-third of the Senate."

Hay's proposal gave the United States the right to build and operate the canal. Tolls would be the same for ships of all nations, as Lord Salisbury had requested. As neutral territory, the passage would not be fortified, and it would remain open to all, in war as well as in peace. A U.S. police force would keep order in the Canal Zone.

On February 5, 1900, after a year of discussion, the American secretary and the English ambassador met in Hay's office to sign their agreement. A block away, on H Street, Henry Adams was composing a letter to Lizzie Cameron. "At this instant, 11 A.M., while I write, Hay is probably signing with Pauncefote an abrogation of the Clayton-Bulwer Treaty! Hay himself actually trembles for fear that he should wake up and find that he dreamt it. He has given nothing for what a dozen Presidents have broken their necks to get."

In the State, War, and Navy Building, Hay and Pauncefote were waiting for the wax seals to harden on the documents. Hay pulled out his watch. Eleven o'clock precisely. He savored the moment. The English had tried to use the canal treaty as a bargaining chip in a long-standing quarrel over the boundary between Canada and Alaska, and Hay had refused on the ground that the two matters had nothing to do with each other. In the end, England surrendered all the advantages of Clayton-Bulwer while the United States conceded nothing. The secretary forwarded his masterpiece to the Senate and waited for the applause.

Capitol Hill responded with a storm of abuse, attacking the secretary for style as well as substance. Hay had not bothered to consult the Foreign Relations Committee during his talks with Pauncefote, an oversight that senators read—correctly—as a sign of disdain. Nor did they share his vision of a neutral unfortified canal.

Senator Henry Cabot Lodge, Hay noted acidly, was "the first to flop." The American people, Senator Lodge told the secretary, "can never be made to understand that if they build a canal at their own expense and at vast cost, which they are afterwards to guard and maintain at their own cost, and keep open and secure for the commerce of the world at equal rates, they can never be made to understand, I repeat, that the control of such a canal should not be absolutely within their own power." Despite years of Nannie's tutelage, Pinky Lodge still could not turn a graceful sentence, but he knew where he stood.

Next an enterprising newspaper reporter thought to ask the governor of New York, a former assistant naval secretary named Theodore Roosevelt, for his opinion of Hay-Pauncefote. Theodore administered a flogging, which the New York *Sun* ran on its front page.

Hay was flabbergasted. *"Et tu?"* he shot back. "Cannot you leave a few things to the President and the Senate, who are charged with them by the Constitution?" Hay had based his plan for a neutral, unarmed zone on the Suez Canal, and naval authorities had assured him that the United States could ably defend its Central American interests with ships based in Puerto Rico and Hawaii.

Unhumbled, Governor Roosevelt told Hay that his proposal was "fraught with very great mischief." If a canal of the sort Hay wanted had been open during the Spanish-American War, Roosevelt argued, the Spanish could have sailed from the Caribbean to the Pacific to attack Dewey or the American West Coast. "If that canal is open to the warships of an enemy, it is a menace to us in time of war; it is an added burden, an additional strategic point to be guarded by our fleet. If fortified by us, it becomes one of the most potent sources of our possible sea strength. Unless so fortified it strengthens against us every nation whose fleet is larger than ours."

Hay was too stunned to perceive the merits of either argument. He accused Cabot of losing his nerve under pressure from Irish constituents, and he suspected Roosevelt of grandstanding for the 1900 Republican presidential nomination. He could not fathom how anyone "outside of a mad house could fail to see that the advantages were all on our side." Convinced that he was right, Hay would concede only one error: "I underrated the power of ignorance and spite, acting upon cowardice."

Watching the hostilities from the safety of the sidelines, Adams at first saw nothing but the humor of his own position. Each afternoon when he and Hay wandered the streets above Lafayette Square, Adams listened in silence while Hay excoriated Cabot, and once a week, when Adams called on the Lodges, he suffered through Cabot's philippics against Hay. Roosevelt's gratuitous intrusion only added to the merriment. "You can imagine to what an extent the fat is in the fire!" Henry told Lizzie. Hay vowed to resign if the Senate defeated his treaty, and if Hay *didn't* quit, Henry predicted, "he will certainly hamstring Teddy. Won't it be fun?"

After considering the likely personal consequences of the brawl, however, Adams grew alarmed. "I foresee the bitterest kind of breach between [Hay] and Cabot," Henry told Lizzie. For Cabot he cared little, "but sister Anne [Nannie Lodge] will feel a quarrel, and if Hay is forced out of office by Cabot's act, as seems to be rather expected, you can judge better than I whether sister Anne will feel it." While Adams had come to loathe the sanctimonious Cabot, he treasured Nannie. And because of his own tie to a woman trapped in a difficult marriage, Henry undoubtedly understood that Nannie's affair with Hay was a much needed antidote to life with Cabot. A permanent rift between Hay and Lodge, which would drastically limit Nannie's opportunities to see Hay, would be a serious loss.

On March 13, exhausted after five weeks under fire, Hay resigned. Because of his impasse with the Senate, he told the president he had concluded that his usefulness was "at an end. I cannot help fearing also that the newspaper attacks upon the State Department, which have so strongly influenced the Senate, may be an injury to you, if I remain in the Cabinet."

McKinley returned Hay's letter as soon as he read it. "Nothing could be more unfortunate than to have you retire from the Cabinet," he insisted. "The personal loss would be great, but the public loss even greater. Your administration of the State Department has had my warm approval." Promising to "cheerfully bear whatever criticism or condemnation may come," McKinley urged Hay to "bear the atmosphere of the hour. It will pass away. We must continue working on the lines of duty and honor. Conscious of high purpose and honorable effort, we cannot yield our posts however the storm may rage."

A week later, revived by the warmth and strength of McKinley's confidence, Hay felt bold enough to send the notes that informed the European powers they had agreed to the Open Door in China. "Hay has had some sunshine to make up for the failure of his Canal Treaty," Henry wrote to Lizzie. The praise for the Open Door mystified Adams since he could not see that it bound anyone to anything, but Hay and Rockhill believed that their Open Door had "secured China's independence and so served the cause of peace and civilization." The secretary and his deft Orientalist were so sure of the permanence of their success that they were wholly unprepared for the anxious dispatches that soon began filtering in from Peking.

According to Edwin H. Conger, the American minister to China, the ruling Manchu dynasty was careening toward collapse. At the heart of the problem was a secret society, the Righteous and Harmonious Fists. Better known as the Boxers, they met behind closed doors to practice martial arts and to plot the overthrow of the im-

In the summer of 1900, when the Boxers began murdering foreigners in China, crowds gathered outside the home of Secretary of State John Hay to wait for news of Americans in Peking. LIBRARY OF CONGRESS

perial dynasty and the expulsion of "foreign devils." As the empress dowager raised taxes and granted ever more commercial concessions to outsiders, the Boxers' fury mounted, and when a drought in the summer of 1899 created an economic crisis, they went on a rampage. Bands of marauders swept through the northern province of Shantung, killing German missionaries and their Chinese converts and setting fire to churches and schools.

When the Boxers ignored orders to stop, Conger shrewdly guessed that at least some parties in the imperial palace sympathized with the uprising. Looking ahead, he saw the overthrow of the dynasty.

Rockhill disagreed. The Manchu dynasty had survived for centuries, and he could not believe it would perish at the hands of a small band of fanatics. Though he himself had not been to China for several years, he felt he understood it better than Conger, a former Iowa congressman who owed his post solely to his friendship with the president.

Conger's alarms continued, and in early June 1900 the Boxers began rioting in Peking. Houses belonging to foreigners were torched. Chinese suspected of being Christians were shot on sight.

Telegraph lines were cut, imperial soldiers defected to the Boxers, the Japanese chancellor and the German minister were murdered, and all the foreign legations were under siege. On June 13, a small expeditionary force organized by the European powers tried to march on Peking, and the empress, desperate to placate the Boxers, ordered her troops to turn back the Europeans. Five days later she decreed that all foreigners be put to death.

"Your open door is already off its hinges," Henry Adams wrote to Hay from Paris at the end of June. "How the deuce are you to get out? For a fortnight I have been utterly aghast about it. First, the unequalled horror of those wretched people shut up in Pekin to be skinned and burned. . . . Make an arrangement with You or Me or Him to let our citizens loose, and we'll promise never to go there again. . . . I hope you may do it, but all know you can't. What *can* you do then? That's where I begin to turn green. You've got literally the world on your shoulders."

Hay's first move was to advise Conger to protect Americans in China as independently as he could: "there must be no alliances," he cabled. Conger, with no time for fine points, moved a large contingent of Americans into the safety of the well-fortified British legation.

Washingtonians anxious for news of friends and relatives in Peking gathered daily outside Hay's house on Lafayette Square. The secretary had little to tell them. For weeks there was no word from Conger, and on July 20, when the minister finally broke through with a cry for help, the secretary worried that it was some sort of Boxer trickery. "Authenticity doubted," he wired Peking. "Answer this by giving your sister's name." Back came the magic word—*Alta*—and the newspapers marveled at Hay's ingenuity.

Three weeks later an international expeditionary force, including two thousand American soldiers from the Philippines, blazed its way into Peking and ended the uprising. The secretary of state received much of the credit and, to his great surprise, none of the abuse he had expected from those who predicted that America's involvement would lead to alliances with other powers. "What a business this has been in China!" Hay wrote to Adams. "So far we have got on, by being honest and naif—I do not clearly see where we are to come the delayed cropper. But it will come. At least we are spared the infamy of an alliance with Germany. I would rather I think be the dupe of China, than the chum of the Kaiser."

On the August day when the expeditionaries stormed Peking, Hay was in bed at Lake Sunapee, where he would stay for two months. The newspapers rumored that he was dying. Obviously hoping to influence the *Tribune*'s coverage of his health, Hay sent Whitelaw Reid a jaunty account of himself, insisting that he was a temporary casualty of his "June and July in Washington, with a crisis per hour, and a temperature of 98°. . . . This old tabernacle which I have inhabited for sixty years is getting quite ramshackle in the furnace, the plumbing and the electrical arrangements. But I have had myself pretty thoroughly overhauled, and they tell me there is nothing much the matter except antiquity, and that I have the right to look forward to a useless and querulous old age."

Clara Hay took a grimmer view. She rarely wrote to Henry Adams, but after a week of nursing her exhausted husband, she begged Henry to spend the winter in Washington rather than Paris. Hay, too weak to sit up and write, dictated a letter to Adams and added a note in his own hand: "I have never known anyone refuse to do as she says without being sorry for it afterwards."

As Hay lay in bed during August and September, he had plenty of time to work out the calculus of his life. His political feud with Senator Henry Cabot Lodge had created the bitter breach foreseen by Henry Adams, and Hay had not seen Nannie for months. This was a loss he could not discuss with anyone but Adams and Lizzie Cameron, and in a letter to George Nicolay, whom he had known for four decades, Hay seemed determined to count himself a fortunate man. Though he admitted his exasperation with the Senate, he declared himself generally pleased with the course of his life. His boyhood dreams had "absolutely and literally been fulfilled," he said. "The most important part of my public life came late, but it came in precisely the shape I dreamed when I was a boy." With this friend who had shared his youthful ambitions, Hay perhaps felt obliged to acknowledge that life had given him much of what Nicolay knew he wanted. But writing to Sir John Clark, whom he had befriended in his forties, Hay said he found little cause for jubilation. What joy was there in scaling a pinnacle if one could not act? he wondered. "So like

many another better man before me," he told Sir John, "I find power
and place when it comes late in life, not much better than dust and
ashes."

Triumph or pointless exercise, Hay's career as secretary of state
would soon be over. Clara had announced that she would not serve
a second term as a cabinet wife. The secretary, who had talked of
resigning from his "little Hell upon earth" for more than a year,
vowed to leave office after the election of 1900. He had only one
worry: "How hideous it would be, if I found private life bored me,
after definitely chucking the public," he told Adams. But after two
grueling years of "twisting the rope of sand which is American
diplomacy," he was willing to run the risk.

To Hay's weary eyes, America seemed to be "wallowing in a fat and
stupid prosperity," but he guessed that prosperity, even the fat and
stupid kind, would suffice to keep William McKinley in the White
House. As the summer conventions approached, the only mystery
seemed to be McKinley's running mate. Vice President Hobart had
died in November 1899 after a long illness. Cabot Lodge and
Thomas Platt, the Republican boss of New York, had immediately
set to work to draft Governor Theodore Roosevelt. Roosevelt
wanted none of it and came to Washington to say so. "It was more
fun than a goat," Hay told Adams. "He came down, with a sombre
resolution throned on his strenuous brow, to let McKinley and
Hanna know, once and for all, that he would not be Vice President,
and found to his stupefaction that nobody in Washington, except
Platt, had ever dreamed of such a thing. He did not even have a
chance to launch his *nolo episcopari* at [McKinley]. That statesman
said he did not want him on the ticket—that he would be far more
valuable in New York. . . . And so he went back, quite eased in his
mind but considerably bruised in his *amour-propre*."

Insisting that the governorship of New York suited his active
mind better than the empty honor of the vice presidency, Roosevelt
nevertheless decided to keep his spot as a delegate to the Republican
convention. When Mark Hanna, the convention chairman, asked
why, Roosevelt explained that it was a question of manliness: only a
coward would have stayed away.

Sensing that the brawny, hyperkinetic Roosevelt was ungovernable, Hanna loathed the prospect of having him on the ticket, and he came close to apoplexy as one delegate after another talked of drafting the Rough Rider. "Don't any of you realize that there's only one life between that madman and the Presidency?" Hanna exploded. When a delegate reminded Hanna that he was in charge, Hanna shouted, "I am not in control! McKinley won't let me use the power of the Administration to defeat Roosevelt. He is blind, or afraid, or something!"

Neither blind nor afraid, McKinley had piously decided that he would have no candidate but the candidate of the convention. Roosevelt, bowing to destiny, allowed himself to be nominated, and in a magnificently ostentatious fit of modesty, cast the only vote against himself.

"Your *duty* to the country," Hanna sputtered to McKinley, "is to *live* for *four* years from next March."

With the boundless energies of Theodore Roosevelt at his disposal, the president did not even bother to campaign from his front porch. Roosevelt whistlestopped from coast to coast, logging twenty-one thousand miles and preaching hundreds of sermons on the "fearful misery" that would follow if William Jennings Bryan lived in the White House. When Bryan, a fervent anti-imperialist, declared that "We dare not educate the Filipinos lest they learn to read the Declaration of Independence and the Constitution of the United States," the Rough Rider jeered. America was "a nation of men, not a nation of weaklings," and Americans were "as ready to face their responsibilities in the Orient as they were ready to face their responsibilities at home." It was absurd to hurl stones at expansionism, Roosevelt said, "for we have already expanded." Contraction was not an option.

Even Andrew Carnegie returned to the fold. Spooked by Bryan's socialism, he announced his support for McKinley in the pages of the *North American Review*. Better to err in the Philippines, Carnegie thought, than to "fail to repel this covert attack upon the reign of law at home." On election day, America decided to sign on for "four more years of the full dinner pail" rather than take a chance on the vague visions of William Jennings Bryan. When the votes were counted, McKinley's sweep was even more commanding than in 1896. "It was," John Hay told his son Del, "the most overwhelming victory in this generation."

20

The Road to Paradise

*F*rom Paris, where he was immersed in the art and literature of the Middle Ages, Adams congratulated Hay on his contributions to McKinley's triumph. The secretary of state had carried out his responsibilities with "infinite patience" and "uncommonly correct judgment," Adams declared, and had done so with exceptional grace: "you have held your tongue." But apart from the vicarious pleasure of a friend's success, Henry felt obliged to confess that to a twelfth-century monk like himself, nothing seemed more fantastical than twentieth-century America.

For five years Henry had lived in two times and places, spending winters in contemporary Washington and summers in medieval France. The deeper he delved into the twelfth century, the more he preferred abbots and troubadors to the politicians who crowded his breakfast table. In Washington, present hurtled toward future at a speed that left him breathless. "Every day opens a new horizon, and the rate we are going gets faster and faster till my twelfth-century head spins, and I hang on to the straps and shut my poor old eyes," he told Lizzie Cameron in February 1900, a few days after his sixty-second birthday.

Returning to France in the spring, he combed the 270 acres of the Paris Exposition for clues to the new century, but as he scrutinized the automobiles, rolling sidewalks, and other wonders of science, he gleaned nothing. "The charm of the show, to me, is that no one pretends to understand even in a remote degree, what these weird things are that they call electricity, Roentgen rays, and what not," he wrote home to Hay.

Again and again he found himself mesmerized by the gleaming dynamos in the machine gallery on the Champs de Mars, where he sat by the hour, "watching them run as noiselessly and as smoothly as the planets, and asking them—with infinite courtesy—where in Hell they are going." He did not understand how they ran, but in their faceless power he read the obituary of his own generation. "The curious mustiness of decay is already over our youth, and all the period from 1840 to 1870," he told Hay. "The period from 1870 to 1900 is closed. . . . The period from 1900 to 1930 is in full swing, and, gee-whacky! how it is going! It will break its damned neck long before it gets through." Awed by the thrumming monsters, unwilling to engage himself with a world in which every advance brought a dozen new perplexities, Adams fled to the comforts of a simpler time.

His escape to the Middle Ages had begun in the summer of 1895, when he toured the cathedrals of northern France with Cabot and Nannie Lodge and their two sons. For ten days they wandered from Amiens to Chartres, with Mont-Saint-Michel and a half dozen other great churches in between. Though he had seen Amiens twice in the past, he had "never thoroughly felt it before," he wrote to Lizzie Cameron. Coutances with its clean lines struck him as "the ideal image of outward austerity and inward refinement." Mont-Saint-Michel, overrun by "gross, shapeless, bare-armed" Frenchwomen, threatened to disappoint, but after a few hours of scrambling over cliffs and moats with the Lodge boys, Henry yielded to the magic of the mount. Even the pugnacious Cabot, he noted, became "natural, simple, interested, cultivated, artistic, liberal—genial." Following a night at Le Mans, the travelers spent an afternoon at Chartres, where Henry "worshipped at last before the splendor of the great glass Gods."

As soon as he arrived in Paris, he sent Lizzie an enthusiastic account of his medieval education. A week later he had second thoughts. "The Gothic church, both in doctrine and in expression, is not my idea of a thoroughly happy illusion," he told his brother Brooks. "It is always restless, grasping and speculative." The pointed arch was "cheap," and the highest compliment he was willing to pay the Gothic style was that it reflected his own "ideals and limitations. It is human." He felt more at home in the sweeping Norman vaults of Coutances, which he imagined his ancestors had helped construct. His soul, he insisted, was "still built into it. I can almost remember the faith that gave me energy, and the sacred boldness that made my towers seem to me so daring . . . Within I had no doubts. There the contrite sinner was welcomed with such tenderness as makes me still wish I were one. There is not a stone in the whole interior which I did not treat as though it were my own child."

But in the end, despite his reservations, it was the Gothic sumptuousness of Chartres, not the simplicity of Coutances, that took hold of his imagination. He understood Chartres no better than the dynamos, but he was content to feel its power. As he mused to Lizzie Cameron after a second visit, "I am not quite sure that there is much religion in glass; but for once I will not require too much." It was enough to sense the "elevation and passion, the absorption of every act and thought in an ideal of infinite beauty and purity." The result was "beyond what I should suppose possible to so mean an animal as man. It gives him a dignity which he is in no other instance entitled to claim."

A year later, after his winter of plotting with Senators Lodge and Cameron and the Cuban revolutionaries, Henry revisited Chartres and decided that the combination of stained glass and Gothic was "the highest ideal ever yet reached by men." Amid the glories of Chartres he could not help thinking about the paltriness of his own time. Foreseeing the victory of William McKinley and his fellow plutocrats, Adams complained that a "materialistic society like ours has no life except in materialistic success." If America had "an earnest impulse, an energy or a thought outside of dollars and cents," he hoped to see it before his descent into senility.

On the surface, the grievance seemed little more than a reflex born of Henry's twin habits of keeping a tight rein on his pleasures and of seeing himself as an alien. Generations of Adamses had perfected the art of nipping their joys in the bud, a vice that Henry cursed but could not break. Politically, he had always insisted on his status as an outsider, relishing his vision of himself as "stable-companion to statesmen." What distinguished his protests in the summer of 1896 from his past raillery was, quite simply, Chartres. However keenly the cathedral sharpened his feeling of dispossession, it also gave him a refuge. In the peace of its great nave, afloat in the pure colors of the glass and the uncomplicated melodies of Gregorian chant, he would begin to sort through the accumulated tensions of a lifetime: between thinking and feeling, between male and female, and between his love for Lizzie Cameron and his guilt over his dead wife.

Henry Adams spent most of 1897 and 1898 in Europe, but there was little time for cathedrals. Life revolved around Ambassador Hay and his family in London and around Lizzie Cameron, whose marriage was in tatters. In the spring of 1897, after Don vacated his Senate seat, Lizzie begged her uncle John Sherman, then secretary of state, to give Don an embassy. Sherman did not oblige, perhaps because of Don's affinity for bourbon. Out of office, the senator had no use for Washington, and he again spoke of retiring to his farm in Pennsylvania. Lizzie promptly collapsed. The breakdown appears to have been as much mental as physical, but when the physician's stethoscope detected a "distinct valvular weakness" in the heart, the episode was labeled a heart attack. The patient was ordered to rest for six months. Don exacted his revenge by leasing their house to Garret Hobart, the new vice president. On learning that she would have to leave 21 Lafayette Square by the end of April, Lizzie suffered a relapse.

By mid-May, the redoubtable Mrs. Cameron was on her way to Europe, having persuaded her doctors that the strains of life with Don outweighed the stress of travel. Don went "on a jag," a friend confided to Hay, but managed to sober up sufficiently to put Lizzie, Martha, and a nurse aboard an ocean liner in New York. The summer was to be a trial separation, Lizzie explained. "I am determined to make a good try at running our broken down machine—if it *won't* go, then I can re-adjust and begin," Lizzie explained to Henry. "But I must *try,* or I shall not feel quite satisfied." The effort was not for her but for Martha: "She has seen more than I thought and remembers from further back—But for her very sake it must be *made* to

Elizabeth Sherman Cameron. Unhappily married, she looked to Henry Adams for under-standing and companionship but did not love him as deeply as he loved her.
ARLINE BOUCHER TEHAN

work." Unable to express all her tumult, she merely noted how "curious" it was that "one shuts up like a jackknife when anything becomes real, or sensitive. . . . I have often wanted to tell you, but cannot. The moment it is of *you,* I cannot talk of you even to yourself. Above all, I cannot say anything of all that I feel to you. Someday I shall go on my knees to you and humbly kiss your hand—even then, you won't know the smallest portion of it, very dearest."

Adams was waiting on the pier when her ship moored in Southampton. He helped Lizzie to London and on to Paris, where the doctors assured her that she needed nothing but rest. As Henry reported to Nannie Lodge, "there is no incurable trouble; only nervous collapse, which is the slowest of all things to repair itself." He dared not voice his terror that Lizzie's psyche might prove as unsalvageable as Clover's. Two years before, when Lizzie's conflicts with Don precipitated a milder breakdown, Adams had warned her that she was "walking into nervous collapse. Most women do as they approach middle life. My own existence went to pieces on the same rocks. . . . As I have said again and again, you have merely to sit still and let things pass—they cannot hurt you."

With several nieces and their schoolmates coming for the summer, Henry had rented a rambling house in a village outside Paris and persuaded Lizzie and her entourage to join them. Lizzie rested, and Henry's most ambitious outings were his occasional rides among the cedars of Lebanon and purple beeches in the neighboring forest. Cecil Spring Rice, the first of his breakfast-table nephews, came down from Berlin to cheer them up. By summer's end, Lizzie had gained weight and could walk a mile, but neither Henry nor Springy approved of her mental condition. As Adams told Hay, "her head still goes to pieces at the least strain, and I venture to predict that the winter at home, under existing circumstances, will finish her career as anything but an invalid. The heart weakness can hardly fail to become chronic and aggravated." To Henry's dismay and against the advice of her French physicians, Lizzie made plans to return to the United States.

The rapprochement was doomed from the start. Landing in New York in mid-December, Lizzie and Martha learned that they would pass Christmas in a hotel. Don spent lavishly on flowers to brighten their rooms and quickly forged an alliance with Martha by giving her a puppy. With Lizzie, he was noncommittal and uncommunicative; she had no idea whether he wanted a reconciliation or not. "The eggs I am walking on have not smashed, but the tension keeps me so absorbed I cannot concentrate on anything else," she wrote her very dearest. To keep friction at a minimum, she dined out twice a day, visited John La Farge in his studio, and went to the theater almost every night. Come morning she could barely recall "what it all was,—where I have been,—whom I have seen."

In January, when the Camerons moved on to Washington and Lizzie found herself reduced to the role of guest in the world where she had once starred as hostess, she was in a state of constant irritation. Apart from a novelist named Edith Wharton, whom she found intelligent and pretty, she met no one she wanted to know. "I lunch, dine, go to balls, but I see no one interesting, no one whom I want to bring home with me and talk to," she grumbled. "I think one must leave society and go among the freaks to find originality or amusement."

After a bitter quarrel in February, Don went off to Pennsylvania to sulk, and Lizzie organized her own expedition to Boston to prolong their time apart. The heaviest burden fell on Martha. Depressed and anxious, the twelve-year-old had no appetite but was gaining weight at alarming speed. "It is very distressing to me," Lizzie told Henry. "I like grace too much to reconcile myself to those enormous hips." Martha did not like them either and worried that she was abnormal.

Longing for respite from the "howling swells" who filled her evenings, Lizzie found her way to a ladies' lecture on architecture. When the speaker began to discourse on the Gothic, she leaped to share the enthusiasm she had caught from Adams. "I tried to explain that it was not just ornament but fundamental construction," she wrote to her mentor. "But they refused to listen." America was impossible. After the *Maine* blew up in Havana in February 1898, she panicked: What if the United States declared war on Spain before she could get back to Europe? "Oh! Dordy Dordy, how I want to see you *just now*. The summer is long in coming—and when it comes what will it bring?"

What it brought was the long house party in the English countryside at Surrenden Dering. Every day for three months Lizzie Cameron wore an air of gaiety, and only the perspicacious Henry James glimpsed the truth behind the mask. Even before Surrenden, Lizzie had decided she could not bear another winter in the United States. In April, as soon as she arrived in Paris, she found an apartment for herself and Martha at 50 Avenue du Bois de Boulogne and signed a lease. "The amount it will cost me is small for the peace of mind it may bring," she told Henry. "So altogether I thought it best. When I return I must put some furniture in it, then either of us can use it *au besoin*. I do hope you will think it right."

The key word was "either." Mr. Adams and Mrs. Cameron would not occupy the apartment together. Henry's extravagant sense of propriety also demanded that as long as Don Cameron was else-where, it would be indelicate of Mr. Adams to spend too much time in Paris with Mrs. Cameron, even in an apartment of his own. And so began the most peculiar phase of their peculiar liaison. For the next two decades they rarely saw each other for more than a few weeks at a stretch and always in the company of other people, whose presence lent the air of innocence on which he insisted. Each summer when Adams went to Paris, Lizzie traveled, sometimes in Europe, sometimes taking Martha home to see Don. In the fall, when they returned for Martha's school year, Adams lingered a bit then left for Washington, usually planning his arrival for sometime after December 6, his "haunting anniversary."

During the winter of 1898–99, her first in Paris, Lizzie reveled in her new freedom and the elegance of her gold-and-white drawing room. Martha, thriving in her convent school, stood first in all her classes. Whenever Lizzie thought of going back to America, she shuddered. "I wonder how a horse feels after a summer in the pasture when the harness goes on again," she asked Henry. In the spring, she could hardly wait for Adams's arrival. "I shall be hanging over the balcony edge waiting for you when your cab drives up," she promised. ". . . And do you think it proper to stop with me? I do!"

Where Adams stayed is not clear, but he soon joined the Lodges for a tour of Italy and Sicily. For a time Lizzie hoped to meet up with them, and then, in the middle of May 1899, decided that her duty compelled her to take Martha home to see her father. "My instinct tells me that I am to go, that I *must* go," she explained. "And I spend my days hoping that I am above the natural animal and have no instinct left. If you knew how I hate it! I love this Paris *appartement,* and the independence, and the liberty,—and the balcony and the birds—how can I leave! You and I could do so much this summer!"

In New York, Don—looking "very hay-seedy indeed," in Lizzie's opinion—announced that they were going to Saratoga Springs for his gout. Beyond that he had made no plans. A summer of "wandering from hotel to hotel is clearly before us," Lizzie seethed. Saratoga was either "painfully funny" or "funnily painful"—she could not decide. Why, she begged of Henry Adams, "do we like feeding in long trough-like rooms, black with flies and negro waiters? And sitting infinite hours, in infinite dozens of rocking chairs rocking infinite miles, on a piazza half a mile long? And the coarseness, the loudness, the cheapness of type, of the people. It is appalling. Have I forgotten?"

As they gypsied about, Don's moods swung so wildly and so rapidly that Lizzie was perpetually off balance. Pleased with himself for the success of several recent business ventures, including an investment in a new typewriter, Don was often the soul of amiability. But when Lizzie raised a question about Martha's inheritance, he flew into a rage. His will, written years before, provided for the children of his first marriage but had not been revised to include Martha. Angered by the suggestion that he did not love Martha, Don refused to say what, if anything, he planned to do. Lizzie was left to worry that if Don died without changing the will, his heirs would feel no obligation to the child of his estranged wife.

Moving from Saratoga to Saranac and from New York to Cleveland and Washington, the Camerons were pursued by letters in an unmistakably feminine hand, which Lizzie recognized. Several years before, Don and this woman had got into what Lizzie called "a scrape," and Lizzie deduced that she had "some claim upon him," most likely a child. Sensing that Don lived in perpetual dread of a scandal, Lizzie even managed to feel sorry for him. But her sympathy turned to pique when Don announced that they could not stay in Henry Adams's empty house in Washington because "it might not be proper." Clover Adams's old friend Anne Palmer Fell was right, Lizzie decided: "one must not be a female if one would have success or happiness."

Worst of all, Don gave no hint of their future. Lizzie could not tell whether he expected—or wanted—her and Martha to stay in the United States, or whether he planned to continue subsidizing their life in Paris. In early October, unable to bear the suspense any longer, she tried to tell him she thought it best to go back to France. Don refused to hear her out. He "gets up and leaves the room as soon as I open the question," Lizzie moaned to Henry. "What *am* I to do?"

Martha rescued them by falling desperately ill with a fever of 104 degrees. It passed in a few days but not before frightening her father into submission. He hovered over her bed and obediently did errands for the voyage to Europe. "Don't leave the *appartement,* welcome us there like visitors," Lizzie instructed Henry on November 1. "Two weeks from today we shall be together. I cannot write!"

★   ★   ★

Alone in Paris during the months Lizzie and Martha spent in the United States, Henry Adams, to his enormous surprise, felt more contentment than he had known since the happiest days of his marriage. He had begun 1899 in a vile mood. Bored with the chattering young people who filled his house, he longed for deliverance from the condition he had diagnosed as "Avunculitis." What he wanted was "to go—go—go—anywhere—to the devil—Sicily—Russia—Siberia—China—only to keep going."

But as soon as Adams settled in Lizzie's apartment near the Bois de Boulogne, his "world-hatred," as Clarence King had called it, melted away. At liberty to fill his days as he pleased, he walked miles through the streets of Paris in a hunt for Gothic spires. He bought architectural photographs by the score, and when the August heat kept him indoors, he plunged into a study of Mont-Saint-Michel. "Paris delights me, but not for its supposed delights," he wrote to Hay. "It is the calm of its seclusion that charms; the religious rest that it diffuses, and the cloister-like peace that it brings to the closing years of life. I reflect on the goodness of all things, and enjoy the peace of God."

He saw almost no one. King's stepbrother, George Howland, was in Paris with his bride, and much as Adams wanted word of King, he refrained from spoiling a honeymoon with an old man's invitations to dinner. "I study my French prepositions and walk in the Bois," he told Lizzie. When Augustus Saint-Gaudens and a young American poet named Joseph Trumbull Stickney came to dine, they had to thread their way through tables and chairs piled high with books on medieval architecture. It was through Saint-Gaudens that Adams discovered the magnitude of his own contentment. The sculptor had taken a studio in Montparnasse but could hardly work because of depression. After listening to his friend's woes, Henry replied that he himself "never felt any other way and rather liked it; that Michelangelo not only live in it, but made his greatest work out of it, in the Penseroso and Medici tombs; that Albert [sic] Dürer made a picture of it; and that it was really very good fun when you got used to it, and knew what a good fellow it was." As Adams told Lizzie, it was a delectable turn of the tables: "Is it not humorously ironic, that I, of all people, should act as a tonic to *égayer* the depressed?"

When he completed his investigation of spires, he took up stained glass. There were many excursions to Chartres, which impressed him more each time. In late October, entranced by the pure blues streaming through the windows and the hymns sailing through the vast spaces, he "felt the charm" as never before. "Color counts for so much in idolatry," he observed. "The glass window is as emotional as music." For the first time since his encounter with the royal family of Tahiti he wanted to write a book. Not a work of any consequence, he assured Lizzie. He would call it *Travels in France with Nothing to Say,* publish it privately, and present it as a gift when visiting friends in the country.

Any study of the twelfth century and Chartres led quickly to the Virgin Mary, and Henry Adams was uniquely equipped to appreciate her grip on the imagination of medieval France. Like Henry James, he had rejected the masculine worlds of politics and business and cherished the fancy that women, unsullied by struggles for power and money, were the superior sex. For twenty-five years Adams had rarely passed up a chance to argue his case. In his 1876 Lowell Institute lecture on the rights of primitive women, he blamed the inferior status of their modern sisters on the patriarchs of the early Christian church. Enlarging the role of their masculine God, the church fathers had dethroned the strong goddesses favored by the pagans and substituted an ideal of female submissiveness that had persisted into modern times. In *Democracy* and *Esther,* he had pitted feminine idealism against masculine power. His heroines met defeat, but they emerged with their integrity unscathed. After Clover's death, Henry had sought comfort in the companionship of her female friends and in Kwannon, the Buddhist goddess of compassion, whose boundless mercy inspired the sculpture at Clover's grave. The old queen of Tahiti, graceful and unaffected, gave Adams another paragon of womanhood. Happening onto the Virgin Mary after a lifetime of contemplating ideal forms of femininity, Adams easily recognized her as one more deity for his female pantheon. Though he could no more pray to the Virgin than he could worship the dynamo, she inspired one of his greatest books. *The Education of Henry Adams* and his great history showed the riches of his intellect, but it was in *Mont-Saint-Michel and Chartres* that he revealed his deepest feelings.

To introduce the world that had created Mont-Saint-Michel and Chartres, Adams posed as an uncle touring France with his nieces. A genial shepherd, Uncle Henry wanted only to share the delights he had found in the French Middle Ages. Pedantry was not to be countenanced, and dates, which he found "stupidly annoying," would be kept to a minimum. His tourists did not need the facts of the Middle Ages but the feeling, and he often reminded them to feel what they could "and let the rest go."

The tour began with the tip of the spire at Mont-Saint-Michel. "The Archangel loved heights," Adams declared. "Standing on the summit of the tower that crowned his church, wings upspread, sword uplifted, the devil crawling beneath, and the cock, symbol of eternal vigilance, perched on his mailed foot, Saint Michael held a place of his own in heaven and on earth." Poised between two worlds, the Archangel represented "Church and State, and both militant. He is the conqueror of Satan, the mightiest of all created spirits, the nearest to God."

Though Adams suspected that his young charges would find the Mont a bit austere, he wanted them to savor its blend of Romanesque and Gothic. The "quiet, restrained strength" of the Romanesque, with its rounded arches and castlelike masculinity, and the delicately feminine curves and "vaulting imagination" of the pointed Gothic arch, made "a union nearer the ideal than is often allowed in marriage," he said. For those who felt the art, there was no discord: "the strength and the grace join hands; the man and woman love each other still." Mont-Saint-Michel marked a turning point: "What the Roman could not express flowered into the Gothic; what the masculine mind could not idealize in the warrior, it idealized in the woman."

Taking his pilgrims to Chartres, Adams hoped that modern prejudices against the Gothic would not sully their pleasures. To most minds, he said, the Gothic meant shadows and fear and death. For Esther Dudley, the protagonist of his second novel, the neo-Gothic cathedral and oppressive theology of the Reverend Stephen Hazard held all of these terrors. But such dread was rooted in misconception,

Adams had learned in his studies of the Middle Ages. Gothic art strove to express light, not gloom. Craving "light and always more light" Gothic architects scoffed at gravity, turning walls into windows and resting ever higher vaults on ever thinner columns.

The quest for light at Chartres was inspired by the Virgin Mary, and to feel Chartres, one had to accept that it was the work of the virgin, not of human artists. Vividly aware that Mary's displeasure could damn them for eternity, architects and sculptors and stained-glass masters paid no attention to the needs of the "flat-eared peasants" and "slow-witted barons" who would pray at Chartres. Hence the greatest of the cathedral's rose windows was set for the gaze of the Virgin, behind the pilgrims kneeling in the nave.

The Virgin had also supervised the lighting of her palace, and no cathedral had light to rival Chartres. Wanting only to please her, the window makers dispensed with realism and "never hesitated to put their colour where they wanted it, or cared whether a green camel or a pink lion looked like a dog or a donkey provided they got their harmony or value," Adams explained. To his mind, the most exquisite light in the palace came from the windows in the Virgin's "boudoir," as he playfully called the apse.

Mary delighted Adams as much for her heresies as for her queenliness. Her apse was regal, but "in the nave and on the porch, among the peasants, she liked to appear as one of themselves; she insisted on lying in bed, in a stable, with the cows and asses about her, and her baby in a cradle by the bedside as though she had suffered like other women, though the Church insisted she had not." (Joseph, Uncle Henry observed, "was notoriously uncomfortable in her court, and always preferred to get as near to the door as he could.") From the earliest days of Christianity the Virgin had occupied the position of honor in the Church, but as her cult swept France, her devotees "seemed bent on absorbing Christ in His Mother, and making the Mother the Church, and Christ the Symbol," Adams said.

The reason was easily grasped. In the Church's hierarchy of supernatural beings, Mary ranked above the saints and just below the Trinity, which made her the ideal mediator—the gentle mother who stood between the prodigal child and the punishing father. With her maternal willingness to shelter and love and forgive, Adams said, "Mary concentrated in herself the whole rebellion of man against fate; the whole protest against divine law; . . . the whole unutterable fury of human nature beating itself against the walls of its prison-house." In a world where Church and State ruled as one and where the Trinity signified Unity, Mary represented "whatever was not Unity; whatever was irregular, exceptional, outlawed; and this was the whole human race." Her pity was infinite, and her subjects longed to believe that she possessed unlimited power as well.

The Virgin's prominence in the Middle Ages corroborated Adams's theory of female superiority in all spheres—mind, body, and society. To Adams, the splendor of Chartres led straight to the Garden of Eden, where feminine superiority had first appeared. "The woman's greater intelligence was to blame for Adam's fall," he declared. "Eve was justly punished because she should have known better, while Adam, as the Devil truly said, was a dull animal." Biologically, women also had an edge. "Nature regards the female as the essential, the male as the superfluity of her world," he insisted. He offered no evidence, but it was a point he had often discussed with Clarence King, who shared his conviction. (As King gamily put it, reproduction was a business in which men played almost no part: "We press the button and they do the rest.") Socially, Adams believed, man was "a mere rooting grunting hog," a creature who could be saved from his instincts only by the grace of woman. If the court of the Queen of Heaven taught anything, it was that love made gentlemen "even of boors." Seeing the Virgin Mary as the finest specimen of the finer sex, Adams proclaimed her "the last and greatest deity of all."

Summing up the age that worshiped the Virgin, Adams noted that it was the moment in history when men were strongest: "never before or since have they shown equal energy in such varied directions, or such intelligence in the direction of their energy." And yet "these marvels of history"—the Plantagenet kings, scholars like Abelard and Aquinas, Robin Hood and Marco Polo, architects, crusaders, and monks—"all, without apparent exception, bowed down before the woman."

At a loss to explain this paradox, Adams dismissed it. But the intensity of his attraction to a world in which men bowed to women opens the question of his own submission to the forces of femininity. Years before, after the painful Paris reunion with Lizzie Cameron at the end of his South Seas journey, he had told her he yearned for "a God to pray to, or better yet, a Goddess" with a child, which he recognized as a substitute for her and Martha. In the Virgin of the French Middle Ages he found the ideal that allowed him to transform his ungratified love into worship and to create a role for himself that was less demeaning than "tame cat." Mrs. Cameron would be his goddess, he would be her votary. It was a noble resolution of a conflict that had tormented them both, since it seemed to settle, once and for all, the question of sex. In his sixties, he freely admitted his lack of sexual desire, and when he learned that one of his contemporaries took a young bride, he overflowed with disgust. "The sexual period in men and women is well-defined," he told Lizzie. "It is even a scientific distinction, like infancy and senility." Goddesses, of course, inhabited a realm beyond physical desire. Or so he hoped.

The Virgin also gave Henry a new prism for looking at his marriage. With her impeccable taste and disdain for convention, the Queen of Heaven was as charmingly defiant as Clover Adams. But the supreme glory of the Virgin was her love, a point Adams stressed so often that he seemed to be trying to persuade himself that her compassion could even encompass a man who had failed to save his wife from suicide. Outcasts in other churches could still hope in hers. To the Virgin, the Last Judgment did not symbolize God's justice or man's corruption but her own infinite mercy. The Trinity judged, the Virgin forgave. "The rudest ruffian of the Middle Ages, when he looked at this Last Judgment, laughed; for what was the Last Judgment to her! . . . Her chief joy was to pardon; her eternal instinct was to love; her deepest passion was pity!" If anyone could commute the sentence Adams feared he deserved, it was the Virgin.

In spite of his longing to believe in the redemptive power of the Virgin's love, she gave him no more serenity than Esther Dudley had found on her spiritual odyssey. To Henry Adams, the outstanding fact of the Virgin worship that created the sublime beauty of Chartres was its impermanence. By the thirteenth century, the universe was growing "more complex and less reducible to a central control," Adams wrote at the end of his tour. "With as much obstinacy as though it were human, it has insisted on expanding its parts. . . . Unity turned itself into complexity, multiplicity, variety, and even contradiction."

Even the unity was an illusion, Adams decided. The essence of the Gothic lay not in the harmonies of its stained glass but in the tension of the masonry—in the "springing motion of the broken arch, the leap downwards of the flying buttress—the visible effort to throw off a visible strain." Danger lurked in every stone.

> The peril of the heavy tower, of the restless vault, of the vagrant buttress; the uncertainty of logic, the inequalities of the syllogism, the irregularities of the mental mirror—all these haunting nightmares of the Church are expressed as strongly by the Gothic cathedral as though it had been the cry of human suffering, and as no emotion had ever been expressed before or is likely to find expression again. The delight of its aspirations is flung up to the sky. The pathos of its self-distrust and anguish of doubt is buried in the earth as its last secret.

It was a telling secret, for the tensions Adams saw in the Gothic were his own. The age in which all energy was bent to the Virgin's purpose had come to an end because the world "could not remain forever balancing between thought and act." Henry Adams could. He could humorously berate himself as a "sexagenarian Hamlet," but he could not live without tension and polarities. For every consoling Virgin he had to find a menacing dynamo, every new joy heightened his own great sorrow, every insight into his feelings became a spur to self-mastery instead of a step toward self-acceptance. He could admire the twelfth century's success in concealing its doubts, but he could not hide his own. Two decades earlier, when he wrote the ending of *Democracy,* he dispatched his shaken protagonist to Egypt, where her desire to hide in the Great Pyramid revealed the author's wish to bury the anxiety created by Clover's unhappiness on the Nile. In *Mont-Saint-Michel and Chartres,* Henry Adams tried once more to bury his anguish. The Virgin, with all her love and forgiveness, was powerless to help him.

Most of the first draft of *Mont-Saint-Michel and Chartres* was written during the summer of 1900 in Lizzie Cameron's Paris apartment. Thoroughly engrossed, Henry stayed in the city even when the temperature rose to 90 degrees. Thomas Aquinas, he told Lizzie, was as fine as "liquid air for cooling the hot blood of my youth." In October, when she and Martha returned from a summer of traveling in

Italy, he was ready to share the manuscript. He hoped that both of
them would tell him of any "hitches" in translation of medieval
verse, and he counted on Martha, now fourteen, to help by pointing
out passages she did not understand. But by the time the Camerons
arrived in Paris, Lizzie was too distracted to appreciate the ramifica-
tions of Henry's ties to the Virgin. While he had worked to transform his love into adoration, she had fallen in love with a younger
man.

Joseph Trumbull Stickney was an enchanter. He had dark hair, an
olive complexion, pensive eyes of deep gray, and he carried his
six-foot-four frame with the grace of a Greek runner. A magna cum
laude graduate of Harvard, he had enjoyed a short but adventurous
career as a newspaper correspondent during the Spanish-American
War, after which he settled in Paris to write poetry and study literature at the Sorbonne. He was twenty-six, sixteen years younger
than Mrs. Cameron.

Henry Adams knew him well. They had met in Paris in 1899, and
Henry immediately adopted him as a nephew. Like the Lodges' son
Bay, another young poet living in Paris, Joe Stickney gave Adams a
bracing change from the "mild sort of Euthanasia" induced by too
much time in the company of his adoring, compliant nieces. With
their agile minds and fierce opinions, Joe and Bay supplied Uncle
Henry with the resistance and disrespect he considered essential to
mental health.

Joe had been a fact of Lizzie's life since February 1900. After one of
her first dinners with him, she had informed Henry that Stickney
intrigued her. "I do not know how he would wear, but I am willing
to try. We have planned some excursions together." Love poems
from Stickney began to arrive in her mail, and she and Martha spent
much of their summer holiday in Italy with Stickney and his mother.
In the fall, when the travelers reconvened in Paris, Bay Lodge
watched in distress as Joe and Lizzie carried on their flirtation in front
of Adams. Bay, furious with Lizzie for her refusal to "conceal the
fact that she likes the attentions of a young man," told his parents
that "Uncle Henry was very rude to Joe on several occasions. It was
quite pathetic." Bay doubted that there was anything in the relationship "to bring a blush to the cheek of innocence," but whether the
dalliance extended to the bedroom or not, it was clear that Joe Stick-

ney was the recipient of a sexually charged form of affection withheld from Henry Adams.

Though Adams chose to believe that he had outlived sexual desire, he had won no exemption from the pain of jealousy. Faced with a goddess who refused his worship, Adams retreated in stunned silence. As autumn sank into winter, he busied himself with the dynamos on the Champs de Mars and waited for the apocalypse. "I cannot doubt that God will very soon bust up the whole circus, and proceed to judgment," he wrote to Nannie Lodge in early December. Having made his "arrangement for paradise through the Virgin Mary and the twelfth-century church," he claimed not to care. In January Adams packed his trunks for America and announced that he would never again return to Paris.

21

A Queer Taste in Fates

*A*dams was somewhere on the Atlantic when Bay Lodge appointed himself to confront Mrs. Cameron. Impetuous and ardent, Bay undoubtedly expected some sign of contrition, and he was furious to find the accused in a "brutally cheerful" frame of mind. Dismissing Bay's charges with a laugh, she seized control of the conversation and adroitly changed course. Uncle Henry, she explained, had reached a point in life where he deserved their sympathy. "She even told me he was losing his mind and gave little instances of his lapses of memory," Bay fumed to his parents. "The whole thing is pretty tragic and I don't think either Mrs. Cameron or Joe have dealt with him fairly."

Understanding the contest better than Bay did, Adams also adopted a strategy of brutal cheer. The moment his ship docked in Manhattan, he departed from character and threw himself into a "mad cyclone" of socializing. As he rushed to tell Mrs. Cameron, he had been welcomed "with tender embraces" by two of New York's most celebrated women—Elsie De Wolfe, an actress-turned-interior decorator, and her friend Elizabeth Marbury, a theatrical agent. By all rights, the parvenus he met in Miss Marbury's salon should have rasped on his patrician nerves, but to Lizzie he would confess no more than amusement and a passing wish to write another satire.

And if America was "fat and greasy with wealth," so much the better for artists like John La Farge, whose atelier was busier than ever.

Back on Lafayette Square, where vice president–elect Theodore Roosevelt and Senator Henry Cabot Lodge had scaled new heights of pomposity, the cheery pose was harder to maintain. Roosevelt, who had never excelled at listening, now felt entitled to barge into conversations whenever he pleased, pontificating in a high-pitched whine and referring to himself (at unnervingly frequent intervals) by the three-syllable pronoun "Aieeee." The "very buffalo must run," Adams shuddered after having him to dinner in February. To a twelfth-century monk it appeared that America had moved "beyond Teddy"—and beyond everyone else, for that matter. "The ball has rolled up so big that no one knows how to steady it." Roaring at it *à la* Theodore simply "makes one tired."

Cabot was a more complicated case. Working quietly in the wings, Secretary of State John Hay had been trying to get Bay Lodge a sinecure at the American consulate in Rome. The diplomatic service had a long tradition of assigning writers, W. D. Howells and Bret Harte among them, to consular posts with light duties, which left them considerable freedom for literary pursuits. In a perverse display of rectitude, Cabot—the same Cabot who wheedled shamelessly on behalf of constituents with diplomatic aspirations—scotched Hay's plan by striking out the necessary appropriation in Congress. Bay concluded that the secretary did not like him and unfortunately said as much to someone who told Hay. "So Hay feels hurt and wounded and Bay feels hurt and the mothers feel hurt, and Cabot feels virtuous," Henry wrote to Lizzie. "If you dare lisp this story, I'll kill you."

Cabot and Teddy grated, but King and Hay were cause for genuine alarm. Felled by pneumonia and a racking cough, King had been banished to the tropics for the winter. Hay, looking "pasty and pale, had barely enough wind for the five-minute walk from Sixteenth and H to the State Department. With no clear diagnosis from his physicians, Hay sometimes swore he was dying of angina pectoris and sometimes insisted the trouble was mere "duckfits." Clara Hay thought that whatever the malady, the cure was a quiet summer at Lake Sunapee. Adams hoped she was right. "So much of Hay's valetudinarianism has always been nervous that I fully admit he may live to be ninety," Henry wrote to Lizzie, "but he is no longer fit to be Secretary. Enfin, he is writing his resignation."

Hay's letter went to the White House in March 1901, at the beginning of McKinley's second term. When the president asked him to wait a few months, he agreed, and when his ailments abated, he shelved the resignation indefinitely. "Hay gains strength, and, as the devil gets well, he cares less for religious retreat," Adams sighed. Henry sympathized with Hay's fear that he was meant to be a first-rate ambassador abroad rather than a third-rate politician at home, but he had no patience with Hay's willingness to die in the act of proving himself wrong. After the debacle of the Panama Canal treaty, Hay had set aside his senatorial antipathies and plunged into the work of negotiating a new pact, this time taking care to consult the Senate. He also renewed discussions for the acquisition of the Caribbean island of St. Thomas, and in China he put new energy into holding Russia and Germany to the terms of the Open Door agreement. In Adams's view, the weight of circumstance—the same big ball that stood in Theodore Roosevelt's way—would make it impossible for Hay to prevail. "Congress and Europe have combined to sit on him hard, and squeeze his breath out," Henry told Lizzie.

For all its faults, Washington was where Henry Adams wanted to be. Though he confessed to Lizzie his "very strong wish" that she and Martha were with him, he had no desire to return to Paris. In Washington one could at least enjoy the sensation of being a polyp in clean water, he said, "while elsewhere the water is dead and rather dirty," like the water in a lagoon. "Paris is at best a lagoon for artistic polyps"—a species that undoubtedly included Joe Stickney.

Henry tried to detach himself from the hurt inflicted by Lizzie and Joe, but he could not resist an occasional barb. When he sent her his new poem, "Prayer to the Virgin of Chartres," she must have understood that he was pitting his poetic talents against Stickney's, and she could not have failed to note the change in his relationship with his beloved goddess. The joy evoked by the Virgin of *Mont-Saint-Michel and Chartres* was gone, replaced by utter despair.

In another bit of spite, Henry called Lizzie's attention to *The Sacred*

Fount, a new novel by Henry James. Set at a house party in the English countryside, the story was told by a James-like narrator who was trying to sort out the secret romances of the guests in order to test a theory that in every relationship one party was fed and the other was fed upon. From the tale and the setting, Mrs. Cameron would have been forced to conclude that James had not enjoyed his time in her ménage at Surrenden Dering.

Lizzie parried with less subtlety, often mentioning Stickney in her letters and blithely ignoring Henry's jealousy. She said nothing of the tiff with Bay but did note that Bay now found Stickney "very reflective," which she assumed to mean older. "I have the guilty feeling that I have done it," she said, almost proudly. "Dear, dear— think of me aging a man when his great attraction is his youth."

However diminished, Stickney's magnetism was still strong enough to pull her to Italy in the spring. She was "stone broke," she told Henry, and could not tell whether Don intended to continue his support. The lease on their Lafayette Square house would expire at the end of April, but Don refused to say what he planned next. "[D]oes Donald mean to re-let the house?" she wondered. "Are we to go home or stay over here? I am tired enough of Europe, but what else is there? Where are we to go?" Don wrote regularly to Martha but offered no clues to their future. "How tired I am of it all. Of course it is Martha who complicates it all. I could cut a straight swathe if it were not for her interests, bless her."

Until Don made up his mind, Lizzie meant to stay in Italy, subsisting on polenta if she had to. She left Paris in March, and in early April, from Florence, sent an unwelcome bit of news to Lafayette Square: "Stickney is here." For the next six weeks, while Henry heard nothing, Bay Lodge heard everything. Mr. Stickney and Mrs. Cameron went everywhere together, Bay's sources reported. "It appears that on the memorial margins of the Arno, Mrs. Cam and Joe flirted together daily for about six weeks—very busy," Bay wrote to his mother.

Unaccustomed to silence after fifteen years of hearing from Lizzie every week, Adams was anxious and hurt. "Still no letter!" he wrote after a month without word from Italy. "I am now seriously uneasy. You can judge, when I say that last night, sitting alone at dinner, I heard Martha's voice calling Dordy. The absurdity made me smile,

for even in my advanced imbecility I recognise that it is . . . I that
calls for help, and needs it too."

Time deepened his uneasiness and sense of loss. Of all his friends,
only John La Farge was well and happy. In March, Clover's last
surviving sibling, Ned Hooper, had hurled himself from a window
on the third floor of his house on Beacon Street. Injured but still
alive, he was taken to an asylum, and even though he seemed to be
recovering, Henry could not help feeling that Ned was fated to
follow the same path as his sisters.

After a winter's rest in Nassau, Clarence King had come north
looking a decade older and helpless against "paroxysms of cough-
ing." What had first shown up in his chest as a thumbnail-sized patch
of tuberculosis was now larger than a hand. "He must go to Arizona
at once, and ought to have gone there three months ago," Henry
wrote to Lizzie. Whether he and Hay would ever see him again was
a question they preferred not to raise.

Hay was also unwell, plagued by mysterious attacks of numbness
on one side of his body. The president was planning a cross-country
trip by rail, and Clara insisted that John go with him. With a shrewdness worthy of Mark Hanna, she saw that the junket would give Hay
a rest without creating the public flap that would attend an official
leave from the State Department. Hay agreed to go and airily suggested that they carry a silk-lined coffin in the baggage car. "As
usual," Henry noted dryly, "the persons who are needed are hit,
while I, who am an unnecessary palaeozoic reptile am only senile."

For solace, Henry rode in the silent woods of Rock Creek, where
the spring earth was thick with anemones and violets. Remembering
that he had first explored Rock Creek when he was thirty-one and
"life was all ahead," he was staggered by the vastness of the changes
he had witnessed. In a mere three decades, the world seemed to have
"tipped itself over." Monstrous dynamos, venal senators, the rise of
Germany and Russia—all, he said, made him "look with yearning
eyes to my happy home at Rock Creek where I can take off my flesh
and sit on my stone bench in the sun, to eternity, and see my friends
in quiet intervals of thousand-year naps." But even then he feared he
would get no peace. The otherworldly figure at Clover's grave had
become the most famous sculpture in the capital, and Henry's visits
were invariably interrupted by the arrival of tourists, all of whom

wanted to know what the figure meant. He felt a particular aversion to the clergymen, who usually came with companions and, "apparently fascinated by their own reflection, broke out passionately against the expression they felt in the figure of despair, of atheism, of denial," he said. "Like the others, the priest saw only what he brought." When the Lodges invited Adams to Europe for the summer, he was grateful. Paris, with all its vexations, had begun to seem preferable to the specters hovering over Washington.

Mrs. Cameron, meanwhile, had ended her affair with Joe Stickney—not out of affection for Adams but from a sense of her own limitations. As she had coldly put it to Adams, the very fact of Martha made it impossible for her to "cut a straight swathe." Lizzie broke the news to Joe during a stroll on the Ponte Vecchio in early May. Then they boarded a train for Paris, parting somewhere along the way in order to avoid being seen together on their arrival.

Back in her apartment near the Etoile, Lizzie read through the stack of anxious letters from Lafayette Square and pounced on the detail that meant most to her: Henry was sailing for England on May 15. Hoping to catch him before he left, she dashed off a note directing him to a London shop where her hairbrushes were being rebuilt and a Sloane Square hosiery establishment from which she wanted a dozen pair of "very fine openwork lisle-thread stockings—tan-colored and no. 9."

President McKinley and his railroad caravan left Washington at the end of April. Eager to expand foreign trade and annoyed by senatorial lassitude in the matter of commercial treaties, the president was taking his case to the people. With the author of the Open Door at his elbow, he planned to tell his audiences that he wanted to open doors for American goods all over the world. Railroads and steamships, telegraphs and telephones had created a new world, he believed: "We have overcome distance," and the powers of the earth were now "tied together." Global trade was not an end in itself but a step toward the larger goal of world peace: "There is nothing in this world that so much promotes the universal brotherhood of man as commerce."

Secretary of State Hay played his part with ease if not with relish. "I have grown quite an adept at saying a word or two absolutely without meaning and without cerebral expense," he bragged to Adams after ten days on the road. "And the peril to my immortal soul when they ask me what I think of their city. I hastily run over all the advantages of London and Paris and Tadmor in the wilderness, and say their town combines all their charms and none of their faults—which is swallowed even as a turkey gobbles a June-bug." Whenever the train was in motion, he and Clara rested in their car, and despite his own ennui, he was pleased to see that she enjoyed the hoopla.

In New Mexico and Arizona, the tracks were lined with children waving flags and chanting "We want statehood!" as the presidential convoy rolled by. "What can they mean by it except that all the adult males want to be Senators?" Hay joshed. As the train neared Phoenix, his interest began to perk up. King was only sixty miles away, in Prescott.

Except for the winter in Nassau, King had worked without rest since 1897. He first signed on as a consultant for yet another silver mine in Mexico and begged Adams to go with him. "It is hard lines to go alone for the only real fun is to watch the other fellow," he said. When he finished his chores in Zacatecas, they could bask at Acapulco. "I will even execute in advance an assignment of half the brown girls we meet. Moreover I will be a second La Farge and never tell." But Adams had already made plans to go to Europe.

From Mexico, King headed north to a job in Telluride, Colorado, where a mild case of heart failure kept him in bed most of the time. Undaunted, he wrote his reports in bed, where he also claimed to be sketching out a series of literary studies of the American female.

When 1897 ended with little gain, King was disappointed and defensive. "Does success and does honor act as good medicine for the insides?" he asked his friend, Ambassador John Hay. "Tell me a little of the way it feels, and what it does to you—this eminence in your career! And say if you enjoy its multifariousness as much as I do the silent spaces of the desert where most of my days are spent." For the last few years, King confessed, he had been

as lonely and isolated as an anchorite. Months go by with no one to talk to but a peon, and I have made the remoteness complete by never having a newspaper sent on my track. And perhaps I oughtn't to admit it, but I have grown to love the uncomplicatedness of it all. You have always thought my alleged savagery of soul a mere attitudinizing but you were wrong. I could not play the primitive like Thoreau in somebody's vegetable garden but I could live and die for the crowd if only you and Henry would come and camp with me now and again.

For the next two years King hopscotched from Arizona copper mines to coal deposits in Colorado to a mining lawsuit in the Supreme Court of British Columbia. Early in 1900 he was hired as an expert witness in a legal battle between two copper baronies in Montana, where he awed his employers with his long hours, painstaking preparation for the trial, and immaculate wardrobe. He still traveled with James Alexander, the valet he had had since the Fortieth Parallel survey, and each morning James sent him off to the mines in well-pressed overalls.

In June, after a dash to the Klondike for a look at the gold rush, King stopped in Seattle for a few days with the brother of an old friend. When King talked of his affinity for dark-skinned women, his host assumed he was being treated to King's famous wit and pronounced the conversation "delicious humbuggery." King was unable to persuade him otherwise.

As King crisscrossed the West, he was desperately lonely for Ada. "I cannot tell you how delighted I was to see your handwriting again," he wrote from one of his trips. "To see something you had touched was almost like feeling the warmth of your hand. My darling, tell me all about yourself. I can see your dear face every night when I lay my head on the pillow and my prayers go up to Heaven for you and the little ones. I feel most lonely and miss you most when I put out the light at night and turn away from the work of the day. Then I sit by my window in the starlight and look up at the dark night sky and think of you. Lonely seems my bed! Lonely is my pillow! I think of you and dream of you and my first waking thought is of your dear face and your loving heart."

At the end of the summer King managed a quick visit to Lake Sunapee, where he spoke enthusiastically of a wealth of new schemes, literary as well as geological. "He has a new book all ready to print, in fact it is all done but the writing," Hay reported to Adams. "Whether it will get any further you can judge as well as I. It is awfully good literature, at least, to hear him talk about it."

King's final assignment, accepted against the advice of the doctor who discovered his tubercles, was an evaluation of a lead mine in Missouri. An appraisal slated to last ten days stretched on for a month because of mishaps and rainy weather, and King's disease flourished in the dampness. It was "virtually suicide for him to stay there," a colleague declared. "He realized this himself but his sense of duty held him to the spot." Four years of dogged work had brought Clarence King nothing but an advanced case of tuberculosis.

May 8, 1901, was the last day King would spend in New York. He spent it with Ada and the children at their house in Flushing, still keeping up the pretense that he was James Todd. After dinner, in the living room, he told her that he wanted them to move to Toronto. They would find less racial prejudice in Canada, there was an excellent school for their children, and they would no longer have to answer the questions of neighbors curious about the comings and goings of the white Mr. Todd. If anyone in Toronto asked about him, he said, "tell them that you and your husband have agreed to separate and that you do not like to discuss your family matters." Money would be no problem: there was $80,000, enough for the rest of their lives. He had left it in the hands of his oldest friend, James Gardiner, who knew of Ada and the children.

Why Clarence King urged Ada Todd to uproot the family and leave the country remains open to conjecture, but there can be little doubt that such a move would have greatly reduced her chances of discovering his true identity after his death.

Though Hay and King did not connect during the president's swing through Arizona, King had other pleasures, including a comfortable house, a cook, and the company of his manservant. Finding the libations and comestibles of Prescott beneath the standards of any self-respecting gourmand, he asked a friend in San Francisco to ship him eight high-grade hams (Smithfield if possible but definitely not "any Chicago make"), twenty-five pounds of bacon ("English or Irish preferred"), a box of "best" macaroni, several bottles of "best European olive oil" and "best old cider vinegar," five or six pounds of "best" prunes, and six dozen pints of "very best" California wine. No microbe known to man had been able to down his spirits, he said, "and I propose to keep gay to the last."

In early June, when a heat wave overtaxed his heart, King moved to Pasadena, California. The new abode was impressively large but stuffed with the "most vulgar dodgy little bits of 'art furniture' from Grand Rapids," he reported to Clara Hay. "Not a thing one can sit on, not a piece that is not the most hideous mockery of taste." The books in the library appeared to have been "bought by the yard," and the walls were grimly festooned with leather hides bearing portraits of Indian chiefs and Evangeline "burnt in with a hot poker." But the rent was cheap, and King spent most of his days outdoors in a hammock, staring beyond the palms and eucalyptus trees at the blue-gray mountains in the distance.

By the middle of June, Hay was back at his desk in the State Department, feeling cheerier than he had in months. The roaring throngs who greeted McKinley at every stop had also been generous with praise for Hay. In a few days, when Harvard blessed him with an honorary LL.D., his stock would rise again. And to his vast delight, the president had just named twenty-four-year-old Del Hay an assistant secretary, the same post John Hay had held in the Lincoln White House. Henry Adams might have thought that the world had "tipped itself over" in the last thirty years, but to the beaming John Hay, it seemed to have come full circle.

Del had caught the president's notice during 1900, when he went to South Africa to serve as U.S. consul at Pretoria. The English and the Dutch were fighting the Boer War, a conflict in which the United States was committed to a policy of neutrality. Secretary Hay's critics, pointing to his affection for England and to Del's inexperience, thought the appointment highly inappropriate. But Del had succeeded—largely by "not shooting off his mouth," his proud father told one of the skeptics. No one, not even the secretary, knew whether Del's personal sympathies lay with the Boers or the British.

Before taking up his new duties at the White House on July 1, Del decided to go up to Yale for his class reunion. Late in the afternoon of June 22, he checked into a room on the third floor of the New Haven House, then joined his fellows from the class of 1898 for dinner and a play. He came back to the hotel at eleven, spent an hour in the smoker, and on the way to his room asked to be awakened at nine the next morning. At two-thirty, he fell out of his window.

A workman in the streets heard Del's body hit the pavement, saw the motionless figure in pajamas, and ran into the hotel for help. The night clerk summoned the proprietor, who telephoned the White House, and at three o'clock John Hay was awakened by the jangling of his own telephone.

Del's room showed no evidence of foul play or suicide. The only clue, a half-finished cigarette on the window ledge, suggested an accident. The night had been hot and close, and it appeared that Del had dozed off as he sat on the sill for a last smoke before turning in.

When the anguished Hay reached New Haven and saw only a small bruise on Del's forehead, he could scarcely believe there was no more life in the husky, six-foot-two frame. He collapsed and was put to bed, leaving his daughter Helen to cope until Clara arrived from Lake Sunapee. After the funeral in Cleveland, the family went straight to Sunapee, where Clara wanted everyone to try to carry on as usual. The children had guests, and Clara stoically decided that Providence had sent Del on long trips to the Philippines and South Africa "just to prepare us for this one, from which he will not return." John saw no comfort in that thought, nor could he feel the tranquility Clara seemed to draw from the green slopes of Mount Sunapee. "There is not an inch of the ground but is associated with our boy," he wrote to McKinley. "Every hope of the future was linked with him in one way or another. Time, I know, is the great healer—but have I time to heal?"

Condolences poured in—from Lizzie Cameron, Andrew Carnegie, Robert Todd Lincoln, President McKinley, Vice President Roosevelt, and eight hundred others. Hay's old friend Mark Twain wrote to offer "all that I have—the sorrow of one who knows." His own heart had been "hurt beyond healing" by the death of his daughter five years before, he said. "I will not torture you with words; they would help if they could, but in all the ages they have not availed." Even the supremely eloquent Henry James was dumbstruck. He thought of the Hays "with boundless tenderness, feeling with you from the bottom of my heart. But I can dream of no 'consoling' word to say to you." Remembering a recent evening in London with Del, James guessed at the Hays' parental pride and hoped it would help them through their "miserable hour." Nannie Lodge, fearful of compromising herself by saying too much, sent Hay a short note most poignant for its omissions. Her heart was

Secretary of State John Hay and his son Del outside the State, War and Navy Building.
LIBRARY OF CONGRESS

heavy with the knowledge of his anguish, she said, and "I only wish that you could read between these poor lines, all that I long to say."

King and Adams telegraphed as soon as they heard the news, and Adams soon followed his wire with letters. "When one is struck by one of these impossible blows, one either has or has not the strength to go on," he told Hay. "If one has it, one picks oneself up, after a time, and limps along, without help, and never really oneself again, but able to walk. If one hasn't it, one goes under and no help serves." Though Adams wished he were with them, he worried that he might do them harm. As he explained to Clara, "It is so long since I have got the habit of thinking that nothing is worthwhile! That sort of habit is catching, and I should not like to risk too close contact at a critical moment with a mind disposed to be affected by it."

Biding his time in Paris until he joined the Lodges in Germany, Adams had the sensation that he was a centipede condemned to die limb by limb. Only three days after Del's death, Ned Hooper, who had languished in an asylum for months, was carried off by pneumonia.

A few weeks of thinking about the Hays led Adams to two conclusions: If Clara held together, John would, and if John stayed in the
State Department, he might be sufficiently distracted to escape the
grief that had permanently crushed Henry Adams. From Bayreuth,
where he and the Lodges were listening to Wagner, Henry pointed
out that he and Hay were approaching their own Götterdämmerung.

> We might as well go on, as drop off, if we still have a road beneath us.
> Perhaps one only begins to be useful to others when one ceases to be
> useful to oneself. At least we make some distant approach then to what
> religion and philosophy pose for our ideals. I hope you will keep the
> reins and the road till you are turned out, or fall from your coach-box.
> You cannot possibly care a straw what road you go; you cannot imag-
> inably have a notion whether one is better, in the long run, than
> another; you have lived long enough, and are suffering enough now,
> to know that the whole phantasmagoria can be directed, like a dream,
> more or less as your mood is, if you don't struggle; you can gain
> neither peace nor energy by stopping the machinery.

Hay suspected that Adams was right but wondered if his nerves
could stand the strain. His mind crawled with "hideous forebod-
ings." All his life, he told Henry, good luck had pursued him "like
a shadow. Now it is gone—it seems to me forever. I expect tomorrow to hear bad news, something insufferable." Hay tried to console
himself with the thought that a long life was not so desirable as a
happy one, and he told King, Del's "little life was very happy. He
had ease and variety; his family idolized him; everybody liked him
and sought his company." These were the thoughts he tried to think,
he said, but they never rang true: "I mock myself. My grief seizes me
like a bulldog and will not let me go. God help me!"

Returning to Lake Sunapee at the end of July, Hay was hurt and
bewildered to find that there was still no letter from King. "I have
heard nothing from you for ages," he cried. "I don't want you to
write if it bores you—but if you ever feel like it we should like very
much to have news of you."

"A fever which has kept my poor head swimming and throbbing has
made it impossible to write you coherently," King explained in a
letter begun two days before Hay wrote his lament. "A sense of your

sad hours has been with me every hour and was about the only clear impression I had." Lying in his hammock and staring at mountains he would never climb, he had "all day without interruption to think of you, and wonder at the strange, undiscernable purpose of Providence in taking away a life of such bright promise."

For two days, "days of fever and discomfort," King's letter lay unfinished. When he picked up his pen again, he pictured the Hays "curtained from the world by those cool draperies" of maple at Sunapee and learning to live with their sorrow. Grief, he thought, was "an unseen companion, domiciled with us, entering into our lives, sitting by our side, and at meat with us, till we are familiar with it and learn at last to love it there, like some mute messenger from beyond the gates." His deepest regret was that he could not go to them. "What I would give to be well and with you and to take my share of the passing shadow and the coming light. But I am a poor sick old fellow uncertain yet of life or death, suffering more than my lot and simply waiting till nature and the foe have done their struggle."

For the moment, the foe had the upper hand. In spite of the Smithfield hams and "very best" California claret, King in his daily fevers had sweated off more than thirty pounds. The Hays had found a San Francisco physician who claimed great success in treating tuberculosis with X rays, but as King now explained to Clara, such treatment was out of the question. His bronchial tubes were clogged by "morbid growths" of an undetermined nature, and until they were understood, the doctors felt it would be "madness to turn them over to the tender mercies of the X rays, which might kill or cure promptly so far as science now knows."

Dismal as King's prospects sounded, he did not expect to die soon. "Even if there is to be a fatal exit to the case, it may last years," he told Clara. From Pasadena, he planned to go to Phoenix for the winter. The moment his case was pronounced hopeless, he would head for the Southeast, "where Mother can come to me and other friends may drop down on me for a glimpse."

Hay's desolation thickened in the August heat. Sick of hearing "the commonplaces of consolation," he told Adams that he finally understood what a "dunce" he had been to use them with friends. Del's smiling face followed him everywhere, and he wished that fate had taken him instead of his son. Though he said nothing about

Clarence King toward the end of his life, in John Hay's library. FROM CLARENCE KING
MEMOIRS, COURTESY OF THE JOHN HAY COLLECTION, JOHN HAY LIBRARY,
BROWN UNIVERSITY LIBRARY

resigning from the State Department, he loathed it with almost morbid intensity. "The meanness of men—the medium in which we all
must work, grows more intolerably bitter," he wrote Whitelaw Reid
on the last day of August. "I can no longer take comfort in regarding
the politicians as black beetles working out the law of their being.
Their greed and malice worry me and break my rest. Moral integrity
and a sense of humor will carry you a long way; but when your sense
of humor fails—woe unto you!"

One week later, Hay was jolted by another calamity. On Friday,
September 6, in a receiving line at the Pan-American Exposition in
Buffalo, a deranged anarchist fired two shots into President Mc-
Kinley at point-blank range. The assailant, a twenty-eight-year-old
mechanic named Leon Czolgosz, had concealed his revolver in a
handkerchief. Arrested at once, Czolgosz identified himself as Fred
Nieman—Fred No-man. He had shot the president, he said, because

he "didn't believe one man should have so much service and another man should have none."

One bullet had merely grazed the president's ribs and had fallen out of his clothing as the doctors prepared him for surgery. The second, which could not be found, had pierced both walls of the stomach. The surgeons treated the wounds, closed the incision, and sighed with relief. President McKinley was sure to recover. Newspaper reporters old enough to remember the long demise of President Garfield in 1882 were assured that times had changed: improved antiseptic technique had made abdominal surgery a routine procedure.

Henry Adams learned of the attack the next morning, over breakfast in Stockholm. It made him uneasy, he wrote Hay, but behind his uneasiness, "silent and awful like the Chicago express, flies the thought of Teddy's luck!"

Vice President Theodore Roosevelt hurried to Buffalo, as did Hay, who could not rid himself of the thought that McKinley was as doomed as Garfield and Lincoln. On Tuesday, heartened by the doctors' prognosis, Roosevelt headed for a family vacation in the Adirondacks. Hay left for Washington on Wednesday, wiring Clara that he would return to Sunapee over the weekend. On Thursday, with fresh assurances from the physicians, Hay composed a memorandum telling the embassies that recovery was now beyond question. But a "black cloud of foreboding" kept him from sending it, and on Friday word came that McKinley's death was imminent. At six in the evening the president asked for a prayer. In the early hours of September 14, 1901, he died whispering the words of his favorite hymn, "Nearer, My God, to Thee."

Three presidents had died by assassination, Hay noted, and it had been his "strange and tragic fate" to serve them all. And once again, as he had after the death of Vice President Hobart in 1899, Secretary of State Hay stood next in line for the presidency.

Reading Adams's letter from Stockholm, Hay shivered at "the awful clairvoyance" of the remark about Teddy's luck. "Well, he is here in the saddle again," Hay sighed. The moment Roosevelt arrived in Union Station, he had collared Hay and told him he must stay on. "I saw of course it was best for him to start off that way," Hay told Adams, "and so said I would stay, forever, of course, for it would be worse to say I would stay a while, than it would be to go out at once. I can still go at any moment he gets tired of me, or when I collapse."

There were more horrors to come—the death of Hay's old White House colleague and fellow Lincoln biographer, John George Nicolay, and the sad finale of Clarence King. Over the years Hay had perpetrated a raft of ingenious ruses in order to put money in King's pockets, and the settlement of Del's financial affairs inspired him to one more. He sent King a keepsake of Del in the form of a check.

Deeply touched, King said he spent hours thinking of Hay's "superhuman" kindness and of his own financial bungling. "In my present condition of uncertainty of folded hands and days of reflection I have been trying to understand why a man as well endowed with intelligence as I should have made such a failure in money matters." During the last several years, he had built his consulting practice to the point where it covered the $10,000 a year he needed to care for his mother and her household, and the $2,000 it took to "keep a decent position" for himself. According to his check stubs, he had spent $275,000 on his dependents over thirty-five years, but he could not fathom why he had not made "abundant money" besides. Casting about for explanations, he supposed he had "stayed too long in pure science and got a bent for the philosophical and ideal side of life too strong for any adaptation to commercial affairs." He could have joined a college faculty and "abandoned the family to sink but really whenever the moment came I could not do it." Nor did he see how he could have succeeded in literature: "that door seemed always shut in my face."

Hay was equally mystified and considerably more embittered. "There you have it in the face!" Hay told Adams. "The best and brightest man of his generation, who with talents immeasurably beyond any of his contemporaries, with industry that has often sickened me to witness it, with everything in his favor but blind luck, hounded by disaster from his cradle, with none of the joy of life to which he was entitled, dying at last, with nameless suffering, alone and uncared-for in a California tavern. *Ça vous amuse, la vie?*"

The news of King loomed like a nightmare, Adams wrote from Europe. "[W]ith my usual pessimism, I had fully realised the danger, when I bade him good-bye, and both of us knew that it was a chance if we met again. Of late I have found my pessimism rather a serious load. One can afford to be pessimistic only in youth when the world sometimes gets a chance to be gay."

Hay's fury grew with every bulletin from the West. When one of King's doctors wrote Hay that the patient was the most delightful creature he had ever met and the other called him "a rare sweet soul," Hay snarled to Adams, "you must admit that you and the Pope and other infallible powers have a queer taste in fates." A few weeks later, thinking of King's fevers and the "long torture" still in front of him, Hay added, "If one of us could go out and kill him, it would be a brotherly act."

As planned, King moved from Pasadena to Phoenix at the beginning of October. The doctor had prescribed an "uninfected" house, but since the owners of such places were disinclined to rent to tuberculars, it took two exhausting weeks to find new quarters. At last he moved into a comfortable brick cottage that was "as clean as a fresh shaving," he told Hay. And the climate was "good enough to bottle."

Frank Emmons, the Fortieth Parallel survey colleague who had introduced King to Adams, had come West on business and stopped in Phoenix to spend a few weeks helping King. Emmons was shocked to see that King's lungs produced more than a pint of fluid per day, and knowing his friend's love of fine food, he understood at once how disheartened King would be in a place where the grocer and the butcher stocked only the cheapest goods. The electricity flickered on and off at will, and even rudimentary services were in short supply. King's mother talked of coming, but Emmons warned against it. In primitive Phoenix, where one was forced to live "more or less in camping style," the exacting Mrs. Howland would be sorely out of place.

King spoke vaguely to Emmons of a "middle-aged lady from Chicago" who might spend the winter with him, which may have been a heavily veiled expression of his wish that Ada come from Toronto. If Emmons knew about Ada, he did not say so in his diary, and events suggest that he did not. King's mail in Phoenix came to a post office box, and since he could no longer be sure that he or his manservant would be the first to see it, he faced the problem of how to account for envelopes addressed to James Todd. After thirteen years of secrecy, someone had to be told. King found it easier to confess his fraud to Ada than to Emmons.

In one of his last letters to her, written in October 1901, King revealed his true identity but still held out the false promise of an inheritance from his "aunt": "You know that it is my strongest desire and intention in life that we should be legally united just as soon as we can do so without risking the loss of the little property which will come to me." In the meantime, she should take the name King "and have the children's name changed in the New York State Court at Albany so as all to have my name. I have studied it all out and consulted a good lawyer about it and my only wish before God and for you is to do the very best thing for us all and I am perfectly sure that what I have advised you is best." Referring to himself as her husband and urging her to do likewise, he also told her to enter the name Clarence King in their family Bible.

By November, King's days were ruled by fevers. "That the microbes do not respect an old and tired constitution shows them to be no better than the Supreme Court," he joked in his last letter to Hay. "You can fancy that it is awfully hard to watch myself waste away till I am little else than bad temper and expectoration. But the sense of humor survives just enough to know that it did not vanish with the calves of my legs or that biceps of which I once felt an ardent pride."

King's humor endured to the end. During a fitful, delirious night in December, when he overheard the doctor say that the heroin must have gone to his head, he shot back, "Many a heroine has gone to better heads than mine is now." King died in his sleep at two o'clock in the morning on December 24. The doctor filled out the death certificate, putting an *M* on the line for marital status, and telegraphed Ada in Toronto.

22

Nearly All the Great Prizes

A few minutes before ten in the morning on New Year's Day, Henry Adams and Frank Emmons and eight other pallbearers assembled in Manhattan at the corner of Fifth Avenue and 37th Street to escort King's coffin up the aisle of the Brick Presbyterian Church. A raw northwest wind warred with the brilliant sunshine, holding the temperature to twelve degrees. Inside the church, the red-and-gilt walls decorated by John La Farge cast a tropical glow that would have delighted Clarence King. At the head of the coffin, atop a bed of palm fronds, lay a large cross of orchids and Southern greenery, from John and Clara Hay.

As the prayers were read and the hymns were sung, Hay was in Washington, suffering through the pleasantries of a breakfast for the diplomatic corps. La Farge was also away, spending the holidays with his family in Newport. But the church was filled. In the crowd of friends, mining colleagues, and fellow members of the Century Club were W. D. Howells, publisher of King's youthful mountaineering sketches; landscape painter Albert Bierstadt, who had briefly traveled with the Fortieth Parallel survey; Whitelaw Reid of the *Tribune;* James Gardiner, who knew the secret of King's black family; Henry Holt, publisher of *Democracy* and *Esther;* Samuel Parsons, the Central Park superintendent who rescued King after his arrest at the zoo; and, from happier times, E. C. Stedman, financier and man of letters, who had crossed the Atlantic with King in 1882, when King, ecstatic at the beginning of his long European idyll, flipped twenty-dollar gold pieces into the air.

At eleven o'clock the mourners filed out into the bitter wind and a brightness that Howells found piercingly bleak. A hearse waited to take the coffin to Grand Central Terminal for the journey to Newport, where King would be buried. Stedman, pleased by the size of the crowd, remarked that King had had "the gift of friendship." Like dozens of others who mistook King's warmth for intimacy, Stedman could not help regretting that his lovable friend had never had a family of his own. King's devotion to his mother and the Howland children was beautiful, Stedman thought, "but there should have been even dearer ones to bear his name and mourn his loss."

Adams, sad and fearful, boarded the first train for Washington. "I have hardly friends enough to go round for many years more, if it is necessary to supply two or three funerals a year, like 1901," he told Lizzie Cameron, "but I will play out the hand somehow." Unhappily, Lafayette Square offered no sedatives. "What a place this is for nerves!" he cried after a few days at home. "Mine are twisting and squirming like worms of steel."

His deepest anxiety was John Hay. Depressed and assailed by mysterious ills, Hay no longer had the energy for a full day at the State Department. At one o'clock he came home to spend afternoons in his library, where he read dispatches and wrote memoranda under the silent watch of a pair of stuffed cranes perched atop a carved settee. If he felt up to it, he called for Adams at four thirty, and together they set off for a walk up Connecticut Avenue. They talked of Congress, the cabinet, the president, the courts, finance, and foreign affairs. The secretary did not ask the historian's counsel nor did the historian volunteer it. Half an hour later they returned for tea with Clara, the Five of Hearts now reduced to three.

To Henry's surprise, Clara seemed ten years younger. Though he perceived "a shady sub-conscious look about her face which tells her story," she was full of laughter, eager to speak of Del, and excited by the prospect of a family wedding. In February the Hays' daughter Helen would marry Payne Whitney, son of a New York tycoon. Judging by the character in the lad's face, Uncle Henry guessed that

Clara Hay toward the end of her life, by Henry Adams.
MASSACHUSETTS HISTORICAL SOCIETY

Payne would make Helen happy, and it was clear that he would make her rich. "Houses, yachts, jewels rain on her," Henry reported to Lizzie. So many diamonds had been delivered to 800 Sixteenth Street that Clara, fearing burglars, carried them about in her voluminous skirts.

John found it hard to share in the merriment. The deaths of King and Nicolay had carried off large pieces of his past, McKinley's assassination had severed his chief tie to the present, and the loss of Del left him feeling disconnected from the future. Even the largest triumphs failed to lift his gloom. In December 1901, the revised Hay-Pauncefote Treaty had sailed through the Senate virtually unopposed. It was Hay who had had to swallow his fury and start over after Senator Henry Cabot Lodge orchestrated the defeat of the first draft of the treaty, and it was Hay who had persuaded England that the United States should have the authority to do whatever it deemed necessary to protect the Central American canal zone. But as the new pact moved toward ratification and Senator Lodge and President Roosevelt began claiming credit for the success, Hay had no energy for correction. He graciously praised Cabot's change of heart and told Theodore that the British considered it "most auspicious" to have settled so large a question at the outset of his administration.

At forty-three, Roosevelt was America's youngest President and twenty years the junior of his secretary of state. Hay dealt smoothly with his new chief by playing the role perfected by Henry Adams—a combination of mandarin and fond uncle. Hay showed him every respect but stopped short of reverence. Soon after McKinley's death Hay let Roosevelt know that he intended to reserve the title "Mr. President" for official business; the rest of the time he would address him as "Theodore." Nor did Hay allow his official courtesy to spoil the fun of watching Theodore wrestle with the social burdens of his new station. Writing Adams soon after Roosevelt moved into the White House, Hay reported, "Teddy said the other day: 'I am not going to be the slave of the tradition that forbids Presidents from seeing their friends. I am going to dine with you and Henry Adams and Cabot whenever I like. But' (here the shadow of the crown sobered him a little), 'of course I must preserve the prerogative of the initiative.' "

With his unbounded energy and definitive opinions on every mote in the cosmos, Theodore offered a marvelous distraction from grief, and Hay was grateful. In a burst of enthusiasm early in 1902, he managed to persuade his wife and Henry Adams to attend a small White House dinner. Clara had not dined out since Del's death in June, and for twenty-five years Henry had adamantly refused to sup at 1600 Pennsylvania Avenue. On a Friday night in January, the Hays called for Adams in their carriage, and a few minutes later they were seated in the Red Room with Cabot and Nannie Lodge. Waiting for the Roosevelts, Henry felt overwhelmed by "bloody and dreary associations" stretching back to the days of his great-grandmother, Abigail Adams. Though he did not mention it, his last visit to the Red Room was in the spring of 1885, when he took H. H. Richardson to meet Grover Cleveland. Clover had been away, nursing her father in his last illness, the experience that precipitated her suicide. By the time the president and Mrs. Roosevelt appeared, Henry had passed beyond all possibility of pleasure. He found the meal indifferent and badly served, the beverages all wrong, the host insufferable. "Edith was very bright and gay," he told Lizzie, "but as usual Theodore absorbed the conversation, and if he tired me ten years ago, he crushes me now." It seemed to Adams that presidential life had deprived Roosevelt of his freshness but not his dogmatism. When Theodore tactlessly lectured him on history, the historian hid his annoyance by feigning ignorance. He came away from the evening with one clear impression: "Hay and I are shoved up to a distinct seniority; we are sages. I felt it not only in Hay's manner, but in Roosevelt's too, and it is my creed now that my generation had better scuttle gracefully, and leave Theodore to surround himself with his own rough-riders."

Adams's exasperation with the "vanity, ambition, dogmatic temper and cephalopodic brain" of Theodore Roosevelt was a reaction to the man and to the age he symbolized. The twentieth century in which Roosevelt gloried made Henry's skin "curl," he told Lizzie. "That nervous tic I have so often told you of—the instinct to roll on the ground and pray to the dynamo, is becoming chronic here with me." "This huge great ghastly automobile of a country seems just about to roll over us all, and squash us into one enormous mince-pie."

Henry took refuge from Theodore and the dynamos in his beloved twelfth century. Closeted in his study, he plunged into a revision of *Mont-Saint-Michel and Chartres,* emerging only to preside over the breakfast table or to entertain Quentin Roosevelt, age four, whom he found "considerably older and less school-boy-like than his father." Once Henry finished the new draft, he meant to have the book printed in a private edition. As the manuscript "swelled to the size of ox," he feared the printing costs, but commercial publication was out of the question. "My only hope of heaven is the Virgin," he explained. "If I tried to vulgarize her, and make her as cheap as cow-boy literature, I should ask for eternal punishment as a favor."

Next door, the Hays were spending the winter in as much seclusion as a cabinet post and a society wedding would permit. Still in mourning, they wrote letters on stationery edged in black, refused invitations, and rarely entertained. Couriers brought wedding presents by the score—silver candelabras from the Astors, a diamond-studded warming pan from the father of the groom, an immense silver punchbowl from Andrew Carnegie, three table services, and, according to Henry Adams, "pitchers, pots and plates enough to supply the Walkyrie and Valhalla." (His own gift was a small Rodin.) On the eve of the wedding Henry grieved to see Helen surrounded by gold and silver, "blind with headache, and stupendously out of place in all that New York menagerie." His little Helen—"simple, foolish, helpless, unstylish, unfashionable, unconventional"—had to become either "a New York swell or a failure," he lamented. Put off by the ostentation, Adams stayed home from the ceremonies. John La Farge got as far as the church portal, felt intimidated by the glittering crowd, and scurried back to Adams in his hermitage. In the evening, when Clara sent John next door to see why Adams and La Farge had not come to the reception, Adams could only shrug. As he told Lizzie, "one can't give one's why."

At the end of February, Hay stood before both houses of Congress to deliver an address in memory of William McKinley. In anger and bewilderment, he observed that the assassination of an American president was as pointless as it was horrific. The death of a dictator could change an empire, the end of a royal line might create an opening for a new dynasty, but in a well-ordered republic, the death of a ruler caused no state tremor. Summing up the achievements of McKinley's brief tenure, Hay declared that he had guided America to unprecedented greatness. The financial center of the world was no longer London's Lombard Street but Wall Street, and through "sheer reasonableness," McKinley had bettered America's position with all the great powers. Courteous to the last, McKinley had apologized for the damage his death would cause the Buffalo exposition. In his life, Hay concluded, President McKinley showed "how a citizen should live, and in his last hour taught us how a gentleman should die."

Adams felt no more inclination to go to Capitol Hill to hear Hay than he had had to go to Helen's wedding, but when he read the eulogy in the newspaper, he thought it excellent. So did Edith Wharton, who admired its "restrained eloquence" and "the way in which idea and expression hold the same high level, and move, all through it, at the same majestic pace." The only objections came from House Democrats, who accused Hay of making a "Republican stump speech." Angered by his praise of McKinley's economic policies, they sourly voted against a resolution thanking the secretary for coming to Congress to deliver the address.

Hay barely noticed. The griefs of 1901 plus four years at the helm of the State Department had dulled his sensitivity to criticism and enabled him to accept the existence of enemies even though he did not understand the reason for their hostility. Henry Adams understood it perfectly. Hay, he told Lizzie, "no more represents the average American than a nightingale represents a hawk. They loathe him instinctively and justly, from their point of view, as they would loathe me. . . . He is personally too much of a so-called gentleman; they don't trust him." On occasion Hay still threatened to resign, but Henry had stopped believing him. "We are sixty-four years old, and we can't step out, except into our graves."

If Adams expected the grave to bring repose, the case of his newly departed friend Clarence King must have given him pause. It is not clear who told Adams and Hay the secret King had hidden for thirteen years, but they quickly became aware of Ada and the children. The family had left Toronto shortly after King's death, moving back to New York, where Ada placed a newspaper advertisement asking King's friend James Gardiner to contact her. Gardiner sent his secretary, a Mr. Dutcher, who assured her that she would have no financial worries because King had left $80,000 for her in Gardiner's care.

Ada soon began receiving sixty-five dollars a month from Gardiner's office. When she brought up the $80,000, she was informed that she would have to wait. There would be no money until King's assets were sold and his debts paid.

King's mother, in her eighties, knew nothing of his debts, and when apprised of the situation (minus the complications of Ada and the children), she responded with more defensive pride than gratitude. "I should have better understood his broken condition if I had known that he had become a borrower," she wrote to Hay. "The only wrong he ever did me was to keep this from my knowledge. It was from mistaken kindness and the ever watchful tenderness with which he sought to guard my declining years."

During the next two years, Gardiner raised at least $120,000 by selling King's paintings, bric-a-brac, library, and securities, the bulk of which went to John Hay in settlement of King's IOUs. For Ada there would be nothing but the monthly check of sixty-five dollars. Inquiring about the source of those funds, she learned only that they came from a benefactor Gardiner had promised not to name.

In June 1903, acting on Gardiner's instructions, Dutcher purchased a house for Ada in his own name. Gardiner promised Ada that she would one day have the deed, but when the title was transferred, it was from Dutcher to Gardiner. Frustrated, Ada went to Gardiner's office and noisily threatened to sue. Dutcher countered with another threat: any legal action would bring an immediate halt to the monthly checks. In desperation she revealed that she possessed a stack of letters from King—evidence that might strengthen her claim to his estate. When Dutcher expressed an interest in the letters, Ada brought them to him, undoubtedly hoping to win him to her point of view. They were never seen again.

King had left other loose ends, which his loyal friends labored to tie up. His stepbrother, George Howland, was under the impression that the U.S. Geological Survey had appropriated $1,200 for a portrait of King, who had served as the agency's first director. George wrote Hay asking for help in securing the commission, and when the agency declined, the imaginative Hay suggested that the Century Club might want to add a picture of King to its portrait collection. The Century agreed to consider it. George finished the portrait in his Paris studio in December 1902, in time for Adams to carry it home on his annual winter crossing. Though Adams shared Hay's low regard for George's talent, he liked the painting. It was a good likeness, he thought, and, as a seated half-length figure, it did not "offend by over-ambition." He deposited it at the Century, where it was hung in the gallery for reaction. A few weeks later the art committee rendered its verdict: "unsuitable."

It is not clear whether the committee considered George's work poor company for the Sargents and Whistlers and La Farges that graced the Century's paneled walls, or whether the spreading gossip about King's subterranean life made them think that the man himself was unsuitable. The tactful Centurions would say only that the art committee was obliged to take "high ground" in making decisions; otherwise the club would be overrun with mediocre paintings commissioned by the families of deceased members. Undaunted, Hay,

Adams, and several others pooled $500 for George and donated the portrait to the U.S. Geological Survey.

Whatever the real objection to the painting, the Century eventually paid an affectionate tribute in *Clarence King Memoirs,* a volume of essays by friends and colleagues. The book was no place to bare the sadder facts of a life, but for those who wondered how an undependable, deceiving scapegrace had won so many hearts, here were the answers. Hay explained that the secret of King's charm lay in his rare blend of humor and kindness, which enabled him to befriend cowboy and clergyman alike, and which gave him an "astonishing power of diffusing happiness wherever he went." W. D. Howells remembered the sweltering summer day thirty years before when the boyish King, with his blond hair and eyes of "blithe blue," arrived in Cambridge to proofread the galleys of *Mountaineering in the Sierra Nevada.* To Howells's everlasting delight, King had paraded through staid old Cambridge in a pith helmet. John La Farge fondly recalled their candlelight suppers, the stained-glass fantasy they concocted for General Grant's tomb, and the midnight forays to the rented room where King's art awaited the mansion he would build as soon as his Mexican silver mines surrendered their treasure.

Adams served up a rollicking account of his adventures with King among the Cuban rebels, in the course of which he dared to hint at King's other life. The geologist's real interest was not science, Adams told the Centurions, but "man, meaning chiefly woman."

> You remember his famous aphorism: "Nature never made more than one mistake, but that was fatal; it was when she differentiated the sexes." In his instincts I think he regarded the male as a sort of defence thrown off by the female, much like the shell of a crab, endowed with no original energy of his own; but it was not the modern woman that interested him; it was the archaic female, with instincts and without intellect. At best King had but a poor opinion of intellect, chiefly because he found it so defective an instrument, but he admitted that it was all the male had to live upon; while the female was rich in the inheritance of every animated energy back to the polyps and the crystals. If he had a choice among women, it was in favor of Indians and negroes.

More than that Adams forbore to tell. King's decision to conceal his deepest emotional tie from his most intimate friends seemed not to matter. "We were his slaves, and he was good to us," said Adams. "He was the ideal companion of our lives."

To Henry Adams in the winter of 1902, it seemed that John Hay no longer cared for anything. While Adams may have mistaken Hay's apathy for his own, it was true that Hay's élan now belonged to the past. Ground down by the incessant wrangling over consulates—"the vast Senatorial suck," as he called it—he also despaired of practicing the gentlemanly art of diplomacy among men who cared more for money and power than principle.

Well before the second Hay-Pauncefote Treaty cleared the Senate, he had begun negotiating for the Canal Zone with the Republic of Colombia, proprietor of the Isthmus of Panama. In the beginning, the Colombians eagerly cooperated in order to persuade the United States to build the canal in Panama rather than Nicaragua. But fellow feeling turned to hostility in the fall of 1902, when the Panamanians launched one of their many revolts against the government in Bogota. As it had on other occasions, the United States dispatched Marines to guard the Panama Railroad, this time moving the troops without Colombia's prior consent. Bogota was furious, its envoy in Washington implacable. After weeks of refusing to see the secretary of state, he resigned.

Peeved, Roosevelt insisted that the new Colombian diplomat, Dr. Tomás Herrán, be made to understand that if Colombia did not agree to the terms Hay had reached with Herrán's predecessors, the United States would dig the canal in Nicaragua. Hay presented Roosevelt's ultimatum on January 21, 1903. The next afternoon, Hay and Herrán signed their treaty. The agreement gave the United States control of a six-mile-wide strip of the isthmus for a century—longer if the United States chose to renew. In exchange, Colombia would receive $10 million in cash and annual rent of $250,000. Zipping through the Senate with only five nays, the treaty went off to Bogota for ratification. The Colombians temporized for months then decided to press for more money and stronger sovereignty in the isthmus.

Roosevelt, furious with "the Bogota lot of jack rabbits," bellowed to Hay that they must not be allowed to bar "one of the future highways of civilization." Hay counseled patience. Roosevelt was

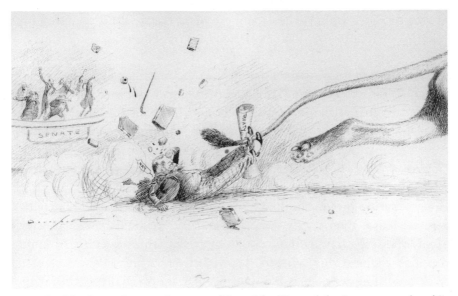

Much of the friction between Secretary of State John Hay and the Senate centered on his friendships with English political figures. In this editorial cartoon, Hay and one of his treaties are being dragged by the British lion while senators assault the secretary with ink-pots, canes, and other missiles. JOHN HAY COLLECTION, JOHN HAY LIBRARY, BROWN UNIVERSITY LIBRARY

summering at Sagamore Hill, Hay was at Lake Sunapee, and nothing of substance could be done before Congress convened in the fall. "I venture to suggest you let your mind play a little about the subject," Hay advised. The United States had alternatives: there was Nicaragua, and there might arise a chance to exploit the perennial tension in Panama.

On November 3, the rebellious Panamanians declared their independence from Colombia. U.S. troops landed the next day, seized the railroad, and prevented Colombian soldiers from crossing the isthmus to quash the revolt. Within days, the United States recognized the new republic.

Neither Hay nor Roosevelt felt the slightest compunction about this course of action. For Hay, it was a simple choice between mayhem and order. To Roosevelt the episode marked the end of a long and melancholy spectacle. For fifty years Colombia had proved "utterly incapable" of keeping order on the isthmus, he said. The United States had acted "in the interest of the commerce and traffic of the whole civilized world." When Roosevelt asked his cabinet's opinion of this defense, Elihu Root, the secretary of war, drew a withering analogy: Theodore, having been accused of seduction, had conclusively proved himself guilty of rape.

The deal-making moved as swiftly as the revolution. On November 9, Philippe Bunau-Varilla, a character who seemed to have stepped from the pages of a Gilbert and Sullivan libretto, lunched alone with John Hay on Lafayette Square. A dapper Frenchman with a waxed mustache, Bunau-Varilla presented himself as Panama's "Envoy Extraordinary and Minister Plenipotentiary near the Government of the United States." Nine days after their lunch, Hay and Bunau-Varilla met in the small blue drawing room at 800 Sixteenth Street to sign their treaty. The Envoy Extraordinary and Minister Plenipotentiary having no seal of his own, the secretary of state supplied a signet ring with the Hay family coat of arms.

Though a new delegation of Panamanians soon challenged Bunau-Varilla's credentials, the treaty was swiftly ratified by both countries. Panama feared that delays might lead the United States to reopen talks with Colombia, and the U.S. Senate, despite grave reservations about America's role in securing Panama's independence, could not hope for better terms than Hay had won. The price remained at $10 million, the same as in the Hay-Herrán compact, but the Canal Zone had widened from six miles to ten, and the United States would hold it in perpetuity. Panama retained sovereignty in name only.

The other pressing piece of business on the secretary of state's agenda, a legacy of the gold rush that had lured Clarence King to the Klondike, pitted Hay's genteel style against the brashness of Theodore Roosevelt and provoked one last battle with his rival in love, Senator Henry Cabot Lodge. Until the discovery of gold in 1896, no one had challenged the Alaskan-Canadian boundary. But when Canadian miners in the Alaska panhandle found themselves without access to the Pacific, the government of Canada claimed that the existing line was incorrect. The boundary set in 1867 when the United States purchased Alaska from Russia had relied on earlier treaties and records, none of which settled the matter with precision.

Guided by his dreams of a new age of Anglo-American harmony, Hay in 1899 had worked out a modus vivendi that allowed Canada

Secretary of State John Hay and President Theodore Roosevelt. The caption of this edito-
rial cartoon read, "A would-be champion, who is somewhat erratic, labors under the dis-
advantage of wielding a very large stick, and insists on playing with a big ball, but they
say that his caddie is fine, and will pull him through." JOHN HAY COLLECTION, JOHN HAY
BROWN UNIVERSITY LIBRARY

to lease a strip of land with a port and to build a railroad through
U.S. territory. The Senate accused Hay of giving away too much,
the Canadians felt he had conceded too little. The standoff continued
until Theodore Roosevelt arrived in the White House. While President McKinley had embraced Hay's notion that a small concession
would further the larger good of amity with England, Roosevelt saw
no reason for compromise. In his view, Canada was behaving in a
"spirit of bumptious truculence." Even the cabinet-room globe,
which had been made by British Admiralty cartographers, showed
the boundary claimed by the United States. The Canadian conten-
tion was "an outrage pure and simple," Roosevelt fumed to his
secretary of state.

Brandishing his Big Stick, Roosevelt ordered eight hundred cav-
alrymen to Alaska on the pretext of assuring order in mining camps.
Hay disapproved of this show of force and continued to press for a

diplomatic solution. Earlier negotiations had led him to think that
Canada might submit the dispute to a tribunal of distinguished jurists, and after months of lobbying, he persuaded Roosevelt to let
him pursue the idea. But the president made it plain that he would
not cede so much as a snowbank: "I should definitely instruct our
three commissioners that they were not to yield any territory what-
soever." They were to insist upon the entire claim and confine themselves to the task of figuring out "the particular line of limitation
which this claim would imply."

On January 23, 1903, in Hay's library, the secretary of state and the
British ambassador signed a treaty creating a panel of "six impartial
jurists of repute," three for each side. The treaty was quickly approved,
and the Canadians named their eminent jurists: the lord chief justice
of England, a former member of the Quebec Supreme Court, and a
respected Ontario attorney. Roosevelt, after extending a halfhearted
invitation to the justices of the U.S. Supreme Court, named three men
who had no standing as jurists and no reputation for impartiality: Secretary of War Elihu Root, Senator George Turner of Washington, and
Senator Henry Cabot Lodge of Massachusetts.

Canada raged, the press hooted, and John Hay winced. Lodge's
genius for giving offense and his personal quarrel with Canada on
another issue made him a particularly abysmal choice. Shortly after
the appointment was announced, Hay moaned that Lodge had already made matters worse: "as if the devil were inspiring him,"
Cabot had gone to Boston and delivered a speech attacking both
Canada and the State Department. "He is a clever man and a man of
a great deal of force in the Senate, but the infirmity of his mind and
character is that he never sees but one subject at a time, and just at
present it is the acceptability of his son-in-law to the voters of
Gloucester." The son-in-law, Augustus Peabody Gardner, was running for Congress in Massachusetts, where fishermen had decided
opinions on a longstanding dispute with Canada over fishing rights
in the North Atlantic.

When Britain asked to delay the boundary talks in order to help
Canada devise a dignified retreat from an embarrassing position,
Hay saw no harm, but Roosevelt angrily threatened to draw the
boundary himself. Hay burned with resentment, partly because he
felt the president had buckled under pressure from Lodge and partly

because it seemed foolhardy not to give an adversary a chance to save face. In the summer of 1903, as the press stoked rumors of a rift between the president and his secretary of state, the two had no choice but to close ranks. Hay insisted to the newspapers that there was not "a shade of difference" between him and Roosevelt, and Roosevelt instructed Hay to ignore the "swine" who invented tales about them: "When I came in I thought you a great Secretary of State, but now I have had a chance to know far more fully what a really great Secretary of State you are. As for those who first of all portray a wholly imaginary difference between us and then attack me because of that difference—for heaven's sake let them go on!"

Soothed, at least for the moment, Hay thanked him "a thousand times" for his letter. What a "comfort" it was to work for a president who "besides being a lot of other things, happened to be born a gentleman." One of Hay's biographers has suggested that he called Roosevelt a gentleman in the hope of inspiring him to act like one. If so, the hope was soon dashed. In a "mutinous and disloyal" letter to his wife, which he asked her to destroy, Hay complained bitterly about Theodore's boorishness. Whenever President McKinley had summoned him to the White House, he had given the secretary of state his full attention for as long as Hay wanted it, he told Clara, "but I always find T.R. engaged with a dozen other people, and it is an hour's wait and a minute's talk—and a certainty that there was no necessity of my coming at all." Only days after swearing publicly that there was no friction between him and the president, Hay wrote out his resignation. Roosevelt kept him waiting for a week then asked him to stay on. "As Secretary of State you stand alone," Roosevelt said. "I could not spare you."

In the end, the settlement of the Alaskan boundary seemed to disprove the fears of both men. After six weeks of negotiations in London, the lord chief justice of England cast his vote with the Americans. The boundary remained as it was on the British Admiralty maps, and Canada came away with nothing but two small islands in the territory in question.

Clashes and all, Secretary of State John Hay had become a personage. He possessed a sheaf of honorary degrees, the Pan American Congress had named him honorary president, and the government of

France would soon tender the Grand Cross of the Legion of Honor. Though he joshed to Adams that the bouquets only reminded him of the daisies soon to grow over his head, they also emboldened him to have himself recorded for posterity.

Like Roosevelt, he sat for John Singer Sargent, and the painter's encounters with the two aptly summarized the differences between the Rough Rider and the gentleman. Hay, a man of refined tastes and a friend of many artists, gave Sargent as much time as he asked, marveled at his intensity, and did all he could to facilitate genius. Theodore paid the artist no more attention than he gave his secretary of state. During his sessions with Sargent he fidgeted, read, bullied his staff, and whined about time taken from his daily fencing matches. Sargent's hours in the White House made him feel "like a rabbit in the presence of a boa constrictor."

The president got the superior portrait—"good Sargent and not very bad Roosevelt," thought Henry Adams. "It is not Theodore, but a young intellectual idealist with a taste for athletics, which I take to be Theodore's idea of himself. It is for once less brutal than its subject." Posed on a staircase, his right hand on the newel post and left planted squarely on his hip, Roosevelt exuded pure will. Hay's portrait, with its abundance of beard and mustache, sharp eyes, and slash of menacing red lip, suggested something smaller than life. Adams considered it "frankly bad" and told Hay that Sargent had glimpsed more meanness in a few hours than Adams had seen in forty years of friendship.

Taking the critique as a joke, Hay sent Sargent next door in the hope that Adams would sit for him. Henry had no such intention. "I am too much of a coward," he admitted. "Sargent gibbets us all, with his everlasting British condescension and patronage. We bore him. He paints it."

Delighted with his Sargent, Hay next commissioned a sculpture. "St. Gaudens is going to bust my head," he informed Clara in the autumn of 1903, shortly after his sixty-fifth birthday. At $10,000 it was "a ruinous expense and folly," he knew, "but I have been a long time in office, and only just now recognized that perhaps I may be considered a bust-worthy name in our annals. So if it is ever done, it may as well be done by the greatest artist of our time. It will be ugly

In 1904, when Augustus Saint-Gaudens was sculpting this bust of John Hay, President
Theodore Roosevelt complained that the chin was weak. Roosevelt, Saint-Gaudens told
Hay, "projected his own powerful jaw on the universe." U.S. DEPARTMENT OF THE
INTERIOR, NATIONAL PARK SERVICE, SAINT-GAUDENS NATIONAL HISTORIC SITE,
CORNISH, NEW HAMPSHIRE

but it will be an object of art: And perhaps the family will be no
poorer for it."

Adams avoided seeing the work in progress for fear of upsetting
the artist with a chance remark, but Roosevelt, unfettered by such
punctilios, insisted on having a look. After first expressing his approval, he walked around to one side, gazed intently for a moment,
then announced that there was "not power enough in the jaw."
When he left, Saint-Gaudens explained with a grin that Theodore
Roosevelt "projected his own powerful jaw on the universe."

During his stay at Lake Sunapee the following summer, Hay rode
over to the sculptor's studio in Cornish, New Hampshire, for a last
round of revisions. Saint-Gaudens tinkered with the cheeks and gave
the whiskers an experimental trim but decided that *"la beauté de la
moustache c'est la longueur."* Hay went home to Sunapee in a furious
thunderstorm and a glorious mood. Saint-Gaudens had made a
statesman of him. The high forehead and straight nose gave his face

an openness that Sargent had missed, and the square shoulders and regal bearing of his head conveyed strength and self-confidence. The jaw showed no hint of weakness.

Hay and Saint-Gaudens also conspired to capture Henry Adams in bronze in spite of his refusal to have himself immortalized in art. (Asked to explain his reticence, Henry coyly replied that his portrait had been done in the Middle Ages. He could be seen in a sculpted Nativity scene at Chartres, he said; he was the ass in the manger.) In August 1904, as soon as Hay's bust went off to the bronze founder, Saint-Gaudens fashioned a circular medallion with a caricature of Adams in flight, his bald head trailing a pair of angel's wings and a body of porcupine quills. Around the border ran the Order of the Garter motto, *Honi soit qui mal y pense* and the words *Porcupinus Angelicus Henricus Adamenso*.

Hay boxed the medallion, adorned it with State Department seals, and sent it by diplomatic courier to Adams in Paris. Henry was charmed. "Your winged and pennated child arrived yesterday by the grace of God and his vicar the Secretary of State," he wrote Saint-Gaudens. ". . . As this is the only way in which the Secretary will ever fulfill his promise of making me Cardinal and Pope I can see why he thinks to satisfy me by giving me medallic rank through you." Speculating that the medal was probably more valuable than a cardinal's hat, Henry wished only that the sculptor could give wings to the secretary: "he needs them more than I who live in holes."

The angelic porcupine and his friend the diplomat clung together after the death of Clarence King, but as they aged they had scarcely more tolerance for each other's faults than for the foibles of the world at large. Hay told W. D. Howells that he and Adams quarreled "like cat and dog. It is wholesome, I know, to be told what an ass I am, and what ignoble company I keep, and Adams deals faithfully with me." For his part, Henry lamented that public office had at last "wreaked its fatal will" on Hay, "as it always does and must on all its victims. He is now the statesman pure and complete. He feels it pathetically but has ceased to struggle. All but the official is dead or paralysed." Hay still came for breakfast on occasion, and the afternoon walks continued, but Adams felt that Hay was irretrievably lost. "He knows it, and is at times miserable about it, but the terror

Henry Adams refused to sit for painters and sculptors, so in 1904 John Hay commissioned Saint-Gaudens to do this small bronze caricature. The angel wings and porcupine body caught the contradictions in Adams's personality. U.S. DEPARTMENT OF THE INTERIOR, NATIONAL PARK SERVICE, ADAMS NATIONAL HISTORIC SITE, QUINCY, MASSACHUSETTS

of the end is over his mind, and he curls up in a helpless heap waiting the coup-de-grace," Henry wrote to Lizzie.

From Roosevelt's first days in the White House, Adams had predicted that Hay would be forced out of the cabinet to make room for a more aggressive type—a Rough Rider in spirit if not in fact. Though Hay suspected that Henry was right, he would not resign even to spare himself the humiliation of being dismissed. As a gentleman, he would go quietly if the president asked; he would not desert. Nor, in spite of large differences with Roosevelt, would he join in Henry's derision. Having cast his lot, Hay strove to be both friend and counselor. He wrote Theodore an effusive sonnet, praised his understanding of history (which would have appalled Adams), and entertained him for an hour every Sunday after the Roosevelts attended services at St. John's.

Unlike Adams, who felt he had stayed too long on earth, Hay derived a certain wry pleasure from his status as an ancient. In 1904, when a delegation of Republicans asked him to speak in Michigan at ceremonies marking the fiftieth anniversary of the party of Abraham Lincoln, Hay merrily reported to Roosevelt that they had "tried to make it as easy for me as they could, said they did not care what sort of speech I made. I was apparently wanted as a sort of relic, and, to clinch the matter and make my acceptance certain, they said I could read my speech. 'Yes,' said another, with large magnanimity, 'you can sit in a chair and read it if you like.' " Clara protested the journey on medical grounds, but John accepted. It was an election year. His chief deserved all the support he could give.

Brought to the White House by accident, Roosevelt had difficulty believing that the public wanted him there, and he was obsessed by the fear of being turned out. He "thinks of nothing, talks of nothing, and lives for nothing but his political interests," Adams complained. "If you remark to him that God is Great, he asks naively at once how that will affect his election." When the New York City newspapers backed the Democratic challenger, a local judge named Alton B. Parker, and when Wall Street vented its displeasure with Roosevelt's trust-busting, he turned panicky and defensive. Defeat would "not in the least alter my conviction that what I have done was both right and wise," he insisted to Hay.

Adams saw that Wall Street was merely trying to scare Roosevelt and prophesied that the financiers would prefer any Republican, even Theodore, to a Democrat. By September, Hay believed that victory was certain. "I am not a rainbow-chaser, but—my dear Theodore— you are elected," he wrote the president. Applauding Roosevelt's adroit courtship of the Irish vote, Hay offered to don a green waist-coat and preface his name with O' if Roosevelt thought it would help. Though the author of *The Bread-Winners* had little use for Irish immigrants, he understood their value on election day. Then an Irishman was better than a mugwump, Hay told the president, be-cause "he goes to the polls while the mug. is apt to take a day off and commune with Nature."

On November 8, three of every five voters cast ballots for Roosevelt, giving him the biggest majority the country had ever seen. Theodore was astounded. "I had no conception that there was such a tide in our favor, and I frankly confess that I do not under-stand it," he told Nannie Lodge.

Hay soon read in the newspapers that Roosevelt expected him to stay in the cabinet until 1909, when he himself left office. The secretary wondered whether his "tenement of clay" would hold together for that long, and he told Adams on an afternoon walk that by 1909 he probably would have lost all faculty for enjoyment. "Make your mind easy on that score, sonny!" Adams retorted. "You've lost it already."

A hundred copies of *Mont-Saint-Michel and Chartres* awaited Henry on his return from Paris at the end of 1904. He packed them off to friends and soon had the pleasure of knowing that they found the book as beguiling as he had found the Virgin. Lizzie Cameron foresaw that it would "creep into the ken of litterateurs" and pronounced it "the best thing done in modern times." William James marveled at the "frolic power" of Adams's prose; his brother Henry read the book with "wonder, sympathy, and applause." From New Hampshire, Augustus Saint-Gaudens sang his delight: "You dear old Porcupinus Poeticus, You old Poeticus under a Bushelibus: I thought I liked you fairly well, but I like you more for the book you sent me the other day." Saint-Gaudens did not know whether to like Adams more because he had given him a fresh view of the twelfth century or because the "general guts and enthusiasm of the work puzzles what courtesy calls my brain. You know (damn you) I never read, but last night I got as far in your work as the Virgin, Eve, and the Bees, and I cannot wait to acknowledge it till I am through. Thank you dear old stick in the mud."

As Adams sat with the large dark-blue volume in his hands and listened to the clanging and honking of streetcars and automobiles on Lafayette Square, he felt more keenly than ever the chasm between Virgin and dynamo. The United States, he remarked to an English friend, "has no character but prodigious force,—at least twenty million horsepower constant." *Mont-Saint-Michel and Chartres* was his protest against this monstrous power, his "declaration of principles as head of the Conservative Christian Anarchists; a party numbering one member. The Virgin and St. Thomas are my vehicles of anarchism. Nobody knows enough to see what they mean, so the Judges will probably not be able to burn me."

To friends who thought the book deserved a larger audience,

Henry replied that the Virgin was not a commercial commodity. Having copyrighted it and presented copies to several libraries, he considered it published in the strictest sense of the word. He would not write for the public because he did not know who the public was. His own public, he imagined, had never exceeded "a score."

> Anything which has helped to bring that score into closer understanding and sympathy, has been worth doing. Any expression which makes on me the illusion of having done anything towards sympathy . . . is as near positive satisfaction as St. Francis or Pascal or I could reach. We never despised the world or its opinions, we only failed to find out its existence. The world, if it exists, feels exactly in the same way towards us, and cares not one straw whether we exist or not. Philosophy has never got beyond this point. There are but two schools; one turns the world into me; the other turns me into the world; and the result is the same. The so-called me is a very, very small and foolish puppy-dog, but it is all that exists, and it tries all its life to get a little bigger by enlarging its energies, and getting dollars or getting friends.

For the dollars he had never cared, but the friends had meant everything. Now they were gone—Clover and her brother and sister to suicide, Clarence King to tuberculosis. Though Lizzie Cameron and John Hay remained, one was lost to Paris, the other to the poison of power. After five years in the State Department, Hay had no more emotional range than a caged rat, it seemed to Adams. "So," he sighed to Lizzie, "I have outlived everybody and everything on the Square, and gaze off into the infinite."

The year 1905 opened with a visit from Henry James. It was his first stay in the capital since 1882, and once again he gravitated to the home of Henry Adams. Above all else in Washington he wanted to see the Saint-Gaudens sculpture at Clover's grave. Unable to put the request to his host, who still forbade any mention of his wife, James confided his predicament to Margaret Chanler, a regular at the breakfast table. Together they slipped away in her brougham and rode out to the snowy slopes of the cemetery at Rock Creek Church. James bared his head and stood silently before the figure for a long time. On the ride home he spoke warmly of Clover's wit and grace. "We never knew how delightful Henry was till he lost her," James told

Mrs. Chanler, "he was so proud of her that he let her shine as he sat back and enjoyed listening to what she said and what she let others say."

As far as James could see, the passage of two decades had left little imprint on Washington. The trees had grown up, softening the skeletal hardness of the architecture, but the city seemed "overweighted by a single Dome and overaccented by a single Shaft." Looking at the hodgepodge of statuary in the Rotunda of the Capitol, he decided that it was, quite inadvertently, a perfect statement of "the collective vibrations of a people; their conscious spirit, their public faith, their bewildered taste, their ceaseless curiosity, their arduous and interrupted education."

James abominated the scale and power of America's industrial society, the ostentation of the rich, the ugliness of the cities. How *could* one admire a land whose greatest source of pride seemed to be the prevalence of the indoor water closet? Punctuating himself into a frenzy, he ranted, "There is NO 'fascination' *whatever,* in anything or anyone: that is exactly what there *isn't.*" Like Clover Adams on the Nile, James rebelled against "the perpetual effort of trying to 'do justice' to what one doesn't like."

Nonetheless, it consoled him to find that Washington was still the "City of Conversation," the title he had bestowed in 1882. It talked incessantly, of itself and nothing else, making for "one of the happiest cases of collective self-consciousness" he knew. As the only American city that did not bow to the great god Business, Washington offered the visitor a view of society as society, and for James, "that rich little fact became the key to everything."

Part of James's affection for Washington sprang from Washington's affection for him. No less a power than Henry Cabot Lodge escorted him to Capitol Hill to watch the Senate at work. Secretary of State John Hay hosted a banquet in his honor, and Theodore Roosevelt, who had once reviled him in print as "a miserable little snob," invited him to dine.

James passed through the high iron palings of the White House and made his way up the drive on January 12, 1905. The executive mansion, alone in a spacious setting, struck him as the noblest edifice in the capital—serene, graceful, unpretentious. The façade scarcely prepared him for the grandiosity within. The president had renounced all imperial ambitions, but as James saw at once, Roosevelt did not need an empire to enjoy playing emperor. "Theodore Rex," as James privately christened him, had created a court complete with crimson silk ropes to cordon the sheep from the goats and platoons of *aides-de-camp* in splendid regalia. (Theodore Rex had succeeded in putting nearly everyone but the diplomatic corps in uniform. In that enterprise he had been stopped cold by Elihu Root, who observed that the only fitting item of apparel for America's envoys would be a coat featuring a tail embroidered with a sprig of mistletoe.) Wondering what the masses made of Theodore's monarchical appetites, James supposed that they tolerated the pomp because they liked the man.

At dinner the president favored the novelist with a seat near his own, which enabled James to see that Roosevelt talked even more, and with even more self-absorption, than Washington itself. Theodore was "a wonderful little machine," James reported to his friend Edith Wharton, "destined to be overstrained perhaps, but not as yet, truly, betraying the least creak."

Events forged one more link between Roosevelt and James before James departed the capital. With Henry Adams and five others, they were nominated to the American Academy of Arts and Letters, a body organized the year before with John Hay, John La Farge, and Augustus Saint-Gaudens among its first seven members. Adams accepted, and James overcame the twinges he felt at being offered the honor after decades of abusing his native land. Only Theodore Roosevelt had qualms. He did not intend to become a member of this "foolish" Academy unless all the other nominees accepted, he told Hay. Even then, he wondered whether he should take part. "Doesn't it seem to you a rather ridiculous thing to try to start such an academy?" In his judgment, such institutions tended to do more for the second-rate than for "permanent literature." By joining, they ran the risk of turning themselves into laughingstocks.

With admirable restraint Hay replied that he considered the list of nominees "unexpectedly good." He speculated that all would accept and pointed out that while the Academy could not possibly enhance Roosevelt's glory, his acceptance would add luster to the Academy.

"All right, I accepted at once," Roosevelt growled. "What is good enough for you is most certainly good enough for me."

Henry James left town with only one worry about the new Academy. Assigning Adams the task of devising a proper uniform, he begged him to "keep it cheap. Think what Theodore will want."

On March 4, Inauguration Day, Theodore Roosevelt went to Capitol Hill wearing the latest version of a gift that John Hay had presented to several other Republican chief executives—a ring containing a few strands of presidential hair, this time from the head of Abraham Lincoln. Deeply touched, Roosevelt had written him, "I wonder if you have any idea what your strength and wisdom and sympathy, what the guidance you have given me and the mere delight in your companionship, have meant to me in these three and a half years?" The softness came easily. Like Hay's other intimates, Roosevelt realized that the secretary of state probably would not live to see another inauguration.

Two weeks into the new administration, Hay boarded an ocean liner with his wife and Henry Adams for a Mediterranean cruise. Exhausted, he stumbled on the pier and had to be helped up the gangplank. The newspapermen who witnessed the fall reported that the secretary of state was dying. Hay hastened to assure his nineteen-year-old son Clarence that the reporters were wrong; after a week of resting in his cabin, he was walking the decks for a mile or two every day.

When the travelers reached the Italian coast in April, Hay had good days and bad. Watching John and Clara set off on a stroll, Adams wondered whether Clara would bring him back on a stretcher or chase him home at a run; both seemed equally possible. Hay wrote Roosevelt that he was "decidedly better" than when he left Washington, "though far from what your Secretary of State ought to be." The doctors diagnosed a heart problem and prescribed a rest cure at Bad Nauheim in Germany. "This involves parting with the Porcupinus Angelicus, and I would almost rather keep the diseases," Hay lamented to Saint-Gaudens. "He has been kindness itself—the Porcupine has 'passed in music out of sight' and the Angel has been perfected in him."

Toward the end of May, when Hay left Nauheim, he was told that he would survive if he continued to rest. The physician told Clara that on landing in New York, they were to go straight to Lake

Sunapee, and Hay was to avoid exertion until autumn. Hay felt sufficiently buoyed to tell Roosevelt that "a complete cure" was in the offing, but he acknowledged that his usefulness in the State Department might be at an end: "I need not say that when you think a change would be, for any reason, advisable, I shall go."

Booked for a June 7 sailing, the Hays spent a few days in Paris with Henry Adams, who whirled them about the city in his latest toy, a 1904 Mercedes. On June 2, Henry drove them to the train station and said farewell. En route to Southampton, they paused in London but saw no one, at the insistence of Hay's physician. Avoiding his English friends made Hay feel furtive and morose, and he was overjoyed when Cecil Spring Rice managed to slip through the net for a short visit.

From their ballroom-size quarters aboard the R.M.S. *Baltic,* Clara sent Henry cheerful notes on John's progress. John, declaring himself "a little to the good since Paris," chatted nonchalantly about European politics. Adams was not deceived. He knew that Hay was doomed.

Hay soon admitted as much to himself, at least in the pages of his diary. On June 13 he recorded a dream in which he had gone to the White House to report to the president, "who turned out to be Mr. Lincoln. He was very kind and considerate, and sympathetic about my illness. He said there was little work of importance on hand. He gave me two unimportant letters to answer. I was pleased that this slight order was in my power to obey." Encountering the hero of his youth had not surprised him, he said, but the dream left him with a feeling of "overpowering melancholy." A day later he summed up his life in a passage obviously meant to soften his family's grief.

I say to myself that I should not rebel at the thought of my life ending at this time. I have lived to be old; something I never expected in my youth. I have had many blessings, domestic happiness being the greatest of all. I have lived my life. I have had success beyond all the dreams of my boyhood. My name is printed in the journals of the world without descriptive qualifications, which may, I suppose, be called fame. By mere length of service I shall occupy a modest place in the history of my time. If I were to live several years more I should probably add nothing to my existing reputation; while I could not reasonably expect any further enjoyment of life, such as falls to the lot

of old men in sound health. I know death is the common lot, and what is universal ought not to be deemed a misfortune; and yet—instead of confronting it with dignity and philosophy, I cling instinctively to life and the things of life, as eagerly as if I had not had my chance at happiness and gained nearly all the great prizes.

Hay died in his bed at Lake Sunapee at 12:25 A.M. on July 1. The next day, swathed in a heavy veil, Clara and her son Clarence rode down Mount Sunapee to the village of Newbury, where a special train waited to carry Hay's body to Cleveland. "As he had told me once he did not care where I laid him and as our boy was there it seemed more like home," she wrote in John's diary after the funeral. Theodore Roosevelt and his entire cabinet came from Washington, but Clara scarcely noticed. "The service was very simple and I could not realize that it was he who was being removed from my sight. All signs of death were concealed and nothing to show that it was the end was visible. I cannot yet realize what has happened. I am paralyzed and numb. I suppose I will wake up some day and will know."

23

Playing Out the Hand

That evening, when word reached Henry Adams in Paris, he thought first of himself. "Hay's death strands me," he mourned. "I am now left quite alone, with no thought or wish except to follow as quietly and easily as possible."

His next thoughts, born of a habit so old and deep it had become instinct, were of his friends. Knowing that Clara would blame herself for the failure of John's medical treatment, Henry hastened to assure her that she had been "superb." He also flew to the side of Nannie Lodge, who was vacationing in Paris with Cabot. But there was little to say. Nannie could not grieve openly for Hay, nor would she care to hear Henry's theory that Hay had been murdered by Cabot and his Senate colleagues. Though Adams struggled to conceal his loathing for Cabot, who had become physically repulsive to him, Nannie saw "every shade" of his feelings, he told Lizzie. "We keep up a sort of mask-play together, each knowing the other to the ground. She kept it up with Hay to the end. It has gone on for years, and may go on for more, but only on condition that I do not let my irritability show itself."

At the White House, Hay's death loosed a torrent of emotion. Calling Hay a "wise and patient advisor" and the most charming of friends, Theodore Roosevelt told Clara that no one in the administration could fill his place. But the secretary of state had been dead for only three weeks when the president turned against him. While Hay's reputation and loyalty were genuine assets, his declining health and his Anglophilia had impeded the business of state, Roosevelt grumbled to Lodge. "I had to do the big things myself, and the other things I always feared would be badly done or not done at all." In Roosevelt's view, Hay's English leanings meant that he could not be trusted to deal with Germany or Britain. Nor did Roosevelt sympathize with Hay's perennial woes in the Senate: "the business of an active politician is not to complain of defects which cannot be changed, but to do the best he can in spite of them."

Theodore's revisionism would not have surprised Henry Adams. After four years of watching Hay writhe, and curse himself for writhing, under the heels of men like Lodge and Roosevelt, Adams knew all. He would wear the mask with Nannie but not with Theodore. After Hay's death, Adams and Roosevelt rarely saw each other.

With his intimate knowledge and impassioned opinions, Adams felt he could not possibly write a memoir of John Hay, and he dreaded the day when Clara might suggest it. In self-defense he began writing a book about his own life, hoping that its portrayal of Hay would exempt him from the task of a full-scale biography. By the end of 1906, *The Education of Henry Adams* was ready for the printer.

The *Education* was not an autobiography, Adams insisted. It was a reflection on an age of multiplicity, a companion to *Mont-Saint-Michel and Chartres,* which had been a study of an age of unity. The title character was "purely imaginary"—a narrative device in service of a larger point. To strengthen the fiction, he wrote in the third person, dissecting Henry Adams as coolly as if he were a corpse on a slab.

Autobiography or no, the *Education* caught the essence of Henry Adams: the deeply divided self that made him both angel and porcupine, a skeptic in search of faith, and powerless friend of the powerful. Born in a climate of bitter winters and blistering summers, he had sensed from earliest childhood that life was "a double thing." As an adult, he felt himself crawling painfully along a knife edge, aware of the Virgin on one side and the dynamo on the other but unable to surrender to either force. The American man was a failure, the woman no better: neither sex seemed to understand that woman should be worshiped because "she was reproduction—the greatest and most mysterious of all energies." He said not a word about his own childless marriage or his wife. The other great feminine presence in his life, Lizzie Cameron, was dismissed in half a line as one of the chief "dispensers of sunshine" on Lafayette Square.

The irony at the heart of the *Education* was the author's abiding ignorance despite a life spent in quest of enlightenment. Harvard College had left nothing but "an autobiographical blank, a mind on which only a water-mark had been stamped." Trained as idealists and reformers, Adams and his classmates had gone forth into a world that had no use for them. There were other disappointments. Hay and Adams had devoted years and vast sums of money to the writing of histories that no one cared to read. The greatest artists of their day—Saint-Gaudens, La Farge, and Richardson—had won little acclaim. Casting about for the organizing principle of such a universe, Adams concluded, "Chaos was the law of nature; Order was the dream of man." To his baffled mind, only chaos and its cognates—chance, luck, fate, accident—could explain how a man as unambitious as John Hay rose to the head of the State Department while the drive and brilliance of Clarence King ended in ruin. King's failure taught "whatever the bystander chose to read in it, but to Adams it seemed singularly full of moral, if he could but understand it."

Understanding eluded Henry Adams, leaving him with little except a hope for some gentler future in which he and Hay and King might be reunited. "Perhaps some day—say 1938, their centenary—they might be allowed to return together for a holiday, to see the mistakes of their own lives made clear in the light of the mistakes of their successors; and perhaps then, for the first time since man began his education among the carnivores, they would find a world that sensitive and timid natures could regard without a shudder."

Adams sent the *Education* to friends for comment and correction but hardly cared whether it inspired praise or condemnation. The book was "a mere shield of protection in the grave," he explained to Henry James. "I advise you to take your own life in the same way, in order to prevent biographers from taking it in theirs." To another friend, he explained that the book could be understood by imagining "a centipede moving along in 20 little sections (each with a mathematical formula carefully concealed in its stomach) to the bottom of a hill; and then laboriously climbing in 15 sections more (each with a new mathematical problem carefully concealed in its stomach) till it can get up on a hill an inch or two high, so as to see ahead a half an inch or so."

Chilled by the cynicism of the *Education,* Clara Hay urged Henry to turn to the Bible for wisdom and consolation. Without directly challenging the book's most peculiar silence, she reminded him, "You have said that all the good in your life has come from women. Will you not listen to the least among your women friends?"

As a ruse to avoid writing a memoir of John Hay, the *Education* stopped just short of success. Instead of a memoir, Clara decided to publish John's letters and portions of his diary. When she asked Adams to serve as editor, he could think of no graceful way to demur. From the outset he suspected that Clara's sense of propriety would lead to censorship, but in the two years he gave to collecting and transcribing hundreds of Hay's letters, he never once imagined the evisceration she had in mind. She cut even the mildest of Hay's profanities, eliminated whole paragraphs with no sign of ellipsis, and slashed all proper nouns to initials. A typical passage, from a harmless letter to Adams, reported that "Mrs. H——— got a letter from Mrs. L——— yesterday saying Mrs. C——— was leaving B———. She is expected in C———, but of course she will not come. We went down to B——— one day to see her. C——— and A——— had a delightful day with M———. Mrs. L——— came over from N———, and we talked, mostly about you till train-time."

Privately printed in November 1908, the three-volume *Letters of John Hay and Extracts from Diary* quickly made its way around Washington. The welter of initials deceived no one. T——— R——— and H——— C——— L——— easily recognized themselves, took deep offense, and exchanged letters meant to record their version of events for posterity. In a tirade that filled fifteen typewritten pages, Roosevelt conceded that Hay was "a man of remarkable ability" and the greatest conversationalist of his age but had not been "a strong or brave man."

He had a very ease-loving nature and a moral timidity which made him shrink from all that was rough in life, and therefore from practical affairs. He was at his best at a dinner table or in a drawing room . . . his temptation was to associate as far as possible only with men of refined and cultivated tastes, who lived apart from the world of affairs, and who, if Americans, were wholly lacking in robustness of fiber. His close intimacy with Henry James and Henry Adams—charming men, but exceedingly undesirable companions for any man not of strong nature—and the tone of satirical cynicism which they admired, and which he always affected in writing them, marked that phase of his character which so impaired his usefulness as a public man. In public life during the time he was Secretary of State under me he accomplished little. . . . his usefulness to me was almost exclusively the usefulness of a fine figurehead. He was always afraid of Senators and Congressmen who possessed any power or robustness, this fear being due in part to timidity and nervousness, and in part to a sheer fastidiousness which made him unwilling to face the rather intimate association which is implied in a fight.

Cabot agreed and vigorously defended the actions of his colleagues on Capitol Hill. It was Hay who had abused the Senate, not vice versa, the senator insisted to the president. "The result was that, although when he first came into office he was very popular with the Senate and Senators were most anxious to do what he wanted, as his term of service drew to a close they had become so embittered by hearing what he said of them that they were inclined to defeat anything he wanted." Cabot disputed Theodore on only one point: the brilliance of Hay's conversation. Once as dazzled as Roosevelt, Cabot had since decided that Hay's rhetorical virtuosity probably ranked behind that of Oliver Wendell Holmes and James Russell Lowell.

Adams quietly filled in the blanks in his copy of Hay's letters and hid his glee when Clara borrowed his volumes to emend her own. Clara, having concluded her business in Washington (apparently without realizing the futility of her editorial stratagem), left Lafayette Square in 1909. She would spend the last five years of her life building a grand palazzo in Cleveland and reigning over a growing brood of grandchildren.

The disaster of editing Hay's letters snuffed the last of Henry's literary desires, but circumstance pressed him into service once again. Bay Lodge died of ptomaine poisoning in 1909, at the age of thirty-five. When his parents decided to publish his poems and plays, they asked Adams to write a brief biography based on Bay's letters. Adams, loving Nannie even more than he despised Cabot, agreed.

The Life of George Cabot Lodge matters less as biography than as a postscript to *The Education of Henry Adams,* for when Uncle Henry peered into Bay's life, he saw his own. Like Adams, Bay proved unamenable to education, loathed puritans and plutocrats, and worried desperately about failure. The Lodges saw nothing to censor, and early in 1911, as the biography and two companion volumes of verse were readied for the press, Cabot came to 1603 H Street to discuss a few last details. "I was beautiful and approved everything, and said that I agreed with everybody," Henry boasted to Lizzie.

The biography of Bay Lodge was Henry Adams's last book but not his last act of friendship. Hoping to shape history's view of John La Farge, he corresponded with and granted interviews to the artist's first biographer, Royal Cortissoz, and allowed him to reproduce Clover's portrait of La Farge.★ (La Farge had died a pauper in 1910. After decades of poverty and neglect, his wife had exacted her retribution. Pleading a "bilious headache," Margaret La Farge stayed away from her husband's funeral. She also ignored his wish to be buried in an expensive plot in New York's Woodlawn Cemetery. The rest of the family preferred to think that the interment would not have troubled La Farge. He had loved to tell his children the tale of a Chinese painter who entered eternity by stepping into one of his pictures and disappearing.)

Lizzie Cameron and Henry Adams saw little of each other from 1904 to 1908 as Lizzie darted from ballroom to ballroom in Paris, London, Newport, and Washington in hopes of mating tall, shy Martha. The hunt ended in 1909, when Martha married Ronald Lindsay, a Scotsman posted to the British embassy in Washington. Mission accomplished, Lizzie returned to Europe for good.

Mrs. Cameron's liaison with Joe Stickney had permanently cooled Henry's ardor, but they continued to write each other weekly, and when he came to Paris each summer, he and his automobile were at her service. Through her, Adams came to know Edith Wharton,

★ The gesture was a tribute to Clover as well as La Farge. The portrait became the first of her photographs to appear in print.

whose elegant apartment in the Faubourg St. Germain became the center of his Parisian social life. Drawn to the white-mustached little man with the dark blue eyes and the warm, husky voice, Mrs. Wharton soon adopted him as her Uncle Henry. She joshed about his superabundance of "wives"; he teased her about her expatriate "saloon." Adams had known and enjoyed Bernard Berenson for several years, and when he discovered that the art historian and Mrs. Wharton held each other in low regard, he went to work at once to right this grievous wrong. Berenson was invited to a restaurant for dinner with Henry Adams. Arriving at dusk, he was led to a dim private room where he found his host surrounded by guests, including Lizzie Cameron and a woman whose face was obscured by a veil of black lace. Berenson did not recognize the woman's voice but was captivated by her artistic prejudices, which matched his own. After sundown, when the lights came on, he saw to his astonishment that she was Edith Wharton. By clearing the brambles, Adams started Bernard Berenson and Edith Wharton on the path to a close friendship that would last until her death, in 1937.

In February 1912, shortly after his seventy-fourth birthday, Henry announced to Lizzie that he planned to sail for Europe on April 20. Still fascinated by advances in science and engineering, he had booked passage on the first return voyage of a new English ocean liner, the *Titanic*. When it sank on April 14, he was deeply shaken, and a few days later he suffered a stroke. In June, as soon as he was well enough to be moved, a private railroad car carried him north to his brother Charles's estate, Birnamwood, in South Lincoln, Massachusetts.

There began a regimen of physical therapy and an elaborate, meanspirited family campaign to prevent Mrs. Cameron from making a visit. Henry's sister, Mary Quincy, cabled Mrs. Cameron that nothing could be done and that Henry would not recognize her. "I won't have her," Mary told Charles. ". . . There has been disagreeable scandal enough about that affair, and we certainly cannot permit people to say that in his last illness she came from Europe to look after him!" Henry James also advised Lizzie against the voyage, perhaps at the instigation of Brooks Adams, who was in London at the time. "To speak crudely and familiarly they clearly—by all their gestures—'don't want you,' " James told her. On learning that she was determined to go, James retreated. Her journey was "heroic," and she was "magnificent," he said. "If you do see Henry Adams but once, you will be glad to the last intensity that you have done so."

Nannie Lodge tried to ease the tension by proposing that Lizzie bring Henry to Nahant for a few days, a suggestion that drew a sharp rebuff. Perhaps this "superannuated honeymoon" would do wonders for the patient, Charles sneered, but "all this time where is Don?—Where?—oh, where?—Henry Adams of Washington, D.C. as 'co-respondent,' and your house as the *locum in quo* will sound good!"

Full of apologies and explanations, Nannie reminded Charles that the idea had come from Henry, who had raised it during the Lodges' recent visit to South Lincoln. "As you know he spoke first to us of the possibility of his going later to Nahant, in the hope a house could be found for him, and it was that fact alone which emboldened me to write to Mrs. Adams and Mrs. Quincy to tell them that our house was at Henry's disposition, if the move should at any time be thought advisable. But I don't wonder that it annoys you to have suggestions of this kind made to Henry, when he is so well off where he is."

Lizzie arrived at the end of July, settling in Boston and making a few excursions to South Lincoln. Except for a slight limp, Henry had recovered most of his powers, and the pleasure of seeing Lizzie did not trigger the overexcitement feared by the Adamses. But their glacial hospitality soon drove her away. Sad to see her go, Henry set his sights on the following winter, when he hoped to join her for a Mediterranean holiday.

By election day, Henry was back on Lafayette Square with a choice seat for a three-ring circus starring the calamitous Theodore Roosevelt. Unhappy with his plodding successor, William Howard Taft, Roosevelt had bolted the Republicans and formed his own party, the Progressives, to run for president in 1912.

Theodore, Adams snorted, was "a chewed-up cud." Feeling no fondness for Taft, whom he considered an imbecile, Adams inclined toward Woodrow Wilson, the Democratic nominee. "Mr. Wilson is a College Professor," he informed Cecil Spring Rice, who was about to come to Washington as British ambassador. "I cannot write a paper to show that a Professor is by essence incapable of acting with

Sir Cecil Spring Rice (Sir Springy to his American friends) returned to Washington as Britain's ambassador in 1913. REPRODUCED FROM *THE LETTERS AND FRIENDSHIPS OF SIR CECIL SPRING-RICE,* EDITED BY STEPHEN GWYNN

other men." On November 5 Roosevelt won more votes than Taft but not enough to defeat Woodrow Wilson.

None of it made the slightest difference to Henry Adams. His mornings were spent walking with a niece, and in the afternoons he explored medieval music with the secretary-companion who had been hired after his stroke. A tall, striking young woman who sang and played the piano, Aileen Tone had come from New York with the understanding that she and Mr. Adams would try each other out. Knowing his passion for the twelfth century, she had brought a book filled with transcriptions of medieval French songs, and as soon as she sang a few, Adams issued a heartfelt command: "Tell your mother you're not going home."

Charmed by the fluidity and the strangeness of melodies that seemed to end "with their tails in the air," Adams acquired a Steinway and sent to France for more music. Back came manuscripts and liturgical tomes filled with songs written in clefs and notes that Aileen could not read. With the help of John La Farge, Jr., a Jesuit, she learned to decode the plain-chant notation and mastered enough of the rhythms and phrasing to perform for her new uncle.

During the summer of 1913, Adams transplanted himself and Aileen and two nieces to a chateau near Paris, where everyone indulged his new enthusiasm. He hired two scholars to ransack the libraries of France for more songs, and the travelers returned to Lafayette Square in November with reams of new melodies, many of which had lain undisturbed for centuries.

Reawakened to the joys of the twelfth century, Adams finally consented to the publication of *Mont-Saint-Michel and Chartres.* He still refused to sully himself by selling the Virgin, but he permitted the book to be published under the aegis of the American Institute of Architects, with royalties set aside to furnish copies for penniless members of the profession. When the book appeared early in 1914, the author read the reviews and laughed. "[I]t is droll! he told a friend. "Here am I, telling everyone that I am quite dotty and bedridden, and the papers reviewing me as a youthful beginner." No one seemed to realize that he had written anything else.

From a chateau fifty miles north of Paris, uncle and nieces watched anxiously in the summer of 1914 as Austria declared war on Serbia, Germany marched on Luxembourg and France, and England entered the conflict. Like other foreigners, Uncle Henry and his charges were evacuated to Paris, and toward the end of August, he decided to shepherd his flock to safety in England. They caught the last boat to Folkestone.

Unnerved by the somber crowds and the wounded soldiers he had seen in France, Henry felt he had narrowly escaped from "what verged on Hell." Martha Cameron Lindsay lent him her country house in Dorset, where he went gratefully to wait for passage to America. Henry James came over from Rye, and Aileen Tone watched the two old friends tumble into each other's arms and hold fast. Their world had been smashed. For James the war was "horrible, unspeakable, iniquitous." He tried to tell himself that it might also prove interesting, but it was no use; the thought made him ill. Adams and James talked deep into the night, with James arguing passionately that the United States had a moral duty to join England in the war. The following summer, outraged by America's continued neutrality, James became a British subject. He died in 1916.

The loss opened a floodgate in Henry Adams. James had not only been a friend for forty years, he wrote to Lizzie, "but he also belonged to the circle of my wife's set long before I knew him or her, and you know how I have clung to all that belonged to my wife. I have been living all day in the seventies. . . . we really were happy then."

Nannie Lodge had died a few months before James, and in the deepening solitude Adams began to imagine himself "a grasshopper in October without legs or wings or song." He left the house only for his daily walk and occasional rides with Aileen Tone to Rock Creek Church Cemetery, where he sat in the enfolding arms of the long stone bench and contemplated the guardian of Clover's grave. When Aileen finally summoned the courage to ask about Clover, Adams paused for a suspensefully long moment then turned to her and said softly, "My child, you have broken a silence of thirty years." He showed her the portrait of Clover on horseback and spoke of "your Aunt Clover" so often that Aileen began to feel as if she had known her.

If they talked of Aunt Clover's suicide, Aileen tactfully kept Uncle Henry's remarks to herself. Judging by the marginal notes he had made a decade earlier in his copy of *The Principles of Psychology* by William James, the event remained a mystery to him. The most he had deduced was that suicide was the act of "people who detest their own identity." But he did not understand how nature was served by passions strong enough to overpower the human will. Feelings "ought to be involuntary nervous reactions incident to self-preservation," he wrote at the end of James's chapter on emotions. "The mystery is in their astounding sensitiveness to the stimulant. How can a whisper kill? How can an external immaterial suggestion act on a physical organ? How can a thought outside the body, penetrate and kill the body? Why is will powerless to control it?"

In spite of the enigma, telling Aileen about Clover freed Henry to face the most tormenting chapter of his past, and in the spring of 1917 he announced that he wanted to spend the summer in the house at Beverly Farms, which he had avoided since Clover's breakdown.

Shortly after Clover Adams's death, Henry Adams commissioned Augustus Saint-Gaudens to sculpt a memorial for her grave in Washington's Rock Creek Church Cemetery. Henry is buried at her side. U.S. DEPARTMENT OF THE INTERIOR, NATIONAL PARK SERVICE, SAINT-GAUDENS NATIONAL HISTORIC SITE, CORNISH, NEW HAMPSHIRE

The holiday passed in a pleasant haze. Beverly seemed a "fantastic dream," he thought. The woods bore no resemblance to the landscape he remembered, and the scores of young relatives who came to call seemed equally unreal. Still, the experience gave him a sense of completion. "I have finished with Beverly, which has been as happy a refuge for me as it was once for you," he wrote to Lizzie. Saying good-bye to Brooks and the rest of the Adamses, Henry supposed that it was for the last time: "nobody seems to expect to see anybody again."

Back on H Street, life revolved around the war. Lizzie Cameron sent dire accounts of her relief work with Edith Wharton in Paris, where the refugees pouring in from the countryside had strained supplies of food and shelter beyond their limits. The United States had entered the war in April 1917, and young men in khaki and young women in Red Cross uniforms talked animatedly at Uncle Henry's breakfast table. Ambassador Spring Rice, nearing sixty and now as bald as his uncle, came daily to vituperate against his new rival, Lord Northcliffe, who had been sent to coordinate the British war effort in the United States. Embarrassed by gossip of the friction between the two men, the Foreign Office recalled them both. Within weeks, Springy was dead.

As the war dragged on into 1918, Adams was forced to admit that the brute force of the dynamo was pure innocence compared to the savage machinery of war. In March, a few weeks after his eightieth birthday, Germany stunned the world with Big Bertha, an artillery piece capable of bombarding Paris from a distance of seventy-five miles. "Life has become intolerable," he told Aileen. "This is no world for an old man to live in when the Germans can shoot to the moon."

Lizzie was in no immediate danger, having gone to England to nurse poor Martha, who was fatally ill with typhoid fever. Worried that the Germans would train the sights of Big Bertha on England, Henry sent cable after cable begging them to seek refuge.

On Tuesday, March 26, Big Bertha was the subject of a jolly dinner conversation at 1603 H Street. Aileen and Henry's niece Elizabeth Ogden Adams had been reading him the war news, and he took a grim delight in the generals who boldly declared Big Bertha an impossibility one day and calmly accepted it the next. At ten,

Aileen and Elizabeth took him up to bed, wound his clock, and bade him good-night. He died quietly in his sleep, lying on his side, curled into his pillows.

When Aileen and Elizabeth found him in the morning, Aileen thought his face looked "marvellously beautiful," with the "strangest expression of *consciousness* and will and intellect." Knowing only that Uncle Henry did not want a church funeral, Aileen went down to his study to see if he had left instructions in his desk. No statement of his wishes could be found, but in a top drawer she discovered a partially filled bottle of potassium cyanide, the instrument of Clover's suicide. And in the kneehole hung a sign, hand-lettered in red ink on white paper, which read *Mme. Marthe, Modiste.* Uncle Henry had made it nearly thirty years before for his first adopted niece, little Martha Cameron, who thought of the kneehole as her hat shop.

Aileen and Elizabeth decided to place the coffin in the library, where it would stand among books and paintings and echoes of Hay and King and Lizzie and Nannie and Spring Rice. Lizzie sent a blanket of white lilacs for the bier, and through the library windows, beyond vases of forsythia and lilac, the first spring leaves on the trees of Lafayette Park made a curtain of softest green. On Thursday afternoon the rector of St. John's Church came to conduct a brief service, attended by a few friends, and on Sunday Henry joined Clover beneath the peaceful gaze of the figure at Rock Creek. Sending the news of Henry's death to one of his friends, Elizabeth remarked that he had closed his life "surrounded by people who would have done anything on earth to make him happy." For a man who treasured his friends, it was an unsurpassable end.

To a literal mind, the Five of Hearts had ceased in 1885 with the death of Clover Adams. But the extraordinary flower of their friendship bloomed until the spring day in 1918 when Henry was buried beside Clover at Rock Creek. In the last summer at Beverly, his eyesight nearly gone, Henry had spent hours listening to his nieces read the philosophy of his old friend William James. It was James, pondering the mysteries of the human mind in *The Principles of Psychology,* who had speculated that perhaps the greatest breach in nature was the breach between one mind and another. For all their intimacy, each of the Hearts felt this isolation as keenly as James.

Love had not saved Clover from suicide, nor had it freed King from the complicated shame of his secret life. Loving another woman more than his wife, Hay too knew the sorrows, and the loneliness, of the masquerade. Clara Hay, never wholly at ease in Washington, had fled to Lake Sunapee, Cleveland, and Europe at every chance. To Henry Adams, master of irony, the separateness of human beings was unbearable—and inevitable. The tragedy of the Five of Hearts was that they could not close the breach. The glory was that they tried.

Epilogue: A Legacy and a Lawsuit

Ada Todd King had her day in court—November 20, 1933. It was a dispiriting autumn Monday, bleak and gray, forty degrees. For the trip from Queens to the New York County Court House in lower Manhattan, Ada bundled up in hat, gloves, and a dark woolen coat trimmed with fur.

On the witness stand, Mrs. King, as she called herself, described her 1888 wedding, her travels to Washington and Newport with her husband, the servants and the large house on Prince Street, and their five children. At seventy-two, she could no longer summon up all the details of their life together, and when the judge asked the children's birthdates, she laughed with embarrassment. "I disremember," she confessed. She recalled only that the first had arrived in 1889, the last in 1897.

The testimony was part of her lawsuit against the heirs of James Gardiner, the friend to whom Clarence King had entrusted his possessions before his last illness. With attorneys from the Legal Aid Society, Mrs. King was seeking $80,000 from Gardiner's heirs. As her lawyers outlined the matter, Gardiner had abused his power as Clarence King's trustee, taking shameless advantage of the fact that King had created no trust in writing. Mr. King had not put his wishes on paper, they added, because he feared that the disclosure of

In 1933 Ada Todd King, then in her seventies, went to court in New York to press her claim for $80,000, which Clarence King told her he had left in the care of an old friend.
NEW YORK DAILY NEWS

such documents would embarrass his mother and his friends, who did not "view the colored race and miscegenation in the same favorable light." Mr. King's course may have been a poor expedient, but he had taken it in the belief that reliance upon Gardiner's honor offered the best hope of protecting his secret family.

The defendants' attorneys moved for a dismissal of the suit. Plaintiffs "ought not to be allowed to litigate for nothing" or to slur persons of high character, they said. If Ada Todd King had truly believed herself entitled to $80,000—a sum that would produce an annual income of $4,000—why had she accepted $600 a year for thirty years from the unnamed benefactor?

In a deposition taken before the hearing, Mrs. King had offered a simple explanation: "I did not know my rights."

Early in 1934, after hearing witnesses from both sides, the judge dismissed the case. While the monthly payments to Mrs. King after

Mr. King's death demonstrated his feelings for her, they did not prove the existence of a trust, the judge held. Nor did the court find that Gardiner had acted improperly in using King's assets to satisfy the IOUs held by John Hay.

Ada Todd King had gambled for large stakes and lost. In spite of her husband's promises, there would be no $80,000. And without the money, she was at last forced to recognize that the blame for her life of hardship rested not with Gardiner but with Clarence King, alias James Todd, the reckless, elusive charmer who had given her lies along with his love.

For two years of legal turmoil she had gained only one thing: the identity of her mysterious benefactor. With the money from the sale of King's possessions, John Hay had established a trust fund to support King's mother as well as his clandestine family. Clara Hay continued the arrangement after John's death, and when Clara died, their children carried on until the litigation began in 1931.

Acknowledgments

$\mathcal{F}$irst and deepest thanks go to Peg Cameron, superb friend and uncompromising editor, who improved the manuscript with scores of suggestions and challenging questions, and who was willing to discuss matters of structure, tone, and interpretation at every stage of the writing.

Research was pure pleasure, thanks to the cooperation of Jennifer B. Lee of the John Hay Library, Peter Drummey of the Massachusetts Historical Society, Peter Blodgett of the Huntington Library, Chuck Kelly and Janice Ruth of the Library of Congress, Ann Sindelar and John Grabowski of the Western Reserve Historical Society, Tom Dunnings of the New-York Historical Society, the staff of the manuscripts and archives division of the Sterling Memorial Library at Yale University, and the reference desk of the Darien (Connecticut) Library, which arranged several interlibrary loans.

Len Fury was a valued colleague in several projects during the years it took to complete this book, and Peggy and Bob Johnson, Casey and Jeff Mesirow, Kathy Hirsch and Mark Morrow, Molly Hughes and Peter Lindgren, and Jerry Jellison and Marilyn Skelton gave me bed, board, and company during research trips to Rhode Island, Massachusetts, and California. For an extended research trip to Washington, I am indebted to Fran Hunter for finding me a place to stay and to Brooke Shearer and Strobe Talbott for the warmth of their hospitality and the opening of many doors.

Judith Daniels, Barbara Grizzuti Harrison, Jane Howard, Chris Miles, and Paul Nagel supported applications for fellowships and grants, which led to a stay at the MacDowell Colony in 1988. Resident director Chris Barnes and the colony staff saw to every comfort, and in the peace of the MacDowell woods, I was able to sort out and write the most complex chapters of the book. Paul Nagel deserves additional thanks for his willingness to entertain the questions of a first-time biographer and his invaluable advice on key points.

In the early stages, Ellen Gruppo assisted with library research. As the book progressed, Katina Lillios took on that task as well as the daunting labor of checking the accuracy of hundreds of quotes and footnotes. Her perseverance rescued the book from more errors than my pride cares to admit; any that remain are my own.

A book has many fates unforeseen by the author in the beginning, and I am grateful to Beverly Cox and her colleagues at the National Portrait Gallery in Washington, D.C., for their willingness to mount an exhibit based on the life and times of the Five of Hearts.

Kate Whitney put me in touch with Mr. and Mrs. James Symington and Mr. and Mrs. Stuart Symington, Jr., who have been generous in sharing photographs and memorabilia of their ancestors John and Clara Hay.

Art historian Henry Adams (great-grandnephew of the Henry Adams in this book) led me to a photograph of one of John La Farge's South Seas paintings, which Mrs. Henry A. La Farge went to great lengths to secure. She also consented to my use of La Farge family papers at the New-York Historical Society and Yale University. Faith Thoron Knapp and Arline Boucher Tehan graciously shared photographs of Surrenden Dering and Elizabeth Cameron.

Though my quest for descendants of Clarence King yielded no clues, I thank Len Panaggio of Newport, Rhode Island, for publicizing it in a column in the *Newport News*. The search for a photograph of a railroad car used by Henry Adams and John La Farge on their 1886 cross-country trip also proved fruitless, but I am grateful to Harvey Turner, Don Snoddy, and Ken Longe of Union Pacific Corp. for their efforts.

Numerous institutions generously granted permission to draw

upon thousands of documents in their collections: the Adams Manuscript Trust, the Houghton Library at Harvard University, the Huntington Library, the John Hay Library at Brown University, the Massachusetts Historical Society, the manuscripts and archives division of the Yale University Library, and the Western Reserve Historical Society. My debt to these preservers of the past is profound.

The support and enthusiasm of Elaine Markson and Sally Cotton Wofford helped me past many doubts.

At Clarkson N. Potter, editor Shirley Wohl was graceful and encouraging in the face of false starts and wrong turns and throughout has given the book all the care and attention an author could wish for. My only regret is that her contributions are invisible to the reader.

Last, in the course of exploring the ties of the Five of Hearts, I realized that the joy I take in my own friendships is the gift of my mother and late father, the most welcoming and loyal people I have ever known. To Henry Adams, a friend was nothing less than "a miracle." Thanks to my parents, I share the wonder.

Sources

*I*n February 1900, shortly after his sixty-second birthday, Henry Adams mentioned to Lizzie Cameron that he had packed all her letters to him in a box with the instruction that his executors deliver them to her personally. "I thought this better than to destroy them myself, especially since they might be of use to you or Martha," he explained; "—as for mine, I count on you to destroy them. Do not leave them knocking about, as a mash for the female pigs who feed out of the magazine-troughs at five dollars a page, to root root in, for scandal and gossip."

"I had no idea that you kept them," Lizzie replied. "Why not destroy them at once. Surely it is better. As for yours, I shall do the same and I promise you that no publisher or compiler shall ever get hold of them. They shall be destroyed."

They were not destroyed, and the story of the Five of Hearts is the richer for it. In addition to the correspondence of Henry Adams and Lizzie Cameron, I have used thousands of other letters and primary sources, a substantial number of which have not previously appeared in print. The search for these materials stretched from the Massachusetts Historical Society in Boston to the Huntington Library in San Marino, California. In between were the Houghton Library at Harvard University in Cambridge, Massachusetts; the John Hay Library at Brown University in Providence, Rhode Island; the Sterling Memorial Library at Yale University in New Haven, Connecticut; the New-York Historical Society, the Pierpont Morgan Library, the Municipal Archives, and the Hall of Records in New York City; the Western Reserve Historical Society in Cleveland; and, in Washington, D.C., the Library of Congress, the Columbia Historical Society, the National Archives, and the Washingtoniana Division of the Martin Luther King, Jr., Library.

Principal collections consulted include the following:

At the John Hay Library, the John Hay Collection. Of particular interest because of the slight use to which they have been put in the past are approximately ninety letters from King to John and Clara Hay; the correspondence between John Hay and Amasa Stone; Constance Fenimore Woolson's letters to Hay; Hay's letters from Europe during his early years as a diplomat; his love letters to Clara Stone; and letters to Hay about King from mutual acquaintances in England.

At the Houghton Library, the architectural drawings of H. H. Richardson and selected letters to and from Henry Adams, Marian Hooper Adams, E. L. Godkin, Ellen Hooper Gurney, Ephraim Whitman Gurney, Clara Stone Hay, John Hay, Leonard Hay, Edward Hooper, Clarence King, and Theodore Roosevelt.

At the Huntington Library, the papers of James T. Fields, James D. Hague, and Clarence King, including King's youthful letters to James T. Gardiner and most of the sources for my account of King's geological and mining activities.

In the manuscript reading room of the Library of Congress, the papers of George F. Becker, Andrew Carnegie, Samuel F. Emmons, John Hay, and the Miles-Cameron families. In the John Hay Papers, correspondence between Hay and the friends of Clarence King sheds new light on the state of King's financial affairs at the time of his death. The Hay papers also contain the school compositions of Clara Stone.

In the prints and photographs division of the Library of Congress, the collections of Wilhelmus Bogard Bryan, James M. Goode, and Frances B. Johnston.

At the Massachusetts Historical Society, the letters of Marian Hooper Adams to Dr. Robert W. Hooper, papers of the Adams family, Henry Adams (including the H. D. Cater Collection), Adams-King, and the Lodge and Shattuck families. The Lodge Papers are silent on the liaison between John Hay and Nannie Lodge, but evidence of the relationship can be found in Lizzie Cameron's letters to Henry Adams during 1890–91 and a box of letters from Hay to Lizzie Cameron, both of which are part of the Henry Adams Papers.

At the New-York Historical Society, the papers of T. M. Coan, the La Farge family, correspondence between Augustus Saint-Gaudens and Stanford White, and the speeches of Carl Schurz.

In the manuscripts and archives division of the Sterling Memorial Library at Yale University, the papers of William H. Brewer, George J. Brush, Thomas Davidson, the La Farge family, William D. Whitney, and, on microfilm, the papers of William McKinley and Theodore Roosevelt.

At the library of the Western Reserve Historical Society, the Mather Papers.

Missing from the record are most of the correspondence between Henry and Clover Adams, Henry's diary (destroyed except for a fragment from 1888–89), nearly all of Hay's and Adams's letters to the rootless King, most of King's letters to Ada Todd King, his letters to his mother, and many letters to and from Clara Hay.

In quoting from these sources, I have occasionally made minor changes in punctuation in the interest of clarity, and I have corrected misspellings that seemed more distracting than enlightening.

Books and magazine articles in the notes below are cited by the author's last name only (except when more information is needed to avoid confusion). Complete citations appear in the bibliography, which begins on page 445.

The following abbreviations are used in the Notes:

CFA	Charles Francis Adams
CFA, Jr.	Charles Francis Adams, Jr.
HA	Henry Adams
EHA	*The Education of Henry Adams*
LHA	*The Letters of Henry Adams*
MHA	Marian Hooper ("Clover") Adams
LMHA	*The Letters of Mrs. Henry Adams*
ESC	Elizabeth Sherman Cameron
JDC	Senator James Donald ("Don") Cameron
AC	Andrew Carnegie
JTG	James T. Gardiner
CSH	Clara Stone Hay
JH	John Hay
LJH	*Letters of John Hay and Extracts from Diary*
RWH	Robert W. Hooper, M.D.
WDH	William Dean Howells
HJ	Henry James
HJL	*Henry James Letters*
CK	Clarence King
CKM	*Clarence King Memoirs*
JL	John La Farge
AL	Anna Cabot Mills ("Nannie") Lodge
HCL	Henry Cabot Lodge
WM	William McKinley
MSMC	*Mont-Saint-Michel and Chartres*
JGN	John George Nicolay
CSR	Cecil Spring Rice
HHR	Henry Hobson Richardson
TR	Theodore Roosevelt
ASG	Augustus Saint-Gaudens
AS	Amasa Stone
CFW	Constance Fenimore Woolson

Notes

Prologue: Farewells

Page
xv flash of red. *New York Tribune* and
   Washington Post, March 5, 1881.
   "out of a scrape." Seale, I, 511.
xvi red leather armchairs. Samuels,
   Henry Adams, II, 145.
   "that we did." *LMHA*, 273.
xvii "calm and grand." CK to JH,
   Aug. 12, 1988.

Page
xvii "tom-cataract." *LMHA*, 277.
   "more than he bites off." *LM-
   HA*, 306.
xviii Kashmir and Kurdistan. Samuels, op. cit., 143–47.
   "the golden age." *LHA*, II, 349.
   to the world. *LHA*, II, 326.
   "a bore." *LMHA*, 284.

1 A Family Fugitive

Page
4 "never be missed." *EHA*, 70.
   "pole-star of humanity, $!"
   Thayer, I, 54–57.
   assistant secretary in the White
   House. Ibid., 87.
   no sign of force. *EHA*, 107.
5 "victim's sympathies." Ibid., 147.
   of Charles Darwin. Ibid., 127.
   self-serving decisions. Samuels,
   Henry Adams, I, 137–38.
   "collisions." *EHA*, 124.
   "they needed a listener." *EHA*,
   138.
6 put down his pen. Samuels, op.
   cit., 97–120.

Page
6 "a long time." *LHA*, I, 269.
   "a humbug." Ibid., 282.
   "very—very bald." Samuels, op.
   cit., 183.
   "not be tutors." *EHA*, 211.
   "useful to the country." CFA to
   HA, Oct. 22, 1868.
7 "silly young women." CFA to
   HA, Feb. 3, 1869.
   a bold chief executive. HA, "The
   Session, 1869–70," in Hochfield,
   193–224. (Originally appeared in
   North American Review, July 1870.)
   "on public opinion." *LHA*, II, 31.
   "my highest ambition." Ibid., 95.

Page
7 "in Christian lands." Ibid., 5.
"the country began.'" *EHA,*
252–53.
"in archaic time." Ibid., 237.
three best dancers. *LHA,* II, 29.
8 "heads of most people." CFA to
HA, Nov. 25, 1868.
"remove this obstacle." CFA to
HA, May 5, 1869.
"dirty whirl-pool." *LHA,* II, 68.
"will lead me." Ibid., 72.
"influence in America." CFA to
HA, July 11, 1870.
"on the subject." *LHA,* II, 81.
for recitation. Friedrich, 183–84.

Page
9 "Look it up." Laughlin, 579.
"deuce with me." *LHA,* II, 112.
"as much as they do." Ibid., 99.
four hundred at best. Samuels, op.
cit., 218.
mean bankruptcy. *EHA,* 308.
"in Siberia." *LHA,* II, 112.
on horseback. Ibid., 115.
11 a single shot. *CKM,* 345.
"in the sage-brush." *EHA,* 312.
"to practice them." *CKM,*
340–43.
"growth or doubt." *EHA,* 311.
13 "chooses to be loved."
LHA, II, 132.

2 A Charming Blue

Page
14 "the commonplace." *LHA,* II,
141.
Morris wallpaper. MHA to
Eleanor Shattuck, March 5, 1871.
"went off charmingly." MHA to
RWH, June 28, 1872.
"quiet weddings." *LHA,* II, 146.
15 "just like her aunt." Friedrich, 138.
"not her style." *LHA,* II, 132.
16 "read the above." Ibid., 133–34.
"utterly unconnected." Ibid., 137.
"intellectual grace." *HJL,* I, 208.
"termites." Clarke, 5, 48–49, 83,
91, 116–17, 145.
"misery can create." Howe, 11,
134–37.
psychic phenomena. Kaledin, 138.
17 Professor Agassiz himself.
Friedrich, 42–54.
"I love Henry Adams very much."
MHA to Eleanor Shattuck, March
8, 1872.
"as long as it shines thro'." Kaledin, 105–06.
"charming blue," *LHA,* II, 133.
18 "brutalities of marriage." Ibid.,
130.

Page
18 "quiet institution." Ibid., 145.
19 "as happy as I can." Ibid., 141.
"on my side." *LMHA,* 45–46.
"disgusted." *LMHA,* 28–30.
20 "anything new about them."
Ibid., 61–62.
sailed, rowed, poled, or towed.
Edwards, 11–12.
"worthy of Paris." *LMHA,* 62.
"proportionately delighted."
Morris, 66.
failed to turn up. *LMHA,* 60.
"we cannot spell." Allen, 661.
21 "appeals to them." *LMHA,* 75.
"and dumb too." Ibid., 64–66.
"on my hands." *LHA,* II, 156.
22 no dismay. *LMHA,* 67.
returned to Boston. Ibid., 80–
87.
"desolate exile." *HJL,* I, 396.
"ancient brilliancy." Dusinberre,
55–56.
"the 'affections.'" *HJL,* I, 368.
"white marble." *LMHA,* 95.
follow them home. *LHA,* II,
179.
23 "an infernal bore." Nagel, 266.

3 The King of Diamonds

24 majesty of Nature. Wilkins, 17–20.
   because of "illness." Ibid., 28.
25 "aided me." CK to JTG, Jan. 4,
   1860.
   not "Clarence." Ibid.
   "mighty inflaming." Ibid.
   his adoration. CK to JTG, Oct. 2,
   1859.
26 "blood of slaves." CK to JH,
   March 1888.
   "no mental power." CK to JTG,
   March 18, 1862.
   key to El Dorado. *EHA,* 309.
   immediately accepted. Bartlett,
   130–34; Wilkins, 46–56.
   "vastness of prospect." CK, *Mountaineering in the Sierra Nevada,*
   249.
28 "joyous, grateful!" Ibid., 255–56.
   "humble admiration." CK, personal notebook. Hague Papers.
   nothing of Yosemite. Ibid.
   "streaming light." CK to James
   T. Fields, March 9 [1871].
   eleven dependents. CK to HA,
   Sept. 25, 1889.
29 gold-bearing deposits. Crosby,
   95–96.
   first ascents. Ibid., 2.
   statehouse at Sacramento. Wilkins, 94–96.
   "want your place." *CKM,* 385.
   ménage. Wilkins, 96–97.
   to Miss Dean. Wilkins, 112–15.
   "same blessing." CK to William
   H. Brewer, Sept. 15, 1868.
   Florence Howland disapproved.
   Wilkins, 131; Crosby, 146.
31 "every good thing." CK to Mr.
   Davis, April 9, 1880.
   prove him right. Wilkins, 117.
   added pictures to the record.
   Ibid., 161.
33 persuasively made. *CKM,* 337–39.
   playing cards. CK, *Mountaineering,* 310–11.

33 purse strings of the survey. HA,
   North American Review, 114, April
   1872, 445–48.
34 window. Crosby, 16.
   scorpion that died. CK to George
   F. Becker, April 4, 1882.
   attack. Crosby, 14.
35 northwestern Colorado. "Notes
   Dictated by James T. Gardiner to
   His Daughter, Mrs. C. S. Fayerweather." Quoted in Crosby, 19–
   22. Rendered years after the fact,
   Gardiner's account is less detailed
   than one written at the time by
   Samuel Franklin Emmons, a Fortieth Parallel survey member who
   was also instrumental in exposing
   the hoax. See National Archives,
   R.G. 57, Emmons's Field Notes,
   "The Diamond Discovery of
   1872," and Bartlett, 187–205.
   "fossils." Bartlett, 194.
   castanets. Ibid., 195.
   short the stock. Ibid., 198–99.
   beyond question. CK to A. A.
   Humphreys, Nov. 27, 1872.
   train for Oakland. Allen D. Wilson, "The Great California Diamond Mines," *Overland Monthly,*
   April 1904, 296.
36 "impossible occurrence in nature." *Report of Clarence King to the
   Board of Directors of the San Francisco and New York Commercial
   Mining Company,* Nov. 11, 1872.
   on the innocent. Wilkins, 168.
   an hour for prospecting. *Report of
   Clarence King . . .*
   yield of the diamond mine. Henry
   Janin, *A Brief Statement of My Part
   in the Unfortunate Diamond Affair,*
   Huntington Library.
   from Amsterdam. Crosby, 28.
37 indictments. Wilkins, 168–70.
   superiors . . . annoyed. CK to
   A. A. Humphreys, op. cit. King

claimed he could not telegraph the news to Humphreys because "the operators all along the line are on the *qui vive* and *no dispatch is safe in their hands.*"

37 "cost of the survey." "The Diamond Bubble and Its Bursting," *Nation,* 15, Dec. 12, 1872, 380.

4 Death of a Hero

38 "will be large." JH to Charles Hay, Dec. 11, 1872; Wilkins, 171.
Illinois bar. Thayer, I, 83.
Abraham Lincoln's secretary. Dennett, 35.

39 "Iowa?" *LJH,* I, 27–28.
"an absurdity." Ibid., 31.
"the fun." Ibid., 190–91.

39–40 new administration. Thayer, I, 218–19.

40 stopped breathing. Ibid., 219–20.
arrondissements. JH to his brother, Aug. 4, 1865.
"threadbare uniform." JH to Helen Leonard Hay, Jan. 16, 1866.

41 "plundering foreigners." JH, letterbook, Aug. 14, 1866.
"his high office." JH to Charles Hay, Sept. 24, 1866.
"lucrative hoe." JH to Leonard Hay, May 24, 1866.
turpentine business. William Alsop to JH, Aug. 29, 1866.
more than $4,000. JH to "Dear Sir," Sept. 26, 1866.
willingness to try. JH to Milton Hay, Sept. 30, 1866.

42 "stupidish fellow." JH to Helen Hay, Sept. 4, 1867.
"very bad present." JH to John R. Young, Aug. 24, 1867.
"moral principle." JH to Jessie

Louise Bross Lloyd, Dec. 24, 1869.

42 "chronic priapism." JH to John Bigelow, July 21, 1870.
"nonentities." JH to Mrs. John Bigelow, April 4, 1870.
"hate your home." JH to Mrs. John Bigelow, Feb. 27, 1868.
"do a little writing." JH to his parents, March 27, 1870.

43 "virtuous and refined." Stoddard, 61.
"for his paper." Ibid., 93.
"your true field." Whitelaw Reid to JH, Dec. 23, 1870.

44 were restored. Thayer, I, 337–39.
"kicked over." New York *Tribune,* Oct. 17, 1871, 1.

45 "man that died for men." JH, *Complete Poetical Works,* 3–5.
"the matter of me." Ibid., 6–9.
"Bret Harte ever wrote." Jannette Ralston Chase to JH [1871?].
as her brother. Henry King to JH, September 1871.

46 "disgraced by it." *LJH,* II, 5.
"anything of the sort." Ibid., 7.
"no more songs." Ibid.

47 "any yet known." Whitman, 937–40, 961.
drop the subject. Josephson, 100, 141, 172.

48 away from the polls. Dennett, 121.

5 A Daughter of the Middle West

Page

49 "must be mad." Whitelaw Reid to JH, Nov. 21, 1872.

the tender "Little Breeches." Buffalo *Enquirer,* March 6, 1897.

"I worship you." JH to CSH [n.d.].

50 "Christian character." JH to CSH, May 4 [1873].

"for eternity." JH to CSH, May 8, 1873.

53 "her fellow beings." Clara Stone's school compositions are part of the John Hay Papers, Library of Congress.

Mountaineering in the Sierra Nevada. JH to CSH, May 9, 1872.

"large, handsome and good." *LJH,* II, 14.

54 "this proposition?" JH to CSH [n.d.].

"living with me." JH to CSH, Sept. 12, 1873.

restaurant menus. *Cleveland Plain Dealer,* Feb. 6, 1874; *Cleveland Daily Herald,* Feb. 5, 1874.

Mr. and Mrs. Henry Adams of Boston. William Blodgett to JH, Feb. 13, 1874.

anywhere but at home. JH to Flora Stone, Feb. 11, 1874.

unable to sleep. Flora Stone to JH, Feb. 13, 1874.

"her happy life." Flora Stone to JH, Feb. 24, 1874.

railroad bonds. AS to JH, April 7, 1874.

Page

56 "carriage and movement." Twain, *Autobiography,* 232–33.

("strict about Sunday.") Ibid., 233–34.

"immediate wealth." JH to A. A. Adee, Nov. 28, 1874.

57 "good things.'" JH to A. A. Adee, Dec. 14, 1875.

even to Clara. JH to JGN, Nov. 6, 1876.

"away from her." *LJH,* II, 23–24.

58 damages of $600,000. Dow, 62–81; CFA, Jr., *Notes on Railroad Accidents,* 100–11.

the pocketbook. WDH, *Harper's,* May 1877, 919.

"high character" of its officials. WDH, *Harper's,* July 1877, 304.

"every word you write." JH to WDH, Aug. 27, 1877.

59 west of the Alleghenies. Brooks, *Howells,* 22.

a short poem. John Hay Papers.

"write some myself." JH to WDH, Oct. 23, 1877.

fifty thousand words. *LJH,* II, 40.

consult S. Weir Mitchell. S. Weir Mitchell to JH, May 2, 1878.

"indifferent success." *LJH,* II, 38–39.

not bow out entirely. AS to JH, March 27, 1878.

60 "lack of self-knowledge." JH to WDH, Nov. 5, 1879.

6 Infinite Mirth

Page

61 impeccable service. Barton, 120; *Washington Star,* Dec. 27, 1936.

"high-toned Southern Congressmen." A. A. Adee to JH, Nov. 18, 1879.

177,000. *New York Times,* Sept.

Page

10, 1880, 2. The official total was 177,638, of whom 118,236 were white.

61 asphalt. Schlesinger, 88–89.

"till wanted again." Moore, 47.

Page

62 Madison. Warnecke. On file at Columbia Historical Society.
but survived. Goode, 24–25.
Antarctica. Warnecke.
"and go home." JH to Amasa Stone, Dec. 8, 1879.
"gentle and ladylike and poor." JH to CSH, Nov. 22, 1879.
"when evening comes." JH to CSH, March 2, 1880.

63 "the Immortal Bilk." Smith and Gibson, I, 326.
neuralgia. Bret Harte to JH, Feb. 11, 1880.
"would suit him." JH to CSH, April 11, 1880.
"it modifies it." Smith and Gibson, I, 277.
"any office in the world." JH to CSH, Dec. 7, 1879.
"will not get it." JH to CSH, Dec. 18, 1879.
gentlemen's club. Holt, 135.

64 as a candidate. Crosby, 251–57.
"a cold potato." JH to WDH, May 10, 1880.
Western secession. Emmons, 228.
Oriental art. JH to CSH, April 10, 1880.
the 1880 census. Wilkins, 245.

65 "salvation." New York *Tribune*, June 27, 1877, 3.
"the 19th century." CK to JH, Aug. 12, 1888.
debauchés . . . diplomatic corps. *New York Times*, Feb. 14, 1881, 1.
notice of his hostess. JH to CSH, Dec. 18, 1879.

66 "Reap the whirlwind!" *CKM*, 402.
if she wished. Crosby, 124.
afraid of him. JH to CSH, Jan. 18 and April 28, 1880.
"spasmodically forward." JH to CSH, Dec. 6, 1879.
her family's house. JH to CSH, Jan. 31, 1880.
"solid old pile." *LMHA*, 227–29.

Page

66 "powerful large." Ibid., 230.

67 Boojum and Pollywog. Samuels, *Henry Adams*, II, 143–47.
"life offers variety." *LHA*, II, 326.
museums of art did not exist. Frothingham, 841, 845–46.

68 "our own generation." *LHA*, I, 315.
on horseback. *LHA*, II, 349.
trails cut by the Union army. *LMHA*, 301.
" 'inside track.' " Ibid., 197.
"as if we were millionaires." *LHA*, II, 309.

69 "chats for two." MHA to RWH, March 3, 1878.

70 "their social superiors." CK to James D. Hague [1887?].
outlive this prejudice. Levenson, 224–26.
any other voters. Bryce, 342–43.
"vulgarity and shrewdness." CFA, Jr., to HA, June 4, 1880.

71 "more amusing than my crowd." *LHA*, II, 477.
hosted a reception. *LMHA*, 254, 256, 263.
wrong side out. Ibid., 183.
robbed the grave. Friedrich, 242.
"why the D. didn't he?" JH to HA, Oct. 12, 1884.
"this practical age." MHA to RWH, March 30, 1884.

72 "wanted to be." *EHA*, 313.
"than I can boast." *LJH*, II, 56.
"can ask of me." Ibid., 50.
"of his interest." *EHA*, 311.

73 "tips of her fingers." Henry Adams, *Democracy*, 11.

74 "might lead her." Ibid., 13–14.
"aggravate failure." Ibid., 47.
"things that crawl." Ibid., 102.
"the mass pure." Ibid.
"repeat the past." Ibid., 49–50.

75 "the polar star!" Ibid., 205.
"were annihilated." Ibid., 188.
"the best society of the Capital." Samuels, op. cit., 86–87.

76 "to get in." *LMHA*, 286.
"relief dragons?" CK to JH, Dec.
17 [1881?].

77 "community of thought."
EHA, 312.
"taste and dexterity." HA to
CFA, Jr., n.d.

7 Arrivals and Departures

81 and nursed. *LHA*, II, 437.
reopen the mine. Wilkins, 264–82.
82 "life and strength." *LMHA*, 248.
"to the mines." *CKM*, 123–24.
"in the same way." *LHA*, II, 429.
"a week afterward." CK to HA,
Sept. 22, 1881.
"months to gnaw." *LMHA*, 279.
83 "of a book." Ibid., 288.
Ned's five daughters. "Mrs. Ward
Thoron's 'Chronology of HA' and
her evaluation of him." Hooper-
Adams Papers.
"from his work." *LMHA*, 272.
84 news of births. Ibid., 447.
"*All* women want children!"
Friedrich, 214.
"or more encouraging." *LHA*,
II, 246.
"never think about the subject."
Ibid., 316.
"very much together." Ibid.,
326–27.
a specific problem. The gynecological treatise was *Clinical Notes
on Uterine Surgery—with special reference to the management of sterile
conditions* by J. Marion Sims,
M.D. (1873). The book is cited in
Ernest Samuels's biography of
Henry Adams but is no longer
listed among the holdings of the
Henry Adams library at the Massachusetts Historical Society.
their presence. *LHA*, II, 433.
85 "serious work." Whitelaw Reid to
JH, March 18, 1881.
"chances of life." *LHA*, II, 431.
"should Prest. Garfield die." AS
to JH, July 6, 1881.

85 closed early. New York *Tribune*,
Sept. 21, 1884, 7.
"do the thing." CK to HA, Oct.
6, 1881.
Republican Party and . . . Chester
Arthur. Josephson, 95–96.
86 "a dull animal." *LHA*, II, 445.
Twain's next opus. Kaplan, *Mr.
Clemens and Mark Twain*,
240–41.
"before doing so." Whitelaw Reid
to JH, Sept. 25, 1881.
chestnuts. *LMHA*, 292–97.
87 "*raw* material." Ibid., 294.
"our civilization." JH, New York
Tribune, Dec. 25, 1881.
" 'big bow-wow style.' "
LMHA, 306.
"deeply interesting." *LHA*,
II, 448.
88 "happy consequences for you."
HJL, II, 361.
"getting out of it." *LHA*, II, 445.
90 " 'asked Guiteau to tea.' "
LMHA, 307–10.
91 "the Cameron Transfer Company." Tehan, 28; *Dictionary of
American Biography*, II, 435.
contemporary of Lizzie's. Tehan,
10, 20, 28–29, 43, 65, 67.
a fifth of bourbon a day. Ibid., 20,
36, 40–41, 43.
92 "fine house." *LMHA*, 306, 352.
"love and respect." *LHA*, II, 497.
home from Europe. Whitelaw
Reid to JH, Oct. 13, 1881.
"four knives in the air." JH to
MHA, Nov. 14, 1881.
"seem fidgety." CK to HA, Sept.
17, 1888.

92 "For you it has." CK to JH, Dec. 17, 1881[?].

"due respect." JH to MHA, Nov. 5, 1881.

92 a book on poker. CK to MHA, Dec. 31, 1881.

"heavy heart." JH to MHA, Nov. 28, 1881.

8 *"My Facts Are Facts, Too"*

94 "pretty little life." *HJL*, II, 373.

"your complicated Kingdom." Ibid., 366.

"enormous streets." Ibid., 367.

95 "ancient world." Ibid., 370.

"a Valhalla." The remarks about Washington and the Capitol come from James's short story "Pandora." Though made by one of James's characters, the observations mirror the author's sentiments.

"real, live, vulgar" America. *LMHA*, 320.

"hung on my lips." Edel, *Henry James*, III, 30.

"desire to please." *HJL*, II, 373.

"tenth-rate cad." *LMHA*, 338–39.

"thieves and noodles." Ibid., 328.

" 'Oscar on a wild toot.' " Ibid., 338.

96 "impossible to live with?" Ibid., 384.

"forbid they should!" James, *Novels, 1881–1886*, 397–98.

"correspondents' are not." *LMHA*, 301.

97 "after you die." Ibid., 321.

98 "the other way." Ibid., 339–41, 348–49, 351, 368.

his promise. Ibid., 438.

delicacy of execution. Ibid., 385.

99 give some to Clover. CK to MHA, Dec. 31, 1881.

a summer sky. *LMHA*, 430.

aesthetic experiences. Ibid., 435.

flowers . . . in Washington. Ibid., 283.

dogwood petals. Ibid., 282, 430, 441.

99 "Medicus.' " Ibid., 334.

"legs and arms." Ibid., 368.

too strenuous. Ibid., 388.

"I detest." Ibid., 404.

100 "reform pretenses." Ibid., 417, 373.

"spiritual food." Ibid., 419.

"new and fresh." Ibid., 364.

"shape and cohesion." *LHA*, II, 451.

"my concerns." Ibid., 448, 454.

a pudding knife. *LMHA*, 407.

"startling degree." Ibid., 406.

"hint at it." Ibid., 424.

"than they give." Ibid., 407.

101 "jostled you daily." Ibid., 412.

"watched others." Ibid., 415.

"very good clothes." Ibid., 448.

"sounded your heart." Moers, 54.

test his affection. MHA to Anne Palmer, April 6, 1883.

102 "ideas in order." MHA to Anne Palmer, April 21, 1883.

acquaintances. *LMHA*, 438–41.

"a big lonely house." MHA to Anne Palmer, April 21, 1883.

"Rock Creek." *LMHA*, 451.

103 only woman present. MHA to RWH, Dec. 31, 1883.

"take photographs." *LHA*, II, 507.

twenty-five acres. Samuels, *Henry Adams*, III, 576.

"hideous but good photo." MHA's notebook is part of the Hooper-Adams Papers.

104 "in time." *LJH*, II, 86–87.

106 "Gilder's prayer." JH to HA, Jan. 30, 1884.

"grovelling genius." *LHA*, II, 527.

106 "ought to be." MHA to RWH, Nov. 11, 1883.
North American Review. LHA, II, 220. HA's unsigned review appeared in April 1875.

107 found it unreadable. *LHA,* II, 476.
"very skillful." MHA to RWH, Nov. 11, 1883.

9 Vagrant Hearts

108 "Knight of the Grail." *CKM,* 204–05.
109 "all my money." JH to HA, May 25, 1882.
"and the like." *LHA,* II, 458.
of letter writing. Florence Howland to JH, 1882.
financiers of Paris. Wilkins, 283–84.
crumbled church walls. *CKM,* 20–23, 36.
110 "more amiable than ever." JH to HA, Sept. 17, 1882.
"vagrant Heart." JH to HA, July 2, 1882.
Italian daggers. CK to JH, Aug. 24, 1882.
$30,000 trove. JH to Samuel Mather, Sept. 8, 1882. Mather Papers.
111 "abuse me." *HJL,* II, 387.
"fairy-godmother." HJ to JH, Feb. 5, 1883.
come tomorrow. *CKM,* 142–46.
Hartford, Connecticut. JH to HA, Sept. 17, 1882.
112 "active pleasure." *LHA,* II, 474.
"power to do." CK to JH, Aug. 31 and Sept. 3, 1882.
about cashmere. Receipt, March 29, 1883.
"not think about it." JH to S. Weir Mitchell, June 10, 1883.
114 "fear of everything." Gay, *The Bourgeois Experience, Victoria to Freud,* II, 344–45.
capital of capitalism. Whitelaw Reid to JH, Jan. 30, 1883.

114 "come here now." AS to JH, Jan. 30, 1883.
return to their galleries. JH to HA, Oct. 22, 1882.
"of nothing else." JH to HA, Oct. 22, 1882.
115 revealed nothing. Edel, *Henry James,* II, 254–57; Moore, 32.
116 "amiable disdain." JH to HA, Oct. 22, 1882.
left his side. Details about Waddesdon Manor from Morton, 159–60.
King, Hay, and James. Menu card, Au Lyon D'Or, Nov. 9, 1882, John Hay Collection.
"life with him." Smith and Gibson, I, 425.
117 "holding me down." CK to JH, Jan. 26, 1883.
famous in Paris. CK to JH, March 8, 1883.
take the other. Anders Zorn to JH, July 19, 1883; Wilkins, 294.
"whupped for the first time." CK to JH, March 8, 1883.
not fully appreciate. JH to HA, Oct. 22, 1882.
"freely about him." *LHA,* II, 488, 493.
118 "as an archangel." Frank H. Mason to JH, Nov. 10, 1883; see also Mason to JH, Sept. 1, 1883.
Queen Victoria. *CKM,* 369.
pure affectation. Lady Charlotte Clark to JH, Feb. 4, 1884.
119 "every good thing." CK to My dear Davis, April 9, 1880, Hague Papers.

Page

119 "happier star." Gay, op. cit., 395.

120 ("blackguards is.") Hudson, 32.
"nasty." JH to Samuel Mather,
Dec. 3, 1882, Mather Papers.
"toad-eating gaiety." JH to Flora
Stone Mather, Feb. 4, 1883,
Mather Papers.
"can possibly know." JH to HA,
Feb. 13, 1883.
"nobody fit for Congress." JH to
HA, Oct. 22, 1882.
losing their votes. JH to AS, July
24, 25, and 27, and Aug. 17, 1877.
"loathing her lineage." JH, The
Bread-Winners, 28–29, 32.

121 "of sawdust." Ibid., 102.
"influencin' the press." Ibid., 85.
"owe a good deal." Ibid., 211.
"to mass." Ibid., 246–47.

122 "churches by the dozen." JH to
HA, Feb. 13, 1883.
verge of collapse. Dow, 98.
come home early. AS to JH, Feb.
3, Feb. 25, and March 7, 1883.
authorship arose. CFW to CSH,
Jan. 8, 1883.
did not rewrite. Edel, Henry
James, III, 90.

123 "matters of taste." LJH, II,
75–76.
"hate him." HJL, III, 551.
"my real home." HJL, III, 551.
at Delmonico's. JH to HA, March
19, 1883.
said he would. LHA, II, 497.
"leave him." JH to HA, April 23
and May 2, 1883.

124 "usefulness and honor." LJH, II,
84–85.
into his heart. Dow, 99–100.
"the picturesque." Smith and
Gibson, I, 431–32.
"Don and Lizzie Cameron." LHA,
II, 502–03, 504.
"[I]nexpressible." JH to HA, May
27, 1883.
"without hilarity or rum." JH to
WDH, July 27, 1883.

Page

124 not enjoyed for years. JH to
WDH, Sept. 9, 1883.
"thousand brother idiots." JH to
HA, Aug. 23, 1883.
Five of Hearts pins. LHA, II,
504.

125 $3,000 a year. Wilkins, 292.
"first long dream." CK to J. D.
Hague, June 27, 1884.
"all over him." LJH, II, 80.
"One good Turner deserves another." CKM, 130.

126 as disillusioning as Washington.
CK to JH, Aug. 15, 1882.
"on a national novel." CK to JH,
Aug. 24, 1882.
"fair shape." CK to JH, March 8,
1883.
taxing their patience. Wilkins,
296–97.
"the Public is!" JH to HA, Nov.
7, 1883.

127 "must be fatal." HA to JH, Aug.
10, 1883.
"75 percent too much." JH to HA
[n.d.].
"monopolies and corporations."
Atlantic, May 1884.
"my own colleagues." Century,
March 1884, 794–96.

128 "our neighborhood." JH to
WDH, March 26, 1883.
"noice clean floy." JH to CSH,
May 27, 1884.
"out of doors." Kaplan, Mr. Clemens and Mark Twain, 152.
"a fairy scene." JH to CSH, May
27, 1884.
country estate. Sir John Clark to
JH, May 29, 1884.
"tri-millionaires." MHA to Anne
Palmer, Nov. 17 [1884?].
beyond his means. JH to CSH,
May 2, May 31, and June 9, 1884.
often called on her. Edel, Henry
James, III, 298.
"to turn to." CFW to JH, Jan. 27,
1884.

Page

128 collaboration with King. CFW to
JH, Jan. 31, 1884.
"superlative." CFW to JH, May
1884.
"cross as a bear." JH to CSH,
May 31, 1884.

Page

129 "steamer back again." CK to JH,
September 1884.
"new to me." CK to HA, Oct. 6,
1884.

10 In Mid-Ocean

Page

130 "I can find." JH to CSH, May 27,
1884.
131 "introduction." MHA to RWH,
Feb. 3, 1884.
was receiving. Ibid.
"leaving us alone." *LHA,* II, 535.
"new experience." Ibid., 560.
132 *"Come home."* Tehan, 76.
"a native." *LHA,* II, 547.
"any food." MHA to E. A. B.
Shattuck, March 5, 1871.
for fun. *EHA,* 232.
any other creed. Samuels, *Henry
Adams,* II, 246.
133 aim of both. Lawrence, 94.
the old order. Hawthorne, 667–
77.
134 "is lost." Adams, *Esther,* 195,
206.

Page

134 "second-rate amateur." Ibid.,
199–200.
135 "not with Miss Brooke's." Ibid.,
223–24.
"that women can't." Ibid., 244.
"Religion is Love." Ibid., 274.
136 "make me?" Ibid., 284–86.
"candlestick of the church."
Ibid., 277.
"would ever hear." Ibid., 314.
"apart from me." Ibid., 332.
137 "not to do that." Ibid., 333.
"I love him." Ibid., 335.
138 with his mate. HA, "The Primitive Rights of Women," in Hochfield, 333–60.
"in reason, absolute." *LHA,*
II, 515.
"a bladder." Ibid., 235.

11 Seeking Shelter

Page

140 "a sure card." *LHA,* II, 543.
141 "than our own." Ibid., 567; Samuels, *Henry Adams,* II, 224.
"smoky chimneys." MHA to
RWH, Dec. 16, 1883.
"such an object." *LHA,* III,
519.
with George Nicolay. JH to HA,
Sept. 13 and Oct. 2, 1883.
"from your door." JH to HA,
n.d. [1883?].
"maladeimaginairity." JH to HA,
Dec. 7, 1883.
just under $75,000. *LHA,* II, 521.
chunk of his lot. Ibid., 520.

Page

142 slice to King. JH to HA, May 12,
1884.
local land market. Furer, 34.
real-estate holdings. JH to HA,
Jan. 30, 1884.
ruined by his extravagance. *LHA,*
II, 524–25.
"not hurt them." MHA to Anne
Palmer, Nov. 24, 1883.
"Neo-Agnostic." JH to HA,
April 25, 1885.
did not work. MHA to RWH,
April 20, 1884.
"most ultimate." *LHA,* II,
508.

Page
142 driven everywhere. Goode, 91.
"vigorous instructions." *LHA,*
II, 531.
143 "all of a sudden." MHA to ESC,
Jan. 11, 1884.
"pet notions." HHR to HA, Feb.
28, 1884.
144 "hence, architects." JH to HA,
March 13, 1884.
"not do worse." HHR to MHA,
June 6, 1884.
"back windows." HHR to MHA,
July 21, 1884.
145 "one of Cleveland's families." JH
to HA, July 29, 1884.
$35,000 to $50,000. *LHA,* II,
546–47.
"his size." Ibid., 553.
to $80,000. JH to HA, Oct. 28,
1884.
Beverly Farms. *LHA,* II, 546.
"I don't know." Ibid., 557, 569.
"fourfold responsibility." JH to
HA, Dec. 20, 1884.
"speech with us." JH to WDH,
Dec. 27, 1884.
146 staircase windows. *LHA,* II,
573, 578.
"heathendom." JH to HA, Feb.
24, 1885.
mother and child for years. Josephson, 365–67.
"to the widow." Smith and Gibson, II, 501.
campaign gossip. *LHA,* II, 551.
H Street windows. Ibid., 556
note.
147 "enjoy her Grover?" CK to JH,
Nov. 5, 1884.
over the White House. MHA to
RWH, March 5, 1885.
"need so much!" *LHA,* II,
579–80.
148 "Love, love, love!" Ibid., 585.
"satisfaction in life." Ibid., 608.
"on our desk." Ibid., 606.
"much spring." Ibid., 604.
the servants. Ibid., 595.

Page
149 Smithsonian. Ibid., 603–04.
"cheered up amazingly."
Ibid., 584.
"a sensation." Ibid., 579.
minister to Chile. Ibid., 598.
wondrously short. Ibid., 601.
"savoir vivre?" Ibid., 596.
150 "Read and tremble!" JH to HA,
May 2, 1885.
more of her. *LHA,* II, 588–89;
Seale, I, 540–41, 554–59.
"advices from you." *LHA,* II, 581.
"five o'clock." Ibid., 586.
151 "in the open air." Ibid., 607.
"not voted for Blaine." Ibid., 593.
"pass the time." Ibid., 600.
"tired traveller." MHA to JH,
April–May 1885.
152 at Beverly Farms. MHA to Anne
Palmer, April 26, 1885.
"to the Yellowstone." HHR to
HA, June 7, 1885.
their cabin. *LHA,* II, 617–18.
his parents in Quincy. Ibid., 621.
153 "towards us." E. W. Gurney to
E. L. Godkin, Oct. 15, 1885.
"can do nothing." *LHA,* II, 623.
offered no details. Ibid., 626.
his did, too. Ibid., 627.
"didn't like 'em." HHR to HA,
Sept. 27, Sept. 28, Oct. 11, 1885.
less than that. JH to HA, May 22,
1885.
mind went blank. *LHA,* II, 630.
in the stonework. Ibid., 559.
154 favored a lion. Ibid., 620.
"with cement." Ibid., 627.
"food for gossip." Ibid., 629–30.
"with terror." Ibid., 622–23.
155 "I never felt so before." HA, *Esther,* 262–63.
"all of you real!" Kaledin, 224.
and the foyer. *LHA,* 636–38.
"grim silence." Ibid., 636.
156 "house like this." Cleveland
Leader, Nov. 13, 1885.
"more robust." JH to HA, Nov.
19, 1885.

Page
156 of her thought. Cater, li.
"tight shut." *LHA,* II, 634.
157 "I could wish." Ibid., 639.
never forget it. Cater, li.
not feeling well. *LHA,* II, 641–42
note.

Page
157 "hour after hour." Ellen Gurney
to E. L. Godkin, Dec. 9, 1885.
for a doctor. Washington *Post,*
Dec. 7, 1885, 1.
"come near me." *LHA,* II, 640.

12 Hearts That Ache

Page
158 Pennsylvania Avenue. Clover's
death certificate lists the undertaker as "Jos. Gawler of 1724
Penn. Ave."
shared with Henry. Kaledin, 224.
"heart paralysis." Washington
Post, Dec. 7, 1885, 1.
denied entry. Samuels, *Henry Adams,* II, 281.
bare trees of Lafayette Park. Ellen
Gurney to E. L. Godkin, Dec. 9,
1885.
159 "at rest." E. W. Gurney to E. L.
Godkin, Dec. 11, 1885.
"cruelty." Kaledin, 223.
"pointed to." *LMHA,* 181.
came to Washington. Ibid., 442.
found it wanting. Ibid., 428.
accepting them. Earnest, 227–
29.
160 to wait years. "Time seems to be
the only remedy, and I hope that
in the course of the winter she will
return to her normal state." E. W.
Gurney to E. L. Godkin, Oct. 16,
1885. See also Kaledin, 223–25.
"thoughtful as possible." Kaledin, 223.
to the floor. Samuels, op. cit., 281.
wildflowers of spring. Kaledin,
223–24.
161 "harder to bear." *LJH,* II, 98–99.
"those who love you." CK to
HA, Dec. 10, 1885.
potassium cyanide. MHA death
certificate.
"failed to become popular."
Washington *Critic,* Dec. 9, 1885.

Page
162 "better things." Samuels, op.
cit., 274.
"to their house." Ibid., 275–
76.
Beacon Hill friends. *LMHA,* 314.
"run away." *LHA,* II, 643.
"Hell!" Ibid., 640–41.
"same place again." HHR to JH,
Dec. 8, 20, and 31, 1885.
163 able to give. *LHA,* II, 642.
"best and truest." Ibid., 641.
"remind you of her?" Ibid., 645.
"thought of you." Ibid., 644.
"human distress." Ibid.
164 "life is a success." *LHA,* III, 5.
"knottiness of existence." *HJL,*
III, 111.
"salon." Ibid., 107.
"very terrible." CFW to JH, Dec.
26, 1885.
165 Oriental rugs. Cater, lxiii–iv.
of Henry's choosing. Corcoran
Gallery of Art to HA, June 15,
1886.
"full of ghosts." *LHA,* III, 8.
"with the rest." Ibid., 9.
"flavor it has." Ibid., 13.
"it's finished." Saint-Gaudens, I,
356–57; Wilkinson, 235–36.
166 "to paint Japan red." CK to JH,
June 1886.
"out of season!" *LHA,* III, 12.
167 "disagreeable somehow." Recollections of Viola Roseboro. La
Farge Family Papers, Sterling Library.
fastidious standards. JH to CSH,
Jan. 18, 1880.

Page

167 but the Almighty. John La Farge, Jr., 30.

168 "I am right." JL to Margaret Perry, Jan. 1, Jan. 22, and March 13, 1860. La Farge Papers, New York Historical Society.
the ladies' privacy. *New York Times*, June 24, July 16, and Sept. 17, 1885.
"be cut out." Cortissoz, 222.
"fairly fitting." Ibid., 255.
missionaries. *LHA*, III, 13.
"wrote it." CK to JH, June 1886.

169 " 'could not suggest it.' " CK to JH, July 4, 1886.
"in ten years." JH to HA, July 18, 1886.

170 "heart's blood." *LHA*, III, 34.
in a web. JL, *An Artist's Letters from Japan*, 1–8.

171 "delicacy and care." Ibid., 8–14.
"repulsive." *LHA*, III, 17, 27.
"open privies." Ibid., 21.
"to Calvinism." Ibid., 24.
"*ewige* Woman." Ibid., 182.
"you can imagine." Ibid., 17.

172 "kill time." Ibid., 19.
"catch up again." Ibid., 20–21.
mountainsides. Ibid., 21–22.
"of the world." Ibid., 27.

173 in the forest. JL, op. cit., 82, 123, 159–60.

Page

173 passion for perfection. JL, "Hokusai," in *Great Masters*, 219–49.
American homes. JL, *An Artist's Letters*, 74, 112, 127.
paint in New York. Ibid., 101, 152.
"90° and 200°." *LHA*, III, 16.
"steamer with it." Ibid., 29–31.

174 "would have had." ESC to CSH, July 15, 1886. Henry Adams Papers.
"rather upset." *LHA*, III, 34.
"scientific classification." Ibid., 34.
"were metallic." Ibid., 40.
"existence afresh." *LHA*, II, 640.
"oily nastiness." *LHA*, III, 18.

175 in the shade. JL, *An Artist's Letters*, 45, 179.
"waves of prayer." Ibid., 231–32.
of his youth. Adams et al., *John La Farge*, 49–54.
wanted to remember. JL, *An Artist's Letters*, 198–99.
spend $2,000. *LHA*, III, 36.
"our joint genius." Ibid., 32, 38.
"this single day." JL, *An Artist's Letters*, 266.

176 live out the year. *LHA*, III, 42–48.
pressure to sketch. JL, *An Artist's Letters*, 199.
"at home." *LHA*, III, 44.

13 Rebellious Ore

Page

179 "he is there." *LJH*, II, 112–13.
such as W. D. Howells, JH to WDH, Sept. 12, 1886.
"disposition." JH to HA, Aug. 29, 1886.

180 twelve hundred acres. *LHA*, III, 71 note.
writing history together. CK to HA, August 1886; CK to JH, August 1886.
"The Impasse Series." *LHA*, III, 61.

Page

180 anything else. *LHA*, III, 49.
"content him?" Ibid., 40.
would ever deliver. Wilkins, 305–07; Agassiz, 191–92.

180–181 Adams admired. CK to HA, Dec. 23, 1886.

181 as collateral. Wilkins, 308.
"roomy, well padded." JH to HA, Feb. 17, 1885.
"and character." Shi, 166.
turn up. *CKM*, 192.

181 *The Divine Comedy*. Ibid., 193.
183 "second century." [King] "Style and the Monument," 443–53.
"too poetic and ideal." *CKM*, 194–95.
might become. King, *Mountaineering in the Sierra Nevada*, 316.
"stuffed with sawdust." JL to HA, Jan. 17, 1887.
"of a mind." [King] "Style and the Monument," 445, 448.
184 "such as I am." CK to JH, May 30, 1885.
"both sides or none." Bronson, 355–56.
"come to grief." *CKM*, 412–13.
a second half. Ibid., 276.
"about everything." CK to JH, July 4, 1886.
185 "in capital form." CK to JH, Aug. 4, 1887.
"huge diamonds." CK to JH, Aug. 4 and 7, 1887.
"in delicious vein." *LJH*, II, 131.
"than ever before." CK to JH, Aug. 12, 1888.
186 "violence befell him." CK to JH, December 1888.
"fewer mugwumps." CK to JH, July 28, 1887.
"moral law." CK to JH, Sept. 8, 1891.
the white race. Wilkins, 320.
187 "as I ever shall." CK to JH, July 28, 1887.
"blood and warmth." CK to JH, Aug. 4, 1887.
"off anything." Ibid.
Yedras mine. *LHA*, III, 53 note.
delays at Sombrerete. CK to JH, April 27, 1887.
an alias. Crosby, 355.
on her behalf. CK to Samuel Barlow, June 18, 1887.
188 went unrecorded. Plaintiff's Trial Memorandum. *King* v. *Peabody et al.*, File No. 26821–1931. Records

of the New York State Supreme Court, New York County.
189 *le roi*—the king. Ibid.
Erie Railroad. Crosby, 352.
"sculptor's chisel." CK to JH, July 28, 1887.
rare contentment. JL to JH, Oct. 21, 1887.
190 "not want her." CK to JH, July 28, 1887.
"my grovelling mind." CK to HA, July 29, 1887.
to Washington. *LHA*, III, 70; CK to JH, July 28, 1887, and Oct. 2, 1889.
"with whites." Tehan, 56.
bills arrived. *LJH*, II, 131.
"by snowfly." CK to JH, July 28 and Aug. 7, 1887.
191 "over again." *LJH*, II, 147–48.
"them there Kings." Ibid., 134.
first draft by spring. Ibid., 135.
"sprouting up as yet." CK to HA, Sept. 10, 1887.
cancel the trip. HA to JH, Oct. 16, 1887.
"not be made?" JH to HA, Sept. 2, 1888.
four little Hays. *LJH*, II, 146.
192 "to do justice unto." JH to HA, March 27, 1885.
"tell anybody anything." *LJH*, II, 299.
Hot Springs, Arkansas. CK to JH, July [?] 1888.
"must work hard." CK to HA, Oct. 6, 1888.
"story and came." CK to JH, June 5, 1888.
194 "modern fiction?" King, "Artium Magister," 369–84.
"they are dead." CK to HA, Sept. 17, 1888.
195 "may never emerge." CK to JH, Aug. 12, 1888.
"Venus." CK to JH, Nov. 5, 1888.
"ever was in." CK to JH, Nov. 12, 1888.
gray as his own. *LHA*, III, 173.

14 Passions and Tensions

Page

196 treasured John Hay. *LHA*, III, 53.
"will send us." Ibid., 46.

197 slate-blue eyes. Elizabeth Sherman Cameron, passport, March 22, 1898. Miles-Cameron Papers. "were ready." Griscom, 17; Cater, lxxiv–lxxv; *LHA*, III, 62. "most charming women going." Ibid., 228.

198 "$500 a month." Ibid., 219. "revised and corrected." Gwynn, I, 54. "rascality." Ibid., 102. "answered the other." Ibid., 59, 68.

199 by party machines. Gwynn, I, 59. hand-picked by senators. Josephson, 444–46. "a pompous ass." Ibid., 57. "all at once." Ibid., 80. "in handshaking." *LHA*, III, 107. wearing orange. Gwynn, I, 72–73.

200 short supply. Furer, 32–33. "terms you like." *LHA*, III, 56.

201 "anything for him?" Ibid., 72–75, 77. "to be like you." Ibid., 78.

202 "before beginning a journey." Ibid., 76. his breakfast table. Ibid., 79. "climb over it." Ibid., 82–83. "most interested." JL to HA, Nov. 20, 1887. prostrate with grief. *LHA*, III, 93–94. "personal sanctity." Strouse, 258–59.

203 vocal cords. *LHA*, III, 106. "horror and danger." CK to JH, Feb. 13 and March [?] 1888. "just lovely." *LHA*, III, 101. wished to buy. Ibid., 103–05. powerless to control. Ibid., 108. "New Zealand." Ibid., 105.

203 jim-jams vanished. Ibid., 114. panel in his library. Cater, lxxvi. son Del. *LHA*, III, 113.

204 mothers were busy. Ibid., 224. "mischief of some kind." Ibid., 137–38. "I am homesick." Ibid., 135. "sad, sad, sad." Ibid., 114, 121. "to go with her." Ibid., 121. "letters to you." Ibid., 124.

205 exercise the horses. Ibid., 137. "Gibbon never conceived." Ibid., 143. "in the distance." Ibid., 142. the destruction. Ibid., 100 note.

206 "I alone seem to fail!" CK to HA, Sept. 25, 1889[?]. "an August beverage." CK to JH, Aug. 12, 1888. "for the suggestion." Tehan, 104. "I should hate him." ESC to HA, March 9, 1891.

207 "his dear fogs." *LHA*, III, 152. cast a ballot. Ibid., 127–28; Robert Cunliffe to JH, Nov. 11, 1888. surpluses. Josephson, 415–33. "politics and politicians." Gwynn, I, 88–89, 91. Sunday school teacher. Josephson, 436–37. went away a Democrat. Morris, 390. "must vote for him." *LJH*, II, 150. "pure waste." *LHA*, III, 160.

208 in his study. Ibid., 168. "rather clumsy." Ibid., 163; Cater, lv. his House colleagues. Schriftgiesser, 58, 98. biggest one for himself. Morris, 397–98. "the poor wretch." *LHA*, III, 175.

209 move into 1603 H Street. Ibid. "condescension." Ibid., 189.

209 "maunderings." Ibid., 218.
210 "hid the truth." HA, *History of the United States of America during the Administrations of Thomas Jefferson*, 127.
"magnificent scheme." Ibid., 23–24.
211 "century of experience." HA, *History of the United States of America during the Administrations of James Madison*, 1345.
"lasting obligation." Francis Parkman to HA, Nov. 25, 1889.
"pleasure." *LJH*, II, 204–05.
"ashen and disembodied." CK to JH, Oct. 2, 1889.
212 "indeed it was." *LHA*, III, 382.
"scenes and adventures." *LHA*, III, 225.
any doubt on the point. Ibid., 191.
in the excursion. Ibid., 202.

213 "hosts are tired." Ibid., 233, 242, 251.
"16th and H." *LJH*, II, 194.
indexing his history. Ibid., 256.
the summer night. HA says little of these evenings, but JH mentions them in two letters to HA (July 12, 1890, and *LJH*, II, 195). They are also noted in Gwynn, I, 67.
a brief visit. *LHA*, III, 255–56.
"luridly solitary." Ibid., 257.
entire British legation. Gwynn, I, 106.
house at Beverly Farms. *LHA*, III, 240.
214 "worse than the regret." *LHA*, III, 259.
"Most beautiful flinging itself away." Ibid., 263–64.

15 *An American Gentleman*

215 as a boy's. JH's appearance is described in an undated London *Star* item sent by him to HA in the summer of 1889. Adams Papers, Reel 600.
Balzac. *LHA*, III, 223.
"Isles of the Sea." *LJH*, II, 197.
"nor will I." Ibid., 202.
oversee the construction. JH to HA, July 30, 1890.
216 clear, sweet voice. Thayer, II, 64.
"rather agreeable." *LJH*, II, 197.
as bracelets. ESC to CSH, Aug. 13, 1893[?].
who would listen. JH to Leonard Hay, Sept. 21, 1889.
"Yabbit Pox." *LJH*, II, 153.
a dunce. JH to HA, Sept. 21, 1889, and Jan. 10, 1891; JH to Leonard Hay, June 25, 1889.
at the line. *LJH*, II, 196.
"of Cordelias." JH to HA, Sept. 23, 1891.

216 "pinfeather boys." JH to HA, Jan. 10, 1891.
217 "the last house." ESC to HA, Oct. 8, 1890.
but never did. W. J. Miller, 420; April 1945 interview with Mrs. Ward Thoron, H. D. Cater Collection.
naval affairs. Schriftgiesser, 27–30, 47, 111.
"Pinky." W. J. Miller, 420.
218 "extremely well." ESC to HA, Oct. 2, 1890.
new boarding school. ESC to HA, Dec. 2, 1890.
219 the following week. ESC to HA, Oct. 29, 1890.
"run Congress." *LHA*, III, 210.
"during the night." *LJH*, II, 206.
"I understand that." ESC to HA, Jan. 10, 1891.
"I cannot endure it forever." ESC to HA, Jan. 27, 1891.

Page

220 "trying to be happy." JH to ESC, n.d. Henry Adams Papers. The box of letters from JH to ESC contains many notes concerning arrangements for luncheons, evenings at the theater, and other outings with Mrs. Lodge.
"fatiguing for me." ESC to HA, Jan. 27, 1891.
"strong indeed here." Gwynn, I, 113–14.

221 "other countries." Schriftgiesser, 115–16.
'desirable condition." Ibid., 104–09; Groves, 23–24.
"pretty amusing." ESC to HA, Dec. 14, 1890.
tense and drained. ESC to HA, Jan. 27, 1891.
"really superb." ESC to HA, Dec. 2, 1890.
as the Roosevelts. In an undated invitation to JH, TR said he and his wife would like Mrs. Hay to come "but we don't know if we ought to ask her, for we understand that she does not go out on Sunday evening . . ."
potatoes and bread. ESC to HA, Sept. 8, 1892.

222 "Hotel Brunswick." JH to Leonard Hay, Sept. 30, 1887.
somewhere else. JH to HA, July 12, 1890.
castle in Scotland. JH to JGN, Aug. 4, 1887.
"for Mrs. Hay." LJH, II, 132.
baffling medical symptoms. Ibid., 152; JH to HA, July 30, 1888.

223 "it was n.g." LJH, II, 166.
"other nationality." London Star. Adams Papers, Reel 600.
"nihilist." CSR to ESC, June 11, 1889. Adams Papers, Reel 600.
"passing show." LJH, II, 171.
"and the trunk." Ibid., 173.

Page

224 "worked in." HJL, III, 135.
"dine with her." HJ to JH, Ibid., 153.
almost nothing about James. CFW to JH, Feb. 23, 1887.
"its beauty." HJ, Literary Criticism: Essays on Literature, American Writers, English Writers, 640–41.
"new schemes of work." JH to Sir John Clark, Aug. 7, 1887.

225 "money-making." LJH, II, 148.
"river of life." CK, "The Biographers of Lincoln," 861–69.
"no adequate expression." WDH, Harper's, February 1891, 478–83.

226 "musty and dry." LJH, II, 185.
"out of my thoughts." Ibid., 215.
"literary execution." Ford, II, 8.
"not written history." Ibid., 8–9 note.
"ornament or fancy." LJH, II, 103; JH to JGN, April 15, 1887.
"I sincerely believe." LJH, II, 189.

226–227 "without any fuss." JH to HA, Oct. 24, 1891.

227 William Seward. LHA, II, 249.
"for all day." JH to Leonard Hay, May 11, 1889.
the Jesuits. LJH, II, 154.
"his campaigns." JH to JGN, July 25, 1891[?].
ministry in Paris. LHA, III, 168 note.
"sorry for him." ESC to HA, April 9, 1891.
"he of Nannie!" ESC to HA, May 7, 1891.

228 English magazines. ESC to HA, May 21, 1891; O'Connor, 245–46; Stewart, 289–99.
"take you in." ESC to HA, May 21, 1891.
choice of words. Ibid.

229 "together again." Dennett, 155.
not to go to China. LJH, II, 228.

230 "much longer." Ibid., 231–32.

16 Tame Cat

231 sandalwood. JL, *Reminiscences of the South Seas,* 14.

"final dissolution." *LHA,* III, 282.

kimonos. JL, op. cit., 61.

humans in distress. *LHA,* III, 270.

guava. JL, op. cit., 20.

mango. *LHA,* III, 270.

acacia. JL, op. cit., 6, 15.

232 "to fix them." *LHA,* III, 414.

trousers and slippers. Ibid., 276.

embroidery. Ibid., 270.

"yearn towards them." Ibid., 282.

"I shall not struggle." Ibid., 285.

233 "your going away." ESC to HA, Oct. 29, 1890.

"your limitation." ESC to HA, Sept. 2, 1890.

his history. *LHA,* III, 409.

to his neck. Ibid., 289.

leave it undrunk. Ibid., 290; JL, op. cit., 114, 171.

234 evil spirits. Stevenson, 180.

well-lighted huts. *LHA,* III, 291–92.

"the devil." Ibid., 294.

"childish." JL, op. cit., 200.

235 "decency." *LHA,* III, 343–44.

"stupid." JL, op. cit., 84, 189.

236 bananas. *LHA,* III, 305–06.

edge of the village. JL, op. cit., 110.

teaball. JL, op. cit., 91.

sketch pad. JL, op. cit., 74, 274.

floating away. JL, op. cit., 181, 191–92.

for royalty. *LHA,* III, 303.

"same style from me." Ibid., 358.

as large as his own. *LHA,* III, 317.

237 with the men. Ibid., 345–46.

"a baby." Ibid., 293.

"he returns." JL, op. cit., 243.

"secret." *LHA,* III, 331.

"mist and *soufflé.*" Ibid., 394.

"very brief passions." Ibid., 346.

238 to rebel against. JL, op. cit., 94.

238 *"Après nous les artistes."* JL to Russell Sturgis, July 30, 1900.

"you have received." JH to HA, Dec. 30, 1890.

"become art." CK to JH, December 1890.

"so very dry a light." CK to JH, 1891.

239 "discerned her." CK to JH, 1891.

barks of the birds. Stevenson, 181.

240 pilgrims would come. *LHA,* III, 331–33; JL, *Reminiscences,* 207–12.

241 "I can stand ten." *LHA,* III, 340, 358.

"to trivialities. . . ." ESC to HA, Jan. 27, 1891.

242 where she sat. ESC to HA, March 9, 1891.

darkroom on H Street. ESC to HA, April 9, 1891.

"truth it has." *LHA,* III, 298.

"as their chemicals." Ibid., 304.

"Please say yes." Ibid., 382.

243 "greatest chief of Samoa." Ibid., 342.

"for ourselves." JL, *Reminiscences,* 143, 153, 227–28, 293.

cigarette in hand. Dryfhout, 173–74.

244 "shirt and drawers." *LHA,* III, 296.

"in the interest of science." JH to HA, Dec. 30, 1890.

"talking incessantly." *LHA,* III, 303.

shoes and stockings. Recollections of Viola Roseboro, La Farge Family Papers, Sterling Library.

"all he has seen." *LHA,* III, 297.

"of the flesh." JL, *New York Times,* Dec. 30, 1894.

245 "fricasseed?" Colvin, II, 255.

Fortnum and Mason. *HJL,* III, 337.

earning a living. JL, *New York Times,* Dec. 30, 1894.

Page
245 "abuse him." *LHA*, III, 442.
246 Rue de la Cathédrale. JL, *Reminiscences*, 301–02.
"decay." *LHA*, III, 404–05.
"give him a chance." Ibid., 406.
more prose than poetry. Ibid., 393.
hymns more polished. Ibid., 424.
247 "They are a fraud." Ibid., 425.
"fifteen or twenty years." Ibid., 460.
"whitey-brown." Ibid., 417.
"drink—drink—drink." Ibid., 406.
"frantic to escape." Ibid., 445.
H. H. Richardson. Ibid., 418.
prized Henry James. Recollections of Viola Roseboro, La Farge Family Papers, Sterling Library.
248 considerable power. *LHA*, III, 420.
"mix rather well." Ibid., 453.
as Clara Hay. Ibid., 409.
sat on the floor. Ibid., 420.
(Prince of the Deep). JL, *Reminiscences*, 320.
"his second son." *LHA*, III, 452.
"more Teva than the Tevas." JL, *Reminiscences*, 351.
"a thousand years back." *LHA*, III, 478.
"a very brief affair." Ibid., 479.
"the standard." Ibid., 494.

Page
249 "nice impulses." Ibid., 466.
"strong and calm." ESC to HA, March 9, 1891.
"dignity and simplicity." JH to HA, March 25, 1891.
"her own soul." CK to JH, May 1891.
"knock his head off." ASG to HA, April 6, 1891.
250 "trial and suffering." CFA, Jr., to HA, May 3, 1891.
"criticism from me." *LHA*, III, 496.
"true God." Ibid., 480–81.
meet her in Paris? ESC to HA, May 21, 1891.
for $2,500. *LHA*, III, 484.
"to see—you." Ibid., 482.
251 "days are over." JL, *Reminiscences*, 478.
"in October." *LHA*, III, 515.
252 "tormenting." Ibid., 549.
"say the reason." ESC to HA, Sept. 26, 1891.
the French countryside. JL to HA, Nov. 10 and 11, 1891.
253 "I was furious!" ESC to HA, November 1891.
"interrupted and unsatisfactory." *LHA*, III, 560.
254 "the more I love." Ibid., 556–58.
"back to you." Ibid., 560–61.

17 House of Madness

Page
255 "used to talk." ESC to HA, Dec. 6, 1891.
for $2,000. JL to My dear Friend, February 1892.
256 "ways of children." CK to JH, January 1892.
" 'never dreamed of.' " CK to JH, November 1892.
257 "ecstatic madness." Gauguin, 1, 9, 66, 132.
"Even their own attention." JL to HA, Nov. 8, 1906.

Page
257 Kansas City. Wilkins, 332–33.
"a year in drawing." *LJH*, II, 203.
258 "my command." Klein, 601–02.
"that's something." *LJH*, II, 187.
more than $100,000. There were two mortgages dated May 14, 1890, one for $43,000 covering three previous notes, and one for $76,000 against the bank stock. *King* v. *Peabody et al.*
"will not go." JH to HA, Dec. 30, 1890.

259 "joyful hope." Florence King Howland to CSH, July 6, 1890.

291 Hudson Street. Birth certificate No. 920, 1891 (Brooklyn), Municipal Archives, New York City.

"the world." Wilkins, 337–38.

260 "act soon." CK to JH, January 1892.

261 "gift of science." CK, "The Education of the Future," 20–33.

probably occurred in 1891. The Municipal Archives in New York City has birth certificates for three of the five children born to James and Ada Todd. The first is for their second child, Grace, born Jan. 24, 1891. The next—No. 998, 1892 (Brooklyn)—for a birth on Jan. 31, 1892, also claims to be for a second child, which suggests that one of their children died sometime between the 1891 and 1892 births.

"in the breach." CK, "The Education of the Future," 20–33.

262 earth's crust. For an understanding of King's hypothesis, I am indebted to the discussion in Wilkins, 326–32.

one more triumph. *LJH,* II, 213.

"curiosities of investigation." CK to JH, January 1892.

263 "stand the racket." *LJH,* II, 234.

"to my back." CK to JH, Sept. 16, 1892.

"discovered us." CK to HA, Aug. 31, 1892.

"only enemies." *EHA,* 320.

264 "cholera germ?" CK to HA, Aug. 31, 1892.

purview of a mere Civil Service commissioner. Morris, 434–37, 452–55.

"fifteenth century!" Wilkinson, 242.

265 spread out below. Smith, 491–

505; Wilkinson, 253–60; Roth, 174–78.

"vile displays." *LHA,* II, 292.

than Paris. *EHA,* 339.

"appreciation of the old." Samuels, *Henry Adams,* III, 113.

the Treasury. Spence, 234–35.

266 home at once. CFA to HA, July 7, 1893.

"and go on." HA to ESC, Aug. 8, 1893.

debtors paid him. *LJH,* II, 261.

"of the Midway." HA to ESC, Oct. 8, 1893.

267 four million. Spence, 235.

"blizzard." HA to JH, Oct. 18, 1893.

"gone under." HA to JH, Oct. 18, 1893.

the point academic. Wilkins, 338–39; Crosby, 359.

another child in July 1893. Birth certificate No. 8698, 1893 (Brooklyn), Municipal Archives, New York City.

could not sleep. R. P. Lincoln, King's physician, New York *Tribune,* Nov. 4, 1893, 7.

got there. JL to HA, Nov. 7, 1893.

disorderly conduct. New York *Tribune,* Oct. 31, 1893, 4; New York *Sun,* Nov. 3, 1893, 1.

268 "health and vigor." R. P. Lincoln, op. cit.

"care to ask." HA to JH, Nov. 5, 1893.

"little while." JL to HA, op. cit.

"intimate with him." JL to HA, op. cit.

269 prescribed by his physicians. JH to HA, Jan. 1, 1894.

"sanity in his madness." Edel, *Henry James,* IV, 238.

corrections and additions. *LHA* IV, pp. 156–57.

beautiful young women. Crosby, 370–71.

Page

269 daily to Bloomingdale. James Gardiner to George Howland, Nov. 9, 1893; J. D. Hague to E. B. Bronson, Dec. 4, 1893, Hague Papers.

270 "gay enough." CK to HA, Dec. 31, 1893.

"longing for." CK to HA, Jan. 1, 1894.

"obstinate silence." JH to HA, Jan. 1 and 24, 1894.

"alter relations." HA to JH, Jan. 16, 1894.

271 *suicidio.* Edward T. James (ed.), *Notable American Women,* III, 670–72.

A Christmas Carol. CFW to Clare Benedict, Dec. 13, 1893, with additions made Dec. 25, Mather Papers.

"joy at release." Ibid.

her grave. *HJL,* III, 459–60.

272 "latent brain-disease." Ibid., 462.

"suicidal mania." Ibid., 463.

"was diseased." Ibid., 464.

"was attached." Ibid., 470.

Roman sunshine. JH to Samuel Mather, Jan. 31, 1894, Mather Papers.

Page

273 "Perhaps he is." HA to JH, Feb. 3, 1894.

"doubt Weir Mitchell?" CK to JH, Feb. 3, 1894.

"thin air." HA to JH, Feb. 27, 1894.

274 "ought to be." HA to JH, Feb. 27, 1894.

"baked in joy and sweat." CK to HA, March 29, 1895.

"Democracy." HA to JH, Feb. 27, 1894.

"among the stones." HA to ESC, March 1 and 16, 1894.

everything he ate. HA to ESC, Feb. 16 and 23, March 8, 1894.

Negro-Cuban variation, *CKM,* 173.

275 "the coming war." CK, "Fire and Sword in Cuba," 32.

"brigand or both." *CKM,* 175.

blood and gore. Ibid., 178.

"doesn't affect him." HA to JH, April 11, 1894.

276 " 'be free!' " CK to JH, May 16, 1894.

"I harbor hopes." CK to HA, May 11, 1894.

18 *A Splendid Little War*

Page

279 the household. *New York Daily Mirror,* Nov. 21, 1933, 3.

280 silver mines. CK to JH, Aug. 30 and Sept. 29, 1894.

"with, or without, reason." *LJH,* II, 336.

"send over the money." Ferdinand de Rothschild to JH, Feb. 12, 1895.

one dependent. JH to HA, Sept. 3, 1895; George Howland to JH, Dec. 25, 1895.

281 "all at once." JH to HA, Nov. 17, 1895.

"mine Cervantes." CK to HA, Nov. 28, 1895; 1896.

Page

281 *Don Quixote.* CK to JH, Nov. 14, 1895.

age of the earth. *LJH,* II, 355.

fabrications. O'Toole, 77–78.

four hundred thousand lives. Ibid., 58 note.

282 "heart of Cuba." CK, "Shall Cuba Be Free?" 57.

"invincible knight." CK, "Fire and Sword in Cuba," 36–37.

"let the Cubans pass." Ibid.

"a garden party." CK, "Shall Cuba Be Free?" 64–65.

283 sovereign nation. O'Toole, 63.

"justice will be poetic." Ibid., 64.

Page

283 Spaniards in battle. W. H. Phillips
to JH, Sept. 20, 1896.
the fray. *CKM,* 181.
"the only real issue." *LHA,*
IV, 362.
"their greed." Ibid., 368–69.
284 Adams's theme. Samuels, *Henry
Adams,* III, 163–64; O'Toole,
64.
285 "concessions granted." ESC to
HA, June 15, 1896. The Miles-
Cameron Papers contain several
letters to ESC from Gonzalo de
Quesada, one of the Cubans' chief
propagandists in Washington.
The letters thank her profusely for
her suggestions (undoubtedly the
suggestions of Henry Adams),
and one letter (undated) contains a
thinly disguised request to see
Senator Cameron: "Would you be
so kind as to let me know when it
will be convenient for you to see
me and give poor Cuba some of
your valuable advice."
286 not . . . intervene in Cuba. Samuels, op. cit., 171–73.
"cross of gold." Josephson, *The
Politicos,* 678.
"the other rats." Smith, 489.
"rests upon them." Josephson,
op. cit., 676.
"has ever had." Samuels, op.
cit., 171.
would elect William McKinley.
LHA, IV, 369.
287 "at the mouth." Boller, 174.
by his staff. Josephson, op. cit.,
695–96.
$1,000 a month for the campaign.
Hay's contributions are discussed
in Mark Hanna to JH, Oct. 12,
1895; Jan. 11, March 2, and March
5, 1896; and JH to WM, Aug. 3,
1896.
agree to help. *LJH,* III, 77–79.
"is tremendous." JH to Whitelaw
Reid, Nov. 10, 1896.

Page

288 perhaps London. *LHA,* IV, 439.
"decides these things." JH to
Whitelaw Reid, Feb. 14, 1897.
precluded an appointment. JH,
Feb. 19, 1897. There are two letters, Hay's and a copy of McKinley's amended version in Hay's
hand.
"useful purpose." JH to WM, n.d.
stag dinner. Leech, 116.
the first president. Ibid., 109.
289 "and lost." *LHA,* IV, 464.
"effectually drowned." Ibid.
over his head. JH to HCL, May 6,
1987.
"things to you?" *LJH,* III, 84.
"no use for me." *LHA,* IV,
471.
290 Turner. Morris, 465–67.
around the globe. Ibid. 424.
"aggression." Leech, 118.
"reticent." W. H. Phillips to HA,
May 4, 1897.
"honor and renown." Morris,
569–71.
"wigging." Leech, 158.
job well done. Morris, 571.
292 to grant. JH to CSH, September
1897.
"out of it!" JH to HA, May 28,
1897.
Bournemouth. Edel, *Henry James,*
IV, 456–57.
top hat . . . brougham. Receipts.
John Hay Library.
satin gowns. English newspaper
clipping, n.d. Scrapbook no. 40,
John Hay Papers, Library of Congress.
"should talk to." Nevins, *Henry
White,* 127.
"rap on wood and stop." JH to
HA, July 17, 1897.
293 wedded to gold. Nevins, op. cit.,
123, 127; Leech, 143–44.
"talk so much." JH to CK, Dec.
13, 1897.
"must go." *LJH,* III, 103.

Page

293 "it is so." HA to JH, Nov. 21, 1897.

stay home and work. HJ to JH, Nov. 26, 1897.

no assignment. CK to JH, December 1897.

"begging him." *LJH*, III, 106.

Saint-Gaudens. *LHA*, IV, 498.

294 "my dinner?" Ibid., 505.

"to my mind." Ibid., 530.

"creases out." Ibid., 538–39.

"Spaniards did it." JH to HA, May 9, 1898.

the same opinion. Morris, 600.

295 "look ahead." *LHA*, IV, 556–57.

"bent on peace." O'Toole, 146.

"chocolate eclair." Morris, 610.

" 'finish up the work.' " JH to WM, March 26 and 29, 1898.

296 "some great thing." O'Toole, 195.

"chance of his life." JH to HA, May 9, 1898.

decrepitude of Spain. *LHA*, IV, 576; Morgan, 66.

"husband and father." Recollections of Viola Roseboro, La Farge Family Papers, Sterling Library.

297 change course. Morris, 602–03.

298 "American character." JH to TR, July 17, 1898.

"coaling station." *LHA*, IV, 594.

"escapes lynching." *LJH*, III, 126.

"out of theirs." JH to HCL, July 27, 1898.

as compensation. JH to William R. Day, June 4, 1898.

Page

299 "responsible for them." JH to WM, Aug. 2, 1898.

"has ever been." JH to William R. Day, July 19, 1898.

for generations. *EHA*, 363.

"without counting me." *LHA*, IV, 581, 604.

"Versailles." *LHA*, IV, 604.

watermelon. Tehan, 150–51.

300 unmentionable in the Adams family. JH to CSH, March 27, 1898.

"than nature intended." Edel, op. cit., 234–35.

301 "clumsiness of rage." Ibid., 231.

"early adolescence." Beisner, 43.

"danger to avoid." HJ, *Literary Criticism: Essays on Literature, American Writers, English Writers,* 663–65.

"chaplain." *LJH*, III, 133.

SEPTEMBER. Thayer, II, 173.

302 of his health. JH to WM, Aug. 15, 1898.

president's request. *EHA*, 365.

one he did not. JH to Samuel Mather, Sept. 24, 1898.

"without reference to me." JH to WM, Aug. 15, 1898.

"so great an honor." JH to WM, Aug. 15, 1898.

303 "satisfy anybody." *LHA*, IV, 610–11.

"—or with me." Ibid., IV, 616.

"your coat-tails." HJ to JH, April 30, 1900.

19 A Taste of Empire

Page

304 "without you." JH to CSH, Sept. 30, 1898.

305 "so absolutely alone." JH to CSH, Oct. 8, 12, 15, 1898.

"in charge of." *LJH*, III, 150.

306 "while I am President!" Leech, 345; Ziff, 221.

"humorous." Neider, 293.

Page

306 chaos of the Philippines. AC, "Distant Possessions—The Parting of the Ways," 239–48.

inalienable right. Beisner, 165.

307 "near future." *Globe Democrat,* n.d. Carnegie was pleased enough with the report to preserve it in his papers (vol. 56).

Page

307 *"thinks best."* AC to JH, Nov. 24, 1898.
"at Homestead." Thayer, II, 199.
to dinner. JH to AC, Dec. 31, 1898; AC Papers (vol. 59).
"staunch Republican." AC to JH, Dec. 27, 1898.

308 "your brains." AC to Carl Schurz, Dec. 17, 1898.
"aunties." JH, Diary, June 27, 1904.
"establish them in the Philippines." Morgan, 112.
"even lyric." *LHA*, IV, 657–58.

309 "to think." Ibid., 678–79.
"his nature." Ibid., 621.
"buffer-state?" Ibid., 630, 635.
pressed for it. Ibid., 626.
"silver platter." Samuels, *Henry Adams,* III, 193.
"for freedom." *LHA*, IV, 695.

310 "of the rest." Ibid., 666–67.
(likely to buy.) Beisner, 102.
"spoliation." Thayer, II, 241.

311 "definitive." Leech, 515–17.
since 1881. McCullough, 131.

312 satisfying news to Hay. Thayer, II, 214–15.
"secret alliances." *LJH*, III, 169–70.
"under Abraham Lincoln." Leech, 512.

313 "one-third of the Senate." *LJH*, III, 136–37.
order in the Canal Zone. McCullough, 256–58.

314 "necks to get." *LHA*, V, 84.
Eleven o'clock precisely. Leech, 504–05.
"first to flop." Nevins, 150–52.
"their own power." Thayer, II, 260.
"by the Constitution?" JH to [TR], Feb. 12, 1900.

315 Puerto Rico and Hawaii. McCullough, 256.
"larger than ours." Thayer, II, 339–40.

Page

315 Irish constituents. Nevins, 150–52.
presidential nomination. JH to CSH, Oct. 15, 1898; Ford, II, 275.
"cowardice." *LJH*, III, 176.
philippics against Hay. *LHA*, V, 94–95.
"Won't it be fun?" Ibid., 92.
"will feel it." HA to ESC, March 5, 1900.

316 "the Cabinet." Thayer, II, 226–27.
"storm may rage." Ibid., 227–28.
"failure of his Canal Treaty." *LHA*, V, 113.

317 sympathized with the uprising. Dennett, 297; Leech, 517–18.

318 "your shoulders." *LHA*, V, 128.
"no alliances." JH to Edwin Conger, June 10, 1900.
cry for help. Edwin Conger to JH, July 20, 1900.
Hay's ingenuity. Thayer, II, 237; Leech, 521–22.

319 "chum of the Kaiser." JH to HA, Nov. 21, 1900.
"querulous old age." *LJH*, III, 186–87.
"sorry for it afterwards." JH to HA, Aug. 22, 1900.
not seen Nannie for months. In JH to ESC, March 17, 1901, Hay says he has seen Mrs. Lodge only once, by accident, in the last year.
"was a boy." *LJH*, III, 184–85.
"dust and ashes." Ibid., 190–91.
a cabinet wife. *LHA*, V, 110.
"little Hell upon earth." JH to HA, Aug. 5, 1899.
"rope of sand . . ." *LJH*, III, 205.
"fat and stupid prosperity." Ibid., 171.
"amour-propre." JH to HA, June 15, 1900.

320 "or something!" Leech, 537.
candidate of the convention. Morris, 726.

Page
320 "next March." Boller, 180.
"fearful misery." Ibid.
"Constitution of the United
States." Leech, 549.

Page
320 not an option. Boller, 180–81.
"law at home." Beisner, 183.
"this generation." Thayer, II, 258.

20 The Road to Paradise

Page
322 "your tongue." *LHA*, V, 167.
"poor old eyes." Ibid., 98.
323 "before it gets through." Ibid.,
148, 169.
"inward refinement." *LHA*, IV,
311–12.
"gross, shapeless, bare-armed."
Ibid., 312.
"liberal—genial." *EHA*, 354.
"glass Gods." *LHA*, IV, 312.
324 "It is human." Ibid., 321–22.
"my own child." Ibid., 319.
"require too much." Ibid., 326.
"beauty and purity." Ibid., 330–
31.
"entitled to claim." Ibid., 327.
"dollars and cents." Ibid., 412–
13.
325 "stable-companion to statesmen."
EHA, 317.
give Don an embassy. Henry
White to JH, Feb. 16, 1897.
"distinct valvular weakness."
ESC to HA, May 14, 1897.
liner in New York. W. H. Phillips to JH, May 4, 1897.
326 "very dearest." ESC to HA, May
7, 1897.
"repair itself." HA to AL, June 3,
1897.
327 "hurt you." *LHA*, IV, 304.
neighboring forest. H. D. Cater
Collection; Ford, II, 130.
cheer them up. CSR to JH, Oct.
6, 1897.
"aggravated." HA to JH, Aug. 6
and Sept. 12, 1897.
a puppy. Tehan, 145–46.
"anything else." ESC to HA,
Dec. 31, 1897.

Page
327 John La Farge. ESC to HA, Dec.
13 and 21, 1897.
"whom I have seen." ESC to HA,
Dec. 31, 1897.
328 "originality or amusement." ESC
to HA, Feb. 22, 1898.
time apart. Ibid.
abnormal. ESC to HA, Feb. 15
and 22, 1898.
"refused to listen." Tehan, 149.
"what will it bring?" ESC to HA,
Feb. 22 and March 7, 1898.
"think it right." ESC to HA,
April 21, 1898.
329 her classes. ESC to HA, Nov. 22,
1898.
"harness goes on again." ESC to
HA, Jan. 4, 1899.
"I do!" ESC to HA, March 9,
1899.
"this summer!" ESC to HA, May
16, 1899.
"before us." ESC to HA, July 25,
1899.
"Have I forgotten?" ESC to HA,
Aug. 12, 1899.
330 new typewriter. ESC to HA, July
19, 1899.
estranged wife. ESC to HA, Sept.
24, 1899.
sorry for him. ESC to HA, Aug.
20, 1899.
"not be proper." ESC to HA,
Sept. 3, 1899.
"success or happiness." ESC to
HA, Aug. 7, 1899.
"What *am* I to do?" ESC to HA,
Oct. 3, 1899.
"I cannot write!" ESC to HA,
Oct. 24 and Nov. 1, 1899.

Page
331   "Avunculitis." *LHA*, IV, 653.
"only to keep going." Ibid., 701.
August heat. *LHA*, V, 23.
"peace of God." Ibid., 14.
"walk in the Bois." Ibid., 9.
books on medieval architecture. Ibid., 51.
"the depressed?" *LHA*, IV, 735–36.
332   "emotional as music." *LHA*, V, 53–54.
friends in the country. Ibid., 11.
333   "annoying." *MSMC*, 169.
"let the rest go." Ibid., 174.
"nearest to God." Ibid., 1.
"idealized in the woman." Ibid., 38–39.
fear and death. Ibid., 95.
334   "always more light." Ibid., 105.
"barons." Ibid., 176–77.
"harmony or value." Ibid., 152.
"boudoir." Ibid., 133.
("as he could.") Ibid., 191–92.
position of honor. Ibid., 98.
"Christ the Symbol." Ibid., 102.
335   "prison-house." Ibid., 307.
"whole human race." Ibid., 290.
"a dull animal." Ibid., 214, 224.
"superfluity of her world." Ibid., 215.
("they do the rest.") JH to HA, Dec. 30, 1890.

Page
335   "grunting hog." *LHA*, V, 45.
"even of boors." *MSMC*, 271.
"greatest deity of all." Ibid., 215.
"before the woman." Ibid., 271–72.
"better yet, a Goddess." *LHA*, III, 561.
"infancy and senility." *LHA*, V, 331.
"passion was pity." *MSMC*, 158–59.
"even contradiction." Ibid., 419–20.
337   "last secret." Ibid., 420–22.
"thought and act." Ibid., 385.
"Hamlet." *LHA*, V, 35.
"of my youth." Ibid., 139.
338   "hitches." Ibid., 160.
did not understand. HA to Martha Cameron, October 10, 1900.
the Sorbonne. Tehan, 158.
"Euthanasia." *LHA*, IV, 494.
"excursions together." ESC to HA, Feb. 8, 1900.
and his mother. ESC to HA, Oct. 24 and 28, 1900.
"quite pathetic." Tehan, 169.
"cheek of innocence." Ibid.
339   "twelfth-century church." *LHA*, V, 179.

21 A Queer Taste in Fates

Page
340   "dealt with him fairly." Tehan, 170.
341   busier than ever. *LHA*, V, 189–90.
"Aieeee." Morris, 22.
"makes one tired." *LHA*, V, 202.
"I'll kill you." Ibid., 214.
"duckfits." Ibid., 197, 230–31.
342   "his resignation." Ibid., 201, 206.
"religious retreat." Ibid., 215.
St. Thomas. Ibid., 212.
"breath out." Ibid., 216.

Page
342   "artistic polyps." Ibid., 203.
utter despair. Ibid., 206–08.
343   at Surrenden Dering. Ibid., 248.
"his youth." ESC to HA, Feb. 17, 1901.
"bless her." ESC to HA, March 31, 1901.
polenta. ESC to HA, Feb. 17, 1901.
"—very busy." Tehan, 176.
344   "needs it too." *LHA*, V, 248.
on Beacon Street. Friedrich, 333.

344 his sisters. *LHA,* V, 224, 226, 230.

a hand. Henry M. Adkinson to J. D. Hague, Aug. 22, 1904.

baggage car. HA to ESC, April 16, 1901; *LHA,* V, 235.

"only senile." Ibid., 213.

arrival of tourists. Ibid., 202, 249.

345 "what he brought." *EHA,* 329.

on their arrival. Tehan, 178.

"no. 9." ESC to HA, May 18, 1901.

"as commerce." Leech, 575–76.

346 in Prescott. *LJH,* III, May 7, 1901.

"and never tell." CK to HA, 1897.

in bed. CK to J. D. Hague, Sept. 7, 1897.

American female. H. H. Lee to James D. Hague, Dec. 18, 1903.

347 "now and again." CK to JH, December 1897.

overalls. Wilkins, 350–51.

"humbuggery." Alexander Becker to Samuel F. Emmons, June 23, 1902.

"your loving heart." *New York Daily News,* Nov. 22, 1933.

"talk about it." JH to HA, Aug. 22, 1900.

348 "to the spot." H. M. Adkinson to James D. Hague, op. cit.

"family matters." Plaintiffs' Trial Memorandum, *King* v. *Peabody et al.*

their lives. *New York Daily News,* Nov. 21, 1933.

"to the last." CK to C. W. Howard, June 7, 1901.

349 mountains in the distance. CK to CSH, Aug. 16, 1901; CK to JH, July 27, 1901.

Lincoln White House. *LJH,* III, 212.

the Boers or the British. JH to James McMillan, July 3, 1900.

350 before turning in. *Washington Evening Times* and *Washington Evening Star,* June 24, 1901.

six-foot-two frame. *LJH,* III, 215.

350 "he will not return." CSH to HA, Aug. 7, 1901.

"time to heal?" JH to WM, June 29, 1901.

eight hundred others. Scrapbooks, John Hay Library.

"not availed." MT to JH, June 28, 1901.

"miserable hour." HJ to JH, June 24, 1901.

351 "I long to say." AL to JH, June 27, 1901.

heard the news. CK to JH, June 24, 1901; *LHA,* V, 258.

"no help serves." *LHA,* V, 258–59.

"affected by it." Ibid., 266.

limb by limb. Ibid., 260.

352 "the machinery." Ibid., 269.

"something insufferable." JH to HA, July 14, 1901.

"God help me!" *LJH,* III, 217–18.

"news of you." JH to CK, July 29, 1901.

353 "have done their struggle." CK to JH, July 27, 1901.

thirty pounds. Samuel F. Emmons to G. F. Becker, Oct. 17, 1900.

X rays. *LJH,* III, 209.

"for a glimpse." CK to CSH, Aug. 16, 1901.

use them with friends. JH to HA, July 14, 1901.

everywhere. JH to Montgomery Schuyler, Aug. 30, 1901.

instead of his son. *LJH,* III, 225–26.

354 "woe unto you!" Ibid., 228.

355 "have none." Leech, 590–94.

routine procedure. Leech, 597.

"Teddy's luck!" *LHA,* V, 291.

Adirondacks. Morris, 738–39.

over the weekend. JH to CSH, Sept. 11, 1901.

"black cloud of foreboding." *LJH,* III, 231.

"Nearer, My God, to Thee." Leech, 599–601.

355 "tragic fate." *LJH,* III, 230.
356 "when I collapse." Ibid., 219.
"shut in my face." CK to JH,
Aug. 22, 1901.
"Ça vous amuse, la vie?" LJH, III,
223.
357 "to be gay." *LHA,* V, 284.
"a queer taste in fates." *LJH,* III,
241–42.
"brotherly act." JH to HA, Nov.
17, 1901.
"good enough to bottle." CK to
JH, Nov. 3, 1901.

357 cheapest goods. Samuel F. Emmons, Diary, October 1901.
"camping style." Samuel F. Emmons to G. F. Becker, Oct. 17,
1901.
358 family Bible. Plaintiffs' Trial
Memorandum, op. cit.
"ardent pride." CK to JH, Nov.
3, 1901.
two o'clock in the morning. Samuel F. Emmons, Diary, Dec. 24,
1901.
telegraphed Ada in Toronto.
Wilkins, 355–56.

22 *Nearly All the Great Prizes*

359 pallbearers. J. D. Hague to JTG,
Dec. 30, 1901.
red-and-gilt walls. Adams, et al.,
John La Farge, 180–81.
John and Clara Hay. JTG to JH,
Dec. 30, 1901.
360 piercingly bleak. *CKM,* 153.
"gift of friendship." R. W. Ray-
mond, undated ms., Hague Papers.
"mourn his loss." New York *Tribune,* Dec. 27, 1901, 7.
"the hand somehow." *LHA,* V,
313.
"worms of steel." Ibid., 317–18.
afternoons in his library. Walter
Wellman, *Review of Reviews,* August 1905.
volunteer it. *LHA,* V, 329, 558–
59.
361 skirts. Ibid., 319.
Central American canal zone. Mc-
Cullough, 258–59; Thayer, II,
260–61.
"most auspicious." JH to TR,
Oct. 17, 1901. See also TR to JH,
Sept. 25 and Oct. 2, 1901; JH to
TR, Sept. 30, 1901.
362 address him as "Theodore." JH to
TR, Sept. 30, 1901.

362 " 'initiative.' " *LJH,* III, 239.
363 "rough-riders." *LHA,* V, 322–23.
"cephalopodic brain." Ibid., 349.
"mince-pie." Ibid., 332.
"than his father." Ibid., 329.
"punishment as a favor." Ibid.,
453.
364 "one's why." Ibid., 335, 338. See
also 329, 333–34, 338; New York
Tribune, Feb. 7, 1902, 9.
"gentleman should die." JH, *Addresses,* 137–75.
thought it excellent. *LHA,* V,
349.
"majestic pace." Edith Wharton
to George Washington Smalley,
scrapbook, John Hay Collection.
"stump speech." Ibid.
365 "our graves." *LHA,* V, 380.
Gardiner's care. *New York Daily
Mirror,* Nov. 21, 1933, 3.
"declining years." Florence King
Howland to JH, April 5, 1902.
securities. JTG to Samuel F. Emmons, Jan. 11, 1902; JTG to JH,
March 22, 1902, and April 7,
1903.
366 not to name. *King* v. *Peabody et
al.,* Plaintiffs' Trial Memorandum.

Page

366 never seen again. *King* v. *Peabody et al.,* op. cit.

securing the commission. George Howland to JH, Jan. 10, 1902.

portrait collection. J. D. Hague to JH, April 16, 1902.

winter crossing. George Howland to JH, Dec. 17, 1902.

"over-ambition." *LHA,* V, 424.

"unsuitable." Art Committee to J. D. Hague, n.d.

deceased members. Arnold Hague to J. D. Hague, Jan. 28, 1903.

367 pooled $500. Arnold Hague to J. D. Hague, Feb. 27, 1903.

"wherever he went." *CKM,* 117–32.

pith helmet. Ibid., 133–56.

their treasure. Ibid., 189–97.

368 "of our lives." Ibid., 157–85.

cared for anything. *LHA,* V, 335.

"vast Senatorial suck." JH to TR, July 21, 1902.

stronger sovereignty. McCullough, 329–39.

"highways of civilization." TR to JH, Aug. 19, 1903.

369 "about the subject." JH to TR, Sept. 13, 1903.

recognized the new republic. Chessman, 98–99.

mayhem and order. *LJH,* III, 287–88.

"civilized world." Blum, 130.

370 rape. Marks, 131.

coat of arms. *LJH,* III, 285–86.

name only. McCullough, 387–98.

with precision. Marks, 105; Clymer, 167.

371 railroad through U.S. territory. Clymer, 168–69.

"bumptious truculence." TR to JH, July 16, 1902.

"pure and simple." TR to JH, July 10, 1902.

372 diplomatic solution. Marks, 62–63, 130.

372 "claim would imply." TR to JH, July 10, 1902.

Hay's library. *LJH,* III, 264.

"repute." Schriftgiesser, 208.

North Atlantic. Ibid., 208–09.

draw the boundary himself. TR to JH, June 29, 1903.

373 "a shade of difference." Clymer, 194–95.

"go on!" TR to JH, July 11, 1903.

"a gentleman." *LJH,* III, 273.

act like one. Clymer, 195.

"coming at all." JH to CSH, July 4, 1903.

Hay wrote out his resignation. JH to TR, July 21, 1903.

"I could not spare you." TR to JH, July 29, 1903.

territory in question. Clymer, 195.

374 over his head. JH to HA, Nov. 17, 1901.

"boa constrictor." Mount, 203–08.

"than its subject." *LHA,* V, 472.

"frankly bad." Ibid., 488.

years of friendship. Ibid., 464.

"He paints it." Ibid., 493.

375 "no poorer for it." JH to CSH, Oct. 16, 1903.

"on the universe." JH, Diary, May 8, 1904.

"c'est la longueur." ASG to JH, Aug. 5, 1904.

glorious mood. *LJH,* III, 301–02; JH to WDH, July 28, 1904.

376 (the manger.) Blackmur, *Henry Adams,* 326.

Adamenso. Dryfhout, 265.

"live in holes." *LHA,* V, 608–09.

"deals faithfully with me." JH to WDH, Sept. 20, 1903.

377 "coup-de-grace." *LHA,* V, 480–81.

effusive sonnet. JH to TR, Dec. 24, 1902. Houghton Library.

understanding of history. JH to TR, July 25, 1902.

Page
378 " 'if you like.' " JH to TR, April 14, 1904.
"affect his election." *LHA,* V, 570.
New York City newspapers. TR, *Autobiography,* 402.
trust-busting. Blum, 63.
"right and wise." TR to JH, July 11, 1904.
"you are elected." JH to TR, Sept. 22, 1904.
"commune with Nature." JH to TR, Sept. 5, 1904.
"I do not understand it." TR to AL, Nov. 10, 1904.
379 "lost it already." *LJH,* III, 324–25.
"modern times." Tehan, 208.
"and applause." Samuels, *Henry Adams,* III, 308.
"stick in the mud." ASG to HA, April 6, 1905.
"burn me." *LHA,* V, 618.
380 sense of the word. *LHA,* VI, 351.
"or getting friends." *LHA,* V, 660.
a caged rat. *EHA,* 365.
"the infinite." *LHA,* V, 481.
381 "let others say." Chanler, 301–03.
"interrupted education." HJ, *The American Scene,* 323–47.
"there *isn't.*" *HJL,* IV, 339.
"doesn't like." Ibid., 355.
"key to everything." HJ, op. cit., 332.
"miserable little snob." Morris, 467.

Page
381 edifice in the capital. HJ, op. cit., 341.
382 (mistletoe.) Morgan, 2.
liked the man. *HJL,* IV, 337, 339.
"the least creak." Ibid., 341.
laughingstocks. TR to JH, Jan. 28, 1905.
"unexpectedly good." JH to TR, Jan. 28, 1905.
"good enough for me." TR to JH, Jan. 28, 1905.
383 "Theodore will want." *HJL,* IV, 343.
head of Abraham Lincoln. *LJH,* III, 328.
"three and a half years?" TR to JH, March 3, 1905.
mile or two every day. JH to Clarence Hay, April 1, 1905.
at a run. HA to EC, April 6, 1905.
"ought to be." JH to TR, April 12, 1905.
"perfected in him." JH to ASG, April 12, 1905.
384 until autumn. Dr. D. Groedel to CSH, May 28, 1905.
"I shall go." JH to TR, May 20, 1905.
1904 Mercedes. *LHA,* V, 596.
said farewell. Ibid., 670.
a short visit. Gwynn, I, 465.
John's progress. CSH to HA, June 15, 1905.
European politics. *LJH,* III, 345–46.
385 "great prizes." Ibid., 350.

23 Playing Out the Hand

Page
386 "easily as possible." *LHA,* V, 682.
"superb." Ibid., 685.
Senate colleagues. Ibid., 689.
"show itself." Ibid., 693.
387 fill his place. TR to CSH, July 1, 1905.
"not done at all." TR to HCL, July 21, 1905.

Page
387 "in spite of them." Gwynn, II, 479.
"imaginary." *LHA,* VI, 130.
"a double thing." *EHA,* 7, 9.
to either force. Ibid., 383.
388 of all energies. Ibid., 384.
"sunshine." Ibid., 332.
"stamped." Ibid., 55.

388 cared to read. Ibid., 326–37.
"dream of man." Ibid., 451.
"but understand it." Ibid., 346.
"without a shudder." Ibid., 505.
The year 1938 marked the hundredth anniversary of the births of Hay and Adams; King was born in 1842.
"taking it in theirs." *LHA,* VI, 136.

389 "a half an inch or so." Ibid., 117.
"your women friends?" CSH to HA, May 6, 1907.
"train-time." *LJH,* II, 199.

390 "implied in a fight." TR to HCL, Jan. 28, 1909.
James Russell Lowell. HCL to TR, Feb. 14, 1909.
emend her own. Samuels, *Henry Adams,* III, 405.
grandchildren. CSH to HA, March 17, 1909.

391 "everybody." *LHA,* VI, 412.
Woodlawn Cemetery. Margaret La Farge to Bancel La Farge, Dec. 6, 1910, and May 29, 1911.
(and disappearing.) JL, *Great Masters,* 249.
embassy in Washington. Tehan, 226–34.

392 "saloon." Lewis, 225.
death, in 1937. Berenson, *Sketch for a Self-Portrait,* 24–25; Samuels, *Bernard Berenson,* II, 388–89.
the *Titanic. LHA,* VI, 511.
"look after him!" Tehan, 245.

393 "have done so." HJ to ESC, July 9 and 12, 1912. Miles-Cameron Papers.
"sound good!" Samuels, *Henry Adams,* III, 535.
"well off where he is." AL to CFA, Jr., n.d. Lodge Papers.
Mediterranean holiday. Ibid., 536.
"cud." *LHA,* VI, 563.

393–394 "acting with other men." Ibid., 560.

394 "you're not going home." Cater, xcvii–xcviii.
"tails in the air." Ibid., xcviii.
rhythms and phrasing. John La Farge, Jr., *The Manner Is Ordinary,* 173–74.

395 hired two scholars. Cater, xcviii.
the profession. Samuels, *Henry Adams,* III, 539–40.
"youthful beginner." *LHA,* VI, 636.
to Folkestone. Cater, c.
"verged on Hell." *LHA,* VI, 663.
hold fast. Edel, *Henry James,* V, 522.
made him ill. HJ to Margaret La Farge, Aug. 2, 1914.

396 British subject. Edel, op. cit., 528–32.
"happy then." *LHA,* VI, 724.
"wings or song." Ibid., 726.
"your Aunt Clover." Cater, cii.
known her. H. D. Cater Collection, Henry Adams Papers.
"their own identity." William James, *The Principles of Psychology,* I, 326–27, Henry Adams Library, Massachusetts Historical Society.
"to control it?" Ibid., II, 485.
Beverly Farms. Cater, civ.

398 "fantastic dream." *LHA,* VI, 754.
equally unreal. Ibid., 758.
"anybody again." Ibid., 768–69.
beyond their limits. EC to HA, Jan. 14, 1917.
breakfast table. *LHA,* VI, 769.
recalled them both. Burk, 7–10, 31, 143, 181.
Springy was dead. *LHA,* VI, 785–86.
"shoot to the moon." Cater, cvi.
typhoid fever. H. D. Cater Collection.

399 his pillows. Elizabeth Ogden Adams to EC, April 1, 1918.
"will and intellect." Samuels, *Henry Adams,* III, 586.

399 bottle of potassium cyanide. H. D. Cater Collection.
her hat shop. Ibid.
figure at Rock Creek. Mrs. Cadwalader Jones to ESC, April 19, 1918.

399 "make him happy." Ford, II, 651.
one mind and another. William James, op. cit., I, 237.

Epilogue: A Legacy and a Lawsuit

401 last in 1897. *New York Daily Mirror,* Nov. 21, 1933, 3; *New York Daily News,* Nov. 21, 1933, 3.
402 secret family. *King* v. *Peabody et al.,* Plaintiffs' Trial Memorandum.
unnamed benefactor? Ibid.
"I did not know my rights." De-

position of Aug. 24, 1931, included in ibid.
403 IOUs held by John Hay. *New York Times,* Jan. 24, 1934, 14.
began in 1931. *King* v. *Peabody et al.,* transcript of testimony of William G. Winne; *New York American,* Nov. 21, 1933, 3.

Bibliography

Adams, Charles Francis (Jr.). *Charles Francis Adams, 1835–1915*. Boston: Houghton Mifflin, 1916.

——————. *Notes on Railroad Accidents*. New York: G. P. Putnam's Sons, 1879.

Adams, Henry. "Bancroft's History of the United States." *North American Review* 20, April 1875, 424–32.

[Adams, Henry]. *Democracy: An American Novel*. 1880. Reprint. New York: Fawcett, 1961.

——————. *The Education of Henry Adams*. Privately printed, 1907. Reprint. Boston: Houghton Mifflin, 1961.

——————. *Esther*. [Frances Snow Compton, pseud.] 1884. In *Novels, Mont Saint Michel, The Education*. Edited by Ernest Samuels and Jayne N. Samuels. New York: Library of America, 1983.

——————. *Historical Essays*. New York: Charles Scribner's Sons, 1891.

——————. *History of the United States of America during the Administrations of Thomas Jefferson*. New York: Library of America, 1986.

——————. *History of the United States of America during the Administrations of James Madison*. New York: Library of America, 1986.

——————. "John La Farge and Japan." *Apollo* 119, February 1984, 120–29.

——————. "King's Mountaineering in the Sierra Nevada." *North American Review*, 114, April 1872, 445–48.

——————. *Letters of Henry Adams, 1858–1918*. Edited by Worthington Chauncey Ford. 2 vols. Boston: Houghton Mifflin, 1930, 1938.

——————. *The Letters of Henry Adams, 1858–1918*. Edited by J. C. Levenson, et. al. 6 vols. Cambridge: Harvard University Press, 1982, 1988.

——————. *The Life of George Cabot Lodge*. Boston: Houghton Mifflin, 1911.

——————. *Memoirs of Marau Taaroa, Last Queen of Tahiti*. Privately printed, 1893.

——————. *Memoirs of Arii Taimai E Marama of Eimeo Teriirere of Tooraai Teriinui of Tahiti*. Privately printed, 1901.

445

——————. *Mont-Saint-Michel and Chartres.* Privately printed, 1904. Reprint. New York: Doubleday Anchor, 1959.

[——————.] "Recognition of Cuban Independence." U.S. Congress. Senate. *Report 1160.* 54th Congress, 2nd session, 1896 (Dec. 21).

Adams, Henry, et al. *John La Farge: Essays.* New York: Abbeville Press, 1987.

Adams, Marian Hooper. *The Letters of Mrs. Henry Adams, 1865–1883.* Edited by Ward Thoron. Boston: Little, Brown, 1936.

Agassiz, G. R., ed. *Letters and Recollections of Alexander Agassiz.* Boston: Houghton Mifflin, 1913.

Allen, Gay Wilson. *Waldo Emerson.* New York: Viking, 1981.

Alvarez, A. *The Savage God: A Study of Suicide.* New York: Random House, 1972.

Bartlett, Richard A. *Great Surveys of the American West.* Norman, Okla: University of Oklahoma Press, 1962.

Barton, E. E., ed. *Historical and Commercial Sketches of Washington and Environs.* Washington: E. E. Barton, 1884.

Beer, Thomas. *Hanna.* New York: Knopf, 1929.

Beisner, Robert L. *Twelve against Empire: The Anti-Imperialists, 1898–1900.* Chicago: University of Chicago Press, 1985.

Bell, Millicent. "Adams' *Esther:* The Morality of Taste." *New England Quarterly* 35, June 1962, 147–61.

Berenson, Bernard. *Sketch for a Self-Portrait.* New York: Pantheon, 1949.

——————. *Sunset and Twilight, from the Diaries of 1947–58.* New York: Harcourt Brace and World, 1963.

Blackmur, R. P. *Henry Adams.* 1936. Reprint. New York: Da Capo, 1980.

——————. *A Primer of Ignorance.* New York: Harcourt Brace and World, 1967.

Blair, Gist. "Lafayette Square." *Columbia Historical Society Records* 28 (1926), 133–73.

Blum, John Morton. *The Republican Roosevelt.* New York: Atheneum, 1965.

Boller, Paul (Jr.). *Presidential Campaigns,* New York: Oxford University Press, 1984.

Boorstin, Daniel. *The Americans: The Democratic Experience.* New York: Random House, 1973.

Bronson, Edgar Beecher. *Cowboy Life on the Western Plains: The Reminiscences of a Ranchman.* New York: McClure, 1910.

Brooks, Van Wyck. *Howells: His Life and World.* New York: E. P. Dutton, 1959.

——————. *New England: Indian Summer, 1865–1915.* New York: E. P. Dutton, 1940.

Bryce, James. *The American Commonwealth.* 1888. Reprint. New York: G. P. Putnam's Sons, 1959. Edited by Louis M. Hacker.

Burk, Kathleen. *Britain, America and the Sinews of War, 1914–1918.* Boston: George Allen and Unwin, 1985.

Byrnes, Joseph F. *The Virgin of Chartres: An Intellectual and Psychological History of the Work of Henry Adams.* Rutherford, N.J.: Fairleigh Dickinson University Press, 1981.

Carnegie, Andrew. "Americanism versus Imperialism." *North American Review* 168, January 1899, 1–13.

——————. *The Autobiography of Andrew Carnegie.* Boston: Houghton Mifflin, 1920.

————————. "Distant Possessions—The Parting of the Ways." *North American Review* 169, August 1898, 239–48.

Cater, Harold Dean, ed. *Henry Adams and His Friends*. Boston: Houghton Mifflin, 1947.

Chanler, Mrs. Winthrop. *Roman Spring*. Boston: Little, Brown, 1934.

Chessman, G. Wallace. *Theodore Roosevelt and the Politics of Power*. Edited by Oscar Handlin. Boston: Little, Brown, 1969.

Clarke, Edward H. *Sex in Education: Or, a Fair Chance for the Girls*. Boston: James R. Osgood, 1873.

Clymer, Kenton J. *John Hay: The Gentleman as Diplomat*. Ann Arbor, Mich.: University of Michigan Press, 1975.

Collier, Peter, and David Horowitz. *The Rockefellers: An American Dynasty*. New York: Simon and Schuster, 1976.

Colvin, Sidney. *The Letters of Robert Louis Stevenson*. New York: Charles Scribner's Sons, 1899.

Cortissoz, Royal. *John La Farge: A Memoir and a Study*. Boston: Houghton Mifflin, 1911.

Crosby, Harry H. "So Deep a Trail: A Biography of Clarence King." Ph.D. diss., Stanford University, 1953.

Dennett, Tyler. *John Hay: From Poetry to Politics*. New York: Dodd, Mead, 1933.

"The Diamond Bubble and Its Bursting." *Nation* 15, December 12, 1872, 379–80.

Dickason, David H. "Henry Adams and Clarence King: The Record of a Friendship." *New England Quarterly* 17, June 1944, 229–54.

Dobson, John M. *America's Ascent: The United States Becomes a Great Power, 1880–1914*. De Kalb, Ill.: Northern Illinois University Press, 1978.

Dow, Burton Smith, III, "Amasa Stone, Jr.: His Triumph and Tragedy." Master's thesis, Western Reserve University, 1956.

Dryfhout, John. *The Work of Augustus Saint-Gaudens*. Hanover, N.H.: University Press of New England, 1982.

Dulles, Foster Rhea. *Prelude to World Power: American Diplomatic History, 1860–1900*. New York: Macmillan, 1965.

Dusinberre, William. *Henry Adams: The Myth of Failure*. Charlottesville, Va.: University Press of Virginia, 1980.

Earnest, Ernest P. *S. Weir Mitchell: Novelist and Physician*. Philadelphia: University of Pennsylvania Press, 1950.

Edel, Leon. *Henry James*. 5 vols. New York: J. B. Lippincott, 1953–72.

Edwards, Amelia B. *A Thousand Miles up the Nile*. 1877. Reprint. Los Angeles: J. P. Tarcher, 1983.

Ellison, Joseph W. *Tusitala of the South Seas: The Story of Robert Louis Stevenson's Life in the South Pacific*. New York: Hastings House, 1953.

Emmons, S. F. "Clarence King." *The American Journal of Science* 13, March 1902, 224–37.

Freud, Sigmund. "Mourning and Melancholia." In *A General Selection from the Works of Sigmund Freud*. Edited by John Rickman. New York: Doubleday Anchor, 1957.

Friedlaender, Marc. "Henry Hobson Richardson, Henry Adams and John Hay." *Journal of the Society of Architectural Historians* 29, 1970, 231–46.

Friedrich, Otto. *Clover*. New York: Simon and Schuster, 1979.

Frothingham, O. B. "Washington as It Should Be." *Atlantic Monthly* 53, June 1884, 841–48.

Furer, Howard B. *Washington: A Chronological and Documentary History.* Dobbs Ferry, N.Y.: Oceana, 1975.

Furnas, J. C. *Voyage to Windward: The Life of Robert Louis Stevenson.* New York: Sloane, 1951.

Gauguin, Paul. *Noa-Noa.* Reprint. New York: Noonday, 1957.

Gay, Peter. *The Bourgeois Experience, Victoria to Freud: Education of the Senses.* 2 vols. New York: Oxford University Press, 1984, 1986.

Goldman, Eric F. *Rendezvous with Destiny: A History of Modern American Reform.* 1952. Reprint. New York: Vintage, 1977.

Goode, James M. *Capital Losses: A Cultural History of Washington's Destroyed Buildings.* Washington: Smithsonian Institution Press, 1979.

Griscom, Lloyd C. *Diplomatically Speaking.* New York: Literary Guild of America, 1940.

Groves, Charles S. *Henry Cabot Lodge: The Statesman.* Boston: Small, Maynard, 1925.

Gwynn, Stephen, ed. *The Letters and Friendships of Sir Cecil Spring-Rice.* 2 vols. Boston: Houghton Mifflin, 1929.

Harte, Geoffrey Bret, ed. *The Letters of Bret Harte.* Boston: Houghton Mifflin, 1926.

Hatcher, Harlan. *The Western Reserve: The Story of New Connecticut in Ohio.* 1949. Revised edition. Cleveland: World, 1966.

Hawthorne, Nathaniel. *Tales and Sketches.* Edited by Roy Harvey Pearce. New York: Library of America, 1982.

Hay, John. *Addresses of John Hay.* New York: Century, 1906.

——————. *Amasa Stone.* Privately printed, 1883.

[Hay, John]. *The Bread-Winners: A Social Study.* 1883. Reprint. New York: Harper and Brothers, 1899.

——————. *Castilian Days.* Boston: James R. Osgood, 1871.

——————. *The Complete Poetical Works of John Hay.* Boston: Houghton Mifflin, 1916.

——————. *Letters of John Hay and Extracts from Diary.* 1908. Reprint. New York: Gordian, 1969.

Hay, John, and John Nicolay. *Abraham Lincoln: A History.* 10 vols. New York: Century, 1890.

Higham, John. "Anti-Semitism in the Gilded Age: A Reinterpretation." *Mississippi Valley Historical Review* 43, March 1957, 559–78.

Hitchcock, Henry-Russell, Jr. *The Architecture of H. H. Richardson and His Times.* New York: Museum of Modern Art, 1936.

Hochfield, George E., ed. *Henry Adams: The Great Secession Winter of 1860–61 and Other Essays.* New York: Sagamore Press, 1958.

Holt, Henry. *Garrulities of an Octogenarian Editor.* Boston: Houghton Mifflin, 1923.

Howe, Julia Ward, ed. *Sex and Education: A Reply to Dr. E. H. Clarke's "Sex in Education."* Boston: Roberts, 1874.

Howells, W. D. "Editor's Easy Chair." *Harper's.* May 1877, 919; and July 1877, 304. (Two commentaries on Amasa Stone's role in the 1876 Ashtabula railroad disaster.)

—————. "Editor's Study."*Harper's* 82, February 1891, 478–83. (A commentary on *Abraham Lincoln: A History* by John Hay and John Nicolay.)

—————. "Hay in Literature." *North American Review* 181, October 1905, 343–51.

—————. "Henry James, Jr." *Century* 25, March 1883, 24–29.

—————. *Novels, 1875–1886.* Edited by Edwin H. Cady. New York: Library of America, 1982.

Hudson, Derek. *Munby: Man of Two Worlds.* Boston: Gambit, 1972.

Hurd, Charles. *Washington Cavalcade.* New York: E. P. Dutton, 1948.

James, Edward T., ed. *Notable American Women.* 3 vols. Cambridge: Harvard University Press, 1971.

James, Henry. *The American Scene.* New York: Harper, 1907.

—————. *The Letters of Henry James.* 4 vols. Edited by Leon Edel. Cambridge: Harvard University Press, 1974–84.

—————. *Literary Criticism: Essays on Literature, American Writers, English Writers.* Edited by Leon Edel with Mark Wilson. New York: Library of America, 1984.

—————. *Novels, 1871–1880.* Edited by William T. Stafford. New York: Library of America, 1983.

—————. *Novels, 1881–1886.* Edited by William T. Stafford. New York: Library of America, 1985.

Janin, Henry. *A Brief Statement of My Part in the Unfortunate Diamond Affair.* Privately printed, 1873.

Josephson, Matthew. *The Politicos, 1865–96.* New York: Harcourt, Brace and World, 1938.

Kaledin, Eugenia. *The Education of Mrs. Henry Adams.* Philadelphia: Temple University Press, 1981.

Kaplan, Justin. *Mr. Clemens and Mark Twain.* New York: Simon and Schuster, 1966.

—————. *Walt Whitman.* New York: Simon and Schuster, 1980.

Kazin, Alfred. *An American Procession.* New York: Knopf, 1984.

King, Clarence. "Artium Magister." *North American Review* 147, October 1888, 369–84.

—————. "The Biographers of Lincoln." *Century* 32, October 1886, 861–69.

—————. "The Education of the Future." *Forum* 13, March 1892, 20–33.

—————. "Fire and Sword in Cuba." *Forum* 22, September 1896, 31–52.

—————. "John Hay." *Scribner's* 7, April 1874, 736–39.

—————. *Mountaineering in the Sierra Nevada.* 1872. Reprint. New York: W. W. Norton, 1935.

—————. *Report of Clarence King to the Board of Directors of the San Francisco and Commercial Mining Company,* November 11, 1872.

—————. "Shall Cuba Be Free?" *Forum* 20, September 1895, 50–65.

[King, Clarence]. "Style and the Monument." *North American Review* 141, November 1885, 443–53.

King Memorial Committee of The Century Association. *Clarence King Memoirs.* New York: G. P. Putnam's Sons, 1904.

King v. *Peabody et al.* New York State Supreme Court, New York County, File No. 26821–1931.

Klein, Maury. *Union Pacific*. New York: Doubleday, 1987.

La Farge, John. *An Artist's Letters from Japan*. New York: Century, 1897.

——————. "Concerning Painters Who Would Express Themselves in Words." *Scribner's* 58, August 1899, 254–56.

——————. *Considerations on Painting*. New York: Macmillan, 1896.

——————. *Great Masters*. New York: McClure, Phillips, 1913.

——————. *Reminiscences of the South Seas*. New York: Doubleday, Page, 1912.

La Farge, John (Jr.), S. J. "Henry James's Letters to the La Farges." *New England Quarterly* 22, June 1949, 173–92.

——————. *The Manner Is Ordinary*. New York, 1954.

La Farge, Mabel. *Letters to a Niece and Prayer to the Virgin of Chartres, by Henry Adams, with a Niece's Memories*. Boston: Houghton Mifflin, 1920.

Laughlin, J. Laurence. "Some Recollections of Henry Adams." *Scribner's* 69, 1921, 576–85.

Lawrence, William. *Life of Phillips Brooks*. New York: Harper, 1930.

Leech, Margaret. *In the Days of McKinley*. New York: Harper and Brothers, 1959.

Levenson, J. C. *The Mind and Art of Henry Adams*. Boston: Houghton Mifflin, 1957.

Lewis, R.W.B. *Edith Wharton*. New York: Harper and Row, 1975.

Lynn, Kenneth S. *William Dean Howells*. New York: Harcourt Brace Jovanovich, 1971.

Marks, Frederick W., III. *Velvet on Iron: The Diplomacy of Theodore Roosevelt*. Lincoln, Neb.: University of Nebraska Press, 1979.

Mather, Frank Jewett. "John La Farge: An Appreciation." *The World's Work* 21, March 1911, 14085–100.

McCullough, David. *The Path Between the Seas*. New York: Touchstone, 1977.

McSpadden, J. Walker. "John La Farge: The Painter of Experiment." In *Famous Painters of America*. New York: Thomas Y. Crowell, 1907.

Miller, Perry. *American Thought, Civil War to World War I*. New York: Rinehart, 1954.

Miller, William J. *Henry Cabot Lodge*. New York: James H. Heineman, 1967.

Moers, Ellen. *Literary Women*. New York: Anchor, 1977.

Monteiro, George. *Henry James and John Hay: The Record of a Friendship*. Providence, R.I.: University Press of New England, 1965.

Monteiro, George, and Brenda Murphy, eds. *John Hay–Howells Letters*. Boston: Twayne, 1980.

Moore, Joseph West. *Picturesque Washington: Pen and Pencil Sketches*. Providence, R.I.: J. A. and R. A. Reid, 1884.

Moore, Rayburn S. *Constance Fenimore Woolson*. United States Authors Series, No. 34. New York: Twayne, 1963.

Morgan, H. Wayne. *America's Road to Empire: The War with Spain and Overseas Expansion*. New York: John Wiley and Sons, 1965.

Morris, Edmund. *The Rise of Theodore Roosevelt*. New York: Ballantine, 1979.

Morrow, Patrick. *Bret Harte*. Boise, Idaho: Boise State College Western Writers Series, No. 5, 1972.

Morton, Frederic. *The Rothschilds*. Greenwich, Conn.: Fawcett, 1963.

Mount, Charles Merrill. *John Singer Sargent*. London: Cresset, 1957.

Mumford, Lewis. *The Brown Decades: A Study of the Arts in America, 1865–1895*. 1931. Reprint. New York: Dover, 1955.

Nagel, Paul. *Descent from Glory: Four Generations of the John Adams Family*. New York: Oxford University Press, 1983.

Neider, Charles, ed. *The Complete Essays of Mark Twain*. New York: Doubleday, 1963.

Nelson, H. L. "Social Washington." *Atlantic Monthly* 52, December 1883, 818–25.

Nevins, Allan. *The Emergence of Modern America, 1865–78*. New York: Macmillan, 1927.

—————. *Henry White: Thirty Years of American Diplomacy*. New York: Harper, 1930.

O'Connor, Richard. *Bret Harte*. Boston: Little, Brown, 1966.

O'Gorman, James F. "A Tragic Circle." *Nineteenth Century,* Autumn 1976, 46–49.

Olszewski, George J. *Lafayette Park*. Washington: U.S. Department of Interior, National Park Service, 1964.

O'Toole, G.J.A. *The Spanish War: An American Epic*. New York: W. W. Norton, 1984.

Parrington, Vernon Louis. *The Beginnings of Critical Realism in America: 1860–1920*. 1930. Reprint. New York: Harcourt Brace and World, 1958.

Reed, Robert. *Old Washington, D.C., in Early Photographs*. New York: Dover, 1980.

Rein, David. *S. Weir Mitchell as a Psychiatric Novelist*. New York: International Universities Press, 1952.

Roosevelt, Theodore. *An Autobiography*. New York: Scribner's, 1913.

Roth, Leland M. *McKim, Mead & White, Architects*. New York: Harper and Row, 1983.

Saint Gaudens, Homer, ed. *The Reminiscences of Augustus Saint Gaudens*. 2 vols. New York: Century, 1913.

Samuels, Ernest. *Bernard Berenson*. 2 vols. Cambridge: Harvard University Press, 1979, 1987.

—————. *Henry Adams*. 3 vols. Cambridge: Harvard University Press, 1947–64.

—————. "Henry Adams and the Gossip Mills." In Max F. Schulz et al., eds., *Essays in American and English Literature, Presented to Bruce Robert McElderry, Jr.* Athens, Ohio: Ohio University Press, 1967.

Scheyer, Ernst. *The Circle of Henry Adams: Art and Artists*. Detroit: Wayne State University Press, 1970.

Schlesinger, Arthur Meier. *The Rise of the City, 1878–1898*. New York: Macmillan, 1933.

Schriftgiesser, Karl. *The Gentleman from Massachusetts: Henry Cabot Lodge*. Boston: Little, Brown, 1944.

Schurz, Carl. *American Imperialism*. Address delivered at 27th convocation of the University of Chicago, January 4, 1899.

—————. *For American Principles and American Honor*. Address delivered at Cooper Union, New York City, May 24, 1900.

Seale, William. *The President's House*. 2 vols. Washington: White House Historical Association and National Geographic Society, 1986.

Shi, David. *The Simple Life: Plain Living and High Thinking in American Culture*. New York: Oxford University Press, 1985.

Simonds, Katherine. "The Tragedy of Mrs. Henry Adams." *New England Quarterly* 9, December 1936, 664–82.

Smith, Henry Nash, and William M. Gibson, eds. *Mark Twain–Howells Letters*. 2 vols. Cambridge: Harvard University Press, 1960.

Smith, Page. *The Rise of Industrial America*. New York: McGraw-Hill, 1984.

Spence, Clark C. *The Sinews of American Capitalism*. New York: Hill and Wang, 1964.

Stevenson, Robert Louis. *In the South Seas, Letters from Samoa, etc*. New York: Bigelow, Brown, n.d.

Stewart, George R., Jr. *Bret Harte: Argonaut and Exile*. Boston: Houghton Mifflin, 1931.

Stoddard, Henry Luther. *Horace Greeley*. New York: G. P. Putnam's Sons, 1946.

Strong, Josiah. *Our Country: Its Possible Future and Its Present Crisis*. 1886. Reprint. Edited by Jurgen Herbst. Cambridge: Harvard University Press, 1963.

Strouse, Jean. *Alice James*. Boston: Houghton Mifflin, 1980.

Tehan, Arline Boucher. *Henry Adams in Love: The Pursuit of Elizabeth Sherman Cameron*. New York: Universe Books, 1983.

Thayer, William Roscoe. *The Life and Letters of John Hay*. 2 vols. Boston: Houghton Mifflin, 1915.

Trask, David F. *The War with Spain in 1898*. New York: Macmillan, 1981.

Twain, Mark. *The Innocents Abroad* and *Roughing It*. Edited by Guy Cardwell. New York: Library of America, 1985.

—————. "To the Person Sitting in Darkness." *North American Review* 172, February 1901, 161–76.

Twain, Mark, and Charles Dudley Warner. *The Gilded Age*. 1873. Reprint. New York: New American Library, 1980.

Van Rensselaer, Mariana Griswold. *Henry Hobson Richardson and His Works*. 1888. Reprint. New York: Dover, 1969.

Warnecke, John Carl and Associates. *Historical Survey of Lafayette Square*, 1963.

Warner, Marina. *Alone of All Her Sex: The Myth and the Cult of the Virgin Mary*. London: Weidenfeld and Nicolson, 1976.

Wharton, Edith. *A Backward Glance*. New York: Appleton-Century, 1934.

Whitman, Walt. *Democratic Vistas*. 1871. In Walt Whitman, *Complete Poetry and Collected Prose*. Edited by Justin Kaplan. New York: Library of America, 1982.

Wilkins, Thurman. *Clarence King*. New York: Macmillan, 1958.

Wilkinson, Burke. *Uncommon Clay: The Life and Works of Augustus Saint Gaudens*. New York: Harcourt Brace Jovanovich, 1985.

Wilson, Allen D. "The Great California Diamond Mines." *Overland Monthly* 43, April 1904, 291–96.

Ziff, Larzer. *The American 1890s: Life and Times of a Lost Generation*. New York: Viking, 1966.

Index

Page numbers in italics refer to illustrations.